# THE
# BUSINESS
## OF
# BUSINESS

# THE
# BUSINESS
## OF
# BUSINESS

## How 100 Businesses Really Work

# David Horowitz
# Dana Shilling

**PERENNIAL LIBRARY**

**HARPER & ROW, PUBLISHERS, New York**

Grand Rapids, Philadelphia, St. Louis, San Francisco
London, Singapore, Sydney, Tokyo

FIRST EDITION

*Designed by Alma Orenstein*

Library of Congress Cataloging-in-Publication Data

Horowitz, David, 1937–
    The business of business.

    1. Consumer protection—United States. 2. Business
enterprises—United States. 3. Retail trade—United
States. I. Shilling, Dana. II. Title.
[HC110.C63H669   1989b]        338.7′4′0973        88-45936
ISBN 0-06-055142-9
ISBN 0-06-096327-1 (pbk.)

89 90 91 92 93 CC/HC 10 9 8 7 6 5 4 3 2 1
89 90 91 92 93 CC/HC 10 9 8 7 6 5 4 3 2 1 (pbk.)

*To Suzanne, Amanda and Tori*
*for their love, support and commitment*

—D. H.

# Contents

PART **C**

# Consuming Passions

PART **D**

# Shop Till You Drop

## PART E
# Getting Around

## PART F
# Leisure

## PART G
# Health, and the Alternatives

PART **H**

# Services, Et Cetera

# Introduction

*"Business is in business to stay in business,*
*and not to give people the business.*
*Otherwise, they are out of business."*

By the time we finally become grown-ups, we know where babies come from, but do we really know where dollars come from? How do businesses earn their money? Why are prices so high? How do we know when we're getting a fair deal and when we're being gouged? And what kind of power do we as consumers have over the way business does business?

In a free market economy like ours, dollars are votes. Every time we buy a product or service, we're casting votes for which companies will survive and which will fail. That's real consumer power! The problem is that we're not always sure how to exercise that power. That's part of what this book is all about. By understanding more about how the businesses we deal with every day work, we can better judge how to vote with our dollars—how to tell which companies are really out to win our confidence by giving us the most for our money.

Shopping is a matter of making choices. Do we want the absolutely lowest price available, or are we willing to pay a little more for service, convenience, and selection? Do we think of ourselves as upscale buyers who want only the best, or are we constantly searching for ways to get the most value from every dollar we spend?

Businesses face similar choices. They must decide whether they are out to attract an image-conscious clientele with high-quality merchandise and personal service in an elegant retail environment or the no-frills discount trade. They must control costs in order to keep prices down and remain competitive. They must choose the right equipment and furnishings, hire and train employees, set wages, plan their advertising, and select a range of products and services that will attract customers to their businesses.

In this book, Dana Shilling and I take a long, close look at a hundred different businesses and how they operate. These are the retail and service trades we all deal with every day. This is not a textbook on retail economics. Instead, we've tried to answer the questions most of us have about how businesses function from day to day, how they determine the prices we pay for goods and services, and why some businesses succeed while others fail.

Here are some of the specific questions we deal with in this book:

▶ How many businesses are there in each trade?
▶ How much does the industry as a whole earn each year?
▶ How do people get started in the business? What are the costs involved, and what special problems do they face?
▶ How many people does the industry employ, and what sort of wages do they earn?
▶ How much of a business's income do its owners or stockholders get to keep as profit?

Building on Dana's extensive research and my years of experience as a consumer reporter, we tried to pull all this information together in a way that helps explain not only how businesses do business, but how we relate to those businesses as consumers. Data came from a wide variety of sources, from trade publications to government statistics and personal interviews.

The U.S. Department of Commerce's *Census of Retail Service Businesses* was very useful, though slightly dated, since the government gathers this data only once every five years. Figures from this source are based on 1982 statistical tables. *Business Week* was another major source, especially its Top 1000 and quarterly "Scoreboards." We also learned a lot from the *Wall Street Journal*, the *New York Times*, Crain's *New York Business*, and a wide variety of trade association publications that offered special insights into the businesses they serve. Other sources included The Dun & Bradstreet Corporation's 1987 compilation of business ratios, Leo Troy's *Almanac of Business and Industrial Financial Ratios*, Fairchild's *Financial Manual of Retail Stores 1987*, and the April 1988 edition of Standard and Poor's *Industry Surveys*.

We also consulted several books on specific industries and businesses. Two deserve special mention here. One was *The 101 Best-Performing Companies in America* by Ronald N. Paul and James W. Taylor (Probus Publishing Co., 1986). The other is Harold I. Vogel's *Entertainment Industry Economics: A Guide for Financial Analysis* (Cambridge University Press, 1986), which, despite its formidable title, is a wonderfully witty and entertaining book about business accounting.

As a general rule, wherever we mention a date, it's the year the figures were gathered, rather than the year they were published. Throughout the book there are also what we call "Retail Raps" where Dana and I discuss the meaning behind the statistics, accounting procedures, franchise agreements, business costs, profit margins, and what these things mean to us as consumers.

And that's really the point of this book. Understanding how business does business gives us the edge as consumers. We're more likely to be satisfied with good service and merchandise and less likely to be ripped off by unscrupulous retailers if we know how the system really works. Dana and I hope that this book will answer such questions as why that boutique charges $200 for a dress and why lightbulbs cost more at a hardware store than at a discount warehouse. As consumers, we'll better appreciate the value of personal service when we know what it costs the merchant to provide that service. For those in business for themselves, we provide new insights into what customers expect of a business and what it takes to succeed in a particular industry. We hope consumers and businessmen alike enjoy the experience.

*—David Horowitz*

# RETAIL RAP:  Business Start-ups

A person starting a new business, like a lemming heading toward the edge of the cliff, knows that the odds of success are not good. But some business owners—rather like lemmings with an inner tube—have survival strategies, in the form of detailed business plans.

The first thing anyone starting a business needs is financing—enough funds to get the business ready to earn money. A retail store needs a location, which in turn must be decorated and stocked with merchandise. A service business needs an office and the equipment necessary to provide the service (mirrors, fabrics, and makeup for a "Color-Me-Beautiful" color consultant; telephones, computers, and listings for an employment agency). The new business needs a marketing plan to attract its first customers—and, crucially, it needs enough capital to hang on until the trickle of customers turns into a torrent.

Where does the money come from? Usually, from the savings of the business owners in addition to whatever they can raise from family and friends. A few businesses, usually high-tech businesses run by people with extensive scientific and business experience, can start up by offering their stock to the public and then using the stockholders' money as capital. Or if the business has a strong chance of success, it may attract "venture capital": private financing from venture capital groups, usually in the form of a package of loans and equity participation. Although venture capitalists like high-tech, they fund other businesses as well—but usually not small local businesses.

Bank loans are a possible but unlikely source of start-up capital. Banks, understandably, prefer to lend to businesses that already have a track record and money coming in. The Small Business Administration has virtually no money and has to use its very limited resources to guarantee bank loans and help out small businesses that have already started, not to lend money directly to start-up businesses. So the business owners are thrown back on their own resources, and whatever Aunt Mildred can be persuaded to contribute to the new venture.

## SUPPLIERS

For many small businesses, a milestone is reached when they stop buying goods retail and move into the wholesale market. Sometimes they lack sophistication and don't know that there's any other way to buy things except retail. Sometimes they are so short of cash that they must buy fabric five yards at a time or butter by the pound because they can't satisfy a distributor's or wholesaler's minimum order.

1

Given more money and more knowledge, the owners of start-up businesses have many alternatives for acquiring supplies and merchandise. In some industries, the trade show is the key. Once or twice a year, manufacturers and distributors set up booths and print literature to alert their customers to the newest trends in toys, appliances, clothing, plumbing supplies, electronics, or whatever. Retailers and service businesses come to the trade shows; make contacts; make plans for a half-year's or year's merchandising; and then place six months' or a year's worth of orders.

The trade show offers convenient "one-stop shopping" for the retailers and service businesses and provides a central location for wholesalers to reach their market—but it also puts high pressure on both buyer and seller to make at once decisions that have long-term consequences. New businesses often avoid trade shows because they don't have enough capital to place very large orders.

Other industries have different buying patterns, and a single business often combines many different ways to buy merchandise for processing or resale to consumers. For instance, a health-food store might buy vitamins by mail order, directly from the manufacturer. But the store might also do business with a number of wholesale distributors: one who trucks in baked goods, another who ships herbal teas by UPS, and a third, local distributor that provides frequent deliveries of perishable grains and produce. Over time, a business develops a network of suppliers and alternate suppliers.

The choice between buying directly from a manufacturer and using a middleman such as a distributor depends on many factors: price; convenience (the wholesaler may handle goods from many manufacturers, so the business owner only needs to place one order, instead of many); minimum orders (manufacturers may not be willing to bother with small orders, leaving that segment of the business to distributors); and payment policy.

In some industries, salespeople come directly to the retailer or service business to take orders. It depends on the balance of power between buyer and seller. A manufacturer or distributor that's hungry for new business will contact potential buyers aggressively and will be flexible about matters such as minimum orders and payment policies. But a well-established manufacturing or wholesale business probably won't bother with a small order, and the cost of a sales call will outweigh the potential profit to be derived from it.

## LOCATION, LOCATION, LOCATION

Except for home businesses, all start-up businesses need a place of business: a factory, office, or store. The challenge is to find a location that's suitable for the business's requirements (whether restaurant stoves, blast furnaces, or twenty-five telephone lines), large enough for present needs and expandable for foreseeable future needs, in a suitable location (the financial district, for a brokerage house; with plenty of foot traffic, for a boutique; in an elegant neighborhood, for an upscale hairdresser or restaurant)—yet at an affordable rent.

Novice business owners often have to choose between a space that must be renovated (which takes time and costs money—but can be tailored to the business's needs) and space that's immediately usable (probably at a higher rent than the "handyman's special"). Frequently, they choose the first alternative—and run out of money before the renovations are finished, much less before the first customer walks through the door.

## MARKETING

The crucial question for any business is how to attract, and keep, customers. A really superior product in an advantageous location (or a much-needed product in a location with no competition) is likely to succeed. If a shop selling a hot new designer's clothes is located amid the haunts of the rich and fashionable, it's likely to earn high revenues. If it can control costs, it's likely to earn high profits. Or if a saloon is the only one in a frontier town, its prosperity is guaranteed; even if its rotgut is the worst for a hundred miles around, it's the *only* rotgut for a hundred miles around.

Most businesses, though, face plenty of competition and need to attract customers to their obscure locations. One strategy is advertising: television, radio, print, or direct mail. Another strategy is to form a network of those who need the product or service. For instance, a business consultant could join the local Chamber of Commerce and meet business owners in need of advice; someone who sells computer accessories could tell members of a local computer user's group about all the problems the accessories can solve. A business can offer discount coupons to entice first-time customers, who, it is hoped, will become repeat customers.

In short, businesses must face many challenges before they even open their doors. A million decisions must be made, and they can't be made casually because they shape the entire course of the business. If that carefully designed layout turns out to be impossible to work with, if it turns out that nobody wants those hand-woven Guatemalan coats, but that everyone wants the Burmese shirts (which were only available as a one-time purchase), if a franchisee decides that buying a franchise was the biggest mistake of his or her life . . . there are solutions to all of these problems, but they call for effort and money.

Every business is a risky business. Many things can go wrong; many predictions must be made, often based on little or no information. Getting things done in business usually takes longer, and costs more, than anticipated. It's understandable that many businesses fail. It's a tribute to the sadder, wiser, cannier, and luckier owners that *any* businesses succeed.

# The Financial Heavy Hitters

# Banking

Number of establishments:    14,100 (commercial banks)
Total receipts:                 $184 billion (industry as a whole)

Willie Sutton chose banks to rob because "that's where the money is." Because of that simple fact, banking is one of the most fundamental and important parts of the American economy. You can avoid contact with the auto industry by refusing to drive. You can wear your old clothes until they fall to pieces and stay out of department stores and clothing stores. But even if you're a recluse who keeps money under your mattress, you can't avoid the banking system: people and government agencies keep sending you checks, and you have to cash them in order to have money to put under the mattress.

The banking industry is huge. The industry as a whole ranked as #24 in the United States in *Business Week*'s 1987 Top 1000. Its assets were $1,886,470 *million*. In 1986, the industry's sales were $184,407 million, and its profits were $122,816 million.

It doesn't cost too much money to run a bank, as the chart shows. But it's a business that spends an unusually large amount on interest expenses. Another business that carries an inventory of toys, Toyotas, or

7

Where the Money Goes (Before Taxes)

| | Cost of Operations | Officers' Compensation | Pensions and Benefits | Rent | Repairs | Depreciation |
|---|---|---|---|---|---|---|
| Mutual savings banks | 0.6% | 1.5 | 1.0 | 0.6 | 0.3 | 1.2 |
| Other banks | 0.1% | 2.8 | 0.9 | 0.9 | 0.4 | 1.8 |
| Savings & loans | 1.0% | 1.1 | 0.6 | 0.8 | 0.3 | 1.2 |
| Personal credit institutions | 20.8% | 1.5 | 0.9 | 1.7 | 0.5 | 4.0 |

| | Interest | Bad Debts | Advertising | State, Local Taxes | Other Expenses | Net Profit Before Tax |
|---|---|---|---|---|---|---|
| Mutual savings banks | 73.4 | 1.2 | 0.7 | 1.5 | 12.5 | 5.5 |
| Other banks | 70.1 | 3.0 | 0.4 | 1.3 | 14.5 | 3.8 |
| Savings & loans | 81.2 | 1.1 | 0.8 | 0.9 | 17.0 | 4.2 |
| Personal credit institutions | 35.3 | 2.3 | 0.8 | 2.0 | 25.7 | 4.5 |

(Troy, '84–'85)

toilet seats might devote much of its accounting attention to the cost of the goods as a major factor in profit or loss. Since banks and related institutions buy, sell, and rent out money (but very few other goods, except for a toaster here and there for new depositors), their interest expenses take the place that "cost of goods sold" occupies in the economics of ordinary businesses.

# Banks

## WHAT BANKS DO

Banks, credit unions, and savings and loan institutions accept deposits from customers; finance companies don't. Instead, they get funds from investors. The institution has to take care of the depositors' money, keeping it in nice safe vaults until the customers demand it back [which they can do by appearing at the bank and making a withdrawal or by writing a check. If the depositors have "time deposit" accounts or certificates of deposit (CDs), they must give the bank a certain amount of notice before taking their money back—or they agree to leave it with the bank for a certain amount of time]. When banks have plenty of money available, they are less hospitable; when they desperately need money (say, when plenty of borrowers are begging for the right to pay high interest), they offer microwave ovens, free teddy bears, and, not incidentally, higher interest rates to depositors (especially depositors who are willing to keep the money in the bank for a dependably long time).

Not all depositors are individuals, of course. Corporations need checking accounts. They also need safe parking places for money that will later be invested. Sometimes banks issue investments (such as "retail repurchase agreements," or *repos*) that are attractive to corporations; it depends on what interest rates the bank can afford to pay and how bank investments compare to other investments of similar safety.

But banks are far more than cold-storage lockers for money. Banks earn enough to satisfy their stockholders, pay their vice presidents and security guards, and pay interest to depositors by lending the bank's own capital and the depositors' money to borrowers. Depending on the institution's location, size, and legal status, the borrower could be anyone from

## CONSUMER TIP

What's the best bank for you? Safety comes first (see below)— some banks and many savings and loan institutions are in deep trouble, and your money may not be there when you need it. Convenience counts, too. Are there accessible branches near home, work, and shopping? Are there long lines or quick service? Are ATMs (automated teller machines) available at bank branches and other convenient locations? Next, match the bank's offerings (interest rates on deposits; types of accounts available) and fee schedules to your own bank balance and banking needs. How much do you really earn on your deposits when fees are taken into account? How much does a loan cost, relative to other local banks? Finally, consider "relationship banking": if you'll need a mortgage or personal loan later on, you may get a lower rate from a bank with which you already have a business relationship.

a college sophomore getting a tuition loan to the government of a Latin American country.

Unless (God forbid) there's a run on a bank, most of the depositors won't show up at the same time for their money. In fact, it's a fairly simple mathematical task to predict how much money will be demanded on a given day. This computation, combined with legal requirements (various kinds of banking institutions are obliged to keep varying percentages of their assets on the premises), sets the level of *reserves* the bank must maintain. The bank can lend the rest of its assets. Its success in finding borrowers, getting them to repay, and in getting them to pay competitive interest rates determines the bank's success.

## WHOOPS!

If the bank falls down in any of these areas, it will have a bad quarter—or it'll go out of business. When that happens, the depositors will be protected, but only if a bank in better financial health can be found to take it (including the depositors' accounts) over. First Interstate Bancorp (of Los Angeles) scored a coup in 1986 when it "bought" an Oklahoma City bank. This was not buying as we usually think of it, though. In this case, bank regulators not only absorbed all the bank's bad loans but actually paid First Interstate to take over the bank.

Depositors are also protected if their accounts are insured. If the institution is federally chartered, theoretically accounts are insured up to $100,000 by the FDIC (Federal Deposit Insurance Corporation—for banks) and the FSLIC or FHLBB (Federal Savings and Loan Insurance Corporation or Federal Home Loan Bank Board—for thrift institutions), so the customers should be OK. However, it *is* theoretical because these federal agencies are heavily pressed by the number and size of bank failures. In 1986, 135 banks failed and the top 100 banks scored $11 billion in loan losses—a sum equalling their 1986 after-tax earnings. Things got even worse in 1987, with 184 bank failures; 44 banks hit the drink in the first quarter of 1988. In 1987, the savings and loan industry lost $6.8 billion. But the losses were lopsided: although over a third of the S and Ls lost money that year, only 20 out of the over 3,000 S and Ls accounted for almost $5 million of the red ink. The worst problems occurred in Texas, which was beset by oil-patch woes.

How are the agencies responsible for bailouts doing? The FSLIC was $11.6 billion in the red in 1987; and the FDIC ended 1987 with a net worth of $18 billion but was on the brink of the first loss in its fifty-four years of operation by March 1988.

Depositors are taking an even bigger risk if they entrust their money to institutions that are insured by a state agency (Utah depositors found this out the hard way in 1986 and 1987) or that are privately insured. Before you put Nickel One into either of these types of institutions, make sure that it's in good shape. (Check the business section of the local papers for a few years back; ask a rival banker; see if *Business Week* or a similar business magazine has covered the institution as the fiscal equivalent of a disaster movie.)

## WHEN BAD LOANS HAPPEN TO GOOD BANKS

Banks are in a dilemma. If they don't make loans, they have no profits. But if they make the wrong loans—or even if they make the right loans but economic conditions change—they not only don't make profits, but they lose a lot of money when loans go sour.

Changes in interest rates can be annoying or upsetting for you if you're looking for a car loan or have to deal with the twists and turns of an adjustable-rate mortgage. Just think how the banks feel when they lend out money at 10 percent and everyone else is lending out money at 11 percent (and therefore making more profit). Imagine their chagrin when they realize that they could have gotten a nice, safe long-term commitment to earn 10 percent when interest rates go even lower.

How could they make what, in hindsight, seem to be appalling mistakes? Everyone's smart in hindsight, of course. But a banker can have a theory about interest rate trends, based on a particular economic factor—the worth of the dollar; unemployment rates; or actions taken by the Federal Reserve Board. But, sooner or later, the theory may prove not to conform to reality. Or everyone can agree that interest rates and loan demand will go up—but they go down, or vice versa.

And when you consider how fast interest rates fluctuate, and how much is involved . . . well, we don't expect you to sympathize with banks; but they do have their troubles, too.

For many years, the conventional banking wisdom was that countries never go bankrupt; so *sovereign loans*—loans to governments—were eagerly sought by banks. The borrowing countries were happy because they had plenty of money to build hydroelectric projects, or to buy bombs, or to transfer into the leader's Swiss bank account; the banks were happy because they had huge loan portfolios. By the mid-1980s, however, it was obvious that many countries wouldn't, or couldn't, repay their loans. Often they wouldn't, or couldn't, even pay the interest on the loans.

The fan got hit in the summer of 1987. Citicorp, one of the largest of all the huge banks, announced that it was setting up a $3 billion reserve to deal with bad foreign loans. (Citicorp had made more than $10 billion of loans to Latin America.) This meant that the bank would report a loss of $2.5 billion dollars for the second quarter of 1987.

Almost fifty other banks followed Citicorp's example, setting aside nearly $17 billion, which caused a second quarter net loss of nearly $13 billion. However, because so much in banking is a matter of attitude (is a loan good, sorta bad, or definitely rotten? How much is it worth?) and because these reserves are a belated recognition of a situation that's existed for a long time, the losses should be taken with a grain of salt (that is, accounting conventions don't always accord with commonsense comparisons between money coming in and money going out.)

Still, banks have other things to worry about. There are plenty of bad loans right here in the United States. For example, New York's Chemical Bank was nicknamed "Comical Bank" for its spot of bad luck in lending $50 million to the late lamented Penn Central Railroad a month before its bankruptcy filing.

When oil prices were higher, lenders were enthusiastic about lending to the "oil patch." Today, with lower oil prices and economic doldrums in the Southwest, many of those loans have already been written off, which is leading to bank failures and to pressure on the federal insurance systems. Many more are in dubious condition.


## WHAT CAN'T BANKS DO?

The Glass-Steagall Act, passed in response to the Great Depression, forced banks to choose between "investment banking" (participating in securities underwriting—see page 31) and "commercial banking" or "savings banking" (accepting deposits and making loans). It's only one of the many state and federal laws controlling banking.

For a long time—from the depression era to the Depository Institutions Deregulation Act of the 1980s—a real distinction existed between "commercial banks," which offered no-interest checking accounts and specialized in business loans, and "savings banks," which did not offer checking accounts but which made personal loans and paid somewhat higher interest rates on savings accounts. (*Forbes* magazine described commercial banks as the "One-Minute Lender" because that's often how long it took to turn down small-business loan applications.)

Since deregulation, banks are permitted to set their own interest rates (but depositors haven't benefited much in the long run—savings account interest rates are just about what they were before deregulation), and savings banks and savings and loans can offer *NOW* accounts (Negotiable Order of Withdrawal), which are not technically checking accounts but which work pretty much the same way.

However, there are still controls on the number of branches banks can have, on whether banks can have branches in more than one state, and on whether banks can buy or merge with banks in other states.

Some analysts feel that removing these controls—and repealing Glass-Steagall so all banks could participate in the lucrative underwriting field—would be a good idea because banks could become more competitive and more profitable. After all, banks are prevented from competing with securities firms, but securities firms are allowed to usurp traditional bank functions. Furthermore, American banks must compete with banks of other nations, few of which are subject to the same strict controls.

The other side of the argument is that banks must be prevented from speculating with their customers' money and that banking offers so many opportunities for dishonesty that it must be subject to strict government controls. The 1988 presidential elections will do a lot to determine whether there will be continuing decontrol of banking institutions, or whether the existing controls will remain or be strengthened.

## BANK TECHNOLOGY

In the nineteenth century, banks kept "bankers' hours" because it took several hours after the 3 P.M. closing for the bank clerks to enter all of the day's transactions in the bank's ledgers. (Before the effete development of the five-day workweek, they also had all day Saturday to catch up.) At first, banks would physically transfer gold bullion from one bank to another if, for example, the customers of the First National Bank wrote more checks to the customers of the Second National Bank than vice versa.

The sheer volume of transactions made this system increasingly impractical, and banks have always been enthusiastic about financial technology: first adding machines; then tabulating machines; and today computers. Without computers, it would be impossible for banks to keep up with the various accounts customers have (often a savings account, a checking account, a credit card offered by the bank, and a CD as well as a car loan, home mortgage, and student loan) and to keep track of financial relationships with other banks.

However, computer professionals sneer at the fact that banks often have many different, quite incompatible, computer systems for different activities since that not only raises costs and processing time, but makes it impossible for the bank to do really sophisticated analyses of the profitability of different bank activities or of the status of a particular customer's accounts.

The ATM is changing the way that banks do business. The ATM liberates the customer from bankers' hours: simple bank transactions can be carried out at the customer's convenience, not the bank's. As long as the bank can afford the initial $25,000 cost of an ATM and the $10,000 to $15,000 it costs to install one, it's a good deal for the bank, too. Machines don't get salaries, don't tire, and don't unionize. Besides, banks often find it hard to recruit and keep tellers. It's an entry-level job with a low salary, yet it calls for considerable reading and math skills (and an unusually high resistance to temptation).

Some bank employees yield spectacularly to temptation: annual bank fraud losses in 1986 were more than $1 billion, about six times those of 1978 and 30 percent over 1985 levels. One factor is deregulation: when thrift institutions can make more kinds of loans, they can make more kinds of *crooked* loans. Then the more sophisticated the technology is that banks use, the more ways there are for smart crooks to tap the till— electronically (until an even smarter law enforcement agency catches up).

## BANK EMPLOYEES

There are really two classes of bank employees. Tellers and clerical workers are the lower class, with low salaries, few benefits, and comparatively little chance for advancement. These jobs also offer little security since there's a real risk that they will disappear as a result of automation, bank failure, or bank merger.

The managers and officers are the upper class. Although the road from being a "platform officer"—the first professional person to rule on a loan application or give out information about the bank's services—to being a bank president or vice president is long (and not everyone makes it), the rewards at the top are substantial. In 1986, A. Brittain III, the chairman of Banker's Trust, earned $1,300,000 in salary and bonus in addition to $1,299,000 in long-term compensation (basically stock options). Citicorp's chairman, J. S. Reed, earned a salary and bonus of $1,143,000, and a bit more than $1.5 million in long-term compensation. About a quarter (192 out of 800) of the best-paid CEOs in America, as identified by *Forbes* in 1986, came from the banking industry; and the industry newsletter *Bank Letter* reports that nine top executives of the ten top banks earned more than $1 million in 1986 in salaries and bonuses. Maybe it's the proximity of all that money: boards of directors find it easy to vote high salaries for top bank executives.

## THE BANK OF THE FUTURE

Yes, there probably will be banks in the future. For a while, it was predicted that everyone would "bank at home" by using their home computers to transfer amounts electronically. But not everyone has a home computer, much less one compatible with the local bank's computer system; and the "cashless society," like the "paperless office," never quite came to pass.

The bank of the future will probably be part of a chain. Banks are likely to acquire other, financially weaker banks. Depending on the way the law changes, they may have free reign to acquire banks in other states. The bank of the future may even be a franchise: Enterprise Bank, for example, hopes to have twenty-five operations targeting small businesses in the Southeast by 1990. Denver's Young Americans Bank starts early to build customer loyalty: it has special, low-to-the-ground tellers' windows and Saturday hours with performances by clowns.

However, customers may have to go further to find a bank branch or squeeze into a smaller one. Given increased rent and payroll costs, banks are considering either closing neighborhood bank branches or moving to tighter quarters.

It's dollars to doughnuts that the bank of the future will charge more for its services. Between deregulation and financial sophistication, customers expect more—more services and more interest. That cuts into bank profit margins; to recoup, banks must charge more for maintaining accounts, for each check written, and for the use of ATMs. A report published by the U.S. General Accounting Office in 1987 shows that as a result of deregulation the percentage of accounts offered without fees was cut (by 1985, only about 20 percent of bank checking accounts did not carry fees; a total fee of $57 a year was typical); minimum balances on no-fee savings accounts were imposed; and charges for printing checks, stop-payment orders, and bounced checks went up about 20 percent over 1977 levels.

The bank of the future is likely to offer comprehensive financial planning services, either on its own (if laws change) or in collaboration with another organization. Maybe the bank will open a branch in a supermarket or discount store. In 1986, K Mart Corporation started a successful pilot program, adding convenience banking centers to K Marts in the Chicago area; expansion to other states continued throughout 1987 and 1988. But maybe the integration will work the other way: by mid-1987, customers of about two-thirds of the largest banks could buy mutual funds from mutual fund issuers operating in bank branches.

## Savings and Loan Institutions

A savings and loan institution, like a savings bank, is a "thrift" institution, set up to provide a place for local savers to earn interest on their money and get home mortgages. In the years following World War II, when the demand for mortgages was high, they flourished.

In the 1970s, as high inflation drove market rates up, other institutions got into the mortgage and savings business, and depositors switched to mutual funds, which offered them higher yields. The savings and loans

## CONSUMER TIP

The bank of the immediate future will have to clear your checks faster. Thanks to the federal Expedited Funds Availability Act, banks, thrifts, and credit unions will have to clear checks within no more than seven business days. The seven-day period can be used to clear checks drawn on out-of-town banks, but checks written on local banks must be cleared within three business days. Cashier's checks, certified checks, and government checks must be credited to the depositor's account the next business day after deposit. However, to protect banks against fraud, deposits over $5,000 can be held four extra days; deposits to new accounts—the most frequent sources of fraud—can be held for eight days. Ninety-nine percent of checks *don't* bounce, but that 1 percent of rubber adds up to $47 billion a year.

In 1990, the time periods will be reduced to two working days for hometown checks; five days for out-of-town checks.

had been holding rates at below what they had to pay depositors, and market forces forced them to diversify; deregulation in 1980 gave them legal sanction to do so. They got into commercial loans, office buildings, condos, and even fast-food franchises. Savings and loans had soon lost their special function, so in order to attract savers they had to pay very high rates for CDs. But mortgage rates were so high that many potential new applicants were scared away (or rejected, because they couldn't pay the elevated interest rates)—and the savings and loans had huge "portfolios" of twenty- and thirty-year mortgages, at rates of 5 and 6 percent. Since the S and Ls then had to pay someone 14 percent to get his new account while their old mortgages were only paying 5.5 percent, they were in big trouble.

The result was a wave of failures, and a shopping spree as healthier institutions bought up sickly ones. Nevertheless, in 1986 the savings and loan industry was far from dead, with assets of $132,396 million, sales of $14,791 million, and a market value of $9,147 million. But by 1988, S and Ls were in a national crisis; of the 3,000 institutions in the country, nearly 1,000 were losing money—over $7 billion by October.

Many of these, particularly in Texas, Colorado, Florida, and California, are insolvent, the loans on their books, as reported in *Business Week,* often worthless.

But to fix this gigantic mess means closing down the savings and loans and paying their federally insured depositors, which could cost taxpayers a mind-boggling amount of money—as much as $100 billion.

Where are S and Ls headed? Probably into the sunset. Congress's 1987 bailout—issuing $10.8 billion in bonds for insolvent thrifts—is not the end of the crisis. The Bank Board is struggling and, with hundreds of S and Ls still operating, even its reforms will probably change little. Meanwhile, don't deposit your money in an S and L unless you know the institution is sound. If you're a gambler at heart, you might rely on state or private insurance or on the chance of a merger if your institution gets into trouble, but healthy thrifts, according to *Business Week,* are being expected to shore up the FSLIC, which they expect to take half of their 1988 profits.

# Credit Unions

Historically, Americans have been suspicious of banks, and politicians have always been able to score points by yelling at the "malefactors of great wealth." Isn't there some way for people to arrange their own financial transactions, to keep their money safe, and to get loans for their modest needs—without marble walls and million-dollar salaries for bank presidents?

Well, yes. A group of people (typically, members of an organization, or employees of a single company) can join together to form a "credit union"—an association that is chartered either by the state or federal government. Credit unions operate very much like savings and loan associations. Credit union members can deposit cash or checks, have payroll deductions from their salaries transferred to the credit union, and can write "share drafts" that work very much like Negotiable Orders of Withdrawal—that is, like checks. Some credit unions issue credit cards.

Credit unions are owned by their members and are operated as not-for-profit corporations. (By the end of 1986, there were 54.5 million credit union members, with total deposits of nearly $160 billion.) They can do quite well in conventional accounting terms.

According to Dun & Bradstreet's 1987 figures, the federal credit unions it sampled had gross profits of 52.9 percent of net sales and net profits after taxes of 10.0 percent. The most successful had a return on sales of 15.9 percent, and even the least successful managed a 3.1 percent return on sales. State credit unions had a lower gross profit (39.4 percent),

## CONSUMER TIP

More than two-thirds of the credit unions that issue credit cards do not charge a fee; about the same percentage offer a grace period (a time during which credit is free as long as the customer pays the entire credit card bill before the scheduled date).

but an even higher after-tax net profit (12.5 percent); return on sales ranged from 5.9 percent to a very impressive 46.0 percent. Credit unions were able to achieve these profits because much of their work is done by volunteers and because they either rent modest quarters or have space donated by employers or community groups.

Traditionally, credit unions have been major auto-loan lenders (in November 1986, they made 17.3 percent of the car loans; banks made about half). However, low-rate financing available through auto manufacturers' incentive programs has made credit union loans less attractive and may lower the credit unions' financial returns in the future.

# The Insurance Industry

| Number of establishments: | 937 life insurance companies |
|---|---|
| | 215 accident/health insurance companies |
| Average net sales: | $27,653,557,000 (life insurance) |
| | $32,134,842,000 (accident/health insurance) |

D&B, '87.

The insurance business is one that often confuses and frustrates consumers. Hundreds of insurers sell each kind of policy, so intelligent financial planning requires research on and comparison of the coverage and services each insurer provides and the premiums it charges. Once you choose what kind of insurance you need (automobile, health, homeowner's, life, long-term care, business, liability, or one of the many others) and an insurer, you still have dozens of options. You'll have to distinguish among fly-by-night companies; companies that provide legitimate coverage, but do so inefficiently and at excessive cost to their policyholders; and companies that provide excellent low-cost coverage. It's great to have a lot of choices, but it's tough and time-consuming to pick, and you might

19

## Where the Money Comes From (Property and Casualty Insurance)

| | |
|---|---|
| (1) Automobile liability insurance (consumers): | 20.9 % |
| (2) Collision and comprehensive (consumers): | 14.32% |
| (3) Workers compensation: | 13.64% |
| (4) Homeowner's multiple peril | 10.26% |
| (5) Commercial multiple peril | 7.03% |
| (6) General liability | 6.57% |
| (7) Commercial auto liability | 4.91% (cars owned by businesses) |
| (8) Commercial collision & comprehensive | 2.73% |
| (9) Medical malpractice | 1.51% |
| (10) All other | 18.54% |

(GAO, '76–85)

## Where the Money Goes

| | Cost of Operations | Officers Comp. | Pensions, Benefits | Rent | Repairs | Depreciation |
|---|---|---|---|---|---|---|
| Life insurers (stock) | 45.9 | 0.4 | 0.9 | 0.5 | — | 0.8 |
| Life insurers (mutual) | 33.2 | 0.4 | 0.6 | 0.4 | — | 1.6 |
| Other insurers | 49.7 | 0.6 | 0.7 | 1.0 | 0.2 | 0.8 |
| Agents, brokers, services | 19.1 | 12.1 | 2.8 | 3.4 | 0.5 | 3.3 |

| | Interest | Bad Debts | Ads | State, Local Taxes | Other | Net Profit Before Taxes |
|---|---|---|---|---|---|---|
| Life insurers (stock) | 1.7 | 0.1 | 0.5 | 1.6 | 45.4 | 2.1 |
| Life insurers (mutual) | 1.8 | — | 0.2 | 1.3 | 57.4 | 3.1 |
| Other insurers | 1.8 | 0.1 | 0.6 | 1.8 | 38.6 | 4.1 |
| Agents, brokers, services | 2.8 | 0.9 | 0.9 | 3.1 | 49.5 | 1.6 |

(Troy, '84–'85)

easily feel dwarfed by the economic might of the insurance companies themselves.

We're talking about a *lot* of money here. *Business Week*'s industry forecast for 1987 called insurance a $160 billion industry, with profits of about $15 billion (about a 40 percent rise from 1986 levels). Much of that profit comes from investments, not "underwriting" (that is, actually carrying on the insurance business). Consider what an insurance company does: it collects premiums from thousands or millions of policyholders. Then it gets to hold on to the premiums either for a while (until the life insurance policyholder either dies or surrenders the policy) or forever (if it's an insurance policy on a car that neither crashes nor is stolen).

If it's a liability insurance policy (for instance, a doctor's medical malpractice insurance), a very large claim—or even a court judgment— isn't an unmitigated disaster for the insurer. It still gets to keep the money in question until the appeals process is complete. Even if the case is lost on appeal and the insurer has to pay up, it has several years' worth of investment income as consolation. However, it gets to cry "poor" by reporting its income as if it paid out the full sum as soon as the jury foreman gave the bad news.

What do insurance companies do with the money? They buy massive amounts of stocks and bonds. They purchase and develop real estate. They provide venture capital for new businesses and lend to existing businesses. They buy mortgages on the "secondary market" (that is, they pay the original lender a discounted amount for the right to receive the continuing mortgage payments), which makes it possible for lenders to give more mortgages. That's why Andrew Tobias's best-selling book about the insurance industry is called *The Invisible Bankers:* insurance companies use their money (or, if you prefer, their policyholders' premium money) to carry out many traditional banking functions.

Insurance companies are also invisible brokers. A property or casualty insurance policy, or a term life insurance policy, has no investment aspects. But a whole-life policy accumulates cash value, which can be "tapped" through policy loans (sort of like home equity loans that allow a homeowner to take advantage of increases in the value of the home). Other kinds of life insurance (single-premium whole life, universal life, variable life, variable universal life) combine investment features with life insurance. For many families, these life insurance policies represent a major part (if not the whole) of their investment portfolio.

Many insurance companies are moving beyond their traditional roles to become visible brokers and financial planners by offering mutual funds or discount brokerage or both through a subsidiary and by offering detailed financial plans, including a number of factors in addition to insurance.

# Life Insurance

Life insurance is different from other forms of insurance in that the insured event is not something that probably won't happen (the house burning down) but something that is a lead-pipe cinch to happen: the insured person is absolutely guaranteed to die, though not necessarily at a time when he has a life insurance policy in force.

There are two kinds of life insurance companies: stock companies, which are owned by stockholders, like ordinary business corporations, and mutual companies, which are owned by their policyholders, who can receive dividends in the form of lower premiums. Some observers believe the mutual insurers are more interested in cost cutting than stock companies both because they have to keep their policyholders happy and because mutual policyholders are more likely to take a greater personal interest in the company's management than stockholders who have a portfolio including many other stocks.

Let's take a look at some of the figures involved. In 1987, Aetna Life & Casualty was #97 on *Business Week*'s Top 1000, with a market value of over $5,155 billion and assets of nearly $72 billion. On sales topping $22 billion, its profits were $867.4 million—that is, a return on invested capital of 13.1 percent and a return on common equity of 14.0 percent. For 1987, its profit margin was 3.9 percent. A smaller company but still a major economic force, US Life had 1987 sales of $1.189 billion and profits of $74.7 million. It had a (comparatively) small staff of 2,000. Its margins were quite a bit higher than Aetna's: a healthy 6.3 percent in 1987.

Farmers Group, Inc., is a management and holding company; its more than 13,000 agents sell both life insurance and accident/health insurance. Its 1987 sales were $1.13 billion; its profits, $289.8 million. There were 14,700 employees handling the company's administrative and clerical work, headed by Leo E. Denlea, Jr., a CEO who earned $551,000 in salary and bonus and 19,000 shares in the company. In 1984, the company took in $183,274,000 in life and annuity premiums. (In an annuity arrangement, a person transfers money to an insurance company—usually a large lump sum—in return for the company's agreement to pay either a set amount or a continuing series of payments starting at an agreed time.)

Farmers Group took in about $177,893,000 each in accident and health premiums for a total premium income of $361,167,000. Then the company earned $107,782,000 in net investment income, so its total revenues were $468,949,000. Naturally, Farmers Group didn't get to keep all the money: it had to pay out nearly $100 million in life and annuity benefits and $138,568,000 in accident and health benefits. So life insurance brought in more premiums, while costing less in benefits.

Next came some accounting fancy footwork. The company reserved about $25 million to cope with "increase in liability for future policy benefits" (that is, coping with increasing health care costs) and about $42 million for "amortization—deferred policy acquisition costs." The agents were paid commissions of $24,839,000, which doesn't sound like all that much considering that the company has 13,000 agents.

The company's total operating expenses were $364,823,000 (about 78 percent of revenues), leaving a pretax income of $104,117,000. The company set aside a little over 10 percent of its pretax income for income taxes, so that its net income from "personal lines" (life, accident, and health insurance) was $92,969,000. The company had about the same amount of net income from property and casualty insurance, leaving a consolidated net income of $185,861,000.

In short, it had to start out with close to $500 million in premiums and other income to end up with about $186 million. Its tax rate is probably a lot lower than yours because insurance companies are entitled to certain favorable accounting assumptions when they tally their income for tax purposes.

# Property and Casualty Insurance

In a way, insurers have a kind of monopoly: everybody who has a mortgage has to have fire insurance, and sensible homeowners supplement the coverage that protects the lender with coverage that reimburses them for their losses if the home is the site of a fire, flood, theft, or other catastrophe.

Similarly, drivers are usually required to maintain a certain (albeit low) amount of liability insurance merely in order to register their cars, and basic common sense (supplemented by pep talks from insurance agents) suggests adding a lot more liability insurance even if the car is a miserable old clunker that doesn't deserve collision coverage.

Nobody requires businesses to maintain property or liability insurance, and some of the businesses at either end of the economic spectrum "go bare" (do without commercial insurance coverage, "self-insure" by investing the amount that would otherwise be spent on insurance premiums so that funds will be available in the situations when insurance claims would be made, or simply close their eyes and hope the problem will go away). The smallest businesses do this because they can't afford the premiums and are fatalistically resigned to going out of business if an otherwise insurable calamity occurs. The biggest businesses do this because they think they can invest wisely enough to make sure funds are available when and if necessary.

Property/casualty insurers are in a very different position from life insurers (although some companies are in both kinds of business). Life insurers can be pretty sure that they'll have to pay, and they know exactly how much they'll have to pay, but they don't know when. Property/casualty insurers know that most policyholders will pay premiums obediently but never make a claim; they don't know when they'll have to pay off on the exceptions, and they don't know how much they'll have to pay. Sure, there are policy limits, but a business or a professional practice often holds a multimillion-dollar policy. If an insurance company can't settle a claim against a liability insured, the case must go to court—and judges and juries can be notably generous to a poor little guy who's up against a big, bad insurance company. (And if the insurer doesn't pay off on a property claim or doesn't treat its liability insureds fairly, it may be sued by the insured person for bad faith: plaintiffs charging bad faith have gotten some pretty impressive judgments against insurance companies.)

That's one reason why insurance companies are in the forefront of so-called tort reform: laws that limit the amount that a plaintiff in a personal injury case can recover for pain and suffering and other essentially subjective elements that are left to the discretion of the judge or jury. Insurance companies point out that the number of court cases just keeps increasing (which is true, though most of the increase is in business-related, not personal injury, cases) and so do judgments (also true, but why penalize some poor devil who has been terribly injured by someone else's negligence? Besides, trial court judges have the power to cut down unreasonable jury awards; jury verdicts can be appealed, and cases are often settled after trial for a lower amount, so the injured person won't have to wait for an appeal and take the risk of having the award overturned). The insurers also tell sad tales of how their once-proud industry has been humbled to the dust and all possibility of profit destroyed by greedy plaintiffs, malignant public-interest lawyers, and profligate juries.

Is this true? Responding to a Congressional call, the federal General Accounting Office issued a report in July 1987 called "Insurance: Profitability of Medical Malpractice and General Liability Lines." According to the report, the insurance industry did have "underwriting losses" for the period 1976–1985: that is, claims paid out and expenses were about $65 billion greater than the net premiums earned for this period. But they had investment gains of more than $144 billion.

That means that they came out about $79.5 billion ahead of the game before taxes and, as a result of the accounting rules applied to insurers, didn't have to pay federal income taxes; in fact, they emerged with "negative income taxes," which can be used to reduce their income tax liability in the somewhat unlikely case that they ever have to pay any. Thanks to this bit of largesse from the Internal Revenue Code, the industry was more than $81 billion ahead during this time period.

## TRADE TALK

The "combined ratio" is a company's claims and expenses divided by its premium income. So, if the combined ratio is less than 100 percent, the company has underwriting profits (premiums coming in are larger than claims and expenses going out); if it's more than 100 percent, there's an underwriting loss. For 1976–1985, the combined ratio for all property/casualty insurance was 105.9 percent—that is, there was an overall underwriting loss, even though some lines were profitable (consumers' collision/comprehensive insurance, fire insurance, and burglary and theft insurance, for instance). In 1985, the Top 10 general liability insurers collected 43.5 percent of all general liability insurance premiums, or a little over $5 billion of the approximately $11 billion total. They absorbed 30.2 percent of the underwriting losses: $1.43 billion out of $4.75 billion. The Top 10 companies (American International, CNA, Crum & Forster, Motors Insurance Group, Travelers, Aetna, Hartford, Chubb Corporation, Liberty Mutual, Continental) had combined ratios of 130.4 percent, which isn't so great. But the industry as a whole did even worse: 145.3 percent. One of the Top Ten companies, Motors Insurance Group, actually managed a sizeable underwriting profit, with a combined ratio of 90 percent, probably because automobile insurance tends to be more profitable than other kinds of property/casualty insurance.

But the combined ratio doesn't tell the whole story. Insurers hardly ever pay a claim as soon as it's filed; usually years elapse, and the insurer can earn money on its reserves (money put away to pay future claims) in the interim. If the insurance industry's figures are discounted (that is, if you assume that they invested the reserves in Treasury bills—a safe, conservative investment), then the industry as a whole did not *lose* $653 million on medical malpractice insurance premiums between 1975–1985, as it reported: it *earned* $2.2 billion. Instead of a rate of return of −4.6 percent, the discounted rate of return is 15.3 percent—quite a difference. And discounting changes the reported profit on general liability insurance from $2 billion (3.4 percent rate of return) to $8 billion (13.4 percent rate of return). Sometimes accountants can make things disappear faster than three-card monte dealers.

# Health Insurance

Health insurance has a tremendous effect on consumers, although it sort of lurks in the background, not attracting attention until people file an insurance claim and find out that they must pay a high deductible or assume part of the premium for the coverage. The outcry would probably be a lot louder if employers didn't pay most of the health insurance premiums, so that employees don't always think about this issue. Of course, salaries are adjusted accordingly, but the amount of premiums that employees pay out of their own pockets is comparatively small. (Self-employed people have to pay much higher premiums and may not be able to get the kind of comprehensive coverage offered by many group policies.)

Similarly, few people pay directly out-of-pocket for their own hospital care, and many people have at least part of the cost of medical and dental visits picked up by health insurance. That means that they don't always notice the full cost of treatment, though they're the ones who really pay for it in the last analysis. Aetna Life and Casualty's James L. Garcia estimates that health-care providers extract an extra $10 billion a year from the system through fraud. Pennsylvania's Blue Shield alone has asked for $2.2 million in refunds from doctors to make up for billing for health care that was never provided or that was provided but not medically necessary. Creative doctors have been known to bill for appointments that never occurred, to turn routine office visits into consultations with august (and nonexistent) specialists, and to turn a single procedure into three or four separate occasions for billing.

In 1986, 77 percent of Americans who lived outside institutions had some kind of health insurance, provided by over 1,200 private insurance companies. About 80 percent of the 176 million "junior citizens" (those under 65) had some health insurance, and 163 million had major medical coverage; about half of the senior citizens had private "Medi-Gap" policies to supplement their coverage under the federal government's Medicare system.

In 1984 (the last year for which the Health Insurance Association of America has compiled statistics), Americans paid $129 billion in health insurance premiums and received almost $109 billion in health insurance benefits. The Blue Cross–Blue Shield system collected about $68.5 billion of the premiums (52.73 percent of the total) and paid out $61.8 billion or so (56.73 percent).

Yet, no matter how high their premiums, health insurers aren't

## TRADE TALK/CONSUMER TIP

A health insurer's "loss ratio" is the percentage of its premiums paid out in claims. Their loss is your gain—one of the most important factors in choosing a health insurer is finding a company with a *high* loss ratio because that means that most of your premiums go to pay claims, not to cushion an entrenched and lazy bureaucracy or to fatten the company's coffers. According to the Gray Panther Network, the Medicare system had the highest loss ratio, 95 percent on $80 billion in claims made by senior citizen beneficiaries. The Blue Cross–Blue Shield system had a loss ratio of 90.4 percent; Prudential took in over $3 billion in health insurance premiums in 1986 and paid out $2.356 billion, for a loss ratio of 77 percent. But Union Fidelity Life's Medi-Gap policy, which was promoted heavily on television by senior celebrities, had a loss ratio of only 42.8 percent, making these policies less than a bargain for senior citizens.

always in clover. They face both customer resistance (employers are desperate to reduce health-care costs by making employees bear more of the burden if necessary or simply by cutting the amount of coverage they provide) and tremendous competition.

HMOs (Health Maintenance Organizations; see page 353) have made big inroads into the health insurance market. Insurers sometimes set up their own HMOs in response but often find that creating an HMO is a lengthy and expensive project; a new HMO often takes almost four years to become profitable. Health insurance premiums are increasing from 20 to 30 percent, and medical costs are rising from 15 to 20 percent, which means that some insurers are beating the rising cost of medical care while others are just keeping in step.

As is usual in the insurance industry, a preliminary round of pleading poverty is under way, as insurers gloomily predict that they will be ruined by the spread of AIDS. However, a comparatively small proportion of the victims of this terrible disease even have health insurance, so the cost impact on health insurers will be fairly small, though of course they'll raise everybody's premiums to compensate for the highest possible estimate of the number of cases of AIDS and the cost of care for AIDS patients.

# Insurance Agents and Brokers

The flip side of an insurance company's loss ratio is its expense ratio: the proportion of the premiums that goes to run the company. Much of the expense ratio represents advertising, especially if the company sells its policies directly to the public, without agents and commissions for insurance agents and brokers. (An agent sells policies issued by a single company; a broker sells policies from several companies.)

Being an insurance agent is a lot like being a stockbroker (except that the licensing requirements aren't as tough)—that is, a lot of people take it up each year, many on a part-time basis. Most of them find out that they're not very well suited to sales work, with its constant cold calls, endless brush-offs, and lengthy follow-ups needed to close a major deal. Insurance agents get a hefty share of the first year's premiums on a new policy they sell, and either a smaller share or nothing at all from policies that continue in force. (One company, LifeUSA, issues shares of its stock to agents based on their commission income.)

The new insurance agent usually starts out by asking friends, relatives, fraternity brothers, and remote acquaintances to buy insurance policies; when that source of business is exhausted, the agent either gives up and goes back to whatever he or she was doing before becoming an insurance agent or finds other sources of leads. Some people are spectacularly successful at this. Insurance companies used to honor successful agents by inducting them into a "Million Dollar Round Table" based on the face value of policies they sold; today, many agents bring in millions of dollars in premiums each year.

Steven E. Hancock, an Aetna marketing manager, has written that his office starts new agents off with an unpaid three- to six-month training period, in which the newcomers get an insurance license, study training materials, and go on joint sales calls with established agents ("How Can You Turn Personal Lines Into a Profit Center?" *Rough Notes,* August 1987). Then they spend six months to two years working in the office before going out on their own. They get a level monthly draw against their commissions, and the office keeps 20 percent of the commissions as an

## TRADE TALK

"Twisting" is the practice of getting a customer to drop a perfectly good policy simply to buy another one that provides a large commission for the agent. It's the equivalent of a broker's "churning" a portfolio.

## CONSUMER TIP

How can you recognize twisting? When the agent can't give you a believable reason why the new policy is better for you than the old one.

overhead charge. Trainees are expected to bring in at least one application for a policy each day: 250 a year.

Mr. Hancock's goal for the office is a 10 percent profit on commissions, with 30 percent of the total commissions brought in to go to the
agents who produced them. Ten cents of each commission dollar goes to
the expenses of developing business (advertising, travel); sixteen cents to
operating and administrative expenses; five cents to agency planning and
"management override," twenty cents to paying the nonsales office staff,
and nine cents for employee benefits. He suggests a commission structure
starting at 50 percent of the first year's premium for new policies, and
maybe 10 to 15 percent for renewal policies, with additional incentives for
agents who can keep customers renewing their policies for three or more
years.

So don't hang up on your brother-in-law when he calls to discuss
his new career in insurance sales. (Mind you, we're not necessarily saying
you should buy a policy, especially if he's trying to "twist" you.) Remember that it can be a very tough way to earn a buck.

# The Securities Industry

Security brokers and dealers: of the 1,654 establishments surveyed, gross profit was 39.7% of sales; net profit after tax was 5.0%. Return on sales ranged from a low of 1.1% to a high of 13.4%; return on assets, from 1.3 to 12.6%. (D & B '87)

Top earners: Alan C. Greenberg, CEO of investment banking firm The Bear Stearns Companies: 1987 earnings of $2,448,000 plus 1,369,000 shares in salary and bonus; Donald B. Marron of Paine, Webber Group, Inc. earned $1,975,000 in salary and bonus, plus 320,000 shares.

In the securities industry, "the good old days" started in the late 1960s (with a few bad months here and there), culminated in a gigantic Reagan era bull market, and ended abruptly on October 19, 1987, when the Dow-Jones average dipped more than 500 points and investors dived for cover. About 15,000 workers in the securities industry lost their jobs; Wall Street firms saw earnings and profits drop or disappear.

If you're muttering "Who cares?" or "Serves them right," remember that the health of the securities market ("Wall Street") affects even those who never buy stocks. Pension benefits, for example, depend on investments made by the pension fund's managers—who invest heavily in stocks and bonds. The value of America's currency is related to the securities market; and that, in turn, affects whether you can afford to vacation

**Where the Money Came From (10 Brokerage Firms)**

| | |
|---|---|
| (1) Trading profits: | 25.18% |
| (2) Merger, acquisition fees: | 21.73% |
| (3) Commissions: | 20.62% |
| (4) Underwriting: | 13.45% |
| (5) Selling mutual funds: | 9.24% |
| (6) Interest on margin accounts: | 6.79% |
| (7) Fees for management and advice: | 2.85% |

(Securities Industry Association, '86)

in Europe or buy a Japanese car as well as whether the company you work for can sell its products abroad. If it can't, you may find yourself out of a job.

If people lose confidence (or all their money), they don't buy new houses or new cars—with bad results for the real estate market and the auto industry (and, indirectly, the steel and glass industries). The securities market and the government's response to its conditions affect interest rates, which in turn determine how much it costs you to get a mortgage or take out a loan.

Also the securities business is a major employer, especially in New York. In the decade 1977–1987, of the 400,000 new jobs created in the New York economy, 75,000 of them were related to Wall Street and 40,000 to banking. It's estimated that 8 percent of jobs in New York are directly affected by the market; for instance, the broker takes a client out for a luncheon of leek flan and duck steak while his secretary "orders in" an egg-salad sandwich and Diet Coke. Investment bankers burn up the telephone wires, pay huge sums of money to law firms, and order expensive office furniture. In short, when Wall Street starts singing the blues, much of America takes up the chorus.

The securities business is highly interrelated, with many firms participating in several parts of it. So a firm we discuss in connection with brokerage may also be a powerhouse in investment banking or commodities, and vice versa.

# Investment Bankers

Just what is it that investment bankers do, and why do they make so much money? Okay, they arrange deals: the "underwriting" (issuance) of stock by corporations and of bonds by corporations and government entities. They also advise and handle the securities aspects of one company's attempt to take over another company (and the potential victim's de-

Where the Money Went (Security Brokers and Dealers)

| | | |
|---|---|---|
| (1) Cost of operations: | 7.8% | (not too high—once you open an office, you're set; basically, the securities industry sells electronic blips, so there's no inventory and no warehouse required, although a lot of "back office" space is needed to process all those transactions) |
| (2) Officers' compensation: | 7.4% | |
| (3) Pensions and benefits: | 1.9% | (the ungenerous nature of this figure was one impulse behind the November 1987 strike of securities-industry clerical workers) |
| (4) Rent: | 2.7% | (back offices can be anywhere where telephone lines are efficient and rents are cheap—even, God help us, New Jersey) |
| (5) Repairs: | 0.2% | (naturally, investment banking firms and brokerages have lots of telephones and computers, but they don't have punch presses or motor pools) |
| (6) Depreciation, depletion, amortization: | 3.3% | (must be on the computer equipment) |
| (7) Interest: | 20.1% | (much higher than other industries because the firms have to borrow huge amounts of money to swing deals) |
| (8) Bad debts: | 0.7% | |
| (9) Advertising: | 1.1% | |
| (10) State, local taxes: | 2.4% | |
| (11) Other expenses: | 44.6% | |
| (12) Net profit before tax: | 7.8% | |

(Troy, '83–'84)

fense). They make so much money because they participate in deals involving billions of dollars. In 1986, the twenty biggest investment banks had revenues of more than $35 billion—after all, they participated in many of the 3,000 mergers and buyouts (where a total of $250 billion was flying around) and handled the underwriting of much of the $50 billion that was issued in "junk bonds" (bonds paying high interest but with a high risk of default, often used to finance takeovers).

When an investment banking firm underwrites an issue of securities (in effect, acting as the "wholesaler" between the "manufacturer," or issuer, and the institutions who buy the stock or the retail brokerage firms that sell it to the public), part of its compensation consists of some of the bonds, or shares of the stock, underwritten. Usually, the price of a security goes up right after it's issued (the way the price of an apartment goes up right after the building goes co-op or becomes a condo), so the investment banking firm can earn a lot more money by selling the stock or bonds.

Sometimes, though, the price goes down; or the investment banking firm can agree to sell securities from its inventory and lose money because conditions change. In April 1987, a kind of mini-crash occurred in the price of bonds. First Boston, Inc. (despite the name, it's on Wall Street) lost about $100 million, at just about the time Merrill Lynch lost $275 million trading mortgage bonds and getting caught in interest rate changes.

In 1986, First Boston's revenues from investment banking were nearly $700 million, and trading and investing its own capital brought in another $400 million in revenues. In 1987, even more revenue came in from investment banking—about $850 million—but trading and investment revenues were approximately halved, to some $212 million. That might not sound so bad, but its net income nose-dived: its 1987 net income was only $108.9 million, way down from the 1986 figure of $180.6 million—and things would have been even worse if the firm hadn't pulled in close to $50 million by selling a building.

In one sense, investment banking firms get their "league standings" when the quarterly results are computed. In another sense, a firm's standing in the profession is measured by the "billing" it receives in the "tombstone" ads (so called because they consist largely of a list of names, in the solemn typeface and arrangement suitable for a headstone) that announce securities underwritings. The lead underwriters (the most important in arranging the transaction and distributing the securities) are listed at the top of the ad. Then there are brackets, with the investment banking firms listed in alphabetical order within the brackets, much as a movie's stars might be billed above the title, with costars and supporting actors billed later on and in smaller type.

## TRADE TALK

An underwriter's fee is based on the *underwriting amount,* the amount of stock it theoretically receives. The fee is set at a certain number of pennies per share of the underwriting amount. However, the amount that the firm actually receives and can sell, called the *retention,* can be either larger or smaller than the underwriting amount.

Firms will go so far as to sacrifice money to have their names appear in a more prestigious position in the tombstone ad. It's even said that when the managing partner of a leading firm found out that his firm was being knocked down to a lower position in the tombstone ad, he reacted by shooting himself. (Nowadays, an investment banker in that situation would probably shoot the underwriter responsible for the ranking.)

In 1982, the Securities and Exchange Commission (SEC) changed its rules to allow corporations to make "shelf registrations": instead of going through the complex and expensive registration process whenever they needed to raise capital by issuing new securities, they could get SEC approval in advance, then issue the securities whenever they needed the money (sort of General Motors Corporation's equivalent of a home equity credit line). The shelf registration rule changed the way that investment bankers do business. Before the rule change, major underwritings used to be handled by very large syndicates (cooperative ventures by many investment banking firms). But shelf registrations are often "bought deals": a single, giant underwriting firm buys all the securities issued by a corporation, then uses its own distribution system to get the securities to investors.

Only very big firms can afford to bid on bought deals (so the start of shelf underwriting was very bad news for the smaller firms); and when these huge firms compete, they can get involved in price wars (very good news for the firms issuing the securities), driving the "spread" (the difference between the price the "buyer" of the bought deal pays for the securities, and the price at which he sells them to investors) to as low as 1 percent on a bond issue. Of course, when billions of dollars are at stake, 1 percent can be a nice chunk of change.

Investment banks not only underwrite securities, but they speculate in them, selling securities earned in underwriting and bought deals and other securities purchased in the hope of later price increases. The more daring firms also do risk arbitrage.

The changes in the nature of investment banking both reflect and lead to changes in the nature of investment bankers. Once a genteel occupation for wealthy WASP males, investment banking now attracts the brilliant, hardworking, and mercenary of both sexes (in 1985, one-third of the entry-level jobs went to women) and many ethnic backgrounds. When one investment banker describes another as "lacking in total greed," that's a deadly insult.

However, investment banking is not a business for the middle-ager or the senior citizen. About half to two-thirds of those working in the financial sector have less than ten years' experience; it's been estimated that half are under thirty-five. Nor is it a business for those who want a small, steady income. Big bucks are available, but not guaranteed.

# TRADE TALK

*Risk arbitrage* means buying stocks that you believe will be involved
in a merger or takeover in the hope that the stock's price will rise.
It's "risk" arbitrage because the investment banking firm can guess
wrong—or succumb to the temptation of (and get caught at) insider
trading, which is illegal. There's also risk-free arbitrage, which consists of taking advantage of price differences in different markets.
If you know you can buy silver in London for $X an ounce, and
immediately sell it in Paris for $X plus $10 an ounce, that's a
successful arbitrage transaction (as long as your transaction costs
are less than $10 an ounce). Sometimes investment banking firms
also put up their own money as temporary, or "bridge," loans until
a takeover plan goes through; the risk in such a case is that the deal
won't go through or that the borrower won't be able to repay the
loan three or six months later when it comes due.

In the summer of 1987, newly minted M.B.A.s from the top
schools could earn as much as $100,000 their first year out of school—
which doesn't work out to all that much per hour given the typical
eighty-hour workweek. In 1983, a single Wall Street firm had six happy
folks with paychecks of over $1 million (not counting their profit share).
An investment banker estimated that about one-third of the five hundred or so partners and managing directors in investment banking
houses earned over $1 million a year. But after the 1987 crash, pay-
checks got slimmer. The top management at Morgan Stanley Group,
Inc., got a pay raise in 1987, and its five top executives each earned
nearly—or more than—$3 million a year; but top management at other
firms earned less in 1987 than in 1986. John H. Gutfreund of Salomon
Brothers, Inc., even passed up his bonus, relying on his $300,000 salary
and stock options (and $800,000 in earnings deferred from 1984). The
pay of William A. Schreyer, the chairman of Merrill Lynch & Co., Inc.,
was cut almost in half: to a cool million in 1987 from an even cooler
$1.9 million in 1986.

In July 1987, Salomon Brothers ranked as the #1 managing underwriter in the United States, acting as lead underwriter on eighty-four issues
totalling over $10 billion. Salomon was #85 on *Business Week*'s Top 1000
list published in April 1987, with 1986 sales of $6.78 billion and profits of
$516 million. Yet by November Salomon's municipal finance department
had been shuttered, and two hundred specialists hit the bricks in search
of new jobs. In 1988, profits were down to $142 million, and Salomon had
slipped to #181. (What's the difference between a pigeon and a twenty-
seven-year-old investment banker with an M.B.A.? At least a pigeon can

still make a deposit on a BMW.) In fact, around Christmas of 1987, former brokers and stock analysts started applying to the classy caterer Glorious Food for jobs as waiters, and some of them even got the jobs; they know how to act around corporate executives and, unlike actors, they never take off for auditions.

In 1982, First Boston had revenues of $500 million. About half of that total came from securities trading, with commissions on First Boston's activities as a brokerage firm and the interest it earned on loans and dividends it received on its own stock portfolio constituting $100 million; the remaining $150 million came from investment banking. In 1983, its investment banking income was up to $198 million, but its trading income declined to $176 million. Sales in 1986 were $3.258 billion, and profits a decidedly modest $180.6 million.

Merrill Lynch, a well-known powerhouse in retail brokerage, also has an investment banking operation. In 1983, it had $1.9 billion in capital to play with, gross revenue of $5.6 billion, and earnings of $230 million. It wasn't the largest investment banking firm (in 1987, it was ranked #3, with seventy-six issues and about 12 percent of the market), but the firm as a whole was so large that it was bound to make an impact: $746 million worth in 1986 in investment banking activities as compared to $675 million trading securities for its own account (not for brokerage clients). In 1986, Merrill Lynch ranked #119 on the Top 1000 list, with sales of nearly $10 billion, profits of over $469 million, and profit margins of 7.1 percent in the fourth quarter of 1986. Those margins narrowed considerably in 1987, to 4.0 percent in the first quarter and to 3.4 percent in the second: those damned bond losses took their toll.

Things looked a lot worse in 1988. In the first quarter of 1988, net earnings were down to about $68 million (2.8 percent of the total revenues of approximately $2.4 billion). A year earlier, net earnings were much higher: $108.6 million, and 4.3 percent of the $2.538 billion total revenues. That 5.2 percent drop in revenues was fairly modest, considering that the stock market laid an egg in the interim, but net earnings were down 37.2 percent. A lot of the problem was that commissions were down 32.9 percent (from about $655 million, and 25.8 percent of revenues, in the first quarter of 1987, to $439 million, and 18.35 percent of revenues, a year later). Investment banking income was down 12 percent, to about $226.5 million.

The October 1987 stock market crash had a profound impact on investment banking. Although by early 1988 the mergers and acquisitions field was beginning to revive, some deals that were planned before the crash never went through; the business community was leery, and corporations became cautious about entering into new deals or issuing new securities. Now maybe kids will go back to idolizing sports heroes instead of investment bankers.

# Brokers

If you want to sell your house, you'll probably save yourself a lot of inconvenience, and even get a better deal, if you hire a real estate broker. But if you want to sell it yourself, you have a legal right to do so. If you want to buy or sell securities, though, you *must* employ the services (and pay the commissions) of a licensed broker. In fact, you pay a commission both when you buy a security and when you sell it—which is one reason why brokerage firms did pretty well in spite of the crash (although it certainly made it hard for them to keep giving advice with straight faces). There are two kinds of brokers: one sells to institutional investors, such as pension funds; the other sells retail to individuals.

Retail brokers, in turn, can be either "full-service" brokers, who not only execute orders (that is, buy and sell securities for clients) but also provide advice and reports compiled by analysts about particular companies, or "discount" brokers, who merely execute the orders of their customers. Discount brokers are so named because they provide lower, discounted commission rates. (Brokerage firms are allowed to set their own commission rates; like other businesses, they must decide whether to appeal to the carriage trade or the mass market.) As you'd expect, there are hybrid firms that are "sort of" discount brokers, providing some services in addition to carrying out trades.

The subject of commissions is a complex one. Theoretically, commissions are negotiable, and customers such as financial institutions with large accounts certainly can negotiate a fee of only a few cents per share. But retail customers have to pay the fees the broker demands and in the way he specifies: the broker can demand a flat fee per share traded, a sliding scale per share that declines as the number of shares traded or their value increases, or a percentage of the value of the shares traded.

In 1985, the average retail stockbroker earned $79,575; in 1986, a startling $97,100. Discount brokerages, however, tend to pay salaries (about a modest $25,000 a year) instead of paying commissions to their brokers. Brokers with institutional clients did even better, earning an average of $227,412 a year. (Institutions pay razor-thin commissions, but they can buy or sell million-share blocks, and they tend to trade actively instead of sitting on their stocks, so it all adds up.) Senior retail brokers

## TRADE TALK
Full-service retail brokerages are called "wirehouses."

## CONSUMER TIP

Watch out—if you are buying or selling a small number of shares, or shares of a low-priced security, a discount broker-age firm may set minimum commissions, so that you'd pay less to have a full-service broker carry out the same transactions at a commission calculated on the number or cost of the shares. If you trade a lot, it may pay to maintain accounts with both discount and full-service brokers, so you can compare the commission rates and pick the lowest for each transaction you plan.

Always ask your full-service broker if a lower commis-sion rate is available. Probably it won't be—unless you trade enough to have some clout with the firm or unless the broker is a rank beginner eager to compile a client list—but it doesn't hurt to ask. Firms often let brokers give discounts but penalize overly generous brokers by cutting the percentage of the commission that they can keep. At Paine, Webber Group, Inc., for instance, a broker who grants a 30 percent discount gets to keep $42 on a trade that generates a $200 commission; on a nondiscounted trade, he or she would be paid $80 on the same commission.

often make more than $125,000 a year, and the top producers earn at least $250,000.

There's hardly such a thing as an unsuccessful, experienced broker: people who can't bring in substantial income to the firm get tossed out on their ears a year to eighteen months after being hired. The broker gets to keep between 20 and 40 percent of the commissions he or she brings in, depending on whether the broker is a novice or a star eligible for all sorts of incentives. The broker's cut also depends on whether the firm is having a banner year or tightening its belt: when times are tough, the broker's share is cut "to encourage them to get on the phone" and sell, sell, sell.

According to the estimate of Terry J. Arnold, a vice president at Merrill Lynch, every dollar that the brokerage takes in costs about twenty cents in administrative costs and five cents in special bonuses (plus the normal forty cents to the broker), leaving thirty-five cents, or about one-third, for other expenses and profits. Discount brokerages, though, aver-age only 25 percent employee costs. Lipper Analytical Services' estimate

## CONSUMER TIP

If you pay more than 10 percent of your account's value in commissions each year, your account may be being "churned" by a "stock jockey" who keeps advising you to change your investments merely to increase his commissions. If you pay more than 20 percent, it's almost certain.

is that 1987 pretax earnings for security firms would be about 8 percent of revenues—way below 1985 or 1986 earnings, which hovered around 10 percent, and much less than the 14 percent earned in 1980.

The product coordinator for a brokerage firm's branch office generally earns a bonus of $10,000 to $30,000 over and above commission income; the branch office manager probably earns a salary of $125,000; the second in command for the region, the regional sales manager, probably knocks down $175,000 to $250,000; and the regional VP, probably $200,000 to $400,000. The very top management probably earn over $200,000, and may earn over $1 million.

In essence, a retail broker (sometimes called an "account executive," which sounds classier) is a kind of upscale Fuller Brush man. Once a would-be broker passes the standard exam given by the SEC and gets hired by a brokerage firm, he (or she—but most brokers are men) gets a desk, a telephone, access to the firm's research reports (if it has any) and recommendations (it always has *those*, whether the recommendations are sincerely meant to enrich the clients or just to get rid of some stock that the firm is desperate to get off its hands), and lists of "leads."

## CONSUMER TIP

If you're unsure of your investment direction, the availability and quality of research reports is an important factor in choosing a broker and a reason to prefer full-service to discount firms. If you know what you want, have your own investment system, or are cynical about the worth of the reports in predicting stock prices, the reports won't be a factor in your choice of broker.

Meanwhile, the broker telephones relatives, old school chums, and third cousins of acquaintances in search of people who'll open brokerage accounts. Once they open accounts, the broker's job is to reassure them in bad patches, spur them on in bull markets, and let them know about investments that might fit into their plans (as well as his own).

The firm itself has several ways to earn money: commissions, of course, being the chief one. And when clients buy securities on margin (credit), the brokerage firm lends them the balance on which it then charges interest. In 1986, for instance, Merrill Lynch earned $533.4 million in interest on margin loans to its clients, which sounds terribly impressive until you realize that that's only 5.8 percent of revenue. Usually, margin loans are pegged to the "broker call rate": the rate that banks charge the brokerage firms for short-term loans, with the firm's own inventory of securities as collateral. Average joes get charged 2 to 2.5 percent over the broker call rate; cossetted customers (those who trade a lot and rack up huge commissions) can borrow for .75 percent more than the brokerage firm itself pays for the money. Since so many investors got stung by the crash and had to meet margin calls, 1987 probably won't be a great year for margin lending. (Clients must pay cash for at least 50 percent of the value of their portfolios; if the value of the stock goes down, the customers have to provide cash until the 50 percent level is reached. If they don't have the cash, they may have to sell the securities—even at a loss.)

Then there's the brokerage firm's own investments in the securities markets. A brokerage firm speculating in securities is like a bartender who drinks: there's nothing illegal about it, the stuff is always around, they're supposed to have the knowledge to pick out the good stuff, and the temptation to indulge is almost irresistible. Similarly, some of them enjoy the experience, and others end up on skid row.

A number of brokerage firms (for example, E. F. Hutton Group, Inc.; Merrill Lynch; First Boston; and Bear Stearns) are public corporations, which means that you can buy stock in them. But the stocks tended to be disappointing performers even before the crash—no doubt a case of the shoemaker's children going barefoot.

Charles Schwab Corporation is the biggest discount broker, with 1.6 million customers and a 21 percent profit margin for 1986 (that is, $66 million pretax earnings on sales of $308 million). The average profit margin for the whole brokerage industry is only half that. (Discount brokers get about $1 billion in revenue each year—about 20 percent of the total brokerage revenue.) Schwab spends $15 million a year on advertising, which sounds dramatic until you realize that Merrill Lynch's advertising/promotion budget is $250 million a year—more than one-third of the total $720 million spent by the industry.

Schwab is five times the size of the next largest discounter, the Quick & Reilly Group, Inc., but Quick & Reilly is the single most profitable brokerage house, discount or full-service, in the United States. Its pretax

## CONSUMER TIP

When you choose a discount broker, look for the lowest commission rate for your trading pattern and adequate back-office capacity to execute your trades fast and accurately. The same considerations apply to a full-service brokerage; but here, you're also looking for brokers with a thorough knowledge of the investment choices open to you, a believable trading philosophy, and access to sound research. The financial press publishes regular reports on how the major brokerage firms are doing, including their success in investing their own assets, but if you take advice from your own broker, you may do noticeably better or worse.

profit for its fiscal year ending February 28, 1987 was a startling 32 percent (that is, $15.8 million, or $2.47 per share, on revenues of $89.1 million); a year earlier, it earned a none-too-shabby $11.8 million, or $1.87 a share, on $73.3 million in revenues.

To put those figures in perspective, the New York Stock Exchange reported that about three-quarters of its 393 member firms earned a profit in the second quarter of 1987; total pretax earnings were $868 million, and after-tax profits were estimated at $134 million. That looks pretty sick compared to $1.09 billion in after-tax profits for the first quarter of 1987 in the glorious era of the bull market.

Even before the crash, brokerages sustained some big losses in bond trading, and "market-makers" (firms that promise to act as buyers-of-last-resort for stocks) lost a lot of money on stocks, especially the over-the-counter stocks that everyone wanted to sell and no one wanted to buy. However, most firms made out all right overall (and a few managed to do very well by getting out of their own investments before prices collapsed and by advising clients to do the same): after all, they got commissions on all the panic sales of stock, and they'll get "round-trip" commissions when investors decide that it's safe to get back into the market and pick up suddenly underpriced stocks.

## Mutual Funds

For many years, millions of investors have favored mutual funds as a relatively safe, convenient, and inexpensive way to invest. By choosing a mutual fund, the investor shares in professional management and has a stake in a multimillion (or billion) dollar diversified portfolio. The mutual fund is kind of like a Model T Ford: a simple, low-priced way for ordinary people to buy what was previously an extremely rare luxury item. In 1985, there were more than 1,500 mutual funds, and more than 25 million share-holders had aggregate investments of about $518 billion—$70.8 billion of that invested in 1985 alone. Mutual-fund sales in 1986 added up to about $211 billion (about one-quarter of the sales were funds investing in stock; the rest, in bond funds and income funds).

In that year, about a quarter of all households in the United States owned mutual funds—and half of households with income over $20,000. In 1987, 350 organizations sold a total of 1,850 mutual funds, which is more than the number of companies listed on the New York Stock Exchange, with a variety of investment choices and objectives. If you haven't heard about mutual funds, you haven't been watching TV, listening to the radio, or reading newspapers or magazines: in 1986, the industry spent $68 million just on print ads.

There are many ways to buy mutual funds: directly from the fund, by mail order; from banks (about two-thirds of banks with assets of more than $1 billion sell mutual funds); and from brokers (about two-thirds of mutual fund sales come from brokers).

Brokers just love to sell mutual funds because they often get to keep 50 percent of the "load" (the commission charge on the fund, which ranges from 1 percent to 8.5 percent), as opposed to the 35 to 40 percent of the commission they keep when they sell other kinds of securities. On the other hand, a mutual-fund sale is a one-time payoff for the broker: he doesn't get a commission when you unload your fund shares, even if the mutual fund gets a "back-end load" when you do. (A few funds give the broker an annual "trailer" fee from the mutual fund's own coffers of, say, 0.1 percent of the value of your fund shares for each year you hang on to them, but it's strictly an act of generosity.) If the broker got you to buy stocks or bonds instead, you might turn over your portfolio several times, with commissions each time.

Banks are more cautious about selling mutual funds. In a sense, every mutual fund is a rival to the banks: mutual-fund investors tend to be the kind of cautious people who would otherwise open savings ac-counts or buy bank certificates of deposit. However, if a bank sells a fund, it earns a commission (part of the "load," if it's a load fund; otherwise, the bank charges a processing fee and also collects a little something from the fund) and gets a chance to tell the investor about its other fabulous financial products.

Originally, all mutual funds were "load" funds: the purchaser paid a one-time charge, typically 8 to 8.5 percent of the value of the initial investment, when he or she bought mutual-fund shares. Some of the load

## CONSUMER TIP

A mutual fund's "expense ratio" is computed by dividing its expenses by the average net assets the fund holds. The average ratio is 1.25 percent; as an investor, you want a fund that cuts back on expenses, not one that fritters away money and reduces the amount of your investment that can go to work for you.

compensated the broker who sold the fund; the fund itself kept the rest. Then some aggressive funds began to market their own shares: "no-load" funds, with no "up-front" commissions. The load could be bypassed because the investor bought the shares directly from the fund. As you'd expect, things soon became more complicated, and now there are "low-load" funds, with a load of 1 to 5 percent. Mutual funds also have different policies about withdrawals: many of them impose a "back-end load" when investors get their money back. A typical back-end load starts out at 7 percent, then phases out at the rate of 1 percent a year, so that patient investors can withdraw their funds without penalty after seven years.

| Income | | |
|---|---|---|
| Management advisory fees: | $ 11,378,000 | |
| Interest and dividends: | 28,731,000 | |
| Other sources: | 3,525,000 | (after expenses) |
| | 43,634,000 | total |

| Expenses | | |
|---|---|---|
| Salaries: | −18,420,000 | |
| Interest: | −17,677,000 | |
| Ads and direct selling expenses: | −13,895,000 | |
| Other selling, general, and administrative expenses: | −17,994,000 | |
| | $ 67,805,000 | |
| Pretax income: | $ 75,829,000 | |
| Federal tax: | −29,500,000 | |
| State tax: | −7,700,000 | |
| **Net Income:** | $ 38,629,000 | |

How do no-load funds make their money? All funds, whether or not they have a front- or back-end load, charge management fees. About 40 percent of funds are "12b-1" funds—funds that take advantage of the SEC's Rule 12b-1, which allows them to charge a special fee for marketing and distributing the fund itself; the average is an annual fee of 0.61 percent of the investor's investment in the fund.

Let's take a look at the old-fashioned way in which one family of mutual funds, the Dreyfus Corporation, earned its money in 1984.

The crash didn't hurt mutual-fund families too badly. Many investors, whether by design or because they couldn't get anyone to answer the phone, either held on to their mutual funds or switched from stock and bond funds to money-market funds offered by the same fund family. So, overall, mutual-fund assets remained fairly stable (although the funds usually earn bigger management fees from stock and bond funds than from money-market funds). The challenge will be keeping investors from

## CONSUMER TIP

SEC rules that went into effect May 1, 1988 impose a new standard of truth in mutual-fund advertising and prospectuses. Funds can no longer select their own time period for quoting yield figures to prospective investors. Instead, they must all use the same formula to derive a thirty-day yield figure, and they must also show how the fund's total return (income and changes in the value of the fund's portfolio of investments) has changed in the past year and the past three, five, and ten years. The prospectus must also include a fee table, in understandable form, showing how much an investor would pay if his or her investment of $1,000 grew by 5 percent a year— and if the investor holds the investment for a year, or for three, five, or ten years.

However, remember that this valuable information doesn't and shouldn't set your own investment strategy. The fund that can quote the highest yield isn't necessarily the best; you must consider if its fees are unusually high, if it's temporarily benefiting by taking too many risks and headed for a fall, or if the fund concentrates on short-term return when you want an investment with the potential for long-term stability or appreciation over time.

cashing in and burying their money under mattresses—and, especially, to find new investors or investors who switch from other forms of investment to mutual funds.

# Money Managers

Really rich people and wealthy institutions such as universities, hospitals, and pension funds don't have to make their own investment decisions; they can hire leading professional "money managers," also called "portfolio managers" or "investment advisers," to choose and carry out their investments. Sure, you'd like to get this kind of expertise for your own money, but money managers won't want to meet you unless you have hundreds of thousands of dollars to invest. Millions is better. The usual charge is 1 percent of the first million, then 0.5 percent for the rest of the account; a really large account, $25 million or over, can usually be managed for only about 0.33 percent of the money in the account.

Overall, money managers handle more than $1 trillion (some estimates say $3 trillion), over $525 billion in stocks, and earn fees of over $6 billion a year. The money-management industry (or art form) employs over 175,000 people. They aim to manage a 20 percent return a year for their clients; the "ulcer factor" for a portfolio manager is the difference between that 20 percent and the return they achieve (a 10 to 15 percent deviation is considered acceptable—that is, a range of 17 to 23 percent return a year.)

Money managers are powerful because they handle such huge sums: in fact, their portfolios are larger than the value of all the stocks on the New York Stock Exchange put together. (This is possible because they have access to many other kinds of investment.) They buy, sell, and hold 60 percent of *all* the stocks and bonds in the United States. As a result, some analysts have blamed them for the crash: their computer-assisted techniques of portfolio insurance and program trading, in some theories, caused stock prices to free-fall instead of taking the gentle downward trend that economic forces dictated.

## SUMMARY

When companies need money to keep operations running, or to invest in new technology or expansion, they must turn either to banks or to the securities market. So millions of jobs depend directly or indirectly on the securities industry's role in raising capital.

Additional millions of jobs depend on the securities industry's other role: keeping money in circulation by buying and selling securities that have already been issued. Even if you don't own stocks or bonds, there's a very good chance that you own mutual funds, and it's almost inevitable that your pension plan will. Your future financial security, and maybe even your job, depend on the way the securities industry functions.

# 12

# Credit Card Issuers

Just about everybody who isn't dead broke (and a lot of people who are, perhaps as a result of credit cards) has at least one credit card. Gas stations would rather have your credit card than your cash, and it's almost impossible to rent a car or check into a hotel room without a credit card, even if you have your personal armored car following close behind with your sacks of cash. The total market for credit cards has been estimated at anywhere from $205 billion to $289 billion, with 80 percent going to the bank cards. Department stores and gas stations issue their own credit cards, which means they have to administer the system and collect the bills, while banks issue credit cards usually as part of the networks set up by Visa and MasterCard.

The three giants are Visa and MasterCard (MasterCard has 135 million cardholders, who rung up $94 billion in 1986 transactions), which are issued by various banks, and American Express (17 million cardholders). Sears's Discover card has 15 million cardholders, but the company managed to lose $100 million (after taxes) on its credit-card operations in 1986.

Back in 1977, MasterCard was the clear winner, claiming 60 percent of the bank-card business; now the position has reversed, with Visa on top with 60 percent, and MasterCard lagging behind at 40 percent of the

Market Share of Top Ten Banks Issuing Credit Cards

| Bank | # of Accounts (Million) | Market Share (op) | Outstanding Balances ($ Billion) |
|---|---|---|---|
| Citibank | 10 | 23.7 | 9.1 |
| Bank of America National Trust and Savings Association | 7.2 | 16.9 | 5.3 |
| Chase Manhattan | 5 | 12.0 | 4.5 |
| First Chicago Corporation | 3.6 | 10.4 | 3.3 |
| Manufacturers Hanover | 3.4 | 10.4 | 2.5 |
| Marine Midland Banks, Inc. | 2.1 | 6.8 | 1.2 |
| Chemical Bank | 2 | 6.4 | 1.27 |
| Maryland National | 2.1 | 5.2 | 2 |
| Wells Fargo | 1.8 | 4.3 | 1.94 |
| Banc One Corporation | 1.36 | 3.8 | unavailable |

(Edison Electric Institute, The Nilson Report, '87)

bank-card business. Visa pulled further ahead in August 1987, when the bank with the largest market share, Citibank, switched its own Choice card to Visa; the Choice card had turned in ten years of disappointing performance because merchants preferred Visa and MasterCard. About 200,000 stores accepted the Choice card, as compared to 500,000 for the Discover card and 5.4 million for Visa.

*The Nilson Report,* a credit-card industry newsletter, estimates that banks make an after-tax profit of 2.5 percent on their credit-card operations, charging their cardholders a fee of about $12 per year. Usually, the bank gets an annual fee from the cardmember ($15 is about typical), collects the interest on the customer's outstanding balance (less a fee to Visa or MasterCard for processing and administration), and splits the fees paid by merchants for participation in a credit-card program.

It's worthwhile for the merchants, despite the fees, because they don't have to worry about bad checks and because customers buy more with credit cards: American Express estimates that their cardholders spend 90 percent more than cash customers, 33 percent more than those who pay by check, and 20 percent more than those who use a bank card.

The card issuer does have to worry about the customers' dishonesty: fraud losses range from about $1.50 to $1.59 per $1,000 of business transacted with credit cards.

The difference between Visa and MasterCard on one side, and American Express (and Diners' Club) on the other, used to be clear. The bank cards were "credit cards"; the others, "travel and entertainment cards" that required their cardholders, with limited exceptions, to pay their entire balances each month. Bank-card customers, as long as they pay a tiny minimum fee each month, are more than welcome to take forever to pay off their balances because the bank that issued the card collects interest at rates that usually range from 17 to 20 percent of the balance. Credit-card interest rates, along with other interest rates, zoomed in the early 1980s and somehow managed to stay high although the prime rate plummeted.

In March 1987, perhaps to take advantage of this source of high-interest lending, American Express (which had about 22 percent of the market) announced a new credit card, the Optima card, that would work like a bank card but at the comparatively low interest rate of 13.5 percent. The card is only available to people who already have an American Express card. American Express expects about 2.5 million of the 10 million eligible customers to sign up, but other analysts are more skeptical because potential Optima customers probably have a fistful of other credit cards.

According to the Opinion Research Corporation, half of the households surveyed had Visa cards and half had Sears Discover cards. Forty-two percent had MasterCards, 40 percent had cards from J. C. Penney, 45 percent had other department-store cards, 17 percent had Montgomery Ward's cards, and 14 percent had American Express green cards. (About a third of households had telephone cards and gasoline cards, too.) Only 18 percent didn't have credit cards; and, since this adds up to well over 100 percent, it's clear that most households have multiple cards.

No matter how Optima turns out, American Express will be a major corporation. In fact, it ranked #18 on the *Business Week* Top 1000, with 1986 sales of $14.56 billion, profits of $1.11 billion, and a profit margin of 6.8 percent for the fourth quarter of 1986 and first quarter of 1987, dipping to 1.1 percent in the second quarter of 1987.

Bank-card issuers are also expanding: both Visa and MasterCard are investing heavily in networks of automated teller machines, so they can use computer technology to process other kinds of transactions (such as cash advances and automatic payment of bills from the customer's bank account) and to get information about customers' financial patterns.

Credit-card issuers have a source of income you might not think of at first: they earned about $20 million in 1986 by sharing in the $100 million in fees that consumers paid to credit-card registration services, which notify all of the customer's card issuers when the cards are lost or stolen or when the customer changes his or her address, and shoulder part of the burden if the cardholder must pay for unauthorized charges. Are these

---

## CONSUMER TIP

New York State has a law requiring registration services to disclose your federal rights. Find out if your state has a similar law; if not, research this area before you spend the twelve bucks. And keep a list of your credit-card numbers and of numbers to call in case of loss or theft (in a nice safe place, *not* with your credit cards) in case you have to handle the notification yourself.

---

services a good deal? Usually they cost $12 a year. Each year, about one out of fifty-three cardholders undergoes a loss or theft; that is, fifty-two out of fifty-three don't. And federal law limits a cardholder's liability if he notifies the issuer promptly of the loss.

### NEW CARD OPTIONS

From the merchant's point of view, credit cards aren't exactly perfect. It takes a lot of paperwork to process a transaction and get reimbursed by the card issuer—and then there are those pesky fees. If it were possible to reach directly into the buyer's bank account and have payment transferred instantaneously into the store's bank account using a Point of Sale (POS) terminal, the problems would be minimized—as long as the equipment costs and fees could be kept down. The debit card, an electronic device for making direct transfers of funds to the merchant's account, does just this.

As of August 1987, about 130 million debit cards were in circulation, many of them issued by stores, gas companies, and banks.

Banks are angry because the Federal Reserve Board, which makes the rules about electronic funds transfer, sets stricter disclosure requirements for bank than for nonbank debit cards. Banks must send out monthly statements to each customer, listing the transactions; other issuers won't have to.

Maybe because they're tired of listening to customers (and politicians) complain about credit-card rates, many banks are finding, uh, *creative* ways to set their rates. Some of them lower the rates, but with a catch: there's no "grace period" (the three weeks or so during which customers can pay their balance in full and escape interest). Other banks set "tiered" rates, with a high rate on the first $1,000 or so owed, a lower

**CONSUMER TIP**

Starting in 1990, bank debit-card issuers must list the exact location of each transaction on your statement. Thanks to the new rules, if you report the loss or theft of a card within four days you are responsible for only $50 in unauthorized charges; before the rule change, you had to act within two days to be protected. The new rules also give you ninety days, rather than the sixty as previously, to report mistakes on a debit-card statement.

rate on the next $1,000, and so forth. Or the rate may be set at the prime lending rate plus a certain number of points (for example, an uncomfortable 6 percent over prime).

Affinity marketing is one way that issuers make their cards stand out. Usually, an affinity card is connected to a particular charity (for example, feminist causes, the Leukemia Society of America, or Vietnam Vets of America). Whenever the card is used, the issuer makes a donation of, perhaps, five cents to the cause; the money comes from the annual card fees, interest charges, and fees paid by merchants. Some banks don't want to do this (Chemical Bank announced in September 1987 that it was throwing in the towel); others think it's worthwhile because cardholders tend to be a little freer with the plastic when they can tell themselves it's all in a good cause. Working Assets Money Fund, which administers a card mak-

**CONSUMER TIP**

New York State allows credit-card issuers to offer cards with no grace period, but customers must also be given the choice of a card with a grace period. Before you switch to a new credit card, see how its costs compare to your old card, taking into account the annual fee and the interest rate you'd pay on each card for your normal spending and payment patterns. Several states have consumer protection laws requiring credit-card applications to contain the information to make these calculations easier.

ing donations to human rights, environmental, and peace groups, has racked up $100,000 in contributions in the first eighteen months of operations and finds that cardholders use the card twice as often as the average Visa cardholder.

Banks sometimes handle affinity cards a little differently. Pittsburgh's Mellon Bank has "life-style" cards that provide skiers, sailors, and golfers with discounts on affinity-related trips and equipment. UniClub combines shopping and barter: its 2,000 members get a 15 percent discount on purchases from the 750 participating merchants; the merchants choose between cash reimbursements (the card issuer keeps twenty cents on the dollar) or credits that can be exchanged for goods and services provided by other merchants. Citibank offers "Citidollars" to its card users.

Vengeance is sweet: Floridian Lottye Carlin spent eight years fighting Southeast Banking Corporation over the $2,064.35 in charges that Mrs. Carlin never made on a MasterCard she didn't ask for. She was denied a mortgage on a condominium she wanted to buy, and she amassed over $8,000 in legal fees; but, at last, she settled with the bank for $150,000 and a written letter of apology. She insisted on the written apology.

It's enough to make you want to tear up your credit cards. But if you don't, and you keep them past the expiration date, maybe you should put them in the vault and wait until they become *really* valuable to the 25,000 people who collect old credit cards instead of coins or stamps. A mint-condition 1958 American Express card now fetches $150, but vintage Sears cards only fetch about $5.

# RETAIL RAP:
## Business by the Numbers—Financial Ratios

Business owners and managers rely on a constant stream of numbers to figure out what to do next and even to determine whether the business is a success or a failure.

There are many measures for judging a business, and very often a business succeeds by some measures while it fails by others. A business may make lots of sales and earn a tidy profit, but its stock price may be low (which annoys stockholders) or the dividends paid to the stockholders may be anemic (which doesn't make their day, either). Two businesses may earn exactly the same amount, have the same stock price, and pay the same dividends, yet one may escape the obligation to pay any income tax, while the other writes a sizeable check to the IRS four times a year. It depends on the decisions the business makes for tax purposes.

Usually, businesses aim at profitability, although sometimes they miss. Profitability depends on a number of things: volume (the dollar amount of sales), the cost of sales (what the IRS calls the cost of sales and operations), the direct costs of buying things for resale, general and administrative expenses (costs of running an office), rent, and interest on funds borrowed to keep the business afloat. Some businesses have to distinguish between operating income—income from manufacturing, or processing, or selling whatever it is they manufacture, process, or sell—and nonoperating income. For instance, the Northwest Frammis Corporation may do a lousy job of selling frammises, but it may earn millions by selling some real estate it picked up many years ago. That's nonoperating income.

Volume of sales doesn't help a business unless the sales are profitable. Sure, a business can get away with a few "loss leaders"—items sold at or below cost to attract shoppers who'll then, it is hoped, buy a basketful of profitable items. But in the long run, a business must analyze, guard, and, if possible, increase its "margins," which are its net income from operations, expressed as a percentage of sales. To improve margins, a business can increase sales, cut costs, or both.

Some costs of doing business are fixed: if you have a business phone, you have to pay a certain amount each month even if you don't make any phone calls. A restaurant must pay its rent and utility bills whether it serves three meals a day and continuous snacks or is open only for lunch from 1 to 2 P.M. Other costs are variable: you need more pasteboard boxes to sell a million one-pound boxes of chocolate truffles than to sell forty-five one-pound boxes. Then other costs are sort of fixed, sort of variable: if you have twenty-two employees, you have to pay certain levels of Social Security tax, but you could fire some of the employees or fire them and rehire them as independent contractors.

With any luck, a business will stay around for a while. Sometimes a business will take steps that make it temporarily unprofitable in the hope that the future rewards will be great indeed. Such a company might, for example, buy plenty of new equipment or hire a raft of new employees who need time to become productive. One of the most common complaints about the American business world is that since executives are judged too much by short-term results they therefore "rob the future" by avoiding decisions that are beneficial in the long run but make this quarter's results look disappointing.

Who judges them? Their bosses, other companies considering taking over their companies, and the stockholders. (Indeed, much of what the bosses say is based on second-guessing what the stockholders are going to say.) Stockholders are interested in two things about a company: the price of its stock, and the dividends it pays. Without income, there can be no dividends. The question of the stock price is more complex. (You better believe that if we knew what determines stock prices, we wouldn't have to even *talk* to you people.) Apart from the stock market's general tendency to reach either for the sky or the bottom of the quicksand pit, the market favors some stocks over others, even if two businesses are apparently similar; in fact, sometimes a stock can be a stock-market darling even though the business is less efficient or less profitable than other, comparable businesses with lower stock prices.

Two of the most important measures of stock prices are EPS (earnings per share—the corporation's earnings, divided by the number of shares of common stock outstanding) and the P/E ratio (price/earnings ratio: the stock's price, divided by the corporation's income from operations). Strangely, it's considered good for a stock to have a *high* P/E ratio, which means that the stock's price is much higher than the company's earnings per share. A decline in a stock's P/E ratio usually means that the market is losing confidence in the stock, which of course tends to become a self-fulfilling prophecy if *everybody* then tries to dispose of the stock at ever-lower prices. A company's market value is simply the price of its stock multiplied by the number of shares.

The scale of operations is also important. Net profits of $1 million a year are terrific for a one-person photography studio but an unimaginable tragedy for Sears, Roebuck & Company. Any profit has to be analyzed in light of the amount of effort, and especially the amount of money, needed to generate it.

That's why analysts look at a company's "ratios": the relationship between certain numbers. *Return on invested capital* (ROIC) is the ratio between a company's profits (its pretax net income) and its investment in the operation. *Return on common equity* (RCE), on the other hand, compares the net income that could be paid to the stockholders as dividends to the total amount of common stock and capital and earnings retained by the corporation. The two numbers can be identical, or very different. It depends on whether the business has a lot of capital or very little (service businesses usually have a lot less capital than manufacturers or retailers). It also depends on how much the stock is worth: a business can have lots of profit but a low stock price, or a tiny trickle of profit and a high stock price. Return on investment is one of the most important tests of a business's skill. After all, if a business with a huge work force and billions of dollars of capital tied up earns a mere 2 percent return, it would be better off taking the money and opening a bank account with it than actually running the business.

Other important ratios measure the business's ability to pay its debts. Often, a basically sound business will get trapped: it's the season during which it orders most of its merchandise, and spends the most, but not the season at which it *sells* the most merchandise, so expenses exceed income. The *current ratio* is the company's current assets (money available now) divided by current liabilities (bills due now). The current assets include the company's inventory and accounts receivable (amounts others are required to pay the company) and its cash on hand, minus its bad debts (amounts others owe the company, but aren't paying). The current liabilities are accounts payable (amounts owed to other businesses), mortgages, and short-term borrowing. The *quick ratio* is similar, but current liabilities are compared to the business's cash and accounts receivable—the money it could raise without selling off its inventory. The *ratio of total liabilities to net worth* compares all amounts owed (including long-term loans) to the total amount of the corporation's stock, capital surplus, and profits already earned but not yet divided up. It shows the extent to which the corporation depends on borrowing, not profits or growth, to raise money.

Then there are the millions of decisions a business must make for tax purposes. Sometimes a transaction can be handled in several ways, each requiring a different amount of money, effort, and borrowing (and associated interest cost), and each affecting differently the company's stock price and availability of tax deductions. The manager's job is to pick the best overall strategy.

There. Now we've explained about half of what you'd learn in business school. Why don't you figure out how much it would cost to go to B-School (including the salary you'd lose if you'd quit your job), and split it with us?

# Home, Sweet Home

# 13

# Real Estate Developers

Real estate developers help to shape the landscape. They decide whether a city will be a vista of skyscrapers or gentle rolling hillocks of lower buildings; whether a cornfield will remain a cornfield or be turned into a housing development or mall. They decide whether buildings that are now rental apartments will be turned into co-ops or condos, and whether buildings that now house low- and middle-income people will be converted to luxury housing or retail or office space. They've been blessed for sweeping away urban blight, damned for displacing poor people and neighborhood businesses, and cursed for driving the price of farmland so high that it becomes uneconomical to keep farming it.

Of course, the dreams of developers are limited by zoning laws and permission (or lack thereof) from local authorities. It may be necessary for a developer to lower his sights and put up a smaller building or to "trade" height for amenities such as public plazas. Often many developers have the same dream at the same time, which can lead to a glut of luxury condominiums (somehow, there never seems to be a glut of inexpensive rental apartments), office space, or stores, for example.

Developers are to real estate what producers are to movies and TV shows: they make things happen. In either case, a "property" is involved, either literally—a parcel of land—or figuratively—a screenplay or novel

Where the Money Went

| | |
|---|---|
| (1) Cost of operations: | 25.3% |
| (2) Officers' compensation: | 5.0% |
| (3) Pensions and benefits: | 0.8% |
| (4) Rent: | 1.8% |
| (5) Repairs: | 1.0% |
| (6) Depreciation, depletion, amortization: | 3.9% |
| (7) Interest: | 15.6% |
| (8) Bad debts: | 0.8% |
| (9) Advertising: | 1.8% |
| (10) State, local taxes: | 3.5% |
| (11) Other expenses: | 33.8% |
| (12) Net profit before tax: | 24.2% |

(Troy, '84–'85)

to be adapted. The developer/producer gets the necessary money (either investing his own or—much more commonly—finding sponsors or investors to put it up) and makes sure that the necessary steps are taken to produce the finished product.

For instance, a developer can "assemble" an entire city block for redevelopment by finding out who owns each of the buildings on the block and convincing each one to sell—preferably without word of the assembly leaking out. Once it does, all the sellers will adamantly refuse to sell or hold out for much higher prices; the last holdout either becomes astronomically wealthy—or gets to stay forever: in Manhattan, for instance, a couple of tiny old restaurants and saloons are tucked into high-rise buildings that were built around them. After that, the task of getting giant high-rises designed, built, and resold or rented out can seem relatively minor.

The relationship between development and the actual building is a complex one. In fact, a contractor can enter the development business because he becomes aware of properties that are inexpensive and in need of renovation—tasks that his employees can undertake when other assignments are scarce. Or a developer can enter into a partnership with a contractor, or start his own contracting firm, to handle the work required on his projects. Another variation is for a developer to work with different contractors on different projects, choosing the one offering the best price for providing the needed skills.

Developers use their own funds and funds borrowed from banks to buy property and to get it into shape for rental or resale. They also appeal to investors for funds. Depending on the scope of the project and their network of relationships, they may just call up a few old friends who have pleasant memories of profitable deals in the past. Or they may use methods such as seminars to appeal to a small number of sophisticated investors—making sure that they avoid a "public offering," which requires expensive legal techniques to comply with federal and state securities laws. Nevertheless, if the project justifies it, they'll make a public offering, which calls for prospectuses and approvals by securities regulators.

Real estate developers frequently act as "syndicators," forming a "syndicate" of investors to provide the capital for a project. Depending on the facts of the case, a syndication can be either a private or a public offering. In 1986, about $3.6 billion dollars of real estate syndications were extant—a huge amount, yes, but way down from the 1985 figure of over $7 billion, or 1984's peak of more than $10 billion. (In contrast, pension funds and insurance companies invest about $30 billion a year in real estate.)

Why the drop? Part of it was market saturation: in 1987, about 18 percent of all office space was vacant. Most of the decline in investor interest was a response to changes in the tax laws. Real estate traditionally benefited from generous treatment under the tax code but took some hard knocks in the 1986 tax reform act. Besides, with lower tax rates, rich people are far less eager to find tax shelters; they often prefer investments that require less patience than real estate does.

Then there's the two-edged sword of leverage. Real estate deals depend heavily on borrowed money or "leverage" (it's called "leverage" because a little of the developer's or investor's money can move a big project). This accounts for the high figure for interest costs in the chart: real estate developers get rich—and sometimes go broke—by mortgaging properties to the hilt to buy more properties. All that borrowing leads to high interest costs. That means that high interest rates add hundreds of thousands, or even millions, of dollars to a project's cost. If it takes longer than expected to resell the property or find tenants, the profit can vanish into the lender's pockets.

But as long as a developer can "float" a successful syndication, he's in a good position. Often the developer buys a piece of raw land and waits until it becomes an appropriate candidate for development (until the suburbs spread further into the country, for instance) and then uses syndication funds to build on it; next, he resells the now-improved property, to the profit of everyone involved in the syndication. Not every real estate transaction is a success story, of course. It may cost more than anticipated to acquire the land; zoning authorities may be resistant; borrowed funds may be unavailable or may cost more than planned; the building unions may strike or raise their wage demands; raw materials costs can soar; and, when it's all done, a building glut may drastically lower the demand for the offices, stores, or apartments.

When the project is successful, the developer is usually the biggest beneficiary of the deal. For instance, investors in one real estate "program" that sold $50 million worth of limited partnership interests paid to the developer an 8 percent selling commission, "organization and offering" expenses of 5 percent, acquisition expenses of 2 percent, and acquisition fees of 7.75 percent—so that the developer got 22.75 percent of the necessary funds immediately, more than recovering his initial investment.

According to a 1986 Dun & Bradstreet survey that included 2,045 real estate "subdividers and developers," the average net sales for a developer—a category that includes everything from billionaire moguls to retirees who own shares in a couple of small apartment buildings or a few acres of raw land—was $1,101,858. The average gross profit for this group was 36.9 percent of net sales (much higher than for most businesses). The after-tax net profits—9.5 percent—were less dramatic but still far above the returns for most businesses.


## MAJOR DEVELOPERS

Some of the major real estate developers, far from coincidentally, are also among the richest people in America. For example, Harry Helmsley—known to New Yorkers for many years as the husband of Leona Helmsley, the "queen" of the Helmsley Palace hotel (today they're perhaps better known as the subjects of indictments for tax fraud)—is one of the biggest landlords in America, with interests in twenty-seven hotels, about 50,000 apartments, and 50 million square feet of office space. To renovate the Helmsley Palace in Manhattan, Mr. Helmsley invested $5 million of his own money; raised $23 million by sale of limited partnership shares (and bought five shares himself), and took out a $50 million mortgage.

Donald Trump (of Trump Towers, Trump Village, the Trump Castle casino, and rumored political ambitions) wants to turn some of the least desirable parts of New York's West Side into a $5 billion high-density project called Television City, which would include the world's tallest building and offices, parks, shops, and apartments. His dreams were stymied in November 1987 when NBC decided not to move in. Mr. Trump was counting on NBC's presence to get city authorities to agree to the plan, but, in a kind of Catch-22, the network wouldn't sign a lease until the approval was forthcoming. He also faces tough opposition from community groups who want a lower-density development. Some observers suggest that, as a result, he'll just put the project on hold until the political climate changes.

However, one of the most successful syndicators, Chicago's JMB Realty Trust, is owned by men who are far less well known than the flamboyant and socially prominent Messrs. Helmsley and Trump. JMB has a net worth of over $1 billion and manages about $10 billion worth of real estate for about 250,000 limited partners. Its president, Neil Bluhm, owns

34 percent of JMB's stock; his high-school buddy, Judd Malkin, now an accountant and vice president of JMB, owns another 34 percent; and the corporation's top executives own the rest.

Successful development ain't hay—or even birdseed—but Leonard Stern of Hartz Group has taken his company from selling pet supplies to developing New Jersey real estate. After Mr. Stern earned his M.B.A. at age nineteen, he got into real estate by leasing some space for pet supplies and began to renovate industrial properties in New Jersey. Then he bought some swamplands and turned them into an industrial park; bought some more marshes and made Harmon Meadow, an office park; and is now building offices, homes, and stores in several parts of New Jersey. Hartz, which owns more than $1 billion of property, is an unusual developer in that it relies heavily on in-house architects and designers: it has forty architects and engineers on its $10 million payroll of three hundred New Jersey employees. (Most development firms have far fewer employees—forty is a typical number.)

## DEVELOPING THE FUTURE

As long as there's money to be borrowed and holes to be dug, real estate developers will be building homes, offices, factories, and "mixed-use" developments, which combine several kinds of tenants. There are probably too many offices, so this is unlikely to be a strong market (except in cities that combine strong economies with limitations on new buildings, such as Boston, New York, and San Francisco).

Throughout the country, developers are betting that current trends will continue: that cities will continue to expand and that our nation's future is urban, not rural, and information-based rather than industrial. However, sometimes they guess wrong, as when four developers rush to construct buildings, each of which ends up less than one-quarter filled. If American investors lose patience, an increasing number of wealthy European, Japanese, and Middle Eastern individuals and corporations want to buy American real estate, a trend that some observers view with alarm.

Tenants and businesses crammed into too-tight spaces have made "miniwarehousing" a new and very profitable form of development. These self-storage warehouses can rent a 5-by-10-foot storage space for $100 a month. Even if the developer has to pay $100 a square foot for the land, it's a good business: returns of 15 percent are common while returns on building offices have sagged to 8 or 9 percent. It costs about $75 a square foot to put up an office building, and about 30 percent of gross revenues to run it; building a miniwarehouse costs about $25 a square foot, and operating costs are a comparatively modest 25 percent of gross revenues.

One of the most important factors in financing a project is being able to prove that it will attract buyers or prime tenants. Major corporations like American Telephone & Telegraph Company (AT & T) have devised a new wrinkle: sure, they'll make a commitment to move into a new project—but only if they get a piece of the action, in the form of an ownership interest in the property.

# 14

# Real Estate Brokers

Some houses are sold directly by their owners to a buyer, but most purchases of real estate are handled by at least one brokerage firm. There's a lot of hassle involved in a real estate deal: analyzing the property, making a judgment about what it's worth and how to present it to potential buyers, finding a buyer, and steering the purchase transaction over the financial and legal rocks.

Real estate brokers are licensed by the state. To be a broker, a person must not only have training (state requirements vary; usually a one-semester, one-year, or two-year course taken part-time by a working person) and pass an exam, but must have put in an apprenticeship as a licensed real estate salesperson, working under the supervision of a licensed broker. Supervision is necessary because brokers and real estate salespeople in effect control important transactions involving a lot of money. Often the entire deal is based on a form contract drawn up by the broker, so the broker had better know what he or she is doing.

There are about two million people in the United States who have valid licenses as real estate brokers or salespeople, but no statistics are kept on how many of them are currently active. Many people get real estate licenses "just in case," or use real estate as a part-time activity (for instance, teachers who sell real estate during summer vacations; parents who sell during the hours when their children are in school). It's equally

## CONSUMER TIP

If you're the seller, make sure that the contract specifies exactly when the broker is entitled to a commission and the circumstances under which you are justified in withdrawing from the sale without having to pay a commission. The standard real estate commission is 6 to 7 percent of the sale price of the property, though this is negotiable, and there are "discount" brokers in real estate as well as securities (though discounting is far less prevalent in real estate, probably because active investors buy and sell securities frequently, but most people engage in only a few real estate transactions in the course of a lifetime).

difficult to get a fix on what brokers earn. Their commissions depend on the number and cost of the properties they sell. Some brokers only deal in multimillion-dollar properties and handle more than a dozen transactions a year; others devote months of work to a single transaction that eventually falls through, then quit brokerage altogether (earning no income for the venture).

A brokerage firm earns a commission when it rounds up a buyer who is "ready, willing, and able" to buy the property on terms that the seller will agree to. (The law books contain the records of many, many cases striving to define those terms.) If the seller backs out, it's his tough luck because he still has to pay the broker's commission and may have to compensate the buyer, too.

Sometimes the seller "lists" the property (offers it for sale) with only one broker. The advantage to the seller (and, of course, to the broker) is that real estate brokers and salespeople, being human, often

## TRADE TALK

A "realtor" is a broker who belongs to the local Board of Realtors, which is a trade association, so "realtor" and "broker" aren't exact synonyms. A "realtist" is a member of the National Association of Real Estate Brokers, a mostly black group formed to combat the perceived exclusivity and prejudice of the "old boys' network" of the National Association of Realtors, which has 719,000 members (again, membership doesn't mean that the member is an active broker or salesperson, just that he or she has the legal right to be).

## TRADE TALK

A listing contract is an "exclusive agency listing" if there's only one broker with a right to sell the property, but the seller doesn't have to pay a commission if he digs up a buyer himself, without the broker's help. In an "exclusive right-to-sell contract" the seller has to pay the commission if the sale goes through, no matter who finds the buyer (including the seller's sister-in-law or the mailman who notices the house is for sale and introduces his cousin Larry to the owners).

work harder on "exclusive" properties because they know the commission will be bigger. However, most sellers prefer either an "open" listing (several real estate firms have the right to show the house; the "winner," the one who produces a buyer, gets the commission) or a "multiple listing" (the house is listed for sale on an information system—usually computer-

## CONSUMER TIP

Where should you list the property you're selling, and which brokers should you contact when you want to buy property? If you're a seller, you want a broker with real sales talent, the time and energy to devote to your property, and access to a large group of qualified buyers. You'll also want a broker who will give you favorable terms on the listing contract—not insisting on an exclusive, for instance, or lowering the commission. If the brokerage offers technological advances such as computerized listings and videotapes of houses for sale, that's a plus.

If you're a buyer, you can go to every broker in town; there's no requirement or reason for exclusivity. (However, if all the realtors participate in multiple listing, all the brokers may have the same "core" of multiple listings and so only a few other properties to show you.) What you want is a broker who handles the kind of property with the right location and in the price range you want. Remember that the broker (who will probably be friendly and persuasive) is working for the seller: the broker's job is to get the highest possible price for the property, not to lower the price so you can afford that wonderful house just outside your price range.

ized—and any broker participating in the multiple-listing service can show the property to potential buyers) because as many potential buyers as possible are thus given information about the property. Brokers pay to participate in the multiple-listing system and often find themselves in the position of sharing their commissions with other brokerages in the system; its advantage is that it gives a broker the ability to participate in commissions for far more properties than he could handle unassisted.

The ideal situation for a real estate brokerage would be an active real estate market, with plenty of properties trading at ever-increasing prices paid by hordes of willing buyers—and no other real estate brokers for miles around. The more usual situation is an imbalance of demand: either buyers seek after a small number of properties (which increases the prices but limits the number of possible commissions) or the market is stagnant and sellers desperately seek the few available buyers. It's also common for there to be plenty of competition.

Real estate brokerage is an easy business to enter: all you need is a license, a desk, and a telephone. The trick is to get good listings and to attract buyers to "shop" at your brokerage. In many areas, a newcomer discovers that homesellers are accustomed to the brokers who have been in business for a long time or that they prefer to list their properties with established or nationwide chains, such as Century 21. Real estate brokerage is also an easy business to leave, if the newly established broker finds that listings are scarce and commissions hard to get.

## INTERVIEW

We spoke to Lea Lowe and Lisa Zerbe, two young salespersons at Murphy Realty. Murphy Realty has two offices in Jersey City, New Jersey, one with forty-five salespeople, the other (which has the exclusive right to sell and lease property in the Newport City mixed-use development on the Jersey City waterfront) with forty salespeople. Lowe and Zerbe seemed a little anxious during the interviews, not because they were less than gracious, but because they were interviewed when they were on "uptime": the time when a real estate salesperson stays in the office to answer the phone, make calls to prospects, keep in touch with sellers and potential sellers, and field queries from walk-in customers.

Murphy Realty is one of about 1,100 affiliates in the House and Garden Realty system. The affiliation relationship is somewhat like franchising; the affiliate offices get the advantage of the well-known name and national advertising, in return for a share of the affiliate's commission income.

Ms. Zerbe says she chose real estate sales because it's an exciting field, and she can control her own time and working hours and set her own pace. She's expected to work several 2 to 2½-hour "up-time" shifts a month and to help staff the Sunday afternoon "open houses" (showing condos to home shoppers); otherwise, she makes her own schedule, usually having two to ten appointments a week. Her specialty is selling condos, nearly all in rehabbed rather than newly constructed buildings. About two-thirds of her customers buy condos as personal residences; the rest are investors.

The real estate salesperson's job extends far beyond the well-worn trek around listed properties. Ms. Zerbe says that it's the agency's job to get people to call; it's her job to work with them. First, she does a thorough interview to find out what a customer's needs and financial abilities are. Next, she shows him or her three carefully selected properties that fit those needs, yet are very different from one another. If the buyer doesn't see anything he or she likes, she'll show another "bouquet" of three; it hasn't been necessary to show more than nine condos to any customer so far. (The prospect sees three properties at a time because that's enough choices to offer a variety but not enough to be confusing.) In contrast, house buyers usually see between nine and thirty houses—but then, there are more variables in a house, and a lot more that can go wrong.

The salesperson has a lot of work "behind the scenes": getting descriptions of properties from sellers; working with lawyers, appraisers, and mortgage brokers; making sure that, once a deal is arranged, it goes through on schedule; filling out reams of paperwork for the office's own records; encouraging dispirited sellers who thought the house would have been sold long before, for unreasonably high sums of money.

Home buying slows down in the winter since it's too cold to schlepp around looking at property, and peaks in the summer since buyers want their families resettled before the new school year. The stock market crash of 1987 did cool off the real estate market a little (unemployed former investment bankers can't buy luxurious new homes; people can't count on stock profits to finance a purchase), but sales continue. In fact, nervous investors who distrust the stock market may find homes or investment real estate more attractive than ever.

The future of real estate brokerage seems utterly certain. Although we may never again see the huge profits in housing of the 1980s (and we hope we'll never see their high mortgage rates again, either), it's guaranteed that people will always need housing and will always "trade up" to better housing as their incomes increase, move into smaller houses when their kids are grown, or move to another state to pursue new jobs. And when that happens, the real estate broker and salesperson will be there, making phone calls, showing photographs (and videocassettes) of the properties, and making deals.

# 15

# Title Companies

Before you buy a house, you want to make sure that the sellers really own it. Apart from the more obvious kinds of fraud, there's the possibility that they've lost court cases, and therefore there are judgments that can be enforced when the house is sold. A disgruntled (and unpaid) contractor could have put a mechanics' lien on the house. There could be unpaid water bills. The sellers can believe that the property extends up to the old oak tree when, in fact, it ends ten feet further in.

Title abstracting companies go through the legal records to find out who really owns the property and whether there are any "clouds" on the title. They also perform similar searches when a homeowner applies for a home equity loan, second mortgage, or mortgage refinancing. Some states and communities have a "Torrens title" system, which makes things a lot easier: title to a house is registered on a simple document (like a car's "pink slip"), which is transferred from owner to owner.

In some states, the title company also handles the entire "closing" (the transfer of ownership from seller to buyer); in others, lawyers handle this. (In general, the western states tend to let the title company handle the chores; in the eastern states, lawyers usually consider a closing a source of fees rather than a pain in the neck.)

If you're buying a property and a lawyer handles the closing, he or she will probably recommend a title company that he or she has worked

---

## CONSUMER TIP

If you're buying a house and read through the list of fees about to be charged, you'll notice a premium for "title insurance." The insurance pays off if, despite the title search, it's discovered that the seller can't convey good title to the property. You might, then, think that this policy protects you. Wrong: it's a "lender's title policy" that pays the bank issuing your mortgage if there's a hassle. To protect yourself, consider getting an "owner's title policy" as well.

---

with in the past. If you prefer, you can shop around, select a title company yourself, and perhaps save a significant amount of money. Where no lawyer is involved, the broker will probably refer the buyer to a title company; again, the buyer has the right to choose the company but will probably be grateful to have the decision taken out of his or her hands. Corporations that buy a lot of property usually develop their own relationships with title companies.

The American Land Title Association has 2,000 members: abstracting companies, title insurers, and agents selling title insurance. It's been estimated that these organizations have at least 100,000 employees, in a hierarchy ascending from title examiners (who dig out the records and earn $18,000 to $20,000 a year), to senior examiners (who earn, well, maybe $30,000), title analysts, and finally clearance officers (who are all lawyers).

### INDUSTRY FIGURES

According to a 1986 survey by Dun & Bradstreet of 112 title abstract companies, their gross profit equalled about two-thirds of net sales (63.9 percent). This is entirely a service business, with few assets required and low operating expenses, so the companies got a return on sales that ranged from 4.7 to 16.9 percent. Their return on assets was higher, from 6.2 to 32.1 percent. Return on assets was higher than return on sales because the companies had few assets in the first place. Net after-tax profit averaged 9.8 percent, which, as you'll see as you read through this book, few businesses can equal.

The same survey included 207 title insurance companies. Their gross profit was higher than that of the abstract companies (65.5 percent of net sales, as compared to 63.9 percent), but their net after-tax profit was

| Income | |
| --- | --- |
| Fees and premiums on title insurance policies: | $121,244,000 |
| Income from mapping out properties: | 2,910,000 |
| Total revenues: | $124,154,000 |
| Investment income: | 7,000,000 |
| Other: | 357,000 |
| Sales of copies of title abstracts: | 500,000 |
| Total income: | $132,011,000 |

| Expenses | |
| --- | --- |
| Salaries and other employee costs: | 58,272,000 |
| Other operating expenses: | 41,712,000 |
| Depreciation and amortization expenses: | 3,000,000 |
| Mapping costs: | 3,000,000 |
| Interest: | 1,255,000 |
| Dividends to holders of minority interests: | 648,000 |
| Total expenses: | $107,887,000 |
| Operating income before taxes: | $ 10,660,000 |
| Income tax: | −3,846,000 |
| Operating income after taxes: | 6,814,000 |
| Investment gains: | 225,000 |
| **Net Income:** | $  7,039,000 |

(Stewart Information Services Corporation, 1984 figures)

lower, at 8 percent instead of 9.8 percent—no doubt because insurance companies sometimes have to pay a claim, so they earn less than companies that deal purely in information, such as title abstract companies. Return on assets and return on sales were also lower for insurance companies than for abstract companies: return on sales ranged from 2.2 to 12.3 percent; return on assets, from 2.6 to 21.3 percent.

Let's take a closer look at one title company's sources of income and expense—the Stewart Information Services Corporation, a title insurer with over 1,400 issuing offices and with agents in forty-three states and the District of Columbia.

There are some factors in the economy that aid the title industry. Housing starts are down, yet plenty of people want to buy houses, which means they're likely to buy older houses and to need title searches and title insurance. The growth of home equity loans is also good news because most home equity loans require a title search.

# Utilities

A forest ranger we know described his job as usually pretty dull; but when it isn't, it's "entirely too exciting." That could serve as a capsule history of the utility industries. Until the early 1970s (for power companies) or early 1980s (for telephone companies), the utilities dreamed their way through a golden era of monopoly or near monopoly, low fuel prices, low interest rates, and ever-increasing demand.

Ever since the oil shock and the breakup of the Bell System's monopoly on long-distance telephone service, utility executives have a new and unwelcome set of considerations to balance: protesters at the gate, nuclear power plants that can't be started up for practical or legal reasons, red ink on the financial statements, and competitors at their heels.

Still, things can't be too bad: according to *Forbes'* June 1987 survey, in 1986 seventy-three out of the eight hundred best-paid CEOs in the United States were power company executives. Number one was Einar Greve of Tucson Electric Power Company, with a mere 1,100 employees. Tucson Electric had sales of $425 million (rather modest for a utility company), profits of $117.4 million (an unusually high margin), and paid Mr. Greve $295,000 in salary, not to mention the $1,625,000 in gains on stock he achieved in that year. (A company doesn't have to be making money to propel its CEO to the best-paid list: Robert J. Harrison of Public

Where the Money Went

| | Cost of Opera- tions | Offi- cers Comp. | Pensions & Benefits | Rent | Repairs | Depre- ciation, Amort. |
|---|---|---|---|---|---|---|
| Electric services | 48.3 | 0.2 | 1.6 | 1.1 | 5.3 | 11.9 |
| Combined utility service | 54.1 | 0.2 | 1.7 | 0.5 | 4.4 | 8.0 |

| | Interest | Bad Debts | Adver- tising | State, Local Taxes | Other | Net Profit Before Tax |
|---|---|---|---|---|---|---|
| Electric services | 12.4 | 0.3 | 0.1 | 6.5 | 8.6 | 3.7 |
| Combined utility service | 8.5 | 0.4 | — | 7.7 | 8.9 | 5.6 |

(Troy, '84–'85)

Service Company of New Hampshire earned $216,000, making him sixty-third among the best-paid power company CEOs, although the company lost almost $200 million on sales of $505 million.) Furthermore, more than one-tenth (111) of the Top 1000 companies in *Business Week*'s ranking are utilities.

According to *Business Week*'s corporate scoreboard, a composite of the entire gas and electric power industry would have had sales of $40.45 billion in the fourth quarter of 1986, dipping to $37.36 billion in the first quarter and to $34 billion in the second quarter of 1987. Yet profits rose before falling again: $3.25 billion in the fourth quarter of 1986, up to $4.49 billion, and down again to $3.72 billion, representing decidedly above-average profit margins of 8 percent, 12 percent, and 10.9 percent respectively.

The utility industry has unusually high expenses in several areas. It spends much more than most industries for repairs—and electric power plants need more repairs than the equipment of gas utilities; when the equipment goes, it really goes. For similar reasons, depreciation and amortization are very high: there's so much expensive hardware to be written off. Interest costs, too, are very high because utilities issue a lot of bonds (that is, borrow a lot of money) to get plants on-line and to keep them running. However, bad debt deductions are very low (if you stop paying your bill, the utility cuts off your service, which takes care of that) and so is advertising (if you're a monopoly or near-monopoly, you can either bypass advertising entirely, or use "bill stuffers" enclosed with the monthly bill to tell your captive audience whatever it is you had in mind).

One of the largest utilities, and one of the profit leaders, is Commonwealth Edison Company in Chicago. In 1987, its sales were $5.674 billion with profits of $1.08 billion and a margin of 19.1 percent. The largest utility company, Pacific Gas & Electric, based in San Francisco, had 1987 sales of approximately $7.186 billion, with profits of $597.2 million, a profit margin of 8.3 percent, and a return on equity of 6.7 percent. The highest electric rates in the United States are exacted in New York and San Diego.

## THE REGULATORY PROCESS

Although utility companies have thousands or millions of customers, in a sense they have only one customer to appeal to: the local utilities commission that sets rates and agrees or disagrees with the utility's contentions about the way costs and losses should be accounted for. Pacific Gas & Electric invested $5.8 billion in its Diablo Canyon nuclear power plants, one of which started commercial operation in 1985, the other in 1986. Naturally, PG & E would like to recover as much of that investment as possible, by raising rates, if necessary. It applied for a rate increase that would cover 54 percent of the plant costs. But in May 1987, the Public Staff Division of the California utilities commission recommended that PG & E be barred from recovering $4.37 billion of the investment through rate increases. That's not the final word—the state of California will probably take until mid-1989 to decide.

The Georgia Power Company faces even more grief over its Plant Vogtle nuclear facility. Oglethorpe Power Corporation and the Municipal Electric Authority of Georgia are also part-owners. The plant was supposed to cost about $800 million but ended up costing nearly $9 billion. To the extent that regulators won't let the company raise rates to compensate, it will have to reduce its reported earnings; as a result, the ratings on its bonds will decline perilously, which means that the utility will have to raise interest rates to get anybody to buy the bonds, and that will further depress earnings.

Utility companies, like other corporations, sometimes make charitable contributions; when they do this and try to raise rates to compensate, New York State's highest court has ruled that the customers have a right to sue and challenge the contributions. They can use the First Amendment to complain about contributions to organizations that offend their religious and political beliefs.

The March 1987 minuet danced by Consolidated Edison of New York, Inc. (Con Ed) is a good illustration of the regulatory process. Con Ed agreed to cut its rates by 3.1 percent (which adds up to $132.5 million for the company, and a $1.10 monthly saving for the average customer) and to keep them down until April 1990. Why? Because the New York Public Service Commission was going to restrict Con Ed's permitted rate of return to 12 percent and impose a one-year, 3.3 percent rate cut. As a result of the compromise, Con Ed can earn a 15.2 percent rate of return, but only 12.9 percent on common equity for a three-year period. If Con Ed earns more than the 12.9 percent "cap," it can keep half the extra revenue but must refund the other half to customers.

## Power Companies

An electric utility has both residential and business customers. The residential customers can do a little to reduce their usage—perhaps by turning off lights or switching to gas appliances—but they're pretty much stuck with whatever rates the utility chooses to charge them. According to the Edison Electric Institute, the average revenues that utility companies earn from selling electric power have risen from a little over two cents per kilowatt-hour in 1980 to over seven cents per kilowatt-hour in 1985.

In 1980, industrial customers paid about one cent a kilowatt-hour; in 1985, they paid more than four cents: the rate of increase was about the same, but obviously residential customers pay a lot more for their power. Since people are getting much more energy-conscious, the demand for electric power is expanding very slowly (1.7 percent a year in the 1980s), which means that many utility companies are stuck with expensive nuclear power plants that don't work very well and, even if they work, would generate lots of electricity that nobody wants.

Industrial customers *use* much more power, but they have more options. They can negotiate with the electric company for special lower rates, tie in with another, more cooperative utility, or even generate their own electricity. In fact, some companies (The Dow Chemical Company is one) generate enough electric power to sell it to residential customers, in competition with the utilities. A 1978 federal law called the Public Utility Regulatory Policies Act lets companies that generate electricity sell it to the utility companies, instead of vice versa.

More than 2,000 communities, including cities as large as Los Angeles, have municipal utility companies that charge about one-third less for power than utility companies owned by investors. Chicago is contemplating either buying out the local utility company, Commonwealth Edison, or finding ways to get electricity elsewhere. The city has a franchise agreement with the company lasting until 1990; when that expires, it would dearly like to find an alternative to the company that has raised its rates six times in a decade. It's been estimated that the city government of Chicago could save $1.3 billion over the next twenty years just by buying bulk power from other utilities to meet its own needs; the utility's three million customers in the Chicago area could save another $12.5 billion over that time period. However, a rival consulting firm, hired by Commonwealth Edison Company, says that the assumptions behind those figures are unrealistic.

The whole process sets up a tug-of-war between utility companies, constantly asking for increases in residential rates (so they can be competitive on commercial rates), and utility regulators. The regulators used to rubber stamp requests for rate increases to build new plants; today, they often modify or turn down the request. If utilities can't get a meaningful rate increase, sometimes they can "unbundle," that is, charge separately for different levels of service, including things that used to be free. As we'll see below, the telephone companies responded similarly after the breakup of the Bell System monopoly.

In the quest for profits, utility companies have other options. They can pursue "vertical integration" by buying other energy-related investments: coal mines or natural gas fields, for instance. Or they can seek partners to distribute the electricity, while keeping control of the generation of power. That could be a way to get more flexibility in operations: the states regulate the sale of power, but the federal government (which now has a pro-business philosophy) regulates wholesale power sales, so the generating companies might be subject to less stringent regulation.

They can deemphasize power generation and distribution as a profit source and concentrate on investments: New York's Con Ed has a venture capital corporation that invests in tax-exempt bonds and preferred stock, among other things; Washington's Potomac Electric Power Company invests in aircraft leasing and solar power plants; Charlotte's Duke Power Company consults with other companies about the design and running of power plants.

St. Petersburg's Florida Progress Corporation (which owns the Mid-Continent Life Insurance Company) even joined the effort to bring a major-league baseball team to Tampa–St. Petersburg. If it eventually succeeds, it would be a godsend to sportscasters, who could talk about the team running out of juice whenever it hits a slump. Florida Power & Light Company also owns an insurance company, Colonial Penn. The Pacific Lighting Corporation owns Thrifty Drug Stores. Yet the effort to diversify is a two-edged sword: if the other businesses bring in too much money, utility regulators are likely to turn down rate increase applications or even demand rate rollbacks. Whatever happens, "current" events are likely to remain interesting.

# Local Telephone Service

Economists have a concept called the "natural monopoly": a company that *has* to control 100 percent of the business in its market sector because it's impossible for there to be more than one provider of the goods or services. For a long time, the telephone company was considered a natural monopoly. Who'd want to install a competing set of telephone wires? How would people who subscribed to one phone company talk to people who subscribed to other companies?

All that changed in the 1980s, for reasons both practical (improved communications technology made it possible to have rival phone systems without rival wiring) and legal (a federal court ordered the breakup of "Ma Bell" into a long-distance company, AT & T, and regional "Baby Bells" providing intrastate service). Now AT & T faces competition from other long-distance companies, including Sprint and MCI. However, AT & T still attracts about two-thirds of the $67 billion long-distance market. AT & T had a tremendous advantage—the sheer inertia of many of its customers, who stayed with AT & T simply to avoid picking another company; besides, customers with rotary phones instead of push-button phones either had to stick with AT & T or get new phones.

Its largest competitor, MCI, had a 4.5 percent share of the market in 1987; U.S. Sprint also had 4.5 percent. (Although the market shares are the same, MCI is a larger company.) The Baby Bells picked up 13 percent (because it's possible to make long-distance calls within large states: from Manhattan to Albany, for instance), and other companies handle the remaining 11 percent.

The effect of the breakup on consumers is ambiguous. Long-distance rates have dropped like a stone (about 30 percent since the breakup), but local rates have generally risen at least as much, so the average person pays more for telephone service. (In late 1986, the Consumer Federation of America estimated that residential bills increased 20 percent as a result of the breakup.) Then there are the new phone bills, which require not only the combined talents of a systems analyst and a psychic to read, but also the need to contact three, four, or five different organizations to figure out what went wrong with the phone. (Corporations who need help can turn to telecommunications consultants. The cynical, and not altogether untrue, view of these consultants is that they were the people who created the mess in their former jobs for the phone company.)

In 1987, AT & T's sales were a tad over $51 billion; its profits, $204 billion; and its assets, close to $39 billion. Its market value was $30.8 billion, so it had a return on equity of 14 percent. Its chairman and CEO, J. E. Olson, earned $1.1 million in salary and bonus in 1986, plus deferred compensation of $266,000.

Four of the "Baby Bells" made it onto *Business Week*'s corporate scoreboard and executive compensation surveys. BellSouth Corporation was the most profitable, managing a profit margin of 13.6 percent in 1987. Profit for 1987 as a whole was $1.66 billion. The BellSouth boss, John L. Clendenin, ranked fifth among the best-paid CEOs in the telephone industry, and #199 in the whole country, with 1987 earnings of $1,120,000 (salary and bonus) and 12,000 shares in deferred compensation.

MCI did *not* have a great year in 1986. Sales were just fine, at $3.59 billion, but the company lost over $448 million. That meant it had a return on invested capital of −7.7 percent, and a return on common equity of −24.5 percent. That didn't stop CEO William G. McGowan from earning a $671,000 salary, making him #429 on the list of best-paid executives for the year. At the highest executive levels, earnings and performance aren't always correlated.

Things looked up in 1987, although much of the $25 million MCI earned in the first quarter came from tax-loss carryforwards and from settling an antitrust suit (that is, not from profitable business). MCI has a problem: although AT & T's rate of return is regulated by the Federal Communications Commission (FCC) but MCI is theoretically free to set its own price levels, whenever AT & T is ordered to drop its prices (for instance, because the giant communications company benefited heavily from the 1986 tax code's changes in corporate taxation), MCI either has to match the price cuts or look bad to its own customers. (In fact, in March 1987, MCI even issued a call for deregulation of AT & T because the federally ordered AT & T rate cuts were so tough on MCI; MCI's hope is that a deregulated AT & T would immediately raise its prices and thus give MCI a chance.)

MCI worked hard on cutting costs (including 2,300 layoffs) and got sales/general/administrative expenses down to $3.939 billion in 1987. But MCI can't do much about its two major costs: access charges to connect MCI to local telephone networks (51 to 52 percent of revenue) and telephone lines leased from other carriers (about 5 percent of revenue). These charges are equivalent to retailers' costs of acquiring merchandise for resale: without access and telephone lines, MCI has nothing to sell. Before the breakup of AT & T, the Federal Communications Commission ordered local companies to let MCI and Sprint connect with their lines for much less than they charged AT & T for the same privilege. That's because the lines were set up to interface with AT & T; MCI and Sprint customers had to dial many extra digits. Now, local phone companies have more sophisticated equipment, so the discount has been reduced to 8 to 9 percent.

MCI's profit margins bounced from 4 percent in 1985 to a hefty 12 percent loss in 1986; its 1987 margin was 2 percent. That looks pretty awful compared to AT & T's estimated 4 percent margin for 1987 but great next to the estimated 16 percent loss for U.S. Sprint, the other major entrant in the long-distance phone sweepstakes. Both MCI and Sprint have been plagued with billing trouble (customers either never get billed, or get billed over and over again for the calls they made or for calls they never made) and other administrative problems.

Sprint, which is owned by GTE Corporation and United Telecommunications, Inc., is risking $2 billion on a fiber-optic network that is intended to provide crystal-clear phone service. Until the network is in place (scheduled for early 1988), Sprint has to patch together a network from AT & T leased lines and from microwave towers and computer switches that are far from state-of-the-art. Maybe that's why Sprint could finish 1987 with a loss of as much as $1 billion, following losses in the third and fourth quarters of 1986.

The deregulated environment has created new opportunities and new kinds of companies, such as the "alternative operator service" (AOS) companies. Charges for operator-assisted long-distance calls run more than $7 billion a year. Before the breakup of the Bell System, AT & T handled all these calls. Since then, AT & T maintained a lock on the business until 1986, when AT & T changed its policy and refused to pay hotels a commission when their guests made long-distance calls. That opened the way to alternative companies. The FCC has gotten hundreds of complaints about the cost of placing a long-distance call with the help of these operators; some of them charge ten times as much as the better-established telephone companies. The FCC recommends that callers ask operators *which* company they work for before they place an operator-assisted call from a pay phone, hospital, or hotel. They should also ask about billing practices (will it go on the hotel bill, or the caller's phone credit card?) and the cost of the call. If the answers are discouraging, the FCC suggests finding another phone, served by another company. But this advice isn't always practical if you need to make a call in a hurry (or you're comfortably settled in your hotel room, with a blizzard outside).

Life will get even tougher for Sprint and MCI if federal courts permit the Baby Bells to edge into the long-distance telephone service market; in September 1987, federal judge Harold Greene quashed the Baby Bells' move into long-distance service, but he approved their entry into the

## CONSUMER TIP

One reason your long-distance rates are so high (whether you do your dialing on AT & T, MCI, Sprint, or one of their competitors) is that "hackers" use computers and other electronic technology to find out the billing codes used by long-distance services; then they sell the codes for about $400 each to "phone hustlers," who promise their customers they'll dial long-distance calls to anywhere for only $2 to $4 each. The phone companies, having to make up the lost revenue somewhere, raise the rates they charge their honest customers.

computerized information business. The regional operating companies are allowed to transmit data but can't enter the home-banking business. The regional companies are appealing this decision.

# Long-Distance Phone Service

As a result of the 1984 breakup of AT & T, seven regional "operating companies" now provide local phone service: Bell Atlantic Corporation, NYNEX Corporation (the New York unit; goodness only knows why they chose to be called NYNEX), BellSouth, American Information Technologies Corporation (Ameritech), Southwestern Bell Corporation, US WEST Inc., and Pacific Telesis Group.

Like utility companies, the Baby Bells are looking for new businesses to expand into: NYNEX wants to run a transoceanic fiber-optic cable to Europe and the Caribbean; Bell Atlantic wants to publish a computerized yellow pages and already has profitable cellular phone and computer maintenance businesses.

The Baby Bells get about 10 percent of their revenues from nontelephone business, ranging from less than 5 percent of revenues at Pacific Telesis, to 10 percent at BellSouth and Southwestern Bell. Since nontelephone business, like computer maintenance, is not regulated while telephone operations are subject to court jurisdiction and state regulation, nontelephone business is frequently more profitable than actually running a phone company.

In the past, state regulators decided the rate of return that phone companies would be permitted to earn; rates charged to customers would be raised or lowered depending on whether the company had reached its target. However, a few states (New York and Wisconsin, for example) are allowing rates that permit a higher rate of return. The changes are intended to provide incentives for cost cutting: the phone companies are allowed to keep half the savings, which is good news for telephone company shareholders.

Phone companies are major employers: at the end of 1984, AT & T had more than 365,000 employees. Although AT & T offered what was considered stable, lifetime employment, its number of employees has dropped significantly: in 1988, only 303,000 were on the AT & T payroll. Most of the Baby Bells have also reduced their work forces. Pacific Telesis had nearly 77,000 workers in 1984 but only about 72,000 in 1988; employment at Southwestern Bell dropped from 71,900 to 67,085 in the same period. However, Bell Atlantic's work force went up a little (77,514 to 78,510); so did BellSouth's, rising from 96,000 to 98,664. Many of these workers are unionized; as a result, there have been some acrimonious negotiations and some bitter strikes because many of these jobs are low paying and very vulnerable to loss through automation and shift of market share away from the descendants of the Bell System to independent companies.

The services provided by utility companies run the gamut from gas heat—a slight technological improvement of the first fire kindled in the first scientist's cave—to the farthest reaches of the information explosion relayed over telephone system fiber optics. You can achieve some savings by conservation (not wasting electricity; making phone calls at times when lower evening, night, or weekend rates are charged); by monitoring your bills; and, in some cases, by selecting the provider of services that provides the best value for your pattern of usage.

# RETAIL RAP: All Kinds of Stores

There are stores the size of several stacked football fields that are ready, willing, and able to sell you just about any item that can be legally sold. There are also stores that sell nothing but teddy bears, or buttons, or items shaped like or decorated with hearts. There are stores where you need an appointment to get in (and it helps to have a current good customer sponsor you), and other stores where they practically drag you in off the street.

In the early days of our nation (and of retailing), only two kinds of stores existed: the store that sold a particular thing (be it feed and grain, or agricultural implements, or saddlery and horse harness) and the "general store" that sold everything that the storekeeper figured a body would rightly need.

The term "dry goods store" probably came about from the division of the general store into two parts. In one, the storekeeper sold "dry goods" (calico, pots and pans, ribbons and trimmings) to the wimmenfolk. In the other, the menfolk gathered around a barrel of "wet goods," generally corn whiskey made on the premises.

Today, with far more kinds of retail operations, the line between one kind of store and another is easily blurred. Furthermore, not all retailing is done in a store. Mail-order catalogs have been a staple ever since there was a Pony Express. At first, catalog merchandising brought goods to settlers too remote and too scattered to support a store. Today, it's the choice of those too busy to shop during conventional store hours, those seeking bargains, or those looking for specialty merchandise that can't be found nearer home. Many a successful store will start a catalog operation for enthusiastic customers too far away to appear in person; conversely, a successful catalog operation will sometimes open a showroom so customers can shop, pay, and take home their merchandise without delay. Another pattern is for a catalog operation to seek success in conventional retailing: Banana Republic (travel and leisure clothes) and Victoria's Secret (lingerie) have taken this route.

## NO MORE STORES?

Computer technology has revolutionized retailing. Computers lighten the endless task of keeping track of inventory and reorders; computers make credit-card buying feasible; and computers and other technical advances may make stores, as we know them, obsolete. (Maybe, but we don't think so. Actually buying things is only a fraction of the joy of shopping: you can't hang out with your friends at the mall, for instance, if there isn't any mall.) For one thing, retailers can penetrate into the home through "home shopping'' shows, where merchandise is displayed on television and orders can be taken directly over a telephone line.

Another possibility is retailing by means of videocassettes. The prospective buyer sends away (or, more likely, telephones) to the retailer for a copy of the video-catalog, borrows it, or, in some cases much relished by the retailer, even rents it from a videocassette rental store. If the viewer sees something attractive, then he or she can call the retailer, whose phone lines will probably be open 24 hours a day, to charge the merchandise to his or her credit card. Or if the electronic debit card catches on, the retailer will be able to make an electronic transfer of money directly from the buyer's account without waiting for payment (and taking the risk that the check will bounce, or that the credit-card number is a phony, or its credit limit exceeded).

## MARKETING PHILOSOPHY

The purpose of introducing this technology is to motivate the customers (who can see the products demonstrated, but can't taste the Capuccino Framboise Smash ice cream—at least, not yet). It also saves money for the retailers. Although there's a high initial investment in getting ready for home shopping or in producing a video catalog, the retailer saves by not having to keep the store open late (or at all); and computers don't yell at customers, get pensions or vacation days, tap the cash register, or take home sweaters.

Until stores entirely disappear, however, you should know about several different types of stores:

▶ Department stores have many different types of merchandise, such as clothing for the whole family, housewares, and kitchenware and small appliances. The appeal of department stores is one-stop shopping; at least theoretically, your favorite department store will carry anything you need. Furthermore, many department stores have their own brand of merchandise; the point here is to rely on the reputation of the store.

Not all department stores carry furniture, major appliances, or electronics because they take up a lot of space and discounters offer stiff competition. Sometimes the store leases out space to an outside retailer; that way, the department store attracts the buyers who want the merchandise, but the department store management doesn't have to worry about tying up its money in an expensive inventory.

Sometimes department stores offer services: personal shoppers, theater ticket brokerage, eye exams, glasses and contact lenses, travel agencies. Again, these can be managed either by the store or by a business that leases space in the store.

- ▶ Specialty stores concentrate on a narrower selection of merchandise: garden tools, or men's clothing, or books.
- ▶ A boutique is narrower still, and somewhat elegant. The term is usually used for clothing stores, but it's applied in other situations as well: a "boutique" investment banking firm or law firm, for instance. The appeal of a boutique is exclusivity, the fact that the owner has "edited" the available merchandise. Theoretically, everything in the boutique will be perfect; you're supposed to dive right in and scoop up armfuls of clothes.
- ▶ On the other hand, a discounter competes on price, sacrificing the amenities to offer bigger bargains. There are discount department stores, appliance discounters, discount computer and electronics stores, discount stationery stores, discount china stores, and many, many discount clothing stores. Sometimes the discounter sells his own brand of merchandise, which he purchases directly from the factory, cutting prices by cutting out a middleman or two. At other times, he buys manufacturers' mistakes (seconds or damaged merchandise); merchandise damaged in shipping; or retailers' mistakes (out-of-fashion or simply unpopular merchandise) or "leftovers" (a few colors or sizes from a range, once the rest sell out). Some discount stores operate as "clubs," offering a lower price to members who pay a membership fee or restricting access to the "warehouse" store to club members.

Every store has an image, whether its owner created it consciously or not. Stores can compete on several bases:

- ▶ Service—the glass of champagne as the models parade past; the willingness to repair the tool Uncle Wilmer bought there twenty-two years ago.
- ▶ Price—either so low as to be an irresistible bargain or so high as to make you feel like a dazzling success to be able to afford it at all.

## CONSUMER TIP

There are no legal requirements about the use of the word "discount"; a store calling itself a discount store may sell some merchandise at normal retail prices, or even at higher prices than stores that don't call themselves discounters. So check price and quality before buying.

▶ Exclusivity—exclusively making/importing/selecting merchandise: if you want it, you have to buy it from that particular retailer.

▶ Quality—"only the best." Usually, this is associated with high price and exclusivity, but some mid-range stores maintain a high-quality image.

▶ Fashion—a constantly changing parade of chic. Again, this is often associated with high price and exclusivity.

▶ Time savings—either through personal shoppers or through the elimination by the store owner of everything he or she doesn't think you'd want to buy.

Stores can combine several, but can't compete on the basis of all these factors at the same time.

Observers have found that the "middle range" is disappearing from American retailing. There are now gigantic department stores and acre-long warehouse clubs; even large department store chains are being swallowed up by even bigger department store chains. The tiny neighborhood stores, either survivors from the days before gentrification or start-ups by hopeful entrepreneurs, can survive if they offer merchandise or services unavailable anywhere else or services that must be done in the neighborhood (you really wouldn't drive for an hour and a half just to get your shoes reheeled or your raincoat cleaned). Otherwise, they go under because of competition from malls (which offer a huge variety of stores for shopping as entertainment, and which provide amenities such as parking and climate control), from discounters, and from mail-order operations.

When it comes to price, the survivors seem to be the most aggressive price cutters (appealing to cash-conscious buyers or to those who can't afford the things they want at conventional retail prices) and the purveyors of the most outrageous luxuries (for those who would light their cigars with hundred-dollar bills—if they hadn't given up smoking to improve their marathon times). Once again, the middle ground is perilous, and long-established retailers such as Gimbel's and Abraham & Straus have gone out of business, merged, or been acquired.

Are these trends good or bad? They sure make it harder for small businesses (already buffeted by high commercial rents and utility rates). They can make neighborhoods less convenient (as the friendly, convenient retailers and services are replaced by yet another franchised clothing store or seller of upscale junk food). But for the survivors of the retail wars, the potential for profit has increased (or it will, once they finish paying off the costs of the takeover battles). Consumers sacrifice some convenience but have new forms of retailing (such as home shopping and videocassette catalogs), more and more specialized stores (Teddy Bear World, Kiwi Kottage), and imports from all over the world to choose from.

# Consuming Passions

# 19

# Supermarkets

Number of establishments:  30,505
Total receipts:  $209.8 billion
Average net sales:  $6,872,000*
Number of employees:  2,031,000
Total payroll:  $21,363,000
*Progressive Grocer, 1985

(Department of Commerce, 1982)

Top earners (1987)
  Salary/bonus   Stock Gains   Deferred Comp.
James Wood (Great Atlantic & Pacific Tea Company, Inc):
  $2,010,000      —              11,000 shares
Israel Cohen (Giant Food, Inc.):
  $991,000       $2,445,000      —
Lyle Everingham (Kroger Company):
  $802,000        —             117,000 shares

(BW '88)

In the supermarket business, little things mean a lot. Supermarket management involves choosing a dizzying variety of products, keeping

| (1) Cost of operations: | 78.0 percent |
|---|---|
| (2) Officers' compensation: | 0.6 percent |
| (3) Pensions and benefits: | 1.7 percent |
| (4) Rent: | 1.4 percent |
| (5) Repairs: | 0.5 percent |
| (6) Depreciation, depletion, amortization: | 1.5 percent |
| (7) Interest: | 0.6 percent |
| (8) Bad debts: | 0.1 percent |
| (9) Advertising: | 1.1 percent |
| (10) State, local taxes: | 1.3 percent |
| (11) Other expenses: | 14.1 percent |
| (12) Net profit before tax: | 0.2 percent |

(Troy, '84–'85)

them fresh and in good condition, and keeping the stock turning over often enough to make up wafer-thin (sorry, it just slipped out) profit margins.

According to Dun & Bradstreet's 1987 survey of 2,338 grocery stores, gross profit was a rather low 20.5 percent; return on sales was also very low, ranging from 0.4 percent to 3.6 percent; and return on assets ranged from 1.5 percent to 12.7 percent, all of which shows that food markets have comparatively low assets, spending most of their money on the saleable—and perishable—stock. The grocery stores surveyed managed after-tax profits averaging 2.2 percent, which is comparable to rates achieved in other industries with higher gross profits, so managers must be doing something right.

The successful supermarketeer must decide how much can be spent on refurbishing the stores in the latest image, and whether to position the chain as the choice of the gourmet yuppie or the place for the down-to-earth homemaker to shop for food bargains. (In fact, one chain hired superdesigner Milton Glaser to make their generic food section look *cheap,* a mission he accomplished with plain-brown-wrapper packaging and demolition of tile floors to show the concrete underneath.)

Grocery stores have to offer enough specials, often as loss leaders, to lure people into the store. The stores also have to avoid getting caught up in a suicidal price war with other supermarket chains. Then there's the problem of coupons. Food manufacturers struggle for shelf space; they want their new products to succeed. So they create demand by offering cents-off coupons, which build traffic for the supermarket and induce customers to try the new product (often, to try it a grand total of once). But the coupons are a giant headache for the supermarkets, especially if some @#$%! competing store offers customers double or triple coupon savings that other stores then have to match or lose sales.

Supermarkets manage to do this every day of the week (literally, because most are open seven days a week; some, twenty-four hours a day). In 1981, supermarkets snagged nearly two-thirds of all food store sales; convenience stores attracted 20.2 percent, and specialty stores 6.8 percent of the food dollar. (Today, specialty store sales probably have a much higher market share because of the increasing "gourmet consciousness" and the ever-expanding desire for convenient prepared foods.) The rest went to "superettes," which stock a moderate selection of merchandise and whose sales are in the $500,000 to $2,000,000 range.

Speaking of chains, the supermarket business is concentrated, dominated by regional and national chains. According to the 53rd annual report compiled by *Progressive Grocer* magazine in 1985, there were 30,505 supermarkets in the United States—17,220 of them part of chains, 13,285 independent. However, most of the highest-earning stores were chain operations. Sometimes chains acquire other chains: for instance, the Great Atlantic & Pacific Tea Company, better known as the A & P, owns Pantry Pride, Inc., Shopwell, Inc., Food Emporium, and Waldbaum's.

Cornell University's study for 1985–1986 placed the average gross margin for fifteen supermarket chains at 24.48 percent, with total expenses of 23.14 percent. The average store rang up $11.1 million in sales—that is, $410 per square foot: a very respectable average for retailing as a whole. This also shows strong gains over the Department of Commerce's 1982 survey, which reported average sales per square foot of selling space at $318.

Top Chains, 1987

| | # of Stores | Sales ($000) | (Profits) Net Income ($000) |
|---|---|---|---|
| Kroger | 1,298 | 17,660,000 | 183,300,000 |
| American Stores Company | 1,498 | 14,272,000 | 154,300,000 |
| Winn-Dixie Stores, Incorporated | 1,262 | 8,824,000 | 114,600,000 |
| A & P | 1,200 | 9,642,000 | 98,900,000 |
| Lucky Stores, Inc. | 579 | 6,925,000 | 119,400,000 |

(*Business Week*, '87)

## DESIGNING TO SELL

In a typical supermarket, the produce department takes up 8 to 10 percent of the selling area but contributes 8 to 20 percent of sales and 11 percent of the store's gross profit. Studies have shown that produce sales go up by 1 to 1.5 percent of the store's volume if the produce aisles are near the front of the store. Gross margin for the supermarket as a whole is 22 percent—lower for groceries (16 to 18 percent), higher for produce (32 percent). (But then, selling produce is a risky business: it has to leave the store fast, one way or another.)

One theme that emerges from this book is that the lines between various forms of retail stores are blurring. As a case in point, an increasing number of supermarkets are selling fully prepared hot take-out dishes, and a few supermarkets even have counters or tables where shoppers can sit down and snack or have a full meal. In 1985, 58 percent of supermarkets had a deli department; 35 percent had a bakery (the smell of fresh-baked bread puts customers in a mellow—and buying—mood); 15 percent of-

## CONSUMER TIP

Millions have been invested in "psyching out" the supermarket customer through store design; you can cut your grocery bills by understanding the way it works. The store is laid out so that the typical customer who wants a loaf of bread, a quart of milk, and a few other items must traipse through the whole store to get them. The most profitable items tend to be up front, while the dreary, low-profit, heavy items like laundry detergent tend to be tucked away. Especially if the store cultivates a gourmet image, you'll have to pass tempting, aromatic displays of baked goods and delicatessen items. Once you get to the checkout, you'll have to pass racks of items designed for impulse sales: magazines (you didn't think they put them there as a public service for those who are too snobbish to admit they read *People* magazine, did you?), candy, small toys for kids. The theory is that your kids will demand the items (or grab them and tear the package open) and that you'll buy the items to avoid a scene.

fered catering services; and 11 percent had a take-out salad bar—a service offered by *no* supermarkets in 1980.

Another theme is the trend toward the "superstore": the enormous operation selling everything imaginable. This trend is clear in supermarkets, where the European-style "hypermarket," which combines gourmet food, an unusually large selection of more prosaic grocery items, and service departments (meat, delicatessen, pharmacy, liquor), accounts for four-fifths of the new construction of supermarkets. In 1985, 21,890 of the 30,505 supermarkets were conventional in format; 4,400 were superstores; 3,365, economy stores; and 850, combined formats. Twenty years ago, supermarkets averaged 20,000 square feet; today, 50,000 square feet (and 40,000 separate items) is more like it. Superstore aisles tend to be 8½ feet wide, not 6 feet wide like traditional supermarket aisles.

Stew Leonard's, in Norwalk, Connecticut, represents yet another kind of superstore. It's absolutely huge (110,000 square feet) and does a huge volume of business ($100 million a year), but it offers deep discounts and tightly restricts the number of items it carries to 750, specializing in dairy foods. Leonard's won't carry an item if it can't move 1,000 units a week—and it has been known to sell five tons of cookies in a week and ten million quarts of milk a year. (The *Wall Street Journal,* home of the execrable pun, titled its September 17, 1987 article about Leonard's "In the Moo.")

As you've seen, a final trend worth exploring is the discount impulse. Ordinary supermarkets have specials every week but tailor their choice of specials to increase volume without serious profit cutting. Discount supermarkets don't advertise, depending on word of mouth to attract customers. Some discount supermarkets buy directly from manufacturers, not wholesalers, or import food items; they may also act as middlemen to other supermarkets. Discount supermarkets either specialize in nonperishable bulk items or avoid selling perishable items altogether. They also have a smaller selection within the categories of items they carry: if they have the jumbo size, tough luck for you if you want the colossal size.

Warehouse stores have an even smaller selection of merchandise than discount supermarkets. In addition, they often expect customers to bag their own groceries at the checkout counter, and, in fact, the customers may have to supply their own grocery bags and even their own shopping carts. Warehouse stores may be organized as clubs, limited to members who pay a small fee to join.

## BIG BROTHER AT THE CHECKOUT?

If a supermarket plans to sell 25,000 quarts of milk, it's going to have to buy at least 25,000 quarts of milk, and nothing can be done about it.

However, if there were some way to run a supermarket with only two checkout clerks instead of a small army of checkers and baggers, the supermarket's payroll would decline dramatically. Computerized systems, based on the UPC (Universal Product Code) markings, now make it possible for a supermarket to handle the checkout process faster and with fewer clerks than conventional cash registers require. Changing over to computerized cash registers calls for a heavy capital investment [say, $100,000 per store], which discourages some chains.

However, the computerized system has other advantages. A supermarket may have 2,000 items with price changes in a single week. They can hire enough stock people to run around sticking new labels on things [it's estimated that it takes an employee more than a full working day to change 600 labels]; or they can furnish each cashier with a printout of all the price changes, demanding that the cashier look up each item. Neither alternative is very satisfactory to owners and managers: even if the customers would stand still while the checkout personnel look everything up, the longer it takes to process a transaction, the more hours go on the payroll each week. A better way is to make sure that the computer system has all the latest prices, so that the items can be scanned rapidly by the computer. Theoretically, the price is supposed to be marked on the shelf (though not necessarily for every item) in a form readable by humans, but in practice, items frequently go unmarked when stickering by hand is relied upon.

An efficiently operating computer system makes it simple for the store's manager to check sales against inventory (and makes it tough for the store's employees to help a turkey or case of beer "walk" out of the store). The trend is for merchandise delivery firms to equip their drivers with hand-held computers to monitor deliveries; if the supermarkets adopt compatible systems, they can speed up deliveries, inventory taking, and accounting. The consulting firm of Arthur D. Little estimates that $500 million a year could be shaved off grocery stores' costs by integrating the delivery and in-store computer systems.

The next step is to use the cash register reports to replace items that are out of stock and to analyze seasonal trends in sales. It doesn't take a marketing genius to figure out that people buy more lemonade in the summer than in the winter, and more hot chocolate in the winter than in the summer—but how much more? When do sales shift? With the computerized system, it's easy to find out. Here the computer system opens up a new source of income for supermarkets: selling data to manufacturers of the products sold in the store. Which brand of cologne sells the best? How many customers responded to the fifty-cents-off coupon for the new ice cream dessert—and how many of them bothered to come back for a second package?

In short, computerized systems are great for supermarkets (as long as they can afford the start-up costs). But are they good for customers? You may feel that Big Brother is watching you if your supermarket can find out whether you pay by check or credit card, and then identify your buying patterns. Hmm, lots of extra purchases . . . the in-laws must be visiting from Chicago. A standing rib roast and imported dried mushrooms bought by a family that usually eats chopped chuck and instant mashed potatoes? The boss must be coming to dinner.

## SECURITY PROBLEMS

Supermarkets don't really want too much cash around. The presence of a lot of cash tempts robbers; the presence of a safe tempts burglars; and the busy, multiple tills are favorite drop spots for counterfeiters because cashiers see so many people a day that it's unlikely they'll remember who handed over that particular $20 bill. An even worse security problem is shoplifting: one-third of incidents occur between 3 and 6 P.M., suggesting that schoolchildren drop over for snacks they don't feel like paying for.

That's one reason why supermarkets are happy to issue check-cashing cards to customers who have an employment and banking history. (The other reason is that paying out cold cash has a sobering effect; customers paying by check are much more likely to toss a dozen or so extra items, or more luxurious items, into the cart.) Alas, that subjects the supermarket to the risk of bad checks. The latest solution is to use the computerized system to permit payment by credit card, or by electronic debit card so that the amount of the order is removed directly from the customer's bank account. Or the supermarket can make an arrangement with a bank to install an ATM in the supermarket, so shoppers will never be more than a few feet away from a source of cash.

## REVENUES AND RESULTS

If the supermarket industry were a single business, it would be the twenty-sixth largest in the country. As of April 1985, the supermarket industry had sales of nearly $75 billion, assets of $18.5 billion, and profits of about $1.132 billion—that is, a very respectable return on invested capital of 14.7 percent, and on common equity of 18.1 percent.

Let's look at a few of the major players and their performances for 1987:

| | Kroger | Food Lion | A & P | American Stores Co.* |
|---|---|---|---|---|
| Number of stores | 1,280 | | | |
| Sales | $17.66 billion | 2.954 billion | 9.642 billion | 14.272 billion |
| Profits | 55.8 million | 85.8 million | 98.9 million | 15.43 million |
| Profit margin | 1.0% | 2.9% | 1.0% | 1.1% |
| Return on invested capital | 11.7% | 21.6% | 10.3% | 10.1% |
| Return on common equity | 18.5% | 27.6% | 12.0% | 15.0% |

*A holding company that owns supermarkets and drugstores, including Jewel and Sav-on stores, ranked #282 in *Business Week.*

(*Business Week,* '87)

As mentioned, supermarkets operate on very small margins; Kroger's and A & P's 1 percent, which would spell failure in most industries, is respectable enough for a major supermarket chain.

## AND TOMORROW?

Cynics have acclaimed the supermarket as a remarkable example of American ingenuity: at last, storekeepers have found a way to put the customers to work! At the turn of the century, shoppers picked out the goods they wanted, which were fetched, packed, and then delivered by store employees. When the telephone appeared, telephone orders became common (a system based on unhesitating trust between shopkeeper and customer—and a small array of simple foods in the grocery store).

Today, there are plenty of singles and families to consume the groceries, and precious few housewives to shop for them. Stores are responding with longer hours, so people can shop in the early morning jogging hours, after work, or on weekends. In fact, sometimes stores even provide (of all things!) delivery and telephone orders.

Prospects for food stores are fairly bright. Supermarket managers will always have the problems of low margins and spoilage; however, demographics are on their side. Food shoppers in their forties spend a lot more than older or younger shoppers (an average of $95 a week, as compared to $74). The baby boomers are aging, moving into the prime grocery-buying years, and having kids, thus making it less likely they'll eat in restaurants and more likely to stock up on baby food, peanut butter, potato chips, and other childhood staples.

When people are flush and extravagant, they chow down on porterhouse and buy out the gourmet counter. When they're trimming the budget, they stop eating in restaurants, shop harder for bargains, and stock up on no-frills products. Either way, the supermarket wins.

# 20

# Convenience Stores

A supermarket (see page 89) earns its money by providing a huge number of items, in a large space, to a large number of customers; it can afford to maintain its low profit margins because it does a volume business and so can buy items in gigantic quantities. A convenience store sells some of the same items as a supermarket but does almost everything else differently.

A convenience store sells only a few items, with little or no choice of brands. Its markups are much higher than supermarket markups: prices are typically 10 to 15 percent higher. Instead of catering to those who drive in to buy bag after bag of groceries, the convenience store sells to those who walk or drive in for an item or two that's run out or that was forgotten during a supermarket shopping trip. That means that the average amount spent at a convenience store is low, though the profit on each transaction can be quite high.

Some convenience stores are run by large chains or are franchised, gaining the advantages of mass purchasing and national advertising. But there are also the neighborhood stores, frequently run by members of an ethnic group and suiting that group's food preferences. These stores (familiar to New Yorkers as "bodegas") provide a kind of neighborhood social club; are often local centers for informal off-track betting and num-

bers games; and sometimes provide credit to customers—a powerful incentive for the customer to forsake the supermarket.

According to the *Progressive Grocer*'s 1985 survey, about one-third
of the grocery stores in the United States—45,400 out of 154,000—were
convenience stores; however, their sales of $20.41 billion represented only
7 percent of the total spent on groceries.

The largest company in the convenience-store industry is The
Southland Corporation, which owns or franchises 7,672 7-Eleven stores,
selling $8 billion worth of gasoline, groceries, cigarettes, sodas, beer, sand-
wiches, and other goods a year. Whether the name was chosen to symbol-
ize its long hours or to trigger pleasant associations in customers more
familiar with dice than with diced carrots, the somewhat macho association is appropriate. Seventy percent of 7-Eleven customers are males,
typically young blue-collar workers who come in three times a week for
food and snacks. The chain is now trying to change its image somewhat
by cutting prices on some items to compete with other convenience
stores, or even supermarkets, and to appeal to women customers.

The highest margins are on items like toiletries; the lowest, on basic
items like milk. The average 7-Eleven store sells about $1 million a year,
with profits of $40,000; overall, the stores provided 93.3 percent of South-
land's sales, and $264 million of its $302 million in operating profits. Gasoline sales brought in profits of $193 million, on sales of $1.77 billion.

One effective new sales technique is to rent videos in convenience
stores because the cassette renter has to come in at least twice (to rent
and to return the movie) and therefore has two opportunities to buy
something—a roll of film, a soda, a newspaper, or some popcorn to munch
as the movie rolls.

Another chain, National Convenience Stores, Inc., has more than
1,000 Stop 'n' Go stores and ShopNGo Markets in the Sun Belt. In 1985, its
sales were $927,507,000. The cost of sales was $683,555,000; operating,
general, and administrative expenses ate up a further $201,229,000. Then
there was a little more than $19 million in interest to pay. The total ex-
penses were $903,969,000, leaving pretax earnings of $23,538,000, and
income taxes just over $8 million, for net earnings of $15,509,000. In other
words, the chain had to bring in about sixty dollars to wind up with a dollar
of net earnings after tax, about par for the course for the industries
discussed in this book.

Given the increasing number of two-income families, in which nobody much has time to cook dinner, convenience stores, which offer
frozen and prepared food as well as grocery staples until late at night (or
around the clock), seem likely to continue expanding and prospering.
Both types of convenience store (either the chain or franchise, or the
neighborhood store) can stay in the market because they tend to be
located in different places (chains and franchises on or near highways and

in industrial areas; neighborhood stores in urban residential areas), to carry different assortments of products (the neighborhood stores' customers often do all their shopping there, so a broader range of products must be carried), and to have different financial goals (the supermarket manager's overall profit target, set by central management; the neighborhood entrepreneur's willingness to hang on as long as the doors can be kept open).

# RETAIL RAP:  Franchising

Originally, there was only one way to open a retail business: raise the capital, pick a location, select merchandise, and put up the pennants for the Grand Opening. With luck, the retail merchant would succeed so splendidly that it would be necessary to open a second store, and perhaps a third, fourth, and fifth, to accommodate all the customers who flocked in to offer their money. However, the merchant would still have to run the entire chain of stores. Wouldn't it be wonderful if someone would not only pay for the privilege of learning the merchant's secrets but would open a store and keep the merchant's name before the public eye?

Would-be storekeepers began to wonder what it would be like to be able to take advantage of an already successful name, trademark, products, and style of doing business. Insecure would-be storekeepers hoped for assistance in setting up the business and continuing advice about possible business problems.

Franchising is the product of both these impulses. When a franchise is created, one operation (the franchisor) permits other operations (the franchisees) to use the name, trademark, store design, and other hallmarks of the franchised business. For instance, if you want to sell hamburgers called Big Macs then you'd better have either a McDonald's franchise or a taste for losing court cases. Usually, the franchisor retains the right to open his own, company-owned, franchise businesses—which can create major problems for the franchisees, who see their "parent" turn into a competitor.

In a typical franchise operation, a prospective franchisee applies and is checked out by the franchisor. Depending on the franchisor's reputation, fiscal soundness, and urgency of need for the money, the franchisee may have to demonstrate a substantial net worth and extensive business experience or merely the ability to breathe regularly and not to have declared bankruptcy recently.

The new franchisee pays a franchise fee (anywhere from a few hundred dollars to over a hundred thousand dollars), and gets access to training (anywhere from a few mimeographed sheets to an intensive training course). Sometimes it's up to the franchisee to find a business location; at other times, the franchisor provides guidance or even a fully featured, ready-to-go franchise location. (In that case, the franchisor can derive a substantial income from canny real estate transactions.) Setting up a franchise business can cost only a few hundred dollars (buying Jazzercise videocassettes and a phonograph) or hundreds of thousands (opened a pizzeria lately?)—$75,000 is a pretty typical figure.

Federal and state laws regulate franchising, requiring franchisors to provide would-be franchisees with extensive disclosure documents and to let the potential franchisee know exactly what is involved in the franchise—how much it costs to start, what the franchisee gets for the money, what kind of training is provided, and what restrictions are imposed on the way the franchise does business. The franchisor must also provide a lot of information on his own financial background and that of his company's officers so the person interested in opening a franchise can distinguish between obvious amateurs and seasoned professionals; between those with a history of financial success and those whose dreams are as passionate—and as speculative—as those of the potential franchisee himself or herself.

However, most of the regulatory requirements focus on disclosure, not on the actual policies of the franchisor. So franchisors can and do vary widely in the extent to which they police the franchisees (to keep up the franchise's good name); the amount of initial training and continuing supervision they provide; and the kind of restrictions placed on the franchise. One fast-food franchise may require only that the franchise conform to the food inspection code; another may specify the exact size and moisture content of the frozen french fries to be purchased and the dimensions of the plastic tableware and paper napkins.

Once the franchise is in operation, the franchisee must pay monthly fees; the typical range is anywhere from 3 to 10 percent of gross sales. Sometimes the franchise fee is the only charge; however, many franchises require a monthly advertising fee. Depending on the franchise, this could give the franchisee the benefit of heavy national and local TV, radio, and print advertising, or, if the franchise is too new or too local or too poor to buy media time, it could give the franchisee a couple of fifth-generation photocopies of articles about advertising strategies.

Franchises are supposed to provide merchandise and services of standard quality. It's the franchisor's job to make sure that this is done. Although it's a violation of the antitrust laws for the franchisor to insist that the franchisee buy supplies from the franchisor, the franchisor can insist on conformity to quality-control standards and can recommend vendors who meet those standards.

If everything works well, the franchisee benefits from the creation of a strong national image. A person traveling on business, faced with a choice between lunch at Hardee's and at Mom's Cafe, may balance the chance that Mom's dishes up the finest down-home eats ever shovelled onto a plate, against the risk that it's a ptomaine palace and opt for Hardee's.

The same thing is true of competition between AAMCO and Ed's Garage or a Glemby hair salon and Michael of Carnaby Street's Shear Drop. If everything works well, the franchisor makes lots of money because many, many franchisees will pony up the fees, and they'll earn enough to keep those franchise fees rolling in. If it doesn't work out, the franchisor can resell the location and perhaps the building to a new franchisee (if anyone wants to try); court records and file cabinets at the various state attorney generals' offices are filled with franchisor-franchisee set-tos.

In short, the purpose of franchising is to generate profits for both franchisor and franchisee by removing elements of insecurity. There are about half a million franchised operations of all types in the United States, and they sell nearly $650 billion worth of goods and services a year—over a third of the total U.S. retail sales. A key to their popularity may be that although more than one-third of all new businesses go under in the first year (and about four out of five have disappeared within five years), about 95 percent of franchisees are still going after the crucial first year; 92 percent are still hanging on after five years. Of course, some of those "successful" franchises are run by overworked franchisees who have a heavy debt load and earn a minimal return for their work and investment; others are part of mini-empires owned by contented millionaires with a leisurely life-style.

Is franchising the only way to go for an ambitious would-be retailer or service provider? Yes, if he or she wants to trade a (perhaps heavy) investment and share of the eventual profits for some degree of training, hand-holding, and the security of an established name. No, if the franchise consists of a trademark no one has ever heard of and products and services no one wants. No, if the entrepreneur has a genuinely new idea with a strong potential to succeed independently—or even be franchised to other business owners.

# Fast Food Operations

| | |
|---|---|
| Number of establishments: | 109,353 |
| Total receipts: | $35.67 billion |
| Average net sales: | $326,200,000 |
| Number of employees: | 1,610,000 |
| Total payroll: | $12,935,000,000 |

(Department of Commerce, '82)

When the archaeologists of the future set up exhibits about twentieth-century American life (assuming that, if there is a future, it has archaeologists), they'll have to include a few pictures of chrome-quilted diners and lots of the bright cardboard and plastic wrappings in which fast-food burgers, franks, fries, pizzas, drumsticks, and tacos were served up and delivered.

The tempo of American life no longer includes a worker's midday break to head home for a hot lunch. For one thing, very few housewives are at home to cook it. Whether it's because we have too little time or too much money, a great deal of the nation's food budget (40.5 percent) goes for meals away from home, and 10 percent of breakfasts are eaten in restaurants. ("Away from home" includes those eaten in someone else's home—a figure that the Department of Commerce doesn't trace.) Of course, some of the away-from-home spending goes to elegant restaurants or neighborhood "tablecloth joints," but most of it goes to fast-food restaurants; and the fast-food market is dominated by franchises.

What kinds of fast foods do Americans eat? Precious little tofu and alfalfa sprouts. The burger segment is the largest part of the fast-food picture, thanks to giants such as McDonald's and Burger King. But fast-food operations also sell pizza, tacos, sandwiches, fried chicken, and many other kinds of food.

Estimates of 1986 spending on franchised fast food range from *Manhattan, Inc.*'s figure of $50 billion and *Business Week*'s $52 billion figure, to *Restaurant Business*'s assertion that $48 billion was spent on quick-service hamburgers alone, out of a total of $60.4 billion in fast-food spending.

# Burgers

In 1986, there were 9,435 McDonald's units in operation, and the average unit did $1.3 million worth of business. The 4,743 Burger Kings averaged $1.1 million in sales; the average sale at the 3,734 Wendy's restaurants was $850,000, and the approximately 2,800 Hardee's averaged more than $800,000.

So the Golden Arches were far and away the leader, with 45.54 percent of the hamburger business (and fourth place among America's largest retailers), with Burger King at 18.5 percent, and Wendy's and Hardee's about equal at approximately 11 percent of the burger traffic apiece. In 1987, McDonald's captured 19 percent of all fast-food sales; PepsiCo, Inc., had a 12.3 percent share; International Dairy Queen had 3.3 percent; and all other fast-food operations shared the remaining two-thirds of the market.

McDonald's also had by far the largest ad budget—$700 million in 1987, which makes Wendy's $110 million and Hardee's $70 million ad budgets seem pretty puny.

However, Wendy's International, Inc., had the best-paid CEO. In 1987, Robert L. Barney earned a salary and bonus of $526,000 and 862,000 shares which made him the eighteenth best-paid CEO of a food-distributing company and #571 among all CEOs in America.

It's been estimated that 95 percent of American consumers ate at McDonald's at least once in 1985 (But *can* that be right? Some people keep kosher, and there are vegetarians, devout eaters of all-natural foods, and people who are horribly rich and snobbish), and that each *day,* 7 percent of the American population eats at McDonald's. The same percentage of the work force once worked at McDonald's, and one worker out of fifteen got his or her first job at McDonald's.

McDonald's fifty-billionth hamburger was scarfed down in 1984. Its 10,000th store opened in the spring of 1988. One out of every twenty Cokes is sold by McDonald's, and if the chain were a country, it would be the sixth-largest market for Coca-Cola in the world. (McDonald's Corporation, like the Coca-Cola Company, has the distinction of having its own line of clothes, sold by Sears and featuring McDonaldland characters.) In addition, McDonald's buys 7.5 percent of America's potato crop.

In fact, in May 1988, McDonald's signed a contract to open a 650-seat McDonald's in Moscow, with up to twenty more restaurants to follow. The biggest problem it faces is not official condemnation of fast food (the Soviet powers-that-be have conveniently rewritten their previous diatribes against fast food) but the ingredients: Soviet potatoes can't be french fried to McDonald's standards. Big Macs will no doubt become a status symbol for Soviet citizens—like Russian caviar for Americans—and status symbols are expensive. A Muscovite Big Mac is scheduled to cost two rubles, or $3—but that's a couple of hours' pay for many in the Soviet Union.

McDonald's is also the leader in fast-food profit margins. In 1987, the margin was 11.7 percent on sales of $5.341 billion.

Wendy's, on the other hand, sold $1.054 billion worth of burgers and other foods in 1988, earning a profit of $3.5 million for a profit margin of 2.43 percent, which was an improvement from 1986 and 1987 when sales were strong but the firm scored a loss of $6.8 million. Analysts believe that the problem stemmed from Wendy's attempt to emphasize cooked-to-order breakfast specialties, which didn't appeal to take-out customers. Now that 60 percent of fast-food sales are made at drive-through windows, cooking-to-order is a fatal error. In fact, fast-food chains are debuting tiny sandwiches, such as Burger King's Burger Bundles, both for drivers' convenience and as snacks that can be quickly reheated in a home microwave oven. (Similar figures for Burger King were not compiled because Burger King is part of the Pillsbury Company food empire. However, the Burger King Corporation's sales are recorded as $4.5 billion for fiscal 1986.)

Want your very own burger franchise? You'd better be prosperous to start with. You can expect to earn revenues of $1.3 million from a typical McDonald's unit—after you put down your $12,500 initial franchise fee and $15,000 deposit, put in $135,000 to build the kitchen and $35,000 to decorate the place, with other expenses (such as your initial supply of styrofoam boxes and hamburger patties) amounting to $78,000 to $132,000. To qualify as a franchisee, you should also have at least 40 percent of the total in cash, without borrowing. You'll probably lease the land on which your burgerama is built from McDonald's, so your rent and service fee will be 11.5 percent per month and a monthly ad fee that varies according to location.

Starting up a Burger King is a tad more expensive, although projected sales are lower (at about $1 million a year): the initial franchise fee is $40,000, and it costs about $275,000 to develop a site for opening. The land on which to build can run you $500,000 to $750,000 more. Once you're up and running, the monthly royalty is 3.5 percent and the ad fee is 4 percent a month, both computed on gross sales.

The Wendy's franchisees who pulled down about $850,000 a year in sales plunked down a $25,000 franchise fee, $150,000 to $225,000 in equipment, and $190,000 to $280,000 in building costs. (That doesn't include the price of the land.) Monthly contributions to the franchisor's coffers are 4 percent each for franchise and ad fees. Hardee's units, which averaged sales of about $800,000, cost about $470,000 to build, a figure that does not include land or construction costs. The franchise fee is a comparatively modest $15,000; the ad fee is 5 percent; and the franchise royalty is 3.5 percent for the first five years of the twenty-year franchise agreement and 4 percent for the balance.

Is that too rich for your blood? Well, plenty of burger franchises can be had for less. If you want to sign up with Nashville's Beefy's, Inc., for example, you need pay only $8,500 as an initial franchise fee (or $5,000 per unit, if you buy several). The building costs for the twenty-five-unit chain (with fifty to one hundred more scheduled for opening in 1987) are projected at $130,000 (which doesn't include land, of course); the royalty fee is a modest 3 percent; the ad fee, an unassuming 1 percent. However, the estimated volume for Beefy's franchises is only $400,000 to $600,000— way below the estimates for the better-known national chains. A McDonald's franchise has the advantage of one of the best-known trademarks in world history (even if he does have to pay a sizeable advertising fee to maintain that degree of public awareness).

## FAST-FOOD NUTRITION: AN ALARMING ASIDE

Sounds like a shortest-book-in-the-world joke, doesn't it? If you eat fast-food burgers, you're probably looking for a guilty pleasure that won't be immediately fatal. But just to let you know the full extent of the damage, a McDonald's Big Mac will run you 563 calories, 33 grams of fat, and 86 milligrams of sodium; a Double Whopper with cheese at Burger King has a whopping 950 calories and 60 grams of fat. Add fries and a shake and you're in a nutritional nightmare.

# Pizza

For hundreds of years, pizza has been a traditional snack or light meal wherever in Italy there was a bit of extra bread dough, a little tomato sauce, an oven, and perhaps a drop of olive oil and a few herbs to sprinkle on top. It took the American genius for excess to transform this simple breadstuff into an extravaganza dripping with cheese, loaded with sausage, or chic-ed up with duck sausage and fennel. There are more than 38,000 pizza parlors in the United States, with one out of every ten restaurants serving up saucy, cheese-topped crusts.

Pizza is a kind of edible Rorschach test; it's whatever you make it. It may be little more than melted American cheese on white bread, or made in shallow pans with a single crust. Then there's Chicago deep-dish pizza, and double-crust pizza. And pizza, unlike Big Macs or Kentucky Fried Chicken, can often be delivered. It adds up to a lot of bread (sorry): about $8 billion in 1986 (with some 25 percent coming from delivered pizzas). Apart from innumerable independents, there are 102 companies franchising pizzerias, for a 1985 total of 4,651 units owned by franchising companies and 9,523 owned by franchisees. Franchised pizzas sold for $6.193 billion in 1985; just the 3,700 units in the Domino's Pizza empire (April 1987 market value: $250 million), which devotes $50 million to the activities of its in-house advertising agency, rang up $1.4 billion in yearly sales.

CEO Thomas S. Monaghan, who owns 95 percent of Domino's, swapped his Volkswagen in 1960, when he was a college student, for his brother's interest in a pizza parlor, in a deal that ranks right up there with Esau's mess of pottage. But even mighty Domino's is only number two in pizza. PepsiCo owns the 5,450-unit Pizza Hut, Inc., the sixth-largest fast-food chain, with 1981 sales of $1.87 billion.

Pizzerias, like all small businesses, face the problem of high (and unpredictably increasing) rents and, of course, high utility bills to keep the ovens fired up. An early marketing decision must be made: should the unit sell whole pizzas only, or pizzas by the slice? The latter decision makes the restaurant more attractive to snackers and quick lunchers but also encourages local adolescents to turn the pizza parlor into their clubhouse. A unit that concentrates on delivery rather than on-the-spot pizza consumption can get by with much less floor space, but it'll need delivery trucks or bicycles and delivery personnel. The major franchises have computerized systems to expedite delivery of the right pizza to the right place, in prime condition; in some cities, Pizza Hut customers can call a single central phone number for delivery anywhere in the city. Domino's boasts that average delivery time is 23.08 minutes, and deliverers get bonuses based on delivery speed. That may create a problem with delivery *speeding:* complaints have been made (some of them leading to lawsuits) that Domino's deliverers sometimes ignore traffic laws and clip slower motorists.

The pizza industry is experimenting with the "take and bake" concept: the pizzeria sells the ingredients, to be baked at home by the buyer. This is attractive to pizzeria operators because they can cut way back on labor costs and seating area in the restaurant. The problems are that a real pizza oven gives better results than an ordinary home oven and that unbaked pizza dough can blossom in the warmth of the buyer's car, turning into something out of *Invasion of the Body Snatchers* or *The Attack of the Killer Tomatoes.* The industry copes with this by selling partially baked crusts that just look uncooked.

The average annual sales of a full-service Pizza Hut (one that has both delivery facilities and in-house consumption of pizza) is $500,000 a year; average unit volume for the financially troubled Godfather's Pizza chain is about $360,000 (it used to be $450,000). In other words, average volume for a successful pizza restaurant is lower than for a successful hamburger franchise. Newcomer Round Table Pizza, based in San Francisco, has a stronger average unit volume, at $504,000. Madison, Wisconsin's Rocky Rococo Corporation has an unusual way of expanding sales of pizza-by-the-slice from its 110 units: test locations are setting up in tiny (500 square foot) portions of 7-Eleven convenience stores, and next door to movie theaters owned by American Multi Cinema, Inc. (Why not? If you can buy booze in London movie theaters, why shouldn't you be able to scarf pizza at Florida movie theaters?)

It takes hundreds of thousands of dollars to get into the franchised pizza business. The minimum fee for a Domino's franchise is $6,500, and the capital to start up is estimated at a minimum of $75,000; the franchise fee of 5.5 percent and the 3 percent advertising fee are assessed weekly. (Although Domino's is a market leader, the capital requirements are somewhat smaller than that of other chains because Domino's specializes in delivery, not in-house service, so a somewhat smaller, inexpensively decorated facility can be used.) The minimum start-up capital for a Round Table Pizza franchise is estimated at $250,000 to $315,000, based on a minimum franchise fee of $20,000 and monthly fees of 4 percent as a royalty, 3 percent as an ad fee. The same fees are charged for a Pizza Inn Express franchise ("Express" means that it has a limited menu, not a full panoply of pizza, hero sandwiches, and other Italian and ethnic dishes), but the minimum franchise fee is $17,500, and the anticipated start-up capital is at least $225,000.

# Fried Chicken

Chicken has outstripped beef as Americans' favorite meat (or, anyway, most-consumed meat; it's possible that consumers would prefer a thick, juicy steak, but for reasons of cost or cholesterol, choose chicken instead). The traditional Sunday dinner featured roast chicken, chicken in the pot, or fried chicken, depending on the family's regional and ethnic background. Add some sophisticated marketing savvy, and the fast-food chicken business flaps its wings and starts flying: in 1986, there were 9,883 fast-food restaurants specializing in chicken, with sales of nearly $5 billion a year.

In 1986, of the 6,575 Kentucky Fried Chicken units, 4,653 were owned by franchisees (one of whom owned 790 stores, which ain't chicken feed) and 1,922 by the company; they sold $3.5 billion worth of chicken and fixin's—way ahead of the nearest competitor, Church's Fried Chicken, Inc., with 273 individual franchises, 1,332 company-owned units, and 1986 sales of $578 million. Popeye's Famous Fried Chicken, another major fried-chicken company, which consists of 112 company-owned units and 546 franchises, realized sales of $409 million (estimated) in 1986. Starting a fried chicken franchise costs between $400,000 and $500,000 (the equipment alone for a Kentucky Fried Chicken franchise runs about $200,000), with a minimum franchise fee of $10,000 (for Kentucky Fried Chicken) to $25,000 (for Popeye's). The franchise fees and ad fees add up to 8 to 9 percent of gross sales a month.

In order to cut costs, Church's is pioneering a modular building program, so franchisees can put up "mini-stores" that'll fit into malls for as little as $114,000 and the cost of digging a foundation and hooking up the plumbing and electricity. It costs $176,000 to build a Church's unit with twenty-two seats, and only a little more—$195,000—to build one seating forty-two customers. However, the more seats, the larger the site, and the higher the rent or cost of purchased land.

Despite success stories like Kentucky Fried Chicken and the smaller, but still prosperous, Pioneer Take Out, this segment of the fast-food industry boasts a notable rate of failure: The Horn & Hardart Company's eighty-three Bojangles' Famous Chicken'N Biscuits are now boarded up after four years and millions of dollars spent in a vain attempt to take a forty-unit Carolina chain national. In 1986, Bojangles' sold $90 million worth of chicken, which would be a pretty good performance if it hadn't lost $47.6 million. The failure is blamed on the company's overly rapid expansion and its lack of attention to the millions of details involved in successful franchising.

Fried chicken operators face a struggle on two fronts: competition from other fast-food chains offering chicken products, such as chicken club sandwiches and nuggets of fried chicken, or nuggets engineered out of chicken meat, skin, and fat, and chains specializing in roasted or broiled chicken. Fried chicken is tasty and easy for restaurant owners to prepare quickly (especially with today's sophisticated, computer-controlled deep fryers), but it isn't exactly the health-food fancier's first choice.

Fried chicken chains (sounds like a new punk fashion, doesn't it?) have two responses: moving into foreign markets such as Indonesia or learning from the experiences of their brethren in the pizza business and starting to offer home delivery as an option.

# Ethnic . . . But Not Too Ethnic

A customer can want a meal in a hurry but be tired of burgers, sandwiches, pizza, and fried chicken. Fast-food ethnic restaurants appeal to the taste for something a little different . . . but not too different, not too far outside the mainstream for mass appeal. Shopping mall patrons encounter a variety of ethnic or quasi-ethnic fast foods, whether Chinese, Mexican, Italian, Middle Eastern, or Japanese. But the economics of mall operation—high rents and the need for high volume—mean that standardized, mass-produced, "smoothed-out" versions of ethnic dishes, market-researched for broad appeal, are more likely to appear than authentic regional specialties.

Some pizzerias broaden their appeal by offering a range of Italian (or Americanized Italian) dishes in addition to the pies; there are also fast-food Italian restaurants that don't sell pizza.

General Mills, Inc., which doesn't just sell groceries but owns a restaurant division with fiscal 1987 sales of nearly $1.2 billion, recently devoted much of its attention (and $100 million) to opening, fine-tuning, and improving its chain of fifty-eight Olive Garden restaurants. General Mills chose Italian cuisine because it's a popular but somewhat underserved market segment: according to the Restaurant Consulting Group, there are 4,800 Italian restaurants (other than pizzerias) in the United States, compared to 17,000 Chinese, Japanese, and other Oriental restaurants, and 14,000 Mexican restaurants.

After 1,000 interviews with restaurateurs, 5,000 with consumers, 80 unsuccessful attempts at creating a tasty spaghetti sauce that clings attractively to pasta, and five years of work, The Olive Garden chain finally paid off for General Mills. The average Olive Garden restaurant turns profitable within six months and manages profits of $300,000 or more on sales in the $2.5 million range. Much of the five years' work was spent finding out what images consumers had of Italy (usually vague but pleasant), and their image of an ideal Italian restaurant (which had better be vague—the "Venetian chicken" is cooked with teriyaki sauce). The decor features plants and a see-through kitchen wall with a view of pasta preparation. The background music was supposed to be provided by an accordion player, until cost considerations sent General Mills back to prerecorded music, including a theme song called "Hospitaliano" (but not opera records—they're "too Italian").

The Sbarro family runs an empire of cafeteria-style Italian fast-food restaurants: the 220 units in the chain, most of which are in malls, rang up 1986 sales of $58.5 million and profits of $4.8 million. Half the sales come from pizza; the other half from a selection of pastas, entrees, and desserts. Nearly all the restaurants are company-owned (as part of a quality-control strategy), although there are sixty-three franchised units, and Sbarro is entering a collaboration with fast-food and lodging giant Marriott Corporation, which will open twenty Sbarro's franchises on highways.

Another Americanized ethnic cuisine, Mexican food, has been a notable success for franchising. In 1987, for instance, projected figures for the thirty-six chains of Mexican-food franchisors who operated 4,951 units (2,236 owned by the companies themselves, 2,715 by franchisees) showed sales of nearly $3 billion (a little more than half going to company-owned units, the rest to the individual franchises).

Not everyone succeeds—Pillsbury had a notable failure with a chain of Mexican restaurants called Juan and Only (Dana Shilling suggests that they should have called it Schlepp Nachos—The Take-Out Food You Can Really Be Proud Of). The leading success is Taco Bell Corporation (part of PepsiCo), which has 2,700 units and claims 56 percent of the $2.5 billion market for Mexican fast food. The chain employs 28,000 people. The minimum franchise fee for the Taco Bell chain is $45,000, and to start up takes at least $75,000; the monthly fees total 10 percent (4.5 percent for advertising, 5.5 percent as a royalty).

Alfonso's, of San Antonio, is a hardworking newcomer with eight units and a 1986 gross of $8 million, which adds up to a lot of meals (the average check is $2.25 for breakfast, $3.35 for lunch and dinner). Its merchandising goal is to match McDonald's average unit sales of $1.3 million. One of its tools is a central commissary, which supplies food to all the units. The stores cost about $800,000 to open—half of that cost goes for land, the rest for the building ($250,000) and restaurant equipment ($150,000).

# Family Restaurants

In addition to fast-food operations where the food is "cooked to inventory," and the counter help just have to toss the appropriate paper bags and cardboard boxes into a sack, there are the slightly slower restaurants that comprise a broad sector of the fast-food market. Here the boundaries between different kinds of operations blur. Depending on the restaurant owner's wishes and local preferences, these restaurants could be steak houses (although steak is expensive, it's well suited to a fast-food operation because steaks can be cooked quickly, and the restaurant can serve a limited menu of steaks, potatoes, salads, and perhaps a dessert), family-style restaurants (wholesome places with bright lighting—and without liquor licenses—that often provide special children's menus, coloring books for the kids, and other incentives to families), or cafeterias (in the South, some of the best home-style cooking is done in cafeterias).

In 1986, the franchised steak-house sector contained 563 units, with average unit sales of $840,000. One of the biggest success stories, Benihana of Tokyo, also ranks as an ethnic restaurant. There were forty-seven Benihana units in 1986 (plus a line of frozen Benihana Oriental entrees in supermarkets). The chain estimated that opening a Benihana franchise (only ten were individually owned, the rest owned by the company) would cost over $1 million in capital (perhaps because of the need to install an unusual Oriental decor, instead of sticking with the prior decorating scheme of the location), with the franchise fee somewhat above average at $50,000 and monthly fees of 4 percent each for the franchise and advertising.

It cost a lot less to open one of the 223 individually owned Ponderosa Steakhouses (the company owns 438 units). Minimum capital is estimated at $75,000, and franchisees pay a minimum franchise fee of $15,000 at the outset, with monthly ad and franchise fees of 4 percent each. In 1986, Ponderosa's sales were $582 million. To open a Bonanza Family Restaurant entails a minimum franchise fee of $30,000, minimum capital of $75,000, and fairly low monthly fees of 2 percent for advertising and 4.8 percent for the franchise. Sales for its five company-owned and 550 franchised units were $458 million.

Luby's Cafeterias, Inc., owns and operates eighty-five cafeterias in the Southwest; the typical Luby's is about 10,000 square feet and seats 300. For the chain as a whole, 1985 sales were almost $200 million. The cost of sales was $104.6 million, and operating, general, and administrative expenses were nearly $59.7 million. That left the chain with operating income of $31,679,000, but that was far from all profit. The chain had $3.15 million in nonoperating income (for example, interest earned and investment income) but paid minor interest expenses ($97,000), leaving it a pretax income of $34,733,000. The federal government inherited more than $15 million of that, leaving Luby's with a net income of $19,585,000, or just about 10 percent of sales.

## A LITTLE SOMETHING SWEET

The fast-food universe includes plenty of desserts (see page 115 for a discussion of doughnut shops, and page 118 for ice cream parlors) and sweets. For instance, thirteen franchise operations sell pancakes and waffles, with projected 1987 sales of $1.285 billion from the 606 company-owned units and 1,375 restaurants owned by franchisees.

No discussion of fast food would be complete without homage to the ubiquitous chocolate chip cookie. Wally (Famous) Amos started the trend with his superpremium version of the candy/cookie hybrid invented in a roadside inn called the Toll House. This feat is comparable to what *The Exorcist* did for the horror book and movie industry: from something that had been around for a long time and that had fallen into a commercial slump, he spawned billions of dollars in profit and hordes of fervent competitors. David's Cookies (owned by David Lederman—one of the many lawyers who has found something else to do for a living) and Mrs. Field's Cookies (a leading success story for women in business) then took up the banner.

However, fast-food experts predict that the next snack-food hit will be the cinnamon roll. Cinnamon rolls have long been popular in the Midwest (especially as a side dish for panfried chicken), and midwestern franchisors are hoping to build hundreds of 1,000 to 1,400 square foot units throughout the country, selling giant half-pound "gourmet" glazed cinnamon rolls and smaller counterparts.

Here's *our* favorite idea, which we offer generously to anyone who wants to take it up: a smoked-fish boutique called Yum Kippers ("so delicious you'll regret how many you ate").

# 26

# Doughnut Shops

| | |
|---|---|
| Number of establishments: | 4,046 (1,077 company-owned; 2,969 franchise-owned) |
| Total receipts: | $1.336 billion ($339,232,000 company-owned; $996,857,000 franchise-owned) |
| Average net sales: | $330,200 |

*(Restaurant Business, '87)*

The doughnut has been an established and honorable part of New England cuisine since Pilgrim days, when few families had ovens but most had a frying pan on the hearth to turn a blob of bread dough into a treat. Some unknown culinary genius realized that, if you cut a hole in the center, the doughnut will cook faster and more evenly (and you will have a second, separate product: the doughnut hole). Doughnuts and coffee were a staple of Red Cross missions during World War I; and "sinkers" and coffee were a standby for killing time during the Great Depression. With all these sorrowful associations, it's a miracle that doughnut shops are still around. Probably the human desire for sweet, rich foods and the fact that doughnuts are easily made out of inexpensive materials explain it.

## FRANCHISES

The doughnut shop market is dominated by franchises; and the doughnut franchise world is dominated by three major chains: Dunkin' Donuts, Winchell's Donut Houses, L.P., and Mister Donut of America, Inc. Here's what the figures for these three look like:

|  | Dunkin' Donuts | Winchell's Donut Houses | Mister Donut |
|---|---|---|---|
| Number of stores | 1,280 | 747 | 602 |
| —company -owned | 65 | 723 | 0 |
| —owned by franchisees | 1,225 | 24 | 602 |
| Franchise fee | $20,000 to 40,000 | $25,000 to 30,000 | $15,000 minimum |
| Start-up costs | $75,000 minimum | $38,400 to 295,000 | $50,000 minimum |
| Advertising fee | 4.5 to 5% monthly | 5% monthly | 4.9% weekly |
| Average sales per store | $474,000 |  |  |

## THE FUTURE PROSPECTS?

Most of a doughnut shop's sales are early in the day for breakfast and coffee breaks. However, since doughnuts are best when freshly made and stale doughnuts are pretty gruesome, new batches must be started throughout the day. That's good, because it means that the expensive equipment is in use throughout the day—and bad, because it means more employees are needed.

To cope with these problems, doughnut shops are moving in two directions. They might cut back on their payrolls by having the customers who eat doughnuts or snacks in the store get their orders from a central counter, then sit down to eat, instead of being waited on individually. Another trend is for the doughnut shops to join forces with convenience or discount stores and to produce doughnuts for sale in those stores. Doughnut shops, like many small businesses, must be wary of rent increases. One New York doughnut shop, for instance, paid $19 a square foot for its space; however, a new landlord bought all the leases in the building for a total of $2.5 million and is waiting with bated breath for the doughnut shop's lease to expire, at which time the landlord will cut up the doughnut shop into three stores and charge $225 a square foot for the space. Maybe you'd better pick up an extra dozen on the way home—your friendly local doughnut shop may soon be replaced by a Benetton.

# 27

# Ice Cream Parlors

| | |
|---|---|
| Number of (franchised) establishments: | 10,211 (9,882 franchise-owned; 329 company-owned) |
| Total receipts: | $1.6 billion ($1,533,369,000 franchise-owned; $67,363,000 company-owned) |
| Average net sales: | $156,800 |
| | (*Restaurant Business,* '87) |

Perhaps the golden age of the ice cream parlor was the late nineteenth century, when marble counters, gleaming brass spigots, and stained glass marked the cathedral where ice cream was dispensed as a very special treat to families and courting couples. You'd think that the romance would have died down as soon as home refrigerators made it possible for everybody to keep gallons of the stuff on hand, but ice cream parlors, frozen yogurt dens, and soft-serve units are, well, not quite selling their wares like hotcakes, but doing a lot of business. It seems that many of the people who shun red meat, brown whiskey, and other unhealthy things relax their scruples when it comes time to top off a two-hour workout with a double-dip cone.

## EIGHT HUNDRED FLAVORS . . . AND COUNTING

One appeal of ice cream parlors has always been the availability of a wide choice of flavors, especially in the days when supermarkets stocked only a few, unimaginative varieties. Director Mike Nichols tells of his days as a starving actor, when he worked at a Howard Johnson's. He got so tired of rattling off the day's special flavors that he began his recitation, "Lasagna Ripple . . . Chicken Fat Chip. . . ." Soon, he was freed to continue his career in the theater.

Baskin-Robbins, of course, has thirty-one flavors (actually it has a lot more, but it sells thirty-one at any given time), and Bressler's has thirty-three. And now fast-food operators can buy a computer-guided system that promises thousands of flavors: the freezer carries a basic, neutral ice cream base and dozens of flavors and ingredients to be mixed in at the customer's request.

## FRANCHISES

In all probability, the idea of "mix-ins"—things like bashed-up Heath Bars, Oreo cookies, or chopped walnuts to be forcibly incorporated into ice cream—comes from Steve's Ice Cream, once a landmark in the Boston suburb of Somerville and now a major franchiser with ninety stores in the Northeast and 450 nationwide as a result of a merger with Swensen's, Inc. The merger is highly understandable, since in 1986 Swensen's had revenues of $9.4 million and lost $1.2 million; Steve's had revenues of $11.8 million and managed to be profitable, but only just ($271,000, which doesn't look like much when you're starting with almost $12 million). It's anticipated that the merged companies can earn revenue of $35 million. The franchise fee for a Swensen's unit ranges from around $20,000 to $25,000; the full start-up costs range from $200,000 for a simple cone dispensary to more than $400,000 for a combined restaurant and ice cream parlor.

Baskin-Robbins has 3,135 stores in forty-nine states and outside the United States. The chain is changing its strategy, from concentrating on attracting franchisees for single units to finding franchisees who can take on several units at once—an expensive business because it costs from $90,000 to $120,000 to get started, with a royalty fee of 5 percent and an ad fee of 1.5 percent per month.

There are nearly 5,000 units in International Dairy Queen, with 175 new units added in 1987. To open a Dairy Queen in a shopping mall, you'd need about $120,000—and much, much more ($450,000 or so) to open a free-standing Dairy Queen store. The minimum franchise fee is $25,000, and a fee of 4 percent and an advertising fee of 3.5 percent must be paid monthly by Dairy Queen franchisees. Another strategy is to combine soft-serve frozen desserts with other fast foods: perhaps doughnuts, to bring in traffic in the mornings, or other fast foods such as hamburgers, to increase the average check (currently $3.65 at Dairy Queen).

## YOGURT

Ice cream, like Gaul, is divided into three parts: plain old ordinary ice cream, premium ice cream (with less air and more butterfat), and super-premium ice cream (even less air, and even richer). Then there are soft-serve frozen desserts, such as those offered by Carvel, and frozen custard, such as that served by Nielsen's.

However, for those who want to feel righteous as they slurp down a frozen dessert, there's nothing like frozen yogurt, which could be why superpremium ice cream stores (like the 313 franchised Haagen-Dazs stores; Haagen Dazs is a unit of the Pillsbury Company) began experiencing flat sales curves while the frozen-yogurt business is booming. (Haagen Dazs responded wisely by creating its own gourmet frozen yogurt.) There are at least four major frozen yogurt franchises, and Baskin-Robbins is adding yogurt to its line.

The largest yogurt franchise chain is TCBY, which stands for The Country's Best Yogurt; it has 475 units and planned to add 400 more in 1987. To get started in TCBY land costs between $90,000 and $150,000; average sales for a TCBY store are about $200,000. However, if you want a yogurt cone in the Northeast, you're more likely to encounter an Every-thing Yogurt store. This chain has been in business since the mid-1970s. The new kids on the block are the 100-unit Zack's Famous Frozen Yogurt (with 125 start-ups scheduled for 1987); and I Can't Believe It's Yogurt (presumably because the stuff is so yummy), which currently has 60 units and 112 scheduled for 1987 openings.

Unless everybody goes on a diet simultaneously, the future looks serene for ice cream parlors—especially as long as there are hot summer days, kids, and young lovers of all chronological ages to share ice cream cones as they stroll and discuss the future of the world.

# 28

# Restaurants

| | |
|---|---|
| Number of establishments: | 122,857 |
| Total receipts: | $47.13 billion |
| Average net sales: | $383,600 |
| Number of employees: | 2,291,000 |
| Total payroll: | $12.935 billion |

(Department of Commerce, 82)

Two of the most common fantasies (that can be discussed in a family publication, anyway) are becoming a movie star or sports hero, and opening a restaurant. (Some people combine the dreams: Mariel Hemingway, Mickey Mantle, and New York Met Keith Hernandez own restaurants.) The attractions of stardom are obvious; the dedicated home gourmet dreams either of new combinations of foie gras and peanut butter or of strolling through an elegant forest of tables and mirrors as glittering celebrities raise their champagne glasses. After all, everybody acts (if only when explaining to the boss why the monthly report is late) and everybody eats.

However, very few wannabees succeed in the acting business (and many end up waiting tables), and very few amateur-turned-professional chefs can stay in business long. The restaurant business is an unusually tough one, with the owner at the mercy of late deliveries, below-par string beans, till-tapping bartenders, restaurant critics, and health inspectors (either peering about for a single flyspeck or holding a hand out for a bribe).

In the first nine months of 1986, more than 2,000 restaurants failed (but at least that was better than the same time a year earlier, when nearly 2,100 restaurants bit the dust). The statistics, developed by Dun & Bradstreet, don't count a restaurant a failure if it shuts up shop with all the creditors paid—even though the owner probably thinks of it that way. The New England region was the most auspicious for success, with the smallest number of failures; the East North Central region of the country had the most. D & B estimated that 142 eating and drinking places out of every thousand would fail, which is pretty risky—but other kinds of businesses are even more risky, such as clothing stores, with 170 failures per 1,000 operations. According to *Business Week,* almost 75 percent of restaurant start-ups either close down or are acquired within five years.

As for the restaurant scene as a whole, Dun & Bradstreet's 1987 survey of 2,155 "eating places" shows gross profits at 51.9 percent of net sales, and net profit after tax averaging 4.2 percent. Return on sales for these restaurants ranged from less than 1 percent to 8.7 percent, so good management (and good luck) can make a significant difference. Return on assets ranged from less than 1 percent to 18.8 percent. Not only do management styles differ, but some restaurants have a lot more assets than others: after all, a restaurant can have either a hundred tables and banquet facilities, served by a state-of-the-art computerized kitchen, or four tables and a four-burner stove.

To open a restaurant with real waiters and real tablecloths (that is, not a coffee shop with three stools and a griddle full of cheeseburgers) is likely to cost over $500,000 and might well cost $2.5 million, like New York's Cafe Society, funded by fifteen limited partners who work in the securities industry. Cafe Society is in an area of Manhattan where rents range from $20 to $40 per square foot—much less than the $100 to $200 per square foot in the most fashionable parts of the borough.

Landlords don't really like to rent to restaurants. Not only are they likely to go bust before the lease runs out, but they also use a lot of space, a lot of energy, and create problems such as late-night noise, garbage disposal, and pest infestation.

Once a restaurant starts, the possibilities for earnings are dazzling indeed. In 1985, Windows on the World (in New York's World Trade Center) was the highest-grossing restaurant in the United States, with sales of $21.275 million; Tavern on the Green was next, with $19 million in sales. The 350 employees (48 in the kitchen) of The Manor in West Orange, New Jersey, serve 6,730 people a week in its eleven dining rooms and gross $12 million. Another huge restaurant, Spenger's Fish Grotto in Berkeley, serves

4,000 meals a day on weekends, covers two square blocks, has 250 employees including 50 cooks, and grosses $12 million (much of that from its retail fish store and fish processing plant; $2 million comes from the restaurant, $800,000 from the 300-seat banquet room).

The average receipts, according to the Minnesota Restaurant Association (1986 figures), are about $1 million a year for a "family-style" restaurant and $3 to $4 million for "fine dining" establishments. However, the possibilities for profit are a little more slender.

The Ark Restaurants Corporation, which operates a chain of twelve restaurants in the New York area, each of which has between 90 and 350 tables, has annual sales per restaurant ranging from $1.2 million to $5 million and an average check around $10 to $25 (depending on the restaurant). The chain's average food costs were 30 percent of sales. Add in about 25 percent for personnel costs, rent, and broken glasses, and you'll see there's not much left. (And, in fact, in 1986, the chain lost money on its total sales of $5,851,000. Gross profits were $4,100,000, but operating income was a mere $167,600, and there was a net loss of $78,718.)

Cravings (Los Angeles) is a fifty-seat cafe/take-out food shop/catering shop that cost $126,000 to open; in its first year, its volume was $500,000, with an average lunch check of $13 and dinner check of $19. Its food costs are 25 to 30 percent of sales; labor cost is kept below 20 percent by staff cutbacks when required.

Smaller, more modest restaurants can do fine. Millie's Country Kitchen, a small regional chain in Southern California, has a sales volume of $15 million (which is about average for a family-style restaurant); its average check is $3.75. Its food costs are somewhat above average, at 32.6 percent; labor costs are somewhat less than 30 percent. The two Hamburger Harry's restaurants in Manhattan have an average check of $8.60 and receipts of $2.5 million a year. The first of the two, an eighty-four-seat, 2,050-square-foot restaurant, cost $350,000 to open while its successor, seating 180 in 3,700 square feet, cost $650,000—a difference attributable not only to its larger size but to inflation in building costs.

Apart from financial problems, many new restaurants founder on the shoals of practical problems. Being a great home cook doesn't always prepare a person to run a business or to be an intelligent personnel manager, a diplomat controlling drunken customers and temperamental chefs, or a sophisticated financier—or even to decide exactly how much trout must be ordered for an unknown number of customers, some of whom will order the trout, the rest of whom will graze on the other nine entrees available that night.

Much of the food ordered for a restaurant is highly perishable. Sometimes sturdier dishes can be substituted but at the cost of sacrificing some creativity and also alienating diners who want fresh seafood and produce. Within reason, diners at a restaurant will wait for their food, but it takes tricky orchestration to make sure that Table 17's cassoulet, roast duck, pan-grilled steak, and crayfish crepes are all ready at the same time. Then Table 19 has to be served four courses in time to leave for the theater; everyone at Table 11 is having the raspberry souffle, which takes half an hour to prepare, and so on.

Restaurant owners often start out trying to do everything themselves. That idea soon loses its savor. Restaurants must buy the best fresh foods when the markets open—usually before dawn. Then there are deliveries to be accepted, preparations to be made for lunch, lunch to be served, dinner reservations to be made, cleaning and housekeeping, bookkeeping, serving dinner, cleaning up, usually ending after midnight.

Once a restaurateur accepts the necessity of co-workers, one set of problems ends, another begins. According to the Department of Commerce's 1982 business census, the average salary per restaurant employee was a very low $5,645. That's partly because there are many unskilled and semiskilled restaurant jobs and because restaurant workers in the "front of the house" (those who deal with the public instead of remaining in the kitchen) earn much of their compensation in the form of tips. Nevertheless, payroll costs absorbed 27.4 percent of restaurant sales, a higher percentage than in most businesses. Add in 25 to 33 percent for food costs and think about rent, utilities, debt service, and the other costs of running a restaurant, and you'll realize there isn't much margin for error.

Restaurants are also plagued by very heavy turnover of personnel. Dishwashers, waiters, waitresses, and bartenders quit when they win an acting role, move on to another town, go back to school, or decide to enter another line of work. At the other end of the pay scale, chefs can quit in a dispute over menu policies (if the owner wants to serve a smaller number of popular dishes or to use more prepared foods to cut down on labor costs and spoilage, and the purist chef wants to create a varied, innovative cuisine—whether the paying public is interested or not), be lured away by a competitor, or open their own restaurants.

If you're determined to be one of the many brand-new restaurateurs, it should be pretty easy to find a nice storefront where someone else went broke running a restaurant. Just be sure to be nice to all your diners—you never can tell who'll turn out to be an influential restaurant critic dining incognito. Mimi Sheraton wears funny hats; others wear sunglasses, even wigs and plano glasses.

# 29

# Bars

| | |
|---|---|
| Number of establishments: | 61,289 |
| Total receipts: | $8.56 billion |
| Average net sales: | $139,400 |
| Number of employees: | 324,900 |
| Total payroll: | $1.72 billion |

(Department of Commerce, '82)

In *Son of Paleface*, Bob Hope swaggers into a frontier saloon, asks the barkeep for a sarsaparilla, then tries to retrieve his macho image by adding, "in a dirty glass!" Today's bar owners face a similar problem: many of their steady patrons have switched from six boilermakers an evening to two white-wine spritzers, or even gone on the wagon entirely.

Former singles-bar patrons, worried about what they might get besides lucky, are staying home in droves. A lot of teenagers would be more than happy to drink, but the legal drinking age has been upped to twenty-one in many states. The *Wall Street Journal* of August 19, 1987 reports that desperate bar owners are resorting to ugly bartender contests, wrestling matches in a field of mashed potatoes, and gerbil races to attract business.

125

Where the Money Goes (Eating and Drinking Places Combined)

| | |
|---|---|
| (1) Cost of operations: | 45.0 percent |
| (2) Officers' compensation: | 3.2 percent |
| (3) Pensions and benefits: | 0.8 percent |
| (4) Rent: | 5.7 percent |
| (5) Repairs: | 1.5 percent |
| (6) Depreciation, depletion, amortization: | 4.3 percent |
| (7) Interest: | 2.3 percent |
| (8) Bad debts: | 0.1 percent |
| (9) Advertising: | 2.7 percent |
| (10) State, local taxes: | 4.2 percent |
| (11) Other expenses: | 34.1 percent |
| (12) Net profit before tax: | 0.7 percent |

(Troy, '84–'85)

At the other end of the scale, bar owners have to worry about their customers who overindulge, then get into an automobile accident. Many states have "dram shop" laws, which allow a person injured by a drunk driver to sue the establishment that kept on supplying drinks to a visibly intoxicated person. Of course, not every bar will be slapped with one of these lawsuits, but the mere possibility is enough to drive liability insurance rates for bars into the stratosphere.

## BAR DESIGN—AND BAR HISTORY

The business of supplying liquor has usually been viewed as a shady, if not reprehensible, one—especially when people get together and drink the stuff on the premises. (In fact, there are still places in the United States where it's legal to buy a bottle of liquor but not to buy liquor by the drink in public restaurants or bars.) It's illegal to sell alcoholic beverages without a license.

In most areas, liquor licenses are like phoenixes: one has to die for another one to be born. Being a reputable person who wants to open up a pleasant drinking place isn't enough to get you a liquor license; you have to acquire an existing liquor license or wait for the area's population to increase enough to persuade the authorities to increase the number of licenses.

According to *Sean Mooney's Practical Guide to Running a Pub* (Mooney is a leading San Francisco publican), colonial topers favored beer, wine, and rum imported from the West Indies, and they did their drinking at taverns, seated at benches. By the nineteenth century, the favorite drink had shifted to whiskey, and the favorite place to the saloon: anything from a small, dingy room to a palace complete with gigantic paintings of well-upholstered nudes, etched-glass mirrors, and magnificent mahogany bars. The saloon patron stood at the bar, drinking beer, whiskey, or whiskey with beer chasers, and perhaps nibbling on the "free lunch" of salty tidbits that created goodwill and increased thirst at the same time.

Then came Prohibition. Not all teetotalers were spoilsports and bluenoses: in the nineteenth century, some companies made a point of issuing their workers' pay packets at a saloon conveniently owned by the company, and many a family's rent and food money vanished as the breadwinner had a few drinks . . . and then a few more . . . on payday, leading social reformers to demand a ban on all alcoholic beverages. But human nature dictates that people still found places to do their drinking. Both men and women went to speakeasies, sat at tables, and drank just about anything, smuggled or home-brewed. Perhaps that's one reason for the growing popularity of the cocktail: to disguise the taste of the hooch.

After Prohibition, many bar owners found themselves confronted by regulations that *insisted* on the presence of bar stools, probably on the theory that a man hell-bent on seducing an unescorted woman at the bar would walk over to her for the purpose, but wouldn't pick himself up from his barstool for the same nefarious purpose.

With that out of the way, bar owners tailor their design to the kind of crowd they want to attract: a long bar for solitary drinkers and those who hope to meet someone at the bar; more private banquettes for younger couples and groups, tables for older couples and groups (who feel less comfortable squirming into banquettes).

Today's bar patrons tend to drink "white goods" (vodka, tequila)

## TRADE TALK

▶ An "on-sale public premises license" is a liquor license for a bar licensed to sell spirits, wine, and beer; an "on-sale general license" is for a restaurant with a full bar; an "on-sale beer and wine license" is for a restaurant that can't sell hard liquor; and an "off-sale license" is for a liquor store.

▶ The "speed rack" is a shelf with bottles of frequently used liquors and mixers, perhaps with a "gun" for sparkling water; the speed rack is hung behind the bar at the bartender's waist level, so he or she can assemble the most popular drinks quickly.

▶ "Marrying" means consolidating two partially full bottles of the same liquor; it's illegal, but a lot of bars do it anyway.

▶ "Dumping" is the less-reputable counterpart: pouring cheap booze into an empty bottle of a more expensive variety.

rather than "brown goods" (dark drinks such as whiskey); they often indulge in fanciful mixed drinks; and many of them love imported beers—the more exotic the better.

## BAR ECONOMICS

A would-be bar owner usually figures on paying either six times the average monthly gross revenue or an amount which can be paid back from

---

## CONSUMER TIPS

▶ A clue to dumping: a really dusty bottle of a premium brand, with a worn, torn label. Even if the bar is a quiet one, even if sales are slow, a bottle of expensive liquor doesn't last forever unless it's the same bottle, with ever-changing contents.

▶ Exotic house drinks (say, a mixture of Irish whiskey, peppermint schnapps, and chocolate syrup) are either the product of a fevered imagination or of the owner's determination not to get stuck with something he bought too much of. If nobody in the entire history of convivial imbibing ever thought up the drink, there might be a good reason.

▶ The "stop pour" is a way of giving customers less than they paid for, while making them think the bartender is dazzlingly generous with the boss's booze. To do this, the bartender starts mixing a drink by pouring in a little liquor; then he starts to squirt in mixer from the gun in the speed rack, which distracts the customer's attention. Meanwhile, the bartender keeps a finger over the pouring device in the liquor bottle, so nothing comes out. Finally, he "finishes off" the drink with a splash of liquor.

The same trick can be played with elaborate mixed drinks: the bartender fills the glass with the pineapple-coconut juice, mango sherbet, or whatever, and limits the alcoholic content to a slick at the top of the glass. The customer tastes the alcohol right away and is thus convinced that the drink is a hefty one, not a virtual Shirley Temple.

six years' profits to buy the bar from its last owner. One surprising source of start-up funds is companies that lease jukeboxes and cigarette machines, which may be willing to lend money to barkeepers who agree to install the machines. Then the barkeeper either pays rent or splits jukebox change 50-50 with the leaser; the bar owner gets to keep 10 to 20 percent of the coins dropped into the cigarette machine.

Under state law, bar owners *must* buy their booze from wholesalers (not from the corner grocery store or liquor store); a typical bar has an army of twelve to seventeen suppliers of potables, glassware, and "groceries" (things like cinnamon sticks and fresh limes). Often a bar owner will deal with six or seven liquor wholesalers (because wholesalers offer only a limited choice of brands), and separate wine and beer wholesalers. Usually, there'll be regular deliveries to the bar (from once to three times a week); the owner can also pick up emergency supplies at the local warehouse.

As a rule of thumb, efficient bar operation requires the liquor inventory to be about one-third the gross monthly sales—that is, it takes $1,000 worth of liquor for every estimated $3,000 in monthly sales. Profitable operation requires "pouring costs" to be kept to 25 percent: the bar has to sell $4 for every $1 spent on liquor. (The difference between the 3:1 and 4:1 ratios pays the other expenses.) A successful bar usually turns over its stock seven times a year; if it keeps $10,000 of liquor in inventory, it must budget $70,000 a year for replacements. That's an average: beer turns over much faster; "call brands" (premium brands of liquor kept behind the bar) turn over more slowly.

If a bar customer orders a call brand, an honest bar will pour that brand; if the customer just orders vodka and tonic or Scotch and soda, the bartender pours the "well brand" (the house brand, often a less expensive generic). Bars often change their well brands, depending on the "post-offs" (discounts) offered by the different wholesalers. You could luck out if your favorite bar overbuys some expensive, exotic tipple: it could end up as a well brand if it moves too slowly to be profitable otherwise.

# 30

# Liquor Stores

Number of establishments:  34,861
Total receipts:            $17.3 billion
Average net sales:         $499,900
Number of employees:       167,300
Total payroll:             $1.31 billion

(Department of Commerce, '82)

In a way, a liquor store is the quintessential retail store. The store *never* makes its own goods on the premises (although some very large liquor stores have "house brands" that they buy from wine bottlers and distillers; they don't home-brew them). Most of the time, customers buy brand-name bottles that are readily available in many other liquor stores. Therefore, the customer doesn't depend very much on the expertise of the store's personnel: the buyer knows he wants a bottle of J & B, or a six-pack of Rolling Rock, or half a gallon of generic gin. Usually, clerks needn't be particularly well educated or highly trained, which lowers the payroll.

According to the Department of Commerce's 1982 census, the average salary per liquor store employee was only $7,829, well below the average for all types of business, and payroll represented only 7.6 percent

**Where the Money Goes (Before Federal Taxes)**

| | |
|---|---|
| (1) Cost of operations: | 79.5 percent |
| (2) Officers' compensation: | 2.2 percent |
| (3) Pensions and benefits: | 0.3 percent |
| (4) Rent: | 2.9 percent |
| (5) Repairs: | 0.4 percent |
| (6) Depreciation, depletion, amortization: | 1.1 percent |
| (7) Interest: | 0.8 percent |
| (8) Bad debts: | 0.1 percent |
| (9) Advertising: | 0.6 percent |
| (10) State, local taxes: | 1.8 percent |
| (11) Other expenses: | 9.5 percent |
| (12) Net profit before tax: | 0.8 percent |

(Troy, '84–'85. However, the 1986 Dun & Bradstreet survey
shows a much rosier picture, with gross profit at 21.6% of sales, and
net profit *after tax* at 3.5%.)

of sales, again quite low. The exceptions are stores selling wines that are either extremely fine, and correspondingly expensive, so an expert's help in selection or perhaps his canny bit of advice on whether Yugoslavia or Algeria offers the superior $2.99 magnum is needed.

In fact, since the customers usually know what they want, advertising is a minor item in the budgets of most liquor stores. Sure, an ad might remind potential customers that the store exists and publicize its specials, but the customers will probably stop in at the neighborhood store, or the one on the way home from work. A good location matters a lot, but the decoration of the store probably doesn't. Some very good locations are unavailable for development as liquor stores: there are still "dry" cities and counties, and some states monopolize liquor sales so that the *only* place you can buy liquor is at a state-run store.

Inventory control takes on a stark importance in the liquor store business. If the owner or manager can select the right balance of inventory and turn it over fast enough, then the store will do all right. Otherwise, a lot of dollars will be tied up in slow-moving or unsaleable merchandise, which is heavy, in breakable bottles, and takes up a lot of storage space. Good wine also has a tendency to go bad if it isn't stored right. Customers usually pay cash on the barrelhead (in fact, the expression probably came from barrels of beer or whiskey), so bad debts aren't much of a problem. Some pay by check or credit card, but no one buys on the installment plan.

No, the real question is what merchandise to stock: the optimum balance between quality brands and low-price merchandise; whether to compete heavily on price (which is a fairly new problem since many states used to forbid stores to *cut* prices below a uniform "retail price"); the best balance between liquor, wine, and beer; and whether to add other merchandise (corkscrews, wineglasses, or snacks ranging from bags of potato chips to sixteen kinds of pâté).

A typical liquor store will have to deal with several wholesalers—either different wholesalers for different types of beverage, or wholesalers who each handle the diverse products of a different major distiller. Liquor stores that are part of chains have the advantage of centralized ordering and of larger orders that can bring more favorable prices. Now that state regulations against discounting have been removed, some stores and some chains also maintain a discount-store image and pricing structure.

## A GOOD YEAR

Whether or not it will prove to be a great year for Burgundy, 1986 was a pretty good year for liquor stores. More than three-quarters of the 1,000 beverage retailers surveyed by *Liquor Store* magazine reported sales increases averaging almost 10 percent; the same percentage reported an average increase in profits of 7.8 percent between 1985 and 1986. (The minority—22 percent—reported an average sales decline of 6.5 percent and a drop in profits of 8.6 percent.) The increases were especially significant in that consumption of liquor dropped 4 percent in 1986. So either stores are selling a lot more wine and beer, or people are buying booze but doling it out very slowly.

The average store saw almost 3,000 customers a week and rang up average sales of about $12 per customer, for yearly sales per square foot of about $475. However, respondents were at both ends of the scale: some had only 200 customers a week, some about 8,500; some expected $4.19 each time the cash register rang, some averaged $45.

The average store did one-third its business in liquor, 30 percent in beer, and 26 percent in wine, with the remaining sales in coolers and nonbeverage items. (For instance, Willie's, a fairly raunchy liquor store in Dana's neighborhood, sells pints of Häagen-Dazs, of all things.) But the stores have widely different experiences, depending on the locality (Californians enjoy drinking the local product; in Minnesota, though, 86 percent of alcoholic beverage sales come from beer, only 7 percent each from wine and liquor) and the image the store cultivates (perhaps a place to load up for keg parties; perhaps a gourmet operation where the finest vintages share space with delicacies).

But the various categories of sales make different contributions to profits. The average markup on wine was 34 percent—just a touch higher than the 32.6 percent markup on nonbeverage items. The markup on coolers is lower—28.6 percent—probably because there are many com-

## TRADE TALK

The Great Divide in wine comes between screw-top (often jug wines) and "cork-finished" wines; wines can also be "premium" or "super-premium." Usually, the markups get higher as the level of quality increases. For one thing, customers are more price sensitive about jug wine; for another, you can get Ripple anyplace, but not every store has Romanee-Conte of a vintage year.

peting brands of coolers available, so suppliers offer generous discounts to get their brands into the stores. Liquor markups are lower still, averaging 23.9 percent (the highest reported was 50 percent; the lowest, a tiny 4 percent). The lowest markup of all is on beer: 13.8 percent.

But markup isn't the only factor that determines what a liquor store will stock. Another consideration is how much effort (and labor cost) is required to take care of a beverage. Canned beer isn't a particularly temperamental substance, and liquor bottles are fine unless you drop them; wine, however, requires more careful storage.

There's also the amount that the store must invest in its stock. Beer is usually the cheapest alcoholic beverage for the retailer to buy, liquor or fine wine the most expensive. In the experience of one Dallas store, soft drinks accounted for 3.3 percent of all cases of beverages sold and only 1.6 percent of revenue. Beer made up 73.1 percent of volume but brought in only 29.8 percent of revenue; coolers were neutral, at 2.3 percent of sales for 2.2 percent of revenues. The big gainers were liquor, which accounted for 11.9 percent of all cases sold and 34.8 percent of revenue, and wine, which comprised 9.4 percent of the total cases sold and 22.7 percent of revenue.

Furthermore, effective wine sales can require customer education (and free samples): 42 percent of *Liquor Store*'s March 1987 survey respondents had wine tastings (and tastings of their other goods).

## STORE LAYOUT

Liquor stores, like icebergs, have quite a bit below the surface: extensive storage space is required—perhaps 7,500 square feet each for warehouse and selling space, or 10,000 square feet of selling space backed up by 5,000 square feet of warehouse space. Discounters tend to have a higher ratio of selling space to storage space, first, because they tend to keep fewer items in inventory; second, because they try to push for high turnover and frequent reorders.

It's hard to generalize about "typical" liquor stores, but clearly it's not a shoestring business: inventories are likely to range from $250,000 to well over $1 million, and annual sales in the millions are quite commonplace. San Francisco's Liquor Barn sells more than $20 million a year; but then, San Franciscans spend an average of $6 a week (twice as much as other Californians) on buying alcoholic beverages from liquor stores.

Some successful stores do well with ten to twelve turnovers of inventory a year; others do better than twenty turnovers on wine and liquor (see page 238 about inventory). A store that really tries to maximize beer sales (for example, by offering favorable prices on twenty-four-can "suitcase" packs) can turn over inventory more than forty times a year.

Once a liquor store picks an image and a product mix, it can use regular pricing, special sale prices, promotions, and advertising to motivate the customers to buy the products that the store wants to sell. A successful store has to respond to a certain extent to customer wishes, of course. But a store featuring wine may not carry beer at all, or only a few brands; a store featuring liquor may have only a few, highly profitable, wines. On the other hand, a store can attract customers by its very large selection or by its high turnover, guaranteeing a fresher product.

Computers are an important part of many stores' operations: 63 percent use computers, with 42 percent using them for general business tasks and 27 percent for keeping inventory; 16 percent have computerized cash registers, which integrate the cash register with the inventory records (and make it much harder for employees to help themselves). (The numbers add up to more than 63 percent because store owners can find multiple uses for computers.)

# Shop Till You Drop

# 31

# Shopping Malls

Shopping malls were born about thirty years ago, when postwar prosperity, low land prices, and low gas prices combined to make it worthwhile to build a gigantic assembly of various kinds of stores—if necessary, in the middle of nowhere. Customers would drive to the mall and enjoy a day's shopping, enlivened with meals and snacks. In 1957, about 5 percent of shopping was done in shopping centers; by 1987, half of all shopping was done in malls.

Real estate prices and gas prices now approach the stratosphere, but malls are still hanging on because they're social and entertainment centers for communities as well as shopping centers. Malls are gathering places (like the ancient Greek *agora,* which means marketplace)—even exercise places: middle-aged and senior citizens keep fit with "mall walking" in enclosed, climate-controlled areas. The mall has displaced the general store and the church social as a place for teenagers to meet their age-mates, and for adults to mull over the affairs of the day.

However, the glory days of limitless expansion are over. In the late 1970s through early 1980s, 120 regional malls were built; in the succeeding five years, only 77 were developed.

The late 1970s were also the golden years for "mini-malls," tiny strips of 100,000 square feet or less. (By comparison, a really large "anchor tenant" in a regular mall can have 100,000 square feet all to itself.) They were often developed on corner lots formerly occupied by gas stations that were made unprofitable by rising gas prices. In the 1970s, about 800 shopping centers went up each year, with nearly three-quarters of them mini-malls. The percentage was even higher in the early 1980s: 85 percent of the 6,700 shopping centers built between 1981 and 1985 were mini-malls. At first, rents were attractive to tenants: only about $12 to $36 per square foot as compared to a yearly $30 to $60 per foot at larger, "regional" malls—and a hefty $100 or more at prime city locations.

However, by 1987, the boom went bust. There were just too many mini-malls, too many vacant stores, and too many mini-mall tenants going out of business because the customers had too many pizza parlors and card shops to choose from. Municipal authorities were cracking down, claiming that the malls' designs were unattractive and led to traffic snarls and trash.

Malls also faced competition from "off-price" malls entirely inhabited by outlets and other discount merchandisers. By 1986, there were over 350 of these, selling more than ten billion dollars' worth of merchandise.

## ANCHORS AWEIGH

Larger malls are usually enclosed, housing a matrix of shops in a gallery of glass, concrete, and brick. The basic model for the mall is two or three levels of shopping, with an "atrium" (central court or plaza in the middle). Mall designs frequently include a second, "side court" with the secondary anchor tenant, the fast-food operations, and more shops.

The developer (the organization that builds and sponsors the mall) must find a suitable site. The quest is for the "100 percent location"—one that every shopper has to pass and one that can stay open twenty-four hours a day. For instance, the junction of two freeways is a 100 percent location. With the location settled, the developer usually gets the project rolling by finding "anchor tenants"—tenants such as department stores that will make a commitment to open large, multilevel stores within the mall. The anchor tenant serves many functions. Its rent is high enough to cure many of the developer's anxieties about the project; it has a broad enough scope of merchandise, and advertises enough, to lure shoppers to the mall (where they will pass many, many other stores); and it sets the style and tone of the mall and gives a clue to the shoppers what they'll find, and even whether they'll be welcome. Compare two New Jersey malls: the Riverside Mall in Hackensack is anchored by Bloomingdale's and Saks; the Newport mall in Jersey City by Sears and Sterns. Guess which one attracts more affluent, more glamorous customers and displays higher-scale merchandise.

The "vertical mall" (one that occupies several stories, instead of extending horizontally) now being constructed on 86th Street in Manhattan is anchored by a 300,000 square foot Abraham & Straus department store. The other tenant stores will occupy a total of 180,000 square feet, and the building will also include eleven stories of offices.

The location started life as a Gimbel's department store, but it's becoming harder and harder for department stores serving a middle-class clientele to pay rents high enough to interest landlords. It's often more profitable for the store to sell its real estate to developers who will change the site's use from department store to mall, condos, offices, or a mixture of all of them.

Once the mall developer has one or more anchor tenants, it's time to recruit tenants for smaller shops. It's a delicate art of orchestration—finding tenants who complement, rather than compete too directly; who maintain the image and attract the kind of shoppers the mall wants; and who can stay in business and yield sturdy profits for the mall. For instance, Olympia & York, the developer of the World Financial Center in Manhattan's Battery Park City, has 220,000 square feet of space to turn into seventy-five shops, and 80,000 square feet allocated to fifteen restaurants. It set the rental at $100 a square foot—the rent it tried to charge at their earlier development at the South Street Seaport (also in Manhattan) before being forced to cut rents down to $60 a square foot there.

For store owners, the dilemma is whether to stay put in traditional "Main Street" locations—and perhaps see their customers shift to shopping at the mall—or move to the mall. At the mall, there'll be plenty of foot traffic and coordinated ad campaigns.

But there'll also be plenty of competition; rents that may be higher than for ordinary store fronts; controls on operations (mall tenants are told when to open and close and how to decorate their stores); and charges in addition to the rent. Usually, mall tenants must pay a basic monthly rent, "overage" (a percentage of all profits over a set amount), and "common area" charges for maintaining the atrium, hallways, and other public spaces in the mall.

Malls have nurtured and been nurtured by chains of stores (many of them franchised) that are perfectly designed for mall operation. The chains such as Pants Place and Ups & Downs have a unified design format that fits in with mall restrictions and an approved list of items to be stocked, based on extensive market research about what the mall shopper wants.

## MALL PRACTICE

Whether a mall will be successful for developers depends on a lot of things: how many shoppers will be attracted; how much they'll spend on an average mall visit; and the unique problems of the area (which can be anything from blizzards to teenage gangs). One of the most important factors is the size of the mall since operating costs decrease as the mall gets bigger. The International Council of Shopping Centers 1987 study reports that it costs about $4.00 a square foot to operate an enclosed mall smaller than 200,000 square feet, but only $2.48 per square foot for a mall bigger than 800,000 square feet. That's a national average; costs are lowest in the South, highest in the East.

About 24 percent of an enclosed mall's total operating costs go for maintenance and repair. Other costs include utilities (keeping those lights on well into the night), debt service (interest on the loans to acquire the land and build the mall; in addition to banks, insurance companies and pension plans are heavy lenders to mall developers), and security.

A really successful mall can be the perfect location for a store owner. Stamford Town Center in Connecticut attracts 12,000 shoppers on an ordinary weekday, twice that many on a holiday. Although rents there are not particularly modest ($30 to $40 a foot), the tenants average sales of $400 per square foot.

## DISNEYMALL?

Stamford Town Center snuggles a performing arts amphitheater into its atrium; it also sports one of the "water features" that are the current rage in mall design: in this case, a fountain that spurts water nine stories high. Other malls have ponds and waterfalls.

Phoenix's Metrocenter (the size of thirty-five football fields) blends public and private uses: thirty restaurants, fourteen card shops, twenty-four shoe stores, nearly forty clothing stores, nine banks, three movie theaters—and a public library and a branch campus of Arizona State University. If the trend of combining malls with housing and offices continues, pretty soon it may be possible to live, work, and shop within a single mall—and perhaps never go outside at all.

# 32

# Department Stores

| | |
|---|---|
| Number of establishments: | 9,991 (5,764 "discount or mass merchandising"; 2,400 "conventional"; 1,817 "national chain") |
| Total receipts: | $99.17 billion ($38.8 billion—"discount or mass merchandisers"; $31.8 billion—"conventional"; $28.6 billion—"national chain") |
| Average net sales: | $9,935,000 |
| Number of employees: | 1,515,000 |
| Total payroll: | $12.495 billion |
| | (Department of Commerce, '82) |

Department stores used to be the great beluga whales of retailing, powerful enough to close down entire factories when they discontinued an order. In fact, for a long time Sears, Roebuck and Company was not just the largest retail operation in the United States, but its five regional divisions were the *five* biggest retail operations.

The stores themselves were marvels of urban architecture and elaborate display, the closest things to palaces many of their customers

141

Top Earners, 1987

|  | Salary/Bonus | Stock Ownership |
|---|---|---|
| David C. Farrell<br>The May Department Stores Company | $1,125,000 | 292,000 shares |
| Kenneth A. Macke<br>Dayton Hudson Corporation | $930,000 | 70,000 shares |
| E. A. Brennan<br>Sears, Roebuck & Company | $1,507,000 | 60,000 shares |

(*Business Week,* October 31, 1988)

would ever see. Today, things aren't so great for department stores. Many factors contributed to their decline. Department stores are a highly middle-class institution—and these days, middle-class people find themselves pushed by tax bills and squeezed by their kids' college tuition. For everyday purchases, they often go to discount stores; for that rare splurge, to specialty retailers who stock unusual merchandise that wouldn't appeal to a department-store buyer, who must order hundreds of dozens of an item at a time.

Then there are so many more places and ways to shop than there used to be. Mail-order buying is more popular, varied, and sophisticated than ever. True, shopping malls are usually anchored by one or more department stores, but the mall contains dozens, even hundreds, of stores all competing to charm the customers' credit cards out of their wallets. There are discount stores, warehouse clubs, and home shopping, all competing for the same share of the household budget.

There are so many more *things* now, so numerous and varied that a department store can no longer hope to offer everything. Sears used to believe that it held a "franchise" on the "80": the 80 percent of Americans who are neither very rich nor very poor. But today, farmers buy designer jeans as well as Can't Bust 'Em overalls; and two families, living side by side and with identical incomes, can have very different beliefs about what to buy, how much to save, and where to spend whatever they do spend. Which is not to say that department stores can't be profitable enterprises (though, like supermarkets, they maintain slender profit margins and depend on turnover), but it takes a skilled merchandiser to anticipate trends and operate efficiently in today's environment.

In Dun & Bradstreet's 1987 survey of 989 department stores, net profit after tax averaged 1.5 percent of net sales—not much left out of the gross profits averaging 34.6 percent of net sales. Fairchild's figures for 1986 show average sales of $3.36 billion for department stores (up 8.7 percent from 1985 levels), but net income was up only 4.8 percent, to an average of $104.87 million.

Top Department Stores, 1987

|  | Sales ($000) | Profits ($000) | Profit as a % of Sales (%) |
|---|---|---|---|
| Federated Department Stores, Inc. (#77) | $11,118,000 | $313,000 | 2.7 |
| The May Department Stores Company (#78) | $10,581,000 | $444,000 | 3.7 |
| Dayton Hudson Corporation | $10,677,000 | $228,400 | 3.7 |
| Carter Hawley Hale Stores, Inc. | $4,089,794 | $4,214 | 0.1 |
| BATUS | $2,471,280 | N/A | N/A |

(Fairchild, '86)

According to the Department of Commerce's 1982 business census, America's department stores covered the huge acreage of 1,021,412,000 square feet. Sixty-nine percent of that was selling space; the rest, storage and administrative space. The average sales per square foot were $141. The national chains did much better, averaging $196 a foot; discount and mass merchandise department stores sold only $119 per square foot; and conventional department stores averaged sales of $136 per square foot.

## MAJOR DOLLARS

Ten department-store chains made *Business Week*'s Top 1000 list. Sears, Roebuck is still the largest (and America's fourteenth-largest company), with 1987 sales of $48,440 billion and profits of $1.65 billion. Sears sells practically everything and owns a major insurance company (Allstate) and Dean Witter Financial Services as well as its 835 retail stores and a powerful catalogue operation.

However, Sears's sales since 1984 have grown only half as fast as those of the department-store industry as a whole, and Sears has a cumbersome intracompany distribution system that costs about 8 percent of sales—four times the amount that more efficient retailers spend on this essential function.

Yet it manages to maintain margins well above average for the department-store industry (3.4 percent for 1987). The margins may be comparatively high because Sears sells so much of its own brands of merchandise (eliminating middlemen) and buys so much that it can push manufacturers for a very good deal. Sears's merchandise mix is unusual: about two-thirds of its merchandise consists of "hard goods" such as furniture and appliances, rather than clothing and other "soft goods," which means that it's at the mercy of seasonal trends in hard-good sales—that is, people tend to buy washers, electric drills, and other "unsentimental" purchases for Christmas, graduation, wedding anniversaries, and other milestones; they're hardly ever impulse purchases.

All in all, Sears's report card is that of a kid who's always been at the top of the class, but perhaps doesn't work as hard as some of the less talented kids and needs polishing up in a few essential subjects. [In April 1988, Sears announced plans to bolster profits by expanding space for appliances and home electronics (both national brands and its own Sears and Kenmore brands) by 50 to 70 percent in its existing stores. New stores are on tap: eighty-five department stores and 147 smaller stores are in the works. Sears is also studying the viability of appliance "superstores" to compete with specialty retailers such as Circuit City Stores, Inc.; freestanding "sleep shops" selling bedding and accessories; and small, freestanding auto service centers.]

The Limited, the department-store chain rated #130 in the Top 1000, sells hardly anything except clothes, and, until recently, only women's clothes. Yet in 1987 The Limited managed sales of $3.528 billion and profits of $235.2 million.

The May Department Stores Company owns Associated Dry Goods Corporation, which means that it also owns Lord & Taylor at one end of the price spectrum and the Caldor, Inc., discount stores at the other. It's the #78 company on the *Business Week* list, with 1987 sales of $10.581 billion and profits of $444.0 million. Its margin was 4.2 percent for 1987.

May Department Stores isn't the only company interested in acquiring department stores. One of 1988's biggest business stories was the epic ten-week battle that ended when Robert Campeau became America's fourth-largest retailer by acquiring Federated Department Stores, Inc., for $6.6 billion. The acquisition rippled throughout retailing. Campeau ended up with Abraham & Straus, Bloomingdale's, Rich's, Goldsmith's, Lazarus, Stern's, and Jordan Marsh; and he agreed to sell Bullock's and I. Magnin to megarival Macy's, Filene's and Foley's to May, and Brooks Brothers to Britain's Marks and Spencer.

An up-and-coming chain, Nordstrom's, from Seattle, is staging an invasion of the East. It already has forty-six stores on the West Coast (all soft goods like clothing—no sofas, no stereos, no stoves), average sales of $310 per square foot (nearly twice the average for department stores), store managers who can earn over $100,000 including their bonuses, and a reputation for service that leaves other stores wondering how to compete. The gift-wrapping and free home delivery other stores offer seem almost prosaic compared to the in-store piano players (London department stores all have piano players, but it's an unusual amenity in the United States); in Alaska, the store clerks at Nordstrom's even warm up customers' cars for them. There are plans to open two stores in Washington, D.C., with others in Chicago, Minneapolis, Atlanta, Boston, and an as-yet-undetermined part of New Jersey.

## LIST PRICE AND OTHER FICTIONS

The trend in merchandising used to be to assign a fairly high list price to merchandise, with markups of 60 to 65 percent. If the merchandise sold at that price, all the better. If it didn't, then it was time to roll out the big red *Sale!* signs, take out full-page ads in the tabloids, and run the After-Christmas Sale, the January (or August) White Sale, the President's Day Sale, the July 4th Sale . . . you get the idea. Less than half the merchandise in department stores sells for its original price; the rest is marked down.

The dogs in Ivan Pavlov's experiment learned to salivate whenever a bell rang because they associated the sound with food. Department-store shoppers have learned not to buy anything unless it's singled out as being marked down. They'd rather go to a discounter, with lower prices all the time, or wait for the department-store sale.

Department stores have responded by lowering everyday markups (say, to 50 to 54 percent) and holding fewer sales. That way, they hope to attract customers by offering a larger selection of merchandise and better service than discount stores and to narrow the price difference between the two. What about non-discount, non-department-store retailers? Department store prices *are* often (though not always) lower because the department store can take advantage of large orders to push for low prices and can have goods manufactured to its own specifications. What the smaller store offers is a more personal selection of goods and often a convenient neighborhood location that doesn't require you to travel to the center of town or to the outlying malls, where the department stores are located.

However, department stores have a lot of options for unsold merchandise. If the store is one of a chain, the merchandise can be sent to another (perhaps less sophisticated) store, in the hope that it'll find favor there. Or it can be sold to a store such as Filenes Basement that specializes in other department stores' mistakes. About all the independent store can do is cut the price, so some phenomenal bargains can be found by shoppers who take pity on the unwanted merchandise.

# 33

# Mail Order Shopping

Number of establishments:    7,433
Total receipts:              $11.25 billion
Average net sales:           $1,514,000
Number of employees:         102,600
Total payroll:               $1.19 billion

(Department of Commerce, '82)

The perpetrators would like you to call it "direct mail marketing," but you probably call it "junk mail." In 1985, 52.5 billion pieces of third-class mail were "dropped" (sent out). Much of this blizzard consisted of catalogues and other sales material. (Much of the rest asked for charitable or political donations. And there's a good chance that the solicitor got the recipient's name and address from a mailing list compiled by a direct-mail merchant.)

At first, catalogue merchandising was used to supply America's remote farm families with items that the tiny general store couldn't carry. The western states, the last to get retail stores, are still the best mail order customers. Today, although hardly any American is out of reach of a shopping mall, the catalogue business is booming nonetheless—to the tune of an anticipated $54 billion for 1987. All kinds of at-home shopping

**Where the Money Comes From**

| | |
|---|---|
| (1) Women's and girls' clothes: | 14.4% |
| (2) Men's and boys' clothes: | 7.1% |
| (3) Books, magazines, newspapers: | 6.7% |
| (4) Curtains, draperies, dry goods: | 6.0% |
| (5) Kitchenware, home furnishings: | 5.9% |
| (6) Audio equipment, musical instruments: | 5.8% |
| (7) Food: | 3.9% |
| (8) Drugs and cosmetics: | 3.4% |
| (9) Major appliances: | 3.5% |
| (10) Sporting goods: | 3.8% |
| (11) Car tires, batteries, accessories: | 3.5% |
| (12) All other: | 36% |

(Department of Commerce, '82)

are growing at the rate of 12 percent a year, and experts think it could reach one-third of the total of all retail sales.

Why do people buy by mail order? Sometimes the merchandise is so special that it would be impossible to earn a profit selling it in a store because it takes a nation's worth of customers to keep going. Sometimes the stuff is so embarrassing that the buyers prefer the anonymity of the proverbial "plain brown wrapper." Or price might be the attraction: a mail order enterprise doesn't have to maintain elegant shops on the best streets in town and can survive with only a warehouse in the middle of nowhere. Mail order merchants who distribute their own products cut out several layers of middlemen; even those who distribute the products of others can eliminate a few costly steps in the distribution chain. Mail order can also be a way to distribute discounted merchandise that didn't sell during an earlier life in department or specialty stores.

However, not all mail order merchandise is low priced. It costs a lot of money to print and mail thick, luscious full-color catalogues—most of which go straight into the recipient's trash can and few of which lead to actual orders. Then again, some mail order firms cater to a "captive audience": if you're the only person selling a particular kind of fudge ice-cream topping or exquisite Chinese antiques or the designs of an avant-garde designer, you can charge the highest amount potential customers will pay because you have no competition.

Depending on the mail order operation's history and sophistication, mailing lists can either be a major expense or a major source of income. Usually, a start-up operation must rent mailing lists developed by other merchandisers or by organizations. For instance, a mail order catalogue selling hunting and fishing equipment might rent a mailing list developed by a conservation organization or the National Rifle Association, or use the subscription list of an outdoor magazine.

Eventually, a mail order house develops its own mailing list from those who write in for the catalogue; who buy the products; and, best of all, those who buy products regularly. If the mailing list can be analyzed in various ways (according to geographic area; according to type of product purchased; according to payment type—check or credit card), it becomes a valuable asset to the company because other companies may want to rent it.

Sometimes mail order customers buy merchandise that *can* be found in stores, but only if they chase all over town. The catalogue offers the convenience of ordering a variety of merchandise, selected for a specific taste, in one place. And sometimes the merchandise is available in stores (maybe even stores run by the catalogue company), but mail order is a convenience for enthusiastic buyers who are too busy with work, school, or family commitments to shop. A really good catalogue can also whet customers' appetite for store merchandise. In 1986, for instance, Banana Republic sent out twelve million of its catalogues (at a cost of nearly $1.5 million) and thus increased sales in its new stores by 27 to 43 percent.

However, a 1986 Gallup poll of 1,559 adults found that 68 percent of the survey respondents would not buy mail order merchandise if they could find it at nearby stores; and almost half those surveyed found it difficult to buy by mail order because of the time it takes for the stuff to be delivered. Catalogue merchants must also overcome the stigma that a few fly-by-night operators have given the entire industry: they must make customers believe that merchandise damaged in shipping, or even merchandise that the customers decide they don't like after it arrives, can be replaced or the customers' money refunded.

## SOME SUCCESSES

One mail order company, Lands' End, Inc., has scrambled onto *Business Week*'s Top 1000 list, at #870. In April 1988, the company had a market value of $421 million and assets of $100 million, with sales of $336 million and profits of $22.1 million. Since 1984, the catalog company's sales have grown by around 28% each year. Lands' End's success seems to come from exemplary management devoted to a thoughtful marketing strategy that emphasizes the character of the company and the Lands' End image.

Lillian Vernon Corporation (so called because it was started in Mount Vernon, by a lady named Lillian) is acclaimed as one of the best-run mail order companies, particularly in its specialty of gifts and household

## CONSUMER TIP

If you have a problem with a mail order company—such as damaged shipments or failure to deliver—write to the Mail Order Action Line (MOAL), which has a high success rate in getting firms to respond. Their address is 6 E. 43rd St., New York, New York 10017. Enclose a copy of (not the original) cancelled check or credit card statement with your letter.

items. To fill its 1.3 million orders and to earn $4.1 million, Lillian Vernon mailed more than eighty-two million catalogues.

But catalogues aren't the only way to sell mail order products. Another common technique is to use "bill stuffers": inserts in a bill that's being sent out anyway (say, by a department store or credit card issuer). American Express's mail order operation, American Express Merchandise Services, achieved sales of $75 million one year by sending a bill insert to each of its eighteen million cardholders.

## THE OUTLOOK

Future mail order sales may not involve printed catalogues at all. A growing trend is to use videocassettes to present merchandise. (But some of the most successful video catalogues are issued by lingerie companies, so perhaps the viewers' motives are not entirely connected with a passionate desire to be informed purchasers of lingerie.) The name "mail order" is becoming something of a misnomer, given widespread telemarketing (telephone sales calls to consumers and toll-free "800" numbers for ordering merchandise) and the heavy use of package delivery services instead of the postal system.

Perhaps someday the home computer will put us in touch with daily updates of information about our favorite products; maybe we'll all watch TV home shopping programs or pop videocassettes into the VCR to get the kick of shopping without ever going out into the cold or the rain. (Even if the mall is enclosed, you've still got to *drive* there.)

# 34

# Home Shopping

What can you do if you've just got to have a shopping fix, but it's snowing, or the kids have the sniffles, or it's four in the morning? Sure, you can browse through your catalogue collection and order up a storm . . . but that's so, well, low-tech. The really modern solution is to flip on the home-shopping show on cable TV or UHF, wait until something catches your eye, then dial the toll-free number and give 'em your credit card number. (If you want to pay by check, you'll have to wait for your check to be delivered and to clear, which diminishes some of the fine impulsive rapture of immediate gratification.)

According to a survey done by Leo J. Shapiro & Associates in March 1987, more than one-third of the 451 households surveyed watch home-shopping shows, typically for two to three hours a week. Only 4 percent of those households actually bought anything, but 70 percent of the buyers were repeat buyers, with an average purchase of $33 a shot.

From the producer's point of view, home shopping is an almost ideal television show. It's cheap to produce since all you need is one set, a few presenters, and a constant parade of merchandise, which retailers are more than happy to provide. No temperamental stars, striking screenwriters (or football players), and no heavy payments for hit syndicated comedies or cop shows. That's one reason why so many companies—

thirty or so, although a shakeout is inevitable—are in the business of home-shopping programs and why the projected total 1987 sales are estimated at anywhere from $1 to $2.25 billion and an expected $3 to $6 billion by the end of the decade. If the $3 billion estimate is correct, that's the equivalent of two hundred gigantic (100,000 square foot) stores, each pulling in a very respectable $150 a square foot, and 7 percent of the amount of consumer products sold by mail order in all of 1986, and 11 percent of Sears's 1986 sales. But, to keep this in perspective, Price Waterhouse estimates overall general merchandise, clothing, furniture, and home furnishings sales of $456.7 billion in 1990, leaving plenty of room for conventional retailers to make a buck.

Television shopping shows aim for a 40 to 50 percent gross margin, which means that the range of prices should be somewhere between $15 and $100 per item. Things that sell for under $15 aren't profitable; things that cost more than a C-note are unlikely to be bought on impulse even by the wildest shopper (anyway, nobody wants customers who can't pay for their purchases).

The best-selling products are those that are being launched through home shopping or those made exclusively for shop-TV; people seem less inclined to buy things that can be found in retail stores. Sometimes the impulse comes from the shopping show, which orders merchandise or even has special items manufactured; at other times, the manufacturers and dealers approach the show and demonstrate that their merchandise fits into the show's demographic and buying patterns.

## WHO SELLS AT HOME?

The largest, and pioneering, service is Home Shopping Network, Inc. (HSN), which is building itself a $25 million headquarters-cum-studio in St. Petersburg, Florida. HSN can be viewed on eleven broadcast stations and by the subscribers to any of ninety-five multisystem cable companies. Its cost of doing business is about 27 to 28 percent of sales; surprisingly, this is higher than those of a typical discount store (about 20 percent of sales) but lower than catalogue sales (about 30 percent).

It was #748 on *Business Week*'s Top 1000 for 1987, with assets of $545 million, sales of $664 million, and profits of $23.1 million, for a not-too-shabby return on invested capital of 8.2 percent and return on common equity of 18.6 percent. During the holiday season, HSN scores with high-priced luxury items such as gold jewelry and fur jackets and in 1986 made a hit with a humbler item—the teddy bear.

HSN did well, but nowhere near as well as it predicted. The network claims that the problem was the fault of its telephone system, which cut off half the customers' calls; it's embroiled in a $1.5 billion lawsuit over alleged misrepresentation of the capacity of the phone system. In addition, it launched a game show that was supposed to be a major hit, but it couldn't stand up to the competition of the "Kukla, Fawn and Ollie Show"—the Iran-Contra hearings.

Another major player is the QVC Network, Inc., which handles the home-shopping tasks for retailers and manufacturers including Sears (after all, retailers don't want to be left behind). QVC is carried by more than five hundred cable systems in forty-four states and has a customer base of about 200,000. Catalogue merchants are getting into the act as well, with an estimated audience of thirty-two million for the American Catalogue Shopping Network, broadcasting from High Point, North Carolina.

Not everyone who tries to get involved in home shopping succeeds: Lorimar Telepictures Corporation formed a joint venture with Fox Television Stations and Horn & Hardart Company to put a one-hour show on seventy-four stations six days a week. Well, Fox hasn't been doing too well on any front (see page 288), and the ol' Automat is not exactly in its glory days. Ratings were disappointing after six months, perhaps because the joint venture took a soft-sell approach that wasn't appealing to home-shopping viewers.


## SHOPPING BY COMPUTER

For the latest in home shopping, you can go beyond ordinary dialing for dishes; if you join the eight million Comp-U-Card members who pay $39 a year for the privilege, you can shop either by phone or by home computer. Comp-U-Card is really a data base, which provides information about more than a quarter of a million items under hundreds of brand names, but it doesn't actually sell goods. Instead, the subscribers call a toll-free number, and Comp-U-Card's computers sort through the prices offered by five hundred participating distributors and dealers (who pay commissions of about 7 percent) and place an order on the most favorable terms available. (It works a lot like a travel agent's computer system for airline reservations.)

Now, maybe someone can set up a system of electrodes that plug directly into the brain and give you the *sensation* of buying things, without the need to actually clutter up your closets.

# 35

# Warehouse Clubs

When you get right down to it, the essence of retailing is that someone who owns merchandise agrees to sell it to someone else. The rest—recessed lighting, elegant window displays, and easy credit terms—is just the trimmings; cash-and-carry is the turkey dinner.

Warehouse clubs are even more basic than discount stores, and their numbers are increasing, with 328 clubs and an estimated $12 billion in sales in 1987, up from 36 outlets in 1983. They offer large savings to their long-suffering customers by buying a small range of items in *large* quantities (if the warehouse club doesn't have quite the model number or shade you want, it has no problems about directing you to take your business elsewhere) and by eliminating every possible frill in order to reduce operating expenses to the bone. A typical warehouse club marks up its goods by only 10 to 15 percent, a far cry from the common practice of doubling the wholesale price to set retail prices. The object is volume, and a successful wholesale club can turn over its inventory fifteen to eighteen times a year.

You may have to pay a membership fee to shop at the warehouse at all, and you'll have to pick up your own merchandise from an intimidating heap of sealed cartons, schlepp it to a single cash register or bank of cash registers, and figure out some way to get it home. However, warehouse clubs eventually offer a fairly wide variety of merchandise. They may stock only two china patterns at a time, but the patterns offered may change six times a year.

In 1986, the ten largest players in the warehouse club market had 202 stores in operation and sold $7.8 billion worth of merchandise. Price Co. and Sam's (whose fifty-two clubs were part of discount giant Wal-Mart Stores, Inc.) were the most profitable. In 1987, several operations had fallen by the wayside, and a further shakeout was expected: when margins are wafer-thin, a rent increase, an extra few bucks on the utility bill, or a few minor mistakes in merchandising can ruin a store. Wal-Mart's vice chairman, Jack Shewmaker, said that warehouse clubs were easier to start up than conventional discount stores because they focus on a very limited assortment of goods. But that very focus makes them harder to run than ordinary discount stores: with so few items in the store, the manager must be certain to choose precisely the right ones.

Since 1984, The Wholesale Club has been taking a slightly different approach. Its seventeen clubs average 100,000 square feet, with 3,500 to 4,000 SKUs ("sales keeping units"—see page 238 on inventory) in stock; its gross margins are about 9.5 percent. About 60 percent of its "members" (the word is in quotation marks because there's no membership fee) are individuals; the rest are companies or groups. They pay 5 percent more than the wholesale price of their purchases.

Price Co., which began in San Diego, had twenty-seven clubs (most of them in the Southwest, some in New Jersey) in March 1987, with plans to further expand to the East by buying a majority interest in the New York discount operation TSS-Seidman's. Warehouse clubs are an exotic flower in New York since high rents make it tough to open a store large enough to hold dozens of crated washing machines and truckloads of toasters.

Another industry leader, PACE Membership Warehouses, Inc., had twenty-five units in 1987, racking up margins of 8 to 9 percent and posting an operating profit of $10 million for the first nine months of 1986, while offering customers savings of 25 to 50 percent over conventional stores' prices. For all of fiscal 1986, sales were $602.7 million—119 percent more than in 1985.

As long as shoppers are willing to do without amenities to get bargains, and as long as they don't insist on one-stop shopping, the warehouse club should have a strong future.

# 36

# Clothing Stores

| | |
|---|---|
| Number of establishments: | 97,860 (50,961 women's; 17,480 men's; 5,325 children's) |
| Total receipts: | $45.59 billion ($22 billion women's; 7.7 billion men's; 1.3 billion children's*) |
| Average net sales: | $465,900 |
| Number of employees: | 790,100 |
| Total payroll: | $5.99 billion |

(Department of Commerce, '82)

We've come a long way since the days when most people had one outfit of clothes for everyday and another for Sundays, and the main class difference was the splendor of the clothing (and perhaps the number of garments worn at one time), not the number of outfits each person had. (One reason why Victorian houses have so few closets is that even well-to-do Victorians seldom had more clothes than would fit into a freestanding armoire.)

Now that clothing can be mass-produced, that much of it is made

*The rest unisex, or sold in stores other than clothing stores.

## Where the Money Comes From (Women's Clothing Stores)

| | |
|---|---|
| (1) Shirts, blouses, sweaters: | 20.4% |
| (2) Slacks, jeans, pants, skirts: | 16.5% |
| (3) Suits, jackets, blazers: | 11.8% |
| (4) Dresses: | 18.4% |
| (5) Coats, jackets, rainwear: | 7.0% |
| (6) Active sportswear: | 4.3% |
| (7) Hosiery: | 2.2% |
| (8) Lingerie, sleepwear, loungewear: | 3.4% |
| (9) Underwear: | 1.9% |
| (10) Furs: | 0.6% |
| (11) Hats, wigs, hairpieces: | 0.1% |
| (12) Accessories: | 5.0% |
| (13) Girls' clothing: | 1.9% |
| (14) Mens' and boys'/wear: | 1.3% |
| (15) Miscellaneous women's wear: | 0.9% |
| (16) Knits: | 1.3% |
| (17) Other income: | 2.4% |

(Deparment of Commerce, '82)

## Where the Money Goes ("Apparel and Accessory Stores")

| | |
|---|---|
| (1) Cost of operations: | 58.7% |
| (2) Officers' compensation: | 2.4% |
| (3) Pensions and benefits: | 0.9% |
| (4) Rent: | 5.5% |
| (5) Repairs: | 0.4% |
| (6) Depreciation, depletion, amortization: | 1.7% |
| (7) Interest: | 1.1% |
| (8) Bad debts: | 0.2% |
| (9) Advertising: | 2.7% |
| (10) State, local taxes: | 2.4% |
| (11) Other expenses: | 21.6% |
| (12) Net profit before tax: | 2.4% |

(Troy, '84–'85)

from synthetic fibers (so that clothing can outpace the production of wool, cotton, or silk), and that it's much easier to wash one's person or one's clothes, we expect that people will have many, many different outfits, suitable for different seasons and activities and reasonably in keeping with

## Financial Ratios for Clothing Stores

Column (1) is gross profit as a percentage of sales; column (2) is net profit after tax; column (3) is the range of return on sales; column (4) is the range of return on assets. (All figures are percentages and come from Dun & Bradstreet's 1986 survey.)

| | Gross Profit as a Percentage of Sales | Net Profit After Tax | Range of Return on Sales | Range of Return on Assets |
|---|---|---|---|---|
| Family clothing stores | 35.2 | 5.1 | not given | not given |
| Women's ready-made clothing | 37.6 | 5.8 | 1.3–11.6 | 2.7–20.4 |
| Women's accessory/specialty stores | 41.7 | 6.5 | 0.6–13.2 | 1.6–24.2 |
| Men's clothing stores | 38.5 | 5.2 | 0.9–9.8 | 1.6–15.2 |
| Children's clothing stores | 37.2 | 5.2 | 0.3–11.8 | 0.3–16.6 |

Note: The range of figures is so broad because of the many variables in retailing, such as a retailer's access to merchandise (not every manufacturer sells small quantities; some sell exclusively to one or two stores in an area; large stores and chains can have merchandise manufactured for their private labels), the price of the merchandise, rent, labor costs (1982 Department of Commerce figures show that payroll averages 13.3 percent of sales for the clothing retail industry as a whole, with the highest for men's and boy's clothing, at 15.8 percent and the lowest for women's clothing, at 12.5 percent—probably because salespeople in men's clothing stores must offer advice on big-ticket purchases).

several yearly changes in fashion. In 1983, the average person spent $670 on clothing, accessories, jewelry, and the repair, washing, and cleaning of clothing.

That's good news for clothing stores. At one time, nearly all clothing was produced at home or by a "little dressmaker" who custom-fitted family members and made up clothes according to their wishes. Today, nearly all clothing is bought ready-made, although some people do make their own or their family's clothes for reasons of self-expression or economy, and others do have their clothes custom-made.

## TRADE TALK

A "discount" store sells cheaply made merchandise at low prices; an "off-price" retailer sells at low prices merchandise that is normally higher priced, a feat managed by paying cash for its merchandise, cossetting wholesalers by avoiding inconvenient returns of merchandise, and turning down co-op advertising money.

### WHERE DO YOU BUY YOUR CLOTHES?

Because clothing is one of the basic necessities of life and because it takes up comparatively little space and doesn't go bad (even if it does become unfashionable), many, many stores and kinds of stores sell clothes. Clothing sales are a mainstay of department stores; you can also buy clothes in supermarkets, discount stores, and not from stores at all (if you're one of the millions of people who buys from catalogues—see page 146). In 1984, 27 percent of clothing was sold in specialty clothing stores and 24 percent in department stores. Nineteen percent was sold by chain stores and 16 percent in discount stores, leaving the rest to be purchased from catalogues and in off-price stores and factory outlets.

In 1984, the off-price clothing business amounted to $8.5 billion, or about 6 percent of all sales. The ten largest off-price chains (including Loehmann's, Hit or Miss, and Filenes Basement) divide 40 percent of the off-price sales.

Some stores sell a very broad range of clothing for every member of the family, while others specialize in clothing either for men,

Top Clothing and Off-Price Stores, 1986

|  | Sales ($000) | Profits ($000) | Profit:Sales (%) |
|---|---|---|---|
| The Limited, Inc. | 3,142,696 | 277,780 | 6.1 |
| The Gap, Inc. | 848,009 | 68,099 | 8.0 |
| Charming Shoppes | 521,234 | 40,469 | 7.8 |
| Merry-Go-Round | 207,483 | 7,485 | 3.6 |
| Deb Shops | 181,412 | 12,615 | 7.0 |
| Burlington Coat Factory Warehouse Corporation | 381,792 | 17,326 | 4.5 |
| Syms Corporation | 223,071 | 14,773 | 6.6 |
| Clothestime | 160,334 | 11,908 | 7.4 |
| Dress Barn | 135,828 | 9,161 | 6.7 |

(Fairchild)

# CONSUMER TIP

A "knockoff" is an imitation of a designer style (and sometimes designers knock off their own lines, producing lower-priced merchandise with less careful detailing or less expensive fabric). But there are also counterfeits of designer merchandise. These can be recognized by lower quality (it's a lot easier to buy a Christian Dior label than a Christian Dior garment) or by the fact that the label is out of focus, not properly attached, or attached in the wrong place.

Sometimes when the retailer gets second-quality garments or odd sizes or garments that didn't sell, he agrees to cut the manufacturer's or designer's name from the label so no one will know that the clothing can be purchased for less than the sacred retail price. However, federal law requires labels to carry the "R.N." or "W.P.L." number assigned to the manufacturer. Savvy shoppers can use an R.N./W.P.L. directory in a library to find out the numbers of their favorite designers and manufacturers and thus recognize designer wares if the number remains on the uncut part of the label.

"Designer" isn't always better. Although some designers insist on fine fabrics and fine workmanship and supervise every detail of the design and manufacturing processes, others cheerfully inflate profits by cutting corners in these areas. Still others license their names (allow manufacturers to use their names on goods produced by the manufacturer), a process that can involve anything from detailed supervision of design themes and quality to nothing more than cashing the checks for licensing fees. The lesson is that consumers must examine each garment to see if it'll last at least as long as the fashion does.

women, or children. There are clothing stores the size of football fields, others the size of a smallish walk-in closet, and still others that specialize in low-low-low prices or that don't sell a thing under $500. There's also a wide variety of ownership forms, including single stores that are operated by someone with a passion for fashion; chains, small and large; and franchises.

## THE BIG SUCCESSES

Probably the most successful clothing store is The Gap, Inc., a chain of clothing stores specializing in denim and other forms of casualwear for men and women. The Gap is the only clothing specialty store in *Business Week*'s Top 1000 (although several department stores deriving much of their prosperity from clothing sales are included). In April 1987, The Gap was rated as the 298th on the list, with 11,500 employees, a market value of over $2 billion, assets of $364 million, and profits of $68.1 million on sales of $848 million. That adds up to a very impressive return on invested capital of 33.6 percent and a return on common equity of 35.5 percent.

But in early 1987, The Gap was suffering, saddled with more inventory than it could move. A year later it had turned itself around, and its stock prices doubled—due in some part to the decision to deemphasize blue jeans and fill its shelves with brightly colored sportswear not unlike that of its archrival, Benetton.

The Limited, Inc. (so called because, although some of its stores are department-store sized, they're limited to selling clothing) is another retailing success story. In 1984, the chain owned more than 1,400 stores doing business under the names of The Limited, Limited Express, Pic-a-Dilly, and Lerner, with substantial catalogue sales. For 1984, the chain's net sales were $1,343,134,000.

Well, of course it didn't get to keep all of that: it paid out nearly $1 billion ($938,813,000) for goods sold, occupancy costs, and buying costs. That left $404,321,000 as gross income. More than half of that—$231,219,000—went to general, administrative, and store operation expenses. Operating income was $173,102,000. Almost $17 million went for interest expenses, but the chain had a little more than $1 million in net income that wasn't counted as operating income. The pretax income for the chain was $157,495,000, and $65 million was set aside for income taxes, leaving it a net income of $92,495,000. In other words, less than one out of every thirteen dollars actually stuck; the rest had to be devoted to some business or IRS purpose.

Things were even rosier in 1987, with sales at $3,528 billion, profits at $235.2 million, and a narrowed margin of 6.7%.

Benetton, a chain of stores imported from Italy, has been called the McDonald's of fashion. Benetton, Benetton 0-12 (for kids), and Benetton Uomo (for men) shops are springing up all over the United States: there are now over six hundred shops here, and the chain plans to own four hundred more by 1988. The empire has a total of over 4,000 stores in sixty countries. In 1986, Benetton earned $85 million in profits on $831 million sales, with a net profit margin of 10.2 percent and a sales growth rate of 20 percent. However, only 15 percent of sales were made in the United

States; to remedy that, the company is moving into manufacturing its own merchandise and developing new T-shirt styles to suit American tastes.

Gantos, Inc., is another kind of immigrant success story. The chain was started by two Lebanese immigrants over fifty years ago; today, the sixty-five Gantos stores sell $75 million worth of women's clothing, in thirty thousand SKUs. The chain's strategy is to buy from many different manufacturers, giving it more bargaining power and giving customers a wider choice of designers. Its 1986 profit margin was a very healthy 8.7 percent, and inventory turned over six times a year—in part, because the chain has its own bargain boutiques, where unsold merchandise is cleared out after sixty days on the selling floor. Gantos, unlike many other stores, makes a point of *ignoring* seasonal trends: customers can buy a winter coat or bathing suit when they want one, not when conventional merchandising wisdom says they should.

## WHERE THE STORES BUY THEIR CLOTHES

There are some six thousand textile companies in the United States, and fifteen thousand clothing makers; and, of course, a great deal of clothing (concentrated at the low-price end, and the high-price fashion and couture segment) is imported.

There are two seasons for men's clothing: lightweight spring/summer clothing and heavier fall/winter clothes. For women's clothes there are five seasons (one more than nature manages): summer, early fall, late fall/winter, resort, and spring. Clothing retailers must operate far in advance and must take enormous chances on the amount of clothing customers will buy (the October 1987 stock market crash naturally shut down the spigot) and *what* they'll buy. The designs that roll off the production lines in November are ordered in January and delivered in March; by that time, consumers may have decided that they hate chalk stripes, or miniskirts, or bright colors. If the retailers try to order something else, or even reorder successful items, they're likely to discover that the manufacturers have moved on to another season, so winter clothes, or pastels, or flower prints are not to be had for love or money.

## TRADE TALK

"Off-shore sourcing" means that the fabric is cut in the United States, then assembled in the Caribbean or somewhere else where wages are lower. It also means that the clothing can be brought back to the United States at a lower customs duty than entirely imported clothes.

And how do retailers know what to buy? Depending on their status and size, major manufacturers and innovative young designers may line up to court them, or they may have to beg that a manufacturer find a few dozen of a popular item for them. Trade shows are extremely important, and the New York Prêt (for *prêt-à-porter*—French for "ready-to-wear" not Cole Porter's younger brother) is one of the most important of all, attracting 1,400 exhibitors (mostly Europeans or less-established American names, selling medium- to high-priced women's clothes) and 28,000 buyers annually. New York City sees it as a boon: each year's Prêt fills 12,000 hotel rooms and adds $15 million to the city's economy.

## IT ALL ADDS UP

Ever wonder why clothes are so expensive? Part of it is the sheer number of middlemen involved. In 1984, *Forbes* traced the progress of a $1,350 designer coat imported from Europe. It cost the manufacturer $272 for fabric and labor and a $28 royalty to the designer; the manufacturer's overhead, taxes, and profit tacked on about $100 more. Getting the coat to the United States involved $150 in customs duties, shipping, and handling. Then the retailer added a 59 percent markup (close to $800). Markups are highest on imported merchandise, on exclusive or semiexclusive designer merchandise (because there's no price-cutting competition), and on private label merchandise. In 1988, the *New York Times* went through the same exercise for a jacket with a $400 retail price, estimating that $50 of that cost paid for the fabric; $50 for the production of the jacket, referred to in the garment business as "CMT," for "cut, measure, and trim"; and $100 paid the manufacturer's overhead. The wholesale price would be about $200, with the price at least doubling again at the retail level.

Private label merchandise is manufactured especially for a particular store. Naturally, only a large store or a chain with extensive capital has its own label. Usually, the clothing manufacturer maintains a design staff and produces merchandise that is fashion-oriented but not too radical. The retailer has more control and eliminates a middleman. No wonder private labels are so popular: Macy's, one of New York's giant department stores, makes 25 percent of its sales in private label merchandise, and the majority of The Limited's sales come from its house brand, Forenza.

As the dollar drops, imports become more expensive. In 1987, hand-knit Italian sweaters cost retailers about $100 and were usually marked up to $220. To maintain the same markup when the same sweater costs $130 in 1988, the price tag must initially read $285.

## RENT AND OTHER STUFF

If you want to convince customers that you have the lowest prices on designer clothing, you can get away with plain pipe racks and communal dressing rooms (and you can increase your profits by sprinkling a few seconds or a bit of outdated or damaged merchandise among the designer goodies, or vice versa). With a bit of luck and good marketing, you can get buyers to drive for hours to seek out your bargains.

However, if you want to maintain an image of exclusivity or appeal to office workers who pass by after payday, you need a prime retail location. That means rents of at least $25 to $30 a square foot—more like $100 a square foot, in an up-and-coming location like New York's lower Broadway—or perhaps even $250 a square foot on a truly elegant street. (A national chain might be willing to pay high, even extortionate, rent to maintain a "flagship" store on Rodeo Drive, Fifth Avenue, or other prime shopping street since the flagship serves as a kind of advertisement, even if it never manages to turn a profit.) There's no rent control for commercial enterprises, so many a successful store has paid its rent cheerfully every month from the booming profits only to find out that the rent triples or quadruples as soon as the lease is up. Exit many a successful store. (The retailing rule of thumb is that rent should not exceed 10 percent of sales. Another way to look at it is that if you can't sell ten times your rent, start printing the flyers for the Going-Out-of-Business Sale.)

The average sales per square foot for women's clothing stores are $150, although the twenty-eight-store chain The Naragansett averages $300 per square foot (as does Ralph Lauren's Madison Avenue store), and the British-owned chain of Warehouse Shops averages $500 per square foot.

A ten-store chain for "big and tall men," He-Man, averages $275 a square foot in sales. (It's been estimated that one-third of American women wear size 14 or over, and about 10 percent of men wear "big and tall" sizes—it's an $8 billion business.) Why are large-size clothes relegated to special shops, instead of being found in department and specialty stores in the same quality and quantity as smaller sizes? One reason is that manufacturers—especially manufacturers of designer merchandise—usually don't cut clothes in larger sizes; the task devolves on specialized manufacturers. A store with a chic image won't want to hang polyester pup tents next to the Lacroix originals. Although the variety of stylish and high-quality clothes in larger sizes is constantly increasing, some stores still refuse to stock these items, insisting not only that customers buy clothes far out of season but that they either diet to clothes-hanger slimness or shop elsewhere.

## MEN'S CLOTHING STORES

In many ways, the men's clothing business is quite different from its feminine counterpart. There is such a thing as men's fashion, but many men ignore it, preferring to buy a conservative business suit or two when the old ones wear out and to knock around on weekends in grubby sweaters and pants proudly saved from Army or college days. (The degree of pride seems to increase as the waistband gets harder and harder to close.) Still and all, the cash registers manage to ring to the tune of $27 billion a year for men's wear.

Retailers of men's clothes, then, know that they have to concentrate on making a few sales of expensive items to buyers who have made careful plans rather than relying on a lot of impulse sales of inexpensive fashion items that will be discarded the next season. That's one reason why mark-ups are often higher on men's clothing than on women's clothing—a markup of 108 to 122 percent over wholesale for men's clothes, as compared to 100 percent for women's, is typical. Men also expect free altera-tions on clothing (women usually just feel guilty if they don't fit the clothes rather than vice versa), so a men's clothing store usually needs an altera-tion staff or an arrangement with an outside firm that does alterations.

Men's clothing stores also face heavy competition from discounters and factory outlets. A woman might very well pay $5 more for a blouse for the convenience of shopping at her favorite store; a man is likely to throw brand loyalty to the winds at the prospect of saving $100 on a suit or overcoat. Discounting is one reason why the price of men's suits has gone up about 21 percent in the past decade while the Consumer Price Index as a whole has gone up 68 percent. A lot of men's clothing is imported (25 percent of all suits; 40 percent of wool suits) from countries with lower wages. However, trends in the late 1980s may change the relationship between men's clothing prices and inflation. A less-valuable dollar means that imports become more expensive. Besides, countries such as China and the Soviet Union are becoming more prosperous—and thus better customers for the world's supply of wool and other textiles.

How much more value do you get in a more expensive suit? You may get more hand tailoring; more expensive fabric; even more fabric—a low-price suit may use only 3.4 yards of fabric, while a top-of-the-line suit may be made from 4.2 yards. However, after a point you're paying for the designer label or the exclusive atmosphere of the store, not for the suit.

Suit sales actually declined 10.4 percent between 1985 and 1986. Retailers would have been in big, big trouble if it weren't for the boom in men's sportswear (especially sweatshirts, whose sales increased 51.2 per-cent; jean sales were up 10.2 percent, swim trunk sales were up 6.2 per-cent, and sales of knit shirts were up 14.9 percent).

## CHILDREN'S CLOTHING STORES

Oh, boy, have things changed from the days when parents picked out their kids' clothes from the Monkey Ward catalogue. Today, kids are highly, even frighteningly, fashion-conscious. Moreover, indulgent parents are often willing to spend large sums on the latest in tyke togs (like the junior baby boomer described in a September 21, 1987 *Business Week* article, who, at the age of eight months, had twenty-five jogging suits, a tuxedo, and a $90 corduroy suit for dress-up occasions). Overall sales of children's clothes are $16 billion. About $800 million goes to specialty chains for children; the rest, to department stores and single-store retailers.

It's been estimated that 3.4 million babies a year will be born in the United States through the end of the century. Sure, some of them will wear hand-me-downs and discount clothes from Kids "R" Us (seventy-two stores) or Woolworth's Kids-Mart (293 locations, with 475 more planned by 1992). But others will wear designer sportswear from Benetton (eighty 0-12 stores for kids) or Esprit (sixteen Esprit Kids stores) or Laura Ashley (six posh Mother and Child stores).

Kids' clothes, like toys, have distinct buying seasons. A third of the business is done in the third quarter, for back-to-school sales. The rest of the business tends to clump at Christmas (gifts) and Easter (new dress-up outfits for the holidays). Of course, kids are learning to be the consumers of the future. As soon as they have allowances of their own, they'll be heading down to the mall to buy the latest in teenwear.

# 37

# Shoe Stores

| | |
|---|---|
| Number of establishments: | 36,277 |
| Total receipts: | $11.27 billion |
| Average net sales: | $245,600 |
| Number of employees: | 188,700 |
| Total payroll: | $1.57 billion |

(Department of Commerce, '82)

Sigmund Freud said that shoes are a powerful sexual symbol because the shape of the foot is similar to that of the sexual organs. We can't see the similarity ourselves, but maybe he had something there: people certainly buy a lot of shoes, and there sure are a lot of shoe stores. The Department of Commerce's 1982 business census found that about a quarter of all stores selling clothing or accessories or both were shoe stores, and shoe stores earned a little less than one-fifth of the total spent on clothing and accessories.

Maybe no dark psychological factors are involved: it's just that shoes are less expensive than many other kinds of apparel (even an expensive pair of shoes costs less than a suit or dress), so buying new shoes can be a splurge, but not a ruinous one. Anyway, shoes wear out more quickly than clothing because you walk on 'em (and if you never got around to going on that diet, your shoe size changes less than your clothing size).

Opening a shoe store takes less capital than many other kinds of business because a shoe store can be minuscule and because the stock turns over so fast that the owner can start with a comparatively small stock and reorder as those pairs sell out. Theoretically, shoes are sold in pre-packaged assortments, with a fixed number of pairs of each size. (That's why Dana, who wears a size 10, finds it so hard to buy shoes: there are never enough 10s in the assortment. Other shoppers say finding narrow sizes is like . . . well, a needle in a haystack. Shoe manufacturers, please note.) However, manufacturers cater to the large stores and the chains of shoe stores, so smaller stores may find that they get an odd assortment of sizes.

Although there are large chains of shoe stores (such as Kinney Shoe Corporation and Fayva), only one shoe retailer is in *Business Week*'s Top 1000: U.S. Shoe, with 1986 sales of $2,168 billion, profits of $36 million, and assets of $1.079 billion. That adds up to a return on invested capital of 7 percent and on common equity of 7.2 percent.

## EIGHTH STREET

Eighth Street is one of the main shopping streets of Greenwich Village, and it just may be the shoe store capital of the world: the shoe stores cluster a few feet apart. Whenever there's a "shoe show" (a trade show in Manhattan), the sales reps all beat a path to Eighth Street, assured of a blizzard of orders.

We talked to the owner of one store on Eighth Street, Richard Joseph Tartaglia, of Joseph's Shoe Imports, who for thirty years has seen shoe stores come and go on Eighth Street; and to the manager of another, Steve Popolizio of Make 10. Both stores sell women's shoes. The three hundred or so styles in the tiny (750 square feet) Joseph's are imported directly from Europe, mostly from France and Italy, some from Spain and Germany. Mr. Tartaglia selects the styles himself, six or eight months before they appear in the store. In December 1988, the store was filled with extravagant pumps, eminently suitable for a glittering New Year's Eve party, and with wild, high-heeled boots, some of them thigh-high. The shoe business is somewhat seasonal, peaking before the Christmas parties and aided by the sale of winter boots (even though the leopard skin stilettos at Joseph's aren't the most practical footwear in a blizzard) and declining in the summer.

About 10 to 15 percent of Joseph's sales come from accessories (mostly sparkling rhinestone jewelry), 20 percent from handbags, and the rest, in about equal proportions, from shoes and boots.

Down the block, the much larger Make 10 store employs four full-time and three part-time employees. Its shoes, while certainly not dowdy, are less fashion-oriented than Joseph's, and there are a lot more flats. Make 10 usually buys shoes (especially fashion items) at least four months in advance, though some of the basic "bread and butter" items like plain pumps, which are always in stock at the manufacturers', can be phone-ordered on short notice. Make 10 aims at selling every last pair of shoes; if necessary, the price will be marked down if a pair has lingered more than two weeks.

The Florsheim Shoe Company's two thousand Florsheim Express stores throughout the United States will soon have the latest in technology: nearly three hundred stores already have an "interactive video network" that shows customers videos of 18,800 SKUs (combinations of size, color, and width for 428 styles of shoes). The customer makes a choice, touches the video unit, a computer transmits the order to a central warehouse, and the shoes are shipped directly to the customer. That not only saves the customer the trouble of carrying them, but also allows Florsheim's stores to sell far more shoes than they could ever stock. Customers with unusual sizes or shoe preferences don't have to wander from store to store to find a suitable pair of shoes.

That's one aspect of the future of shoe stores. As for fashion trends, Mr. Tartaglia sees the first faint signs, way in the distance, of a revival of platform shoes. We thought you'd like to know.

# 38

# Furriers

With sales of $1.65 billion, 1985 was a pretty good year for the fur business. The following year was even better, with sales approaching $2 billion—that is, it was a great year overall but a bad year in the "oil patch," where declining oil prices combined with warm weather to make fur coats seem like excessive luxuries, when previously they had seemed like a standard part of an affluent life-style. Before the crash, 1987 also looked good, but then yuppies contemplating second sables began to worry about the maintenance on their co-ops. When the stock market sneezes, the fur business catches pneumonia: about one-third of U.S. fur sales are either in New York City or within a fifty-mile radius.

Two factors one might not have thought about in connection with fur—feminism and democratization—helped fur sales. No longer were fur coats something that men bought for their wives, as a conspicuous way of showing off their own success. More and more women were buying fur coats for themselves, and more and more women earned enough to afford furs (or anyway, to qualify for credit cards with a limit high enough to charge furs). Eighty-five percent of fur sales are now made at prices under $5,000, which used to be considered chump change in the fur industry.

In addition, men were starting to buy fur coats for themselves. In 1985, men's furs added $2.4 million to furriers' coffers—15 percent of the total. However, at least half of a furrier's sales to women will be mink; men's furs are only 10 percent mink while 50 percent are "macho" long-haired furs like coyote and raccoon.

As for democratization, why envy the Carringtons and Colbys when you can dress like them? If you can't have a $100,000 sable cape, at least you can have a $500 fox jacket. And if you can't afford the prices at a "designer" furrier or at a traditional old-line furrier, you can go to a department store with a fur department (which is probably leased to a furrier rather than operated by the department store itself).

This is a fairly recent development: before the 1960s, little attempt was made to mass-market furs. Since then, many other countries (most of them in the Orient) have begun ranching furs and manufacturing fur coats. These inexpensive imports and luxury furs that can be imported now that relations with the Soviet Union have improved increase the available supply of furs; marketing and increased feelings of prosperity create the demand.

Even Sears, Roebuck, which used to be the home of the overall and the housedress, now carries fur coats as well as other fashion apparel. Discount stores such as Loehmann's and factory outlets such as Burlington Coat Factory Warehouse Corporation often carry fur.

A few furriers are publicly held companies: Evans, Inc., the Fur Vault, Inc., and Antonovich, Inc., for example. Evans is about twice as large as Fur Vault: it sells over $130 million a year. Evans leases fur departments (usually 5,000 to 6,000 square feet) in 160 stores run by thirteen department-store chains. It's also opening its own, smaller stores (say, 1,500 to 2,000 square feet) in malls, under the name of Arctic Legends, to sell affordable furs. Sales for each of these stores are projected at $800,000 to $1,200,000 a year.

The Fur Vault, famous to ad readers as the domain of Fred the Furrier, pioneered the idea of advertising furs as an enjoyable yet practical indulgence that working women can buy for themselves to celebrate a promotion or the closing of a big deal. Annual sales for the six Fur Vault stores, its ten salons operated in Bloomingdale's stores, its two outlets, and its fur department leased from Rich's in Atlanta are over $61 million. But Fur Vault, Inc., showed a loss for its fiscal year ending May 31, 1988, after 1987 profits of $4.13 million. FY 1988 sales nearly reached the $100 million level because three new stores were opened, but sales at existing operations were nearly flat.

Antonovich, Inc., sold $22 million worth of furs for the nine-month period ending December 31, 1987—almost 11 percent over 1986 levels—but lost $1.3 million after earning $832,000 the year before.

Not all furs are bought from regular furriers or department stores: many are purchased from special "weekend" sales held by retailers who hold a short-term sale in a hotel ballroom, convention arena, or even an

## CONSUMER TIP

Before you buy a fur at a weekend sale, find out if the sale is run by reputable merchants or fly-by-nighters. How long have they been in business? Where else have they held sales? Have complaints been made to local consumer protection authorities, sales tax authorities, or the Better Business Bureau? Check back issues of the "city" magazine covering your area to see if it has run stories about cheated customers. Find out where you can get your fur cleaned, stored, altered, or repaired *before* money changes hands. A number of states have "transient vendor" laws regulating the actions of out-of-state sellers. Many of these laws were passed to control sales of furniture, not furs, but they can protect you from being taken on a major purchase.

armory—any place where there's lots of room to try on furs. It costs less to rent a room for the weekend than to maintain an elegant, fully staffed fur salon year-round, so the savings can be passed on to the customers. However, these sales can also be a haven for quick-buck operators, who are conveniently unavailable when the coat needs alterations or repairs.

The fur market seems to be following a general trend: there's a lot of activity at the discount and high ends of the market. Rare furs such as sable, priced at $20,000 or even $100,000 or more, sell well; the "middle" is sagging. It's as if consumers are willing to treat a fur either as a mad extravagance and pull out all the stops or as an important purchase of a durable item (almost like a washing machine) and comparison shop, shop, shop, for the best bargain. It's less common to treat it as an ordinary clothing purchase from a conventional store.

# 39

# Fabric Stores

| | |
|---|---|
| Number of establishments: | 9,774 |
| Total receipts: | $2.49 billion |
| Average net sales: | $255,200 |
| Number of employees: | 62,600 |
| Total payroll: | $350 million |

(Department of Commerce, '82)

People who sew at home (most, but not all, of them women) do so for a variety of reasons. Some want to save money on clothes and home furnishings; others find it a relaxing hobby. Some of them can't find the clothing they want, in the quality and fit they want, unless they sew it themselves. You'd think that the increasing number of married women who have paid jobs would cut down on home sewing by both increasing family income and decreasing the time available for sewing, but the 126 stores surveyed by *Sew Business* (September 1987), the industry's trade magazine, projected that 1987 sales would increase 6.4 percent over 1986 levels.

On the average, fabric stores each grossed close to $250,000. But bolts of fabric, sewing machines, and other goods take up a lot of space, so average sales per square foot for 1986 were $100.79—a pretty common

**Where the Money Came From**

| | |
|---|---|
| (1) Clothing fabrics: | 33.7% |
| (2) Sewing notions (thread, zippers, etc.): | 15.2% |
| (3) Sewing machines: | 9.3% |
| (4) Fabrics for home decorating: | 7.1% |
| (5) Sewing patterns: | 5.9% |
| (6) Trimmings and lace: | 5.0% |
| (7) Linings, interfacing: | 4.4% |
| (8) Other (supplies for quilting, other needlework, crafts, etc.): | 19.4% |

*(Sew Business, '86)*

level for retail stores as a whole. However, almost one-third (30.8 percent) of the stores had sales between $50,000 to $99,999; one-fifth (20.6 percent) had sales of more than $300,000. The western states were the best place for fabric stores, with average sales more than double that for stores in the North Central states.

Stores spent at least half of their gross sales on the cost of goods sold (not counting freight). Costs were lowest in the South and West (about 50 percent of sales) and highest in the Northeast (56.3 percent), which is tough because average sales per square foot were quite a bit lower in the high-cost Northeast than in the low-cost West. The average sale per customer was about $20.00, but here the Northeast starred, with average sales of $26.76, as compared to average sales in the West of $12.73. Obviously, then, the stores in the West triumph because they have more paying customers and lower costs.

The stores surveyed by *Sew Business,* like those in the Department of Commerce study, paid about 10 percent of sales for salaries and commissions for personnel (about half the stores had one full-time employee year-round—probably the store's owner; about a quarter of the stores also had a part-timer on staff), and rent was the third-biggest expense, at an average of 8.7 percent of sales. The average fabric store in the survey had 2,250 square feet of selling space.

Fabric store sales are not very seasonal, but some patterns are observable: October is the best month, with 11.1 percent of sales, and summer the slowest time.

Speaking of patterns, many stores find it inconvenient to carry certain brands of sewing patterns. Sewing patterns, like books and records, can be returned to the distributor for credit. In a way, this benefits the retailer, who can place a larger order, knowing that unsold merchandise can be returned; in a way, it's a nuisance because there's a lot of bookkeeping involved. Some lines of sewing patterns are highly fashion-oriented, so there are many returns to be handled when a particular pattern goes out of style. Sometimes fabric stores find it hard to get credit for returned patterns. There's also a lot of competition in pattern sales: these items have traditionally been sold in five-and-dime and discount stores. Patterns are nearly always sold at list price, but a customer won't even enter a fabric store to buy a pattern or a spool of thread if she thinks the fabric store is too pricey.

Discounters also create problems for fabric sales by offering yardage at low prices. Fabric stores can overcome the problem by offering couture or other specialty fabrics or by providing knowledgeable salespeople and such services as classes in sewing or needlework.

# 40

# Furniture Stores

| | |
|---|---|
| Number of establishments: | 24,837 |
| Total receipts: | $17.22 billion |
| Average net sales: | $693,400 |
| Number of employees: | 213,800 |
| Total payroll: | $2.607 billion |

(Department of Commerce, '82)

There's a distinct class system in operation in the furniture business. Some furniture stores will do practically anything to get you in off the street—offer "easy credit terms" (sometimes a misnomer for high interest rates and crummy furniture at inflated prices) and balloons for the kiddies, or run huge newspaper ads and a constant blare of commercials on the radio and late-night TV. Some furniture salespeople are salaried, and payroll represents a fairly high percentage—15.1 percent—of furniture store sales, according to the Department of Commerce's 1982 survey. Other salespeople get much of their income from commissions, which gives them an incentive to make a hard sell or even to misrepresent the quality of the furniture or the terms of sale.

You might think of department store furniture departments as the

**Where the Money Goes (Furniture and Home Furnishings Stores)**

| | |
|---|---|
| (1) Cost of operations: | 62.9% |
| (2) Officers' compensation: | 3.3% |
| (3) Pensions and benefits: | 0.7% |
| (4) Rent: | 3.2% |
| (5) Repairs: | 0.4% |
| (6) Depreciation, depletion, amortization: | 1.2% |
| (7) Interest: | 1.1% |
| (8) Bad debts: | 0.4% |
| (9) Advertising: | 4.1% |
| (10) State, local taxes: | 2.2% |
| (11) Other expenses: | 18.3% |
| (12) Net profit before tax: | 2.2% |

(Troy, '84–'85)

industry's solid middle class—perhaps a bit stodgy but likely to be honest and respectable. Department stores, however, are shifting out of the furniture business for the same reasons they're shifting out of the appliance business: the inventory is large, heavy, and expensive and ties up a lot of floor space and capital until it's sold.

There are also furniture specialty stores in the middle of the market. For instance, British-owned Conran's, which had fifteen U.S. stores at the beginning of 1987 with three more planned, took in $60 million a year by selling 6,000 SKUs of furniture, housewares, and kitchen accessories. Its moderately priced products with a modern (but not radical) design sensibility are marketed to appeal to young singles and families; it fits into about the same market niche as its rival, The Workbench, Inc., which had thirty-six corporate-owned and twenty-seven franchised stores in 1987. Scandinavian Design's seventy stores ring the registers to the tune of $100 million a year. Seaman's Furniture Corporation, Inc. (primarily furniture, not housewares; mostly traditional designs) sold almost $230 million worth of furniture in 1986 but suffered a sales decline in the first quarter of 1987.

Pier 1 Imports, Inc., once a prime source of camel saddles and Indian print bedspreads for hippie households, has yupped up its image while increasing the number of its stores (from 240 in 1983 to 350 in thirty-seven states in 1987), its sales (from $130 million in 1983 to over $250 million in 1987), and its gross margin (from 52.5 percent in 1983 to 57.3 percent in 1987). Pier 1 still sells candles and incense, but they're tucked away in the back of the store; the focus now is on better furniture, much of it imported from the sixty countries where Pier 1 does business.

The 1987 Dun & Bradstreet survey shows that gross profit averaged 38.1 percent of net sales. The net profit after tax averaged 4.8 percent (a better result than most department stores can achieve and far higher than most supermarket profits, but not as good as top clothing specialty stores).

## TO THE TRADE

The *really* classy furniture stores actually try to keep you *out;* they're devoted to selling furniture to the trade (that is, to decorators and designers). The professionals pay the net, or wholesale, price, which is usually 40 percent below the list price; then they resell the furniture to their customers for the list price. This makes up all, or a major part of, their compensation for the design job.

Frequently, these elegant showrooms specialize in "contract" work (furniture for corporate offices) or "custom" work ("COM" is trade-talk for "customer's own material," or custom-upholstery instead of ready-to-go furniture). Either you'll have to rely on your decorator to pick out and buy the furniture for you, or you'll need a decorator or designer as a chaperone to enter a store or showroom that claims to be limited to the trade only.

A design center or "mart" is a collection of showrooms maintained by various furniture manufacturers. You *may* be able to get in on your own if you have a sales tax "resale" number, a business card that belongs or could belong to a designer, or simply the divine self-confidence to sail in uninvited.

Maybe you can find a designer who'll buy the furniture for you, charging a commission for the trouble (usually 10 percent over the net, or designer's price).

## CONSUMER TIP

If you do make it into a trade showroom only to find that the price tags are written in code, try this code key: subtract five from the first number and ten from the second, then add the two resulting numbers. The net price of an item marked 405-35, for instance, would be $425.

**CONSUMER TIP**

If you have a certain amount of patience and can shop from catalogues, consider the discount operations working out of High Point, North Carolina (where much of America's furniture is built). Large public libraries often have out-of-state telephone directories on microfiche: see if anything in the North Carolina Yellow Pages strikes your fancy, then call or write for a catalogue.

### FURNITURE FRANCHISE FUMBLE

Maybe as a result of the trend toward greater elegance, formality, and conservatism of taste, Naked Furniture, an unpainted-furniture franchise, went into bankruptcy in January 1984. The chain was purchased by General Home Furnishings, Inc., with a view to a turnaround; but GHF closed down seventeen of the fifty-nine stores and added only seven new ones. However, the stores are now better looking, the salespeople are better trained, and the average monthly sales for the surviving stores are $35,000 (as compared to $21,000 before the takeover). The stores earn a total of $20.1 million a year, yielding franchise fees of only $725,000 for GHF in 1987, which has to spend a lot on overhead and refurbishing the stores' image. GHF plans to sell about ten more franchises a year. If you think you'd like one, it'll cost you about $100,000 to $150,000 to see if you can buck the trend.

For a while in the 1960s, it looked like the trend was for kicky, kinky, disposable furniture. Today, it seems clear that solid, stable, perhaps antique, furniture is here to stay. In 1986, the furniture industry achieved an overall growth rate of 10 percent—about twice the growth rate of retailing in general. The newest trend may be for custom mini-furniture, sold by condo developers along with the condo because conventional furniture won't fit into tiny urban apartments.

# 41

# Carpet Stores

| | |
|---|---|
| Number of establishments: | 11,125 |
| Total receipts: | $5.01 billion |
| Average net sales: | $447,200 |
| Number of employees: | 53,600 |
| Total payroll: | $721,300,000 |

(Department of Commerce, '82)

In a pioneer's austere cabin, a handmade braided rug or hooked rug on the dirt floor may have been the first item of comfort and decoration, the first item that was not strictly utilitarian. In a modern tract house, it's likely that all the rooms except the kitchen and bathroom (and maybe even those) will have wall-to-wall carpeting because it's easier and cheaper to put down a subfloor of inexpensive chipboard or hardboard, then carpet over it. In the kinds of houses or apartments featured in a decorating magazine, it's likely that the floors will be hardwood or parquet, only partially covered with luxurious rugs—probably museum-quality Orientals or reproductions of rugs designed by great twentieth-century designers.

Wall-to-wall carpeting is a nineteenth-century development. Earlier than that, there weren't enough people who could afford such fripperies—

179

and there weren't looms that could weave carpet wide enough. (That's why carpeting is often called "broadloom": a small room can be covered with a single width of carpeting; there may be seams in a larger room.) The mid-1980s saw the introduction of a new, antistatic nylon carpeting that repels stains—even red wine and coffee. (Sorry, puppy misbehavior is still likely to stain the carpet permanently.) This carpeting was so popular that it spurred a six percent increase in carpet production in 1986.

Except for factory outlets, carpet stores don't make their own carpets; they buy them from mills. Don't be confused by the common practice of labelling the carpet with the store's name instead of the mill's; this is done to make it tougher for you to comparison shop by brand. As a result, if you're a dedicated consumer, you can get comparative price quotes for high-quality, 100 percent nylon stain-proof carpet, but it'll be hard to compare prices on Du Pont's Stainmaster.

The price the store quotes depends on how good a deal it can get from the mill. That explains why many huge carpet discount stores depend on volume purchasing and compete based on price. Depending on their marketing strategies, they may have a very wide selection, or they may stock only the most popular lines. However, department stores that sell carpet often have in-store decorators, who can give you advice about choosing carpet to match your decorating scheme; and smaller carpet stores may have access to the highest quality, most exclusive designs that don't attract enough customers to interest a discounter or department store.

For instance, New York's ABC Carpet Company has more than 150,000 square feet of selling space for broadloom and rugs—enough to display entire rolls of carpet, not just samples—and a 100,000 square foot warehouse so it can offer speedy delivery. It sells more than $85 million worth of the 5,000 varieties of carpet and 5,000 varieties of rug it stocks; it also designs and develops 10 percent of its rugs and 30 percent of its broadloom. ABC spent $1.5 million on ads in 1986, which is lower than the average for the industry, but ABC wants to phase out its advertising and depend on word-of-mouth. ABC also sells 95 percent of its rugs and carpets on a cash-and-carry basis, which is unusual; Rich's, Inc., a chain of nineteen stores owned by Federated Department Stores and based in Atlanta, makes 90 percent of its sales of fine area rugs (usually $400 to $1,200 apiece) on credit.

According to the Retail Floor Covering Institute, the average that Americans spent on carpeting in 1987 was $19.99 a square yard, including padding and installation. Because the cost of installation and padding usually adds about $10 per square yard to the price tag, the Institute's figure suggests some very inexpensive carpets are popular. Olefin indoor-outdoor carpets can be as inexpensive as $2 per square yard while wool carpeting can easily cost more than $100 per square yard, so obviously the market is concentrated at the low-price end.

## CONSUMER TIP

▶ Does the store offer shop-at-home service, so that a sales-person will bring carpet samples to your home where you can see them with your own furniture and lighting? (Shop-at-home service is convenient, but watch out for high-pressure sales-manship.) If not, can you rent or borrow samples and keep them for a long enough time to make a realistic judgment?

▶ How long will it take to get your carpet delivered after you order? Does the store make appointments for the carpeting to be installed by its own personnel, or does it hire an outside service (which may be less reliable and hard to contact if the installers don't show up)?

▶ A good carpet passes the "grin test": bend the carpet sample, with the pile facing up. A good carpet will show hardly any of the backing; an inferior carpet will "grin" widely.

▶ When you order, ask for a sample swatch so you can make sure the carpet actually delivered matches your order.

Most carpet stores mark up their wares by about 40 percent, which includes 28 percent for operating expenses such as salaries and another 5 to 6 percent for advertising. Sears achieves a higher markup, of 60 to 65 percent.

Dun & Bradstreet's 1987 survey of 2,280 carpet stores showed that the average gross profit was only 30.7 percent of sales (as you've seen throughout this book, many sectors achieve much higher gross profits). Still, net profit after tax was 5.7 percent, which isn't too bad comparatively. Return on sales ranged from 1.6 to 9.9 percent, and return on assets ranged from 4.1 to 24.9 percent. The fact that return on assets was higher shows that carpet stores had quite high sales in comparison to assets: that is, they turned over their inventory frequently instead of buying and holding inventory.

# Discount Stores

| | |
|---|---|
| Number of establishments: | 10,989 (variety stores—e.g., Woolworth's) |
| Total receipts: | $8 billion |
| Average net sales: | $736,200 |
| Number of employees: | 160,500 |
| Total payroll: | $1.08 billion |
| | (Department of Commerce, '82) |

There's only one reason why a merchant would want to cut prices: to increase the volume of sales. There are several ways to do this and still earn a profit. The retailer can sell low-quality merchandise that's designed to sell for low prices. If the retailer chooses this option, his margins are not necessarily lower than for better-quality goods and can even be higher. For example, if you buy something for $1 and sell it for $5, your margin is higher than if you buy something for $200 and sell it for $500.

Another approach is for the retailer to become a supershopper, finding odds and ends of merchandise (some of it of superior quality) available for some reason at low cost. Maybe only a few odd colors and sizes are available; maybe the stuff was so fashionable that buyers are just catching up with it. Maybe the merchandise was manufactured for a store that went out of business, or is saleable but doesn't meet the needs of the store that originally ordered it. Sometimes the items are intended for the "gray market," that is, they are designed to be sold outside the United States and imported without the consent (and warranty protection) of the manufacturer. The discounter can also get prices down to rock-bottom by cutting costs: building a forbidding-looking store with plain pipe racks, locating it in no-place-much, and expecting the customers to select their own merchandise (and perhaps even to pack it).

## TWO SECTORS OF THE DISCOUNT MARKET

The discount stores of the past—the Woolworth's, W. T. Grant's, or Lamston's—sold a wide range of low-priced merchandise, with its central core of always available merchandise augmented by seasonal changes in the rest of the stock. For instance, you could always count on finding a pair of socks, as well as Christmas decorations in November and barbecue grills in June.

The newer "job lot" or "odd lot" stores buy closeouts (items that are no longer being manufactured), merchandise from bankrupt stores, fire-sale merchandise, and other odds and ends—anything from a slightly bent screwdriver to a four-slice toaster to a Christian Dior dress. (Sometimes it's a slightly toasted Christian Dior dress, if it comes from a fire sale.) Much of the merchandise is undamaged, but everything must be examined carefully before purchase. It's hard to generalize about margins and markups in this sector: sometimes the merchant is willing to earn a lower profit in exchange for higher volume. Sometimes the markup is equal to or greater than normal retail markups, but prices can be lower because the discounter passes along savings in rent, decoration, payroll, and cost of goods sold.

Because so many discount stores depend on low prices for bulk orders, chain stores dominate the discount industry. However, they don't control the entire field. There are many neighborhood *schlock* (Yiddish for "junk") stores that offer a start-up retailer a toehold. It costs comparatively little to start up a business where low rent, bare-bones store design, and cheap merchandise are expected.

Discounting is big business. Wal-Mart Stores, Inc., a discount department chain in twenty-three states concentrated in the Sun Belt, is rated as #14 on *Business Week*'s Top 1000 corporations list. In 1987, it had sales of nearly $16 billion, making it the largest retailer in the United States with profits of $627 million and assets of $5.93 billion. Wal-Mart also owns a wholesale club (see page 154) and is beginning to introduce European-style "hypermarkets" to the U.S. retail scene. Things must be pretty good because Sam Walton, who created Wal-Mart, is (according to *Forbes* magazine) the richest person in America, with a net worth of $4.5 billion as of June 1987.

Two other discount retailers made the Top 1000: J. C. Penney Company, Inc., and K Mart Corporation (reborn from the sagging Kresge's chain in 1977) which is now the #2 retailer in the country and powerful enough to give once-invulnerable retailer Sears a bad case of heartburn. K Mart also owns Waldenbooks, Pay Less Drugstores, and a number of specialty stores. Let's take a look at the numbers:

|  | Wal-Mart (#14)* | K Mart (#54) | J. C. Penney (#60) |
|---|---|---|---|
| Sales | $15.95 billion | $25.95 billion | $15.33 billion |
| Profits | $727.6 million | $692 million | $608 million |
| Profit margin | 3.9% | 2.7% | 4% |
| Return on invested capital | 22.6% | 12.9% | 12.1% |
| Return on common equity | 31.0% | 16.4% | 15% |

**#s refer to placement on *Business Week*'s Top 1000 listing for the year 1987.

For more than twenty years, K Mart has been the scene of one of the more dramatic innovations in American retailing: the blue-light sale. For anywhere from five to fifteen minutes, while the blue light flashes, up to thirty times a day, shoppers grab for the special-sale merchandise and take it to the cashier to be retagged. K Mart makes sure that the specials are both totable and inexpensive enough to be purchased on impulse and also that shoppers must pass through parts of the store where business is slow in order to pick up the sale items.

Woolworth's continues to operate the traditional, red-fronted five-and-tens, but it's the specialty stores (such as Kinney Shoes) that are the real million-dollar babies. Woolworth's earns an operating profit of 5.1 percent from its variety stores, and a handsome 10.5 percent from specialty stores. Its CEO, John W. Lynn, was the third best-paid retailer in 1986.

Unlike many retailers, Woolworth's needn't worry very much about rent increases or the possibility of being closed down by a greedy landlord. Woolworth's doesn't literally own the sites of its stores, but in many cases it might as well: many of the stores have ten- or even twenty-year leases, with options to renew for thirty or fifty years more, which were negotiated when Woolworth's was one of a small group of leading retailers in the country.

Let's take a closer look at business dollars for one corporation—Pic-n-Save, which in 1984 had ninety retail stores in the Southwest that specialized in closeout merchandise. In that year, net sales were $235,147,000. Cost of sales was $108,954,000 (in other words, about half the income gone right there), and store expenses were over $40 million. Warehouse and administrative expenses came to approximately $13.5 million more, which left pretax earnings of $72,281,000. Pic-n-Save paid nearly $36 million in income taxes, leaving it a net after-tax income of just about $36.5 million.

## FACTORY OUTLETS AND OFF-PRICE MALLS

Sometimes a manufacturer is unwilling to go through the hassles of full-scale retailing but is willing to risk the wrath of the retailers who buy its products by operating an outlet store, selling seconds or excess merchandise in order to add a few dollars to the company coffers without too much expense.

The typical factory outlet store is a decidedly no-frills operation in a decidedly low-rent area. More and more, it is found in an off-price mall, amid other factory outlets. That way, bargain hunters can make a day (or even a vacation) of shopping. In fact, one off-price mall even has a hotel for those who need more than a day to do the grand tour. Off-price malls can have more than a million square feet and more than 200 shops to attract the eager buyer.

## CLOSEOUTS AND ODD LOTS

But for the true lover of bargains—and serendipity—nothing will do but an odd-lot store. Probably the king of the closeout is Consolidated Stores Corporation, which is centered in Columbus, Ohio, and operates more than 220 stores in small and smallish cities in twelve southern and midwestern states. The stores themselves are fairly sizeable—between 15,000 and 35,000 square feet—and sales are a very decent $140 per square foot, on the average. The favored location for a Consolidated store is a strip mall, and since its stores contribute so much money to the mall through the fee based on monthly percentage of sales, Consolidated can negotiate very low base rents; sometimes it manages to knock rents down to $1 per square foot.

Eighty percent of Consolidated's merchandise consists of hard goods—small appliances, for instance; nearly all its inventory is a one-time closeout of merchandise that, for some reason, the manufacturer wants kept out of ordinary retailing channels. Consolidated's gross margin is about 40 to 42 percent, so its buyers must find items that can be bought for about half the price it will sell for in the store.

The chain has a huge warehouse (2 million square feet), a 420,000-

square-foot distribution center, and four smaller, but still sizeable, 150,000-square-foot distribution centers. Consolidated "pushes" the merchandise into its stores, so the managers of individual stores have very little control over what they sell.

At last we come to a small chain that's one of Dana's very favorite stores in the whole world: New York's Odd-Job. (Its insignia is a little bowler, like the derby hat worn by Odd-Job in the James Bond movies, and three of its employees do nothing but write prices and merchandise descriptions on tiny pasteboard bowler-shaped posters.) Odd-Job buys (and, with a bit of luck, sells) things that are out of season (Christmas decorations in January), the wrong color (my dear, fuchsia is no longer worn), or even things that were enormous sellers and manufactured in even more enormous quantities. The Odd-Job chain includes three New York City stores and eleven stores in two other states, with total sales for 1987 estimated at $70 million. The chain claims that its inventory turns over a dozen times a year. But even Odd-Job has its failures: the paperback biography of Harry Truman, for instance, reduced from $4.95 to twenty-nine cents . . . and still unsaleable. (In that case, the merchandise is given to charity.)

If you want elegance, carpeting, complementary coffee in a bone china cup, or the gracious attention of a well-informed salesperson, you'd better turn around and go home. But if you want the unexpected, the deeply discounted, and, sometimes, the frankly awful (like the panty hose Dana's mom bought that turned out to have one leg per pair), climb on the bus heading to the nearest outlet mall or discount store—and watch for the blue light.

# 43

# Appliance Stores

| | |
|---|---|
| Number of establishments: | 10,582 |
| Total receipts: | $5.7 billion |
| Average net sales: | $540,400 |
| Number of employees: | 59,300 |
| Total payroll: | $696,000,000 |

(Department of Commerce, '82)

Where did you buy your toaster (if you didn't get it free from the bank when you bought a Certificate of Deposit)? There's a very good chance that you got it at a department store or an appliance/electronics super-store that can cut prices because it does such a high volume of business (and, of course, does a high volume of business because it can cut prices). That makes life awfully tough for the neighborhood appliance store, which is becoming an endangered species.

The neighborhood store has to pay rent and maintain an inventory of expensive gadgets, some of which (refrigerators and washing machines, for instance) take up a lot of floor and warehouse space. Although the problem of moving merchandise isn't as acute as in a produce store—a rotten banana is a write-off but an unsold microwave oven can always be sold to a company that buys odd lots of merchandise—the manufacturers constantly introduce new models, so customers may turn their noses up at the older ones unless they get a generous discount.

Take microwave ovens as an example. Only 25 percent are sold by appliance/television dealers while the rest are sold by assorted competitors: 7 percent are sold by superstores; 18 percent, by Sears; 8 percent, by other department stores; 10 percent, by discounters; 5 percent, by catalog showrooms; and 4 percent each, by K Mart and J. C. Penney.

Sometimes an appliance retailer starts small: the Florida chain of Kaufman & Roberts, with thirty-six stores (some superstores of up to 15,000 square feet), began with $30,000 in start-up capital ($10,000 in savings, the rest in loans) and one 5,000-square-foot store—but that store generated close to $900,000 in first-year sales. Sales for the chain in 1986 were over $100 million and were about evenly divided between appliances and electronics. There's no Kaufman or Roberts on board; the names were picked from the phone book by the real owners, Jose and Irela Saumat, to show that the store appeals to all ethnic groups.

Kaufman and Roberts' marketing efforts include more than $11 million worth of advertising (three-quarters of it in newspapers) in both Spanish and English. Courteous yet implacable salespeople close a sale with 60 to 70 percent of the customers who enter the store.

When they buy appliances from manufacturers, small stores and chains make different demands. The small stores want longer to pay; the "power retailers" are interested in bigger and bigger discounts. To a certain extent, small stores can exercise the clout of large ones by joining together in buying groups.

The market for standard appliances such as refrigerators is somewhat saturated. However, there's a strong market for more sophisticated washing machines and dryers and for kitchen equipment that either saves time and trouble or fits in with the yuppie interest in haute cuisine as a hobby. The combination of appliances and consumer electronics should also be a strong one: after all, many of the same manufacturers produce both kinds of goods, and it's hard to draw a hard-and-fast line between electronic items and home appliances, especially as appliances get "smarter" thanks to more sophisticated microchip "brains."

According to the 1986 Dun & Bradstreet survey of 1,376 "household appliance stores," gross profit was a little lower than average, at 30.7 percent of net sales; gross profit after tax was about average, at 5.3 percent of net sales. The stores surveyed ranged in their return on sales from 1.1 to 8.8 percent (that is, you have to sell somewhere between $12 and $100 worth of merchandise to keep a dollar) and in return on assets from 2.8 to 16.8 percent. The fact that return on assets is higher than return on sales shows that the stores turn over their inventory rapidly.

Not every marketing technique that lures customers turns out to be

## TRADE TALK

"Floor planning," the usual way of financing purchases from manufacturers, includes ninety free days before interest starts running on the store's purchases of inventory. Finance companies (often run by the manufacturers) set up a payment schedule: unless the retailer pays in full within ninety days, interest is charged at the "extension rate." Usually, retailers prefer to make payments on a monthly schedule instead of paying for each item when a customer purchases it.

Although ninety days is the standard free ride period, it can be extended to 120 days if the manufacturer offers a longer period as an incentive to buy certain models. To a certain extent, appliance stores (like all businesses using a lot of credit) are speculating on the movements of the prime interest rate. The interest rate on merchandise purchased through floor planning is usually a point or so above prime, so an increase in the prime rate can tweak away much of the retailer's profit margin, even if sales are good.

a success. In 1986, a discount appliance chain called Silo took its name a little too seriously, and advertised a stereo costing a mere "249 bananas." About four hundred customers took the commercial a little too seriously and demanded to swap fruit for components. The store complied, losing over $10,000 on the deal. History does not record what they did with the bananas—either the stores developed a sideline in wholesale produce or gave away bananas with every purchase, or their personnel made a lot of banana bread.

# 44

# Electronics Stores

| | |
|---|---|
| Number of establishments: | 19,462 ("radio and TV stores") |
| Total receipts: | $9.76 billion |
| Average net sales: | $501,700 |
| Number of employees: | 92,800 |
| Total payroll: | $1.175 billion |
| | (Department of Commerce, '82) |

Although the similarities are a little obscure at first sight, running an electronics store is a lot like running a liquor store. In either case, you're selling a product that people may *want* a lot but don't really need for survival; you have to keep a lot of expensive inventory on hand, so you need a lot of storage space or a separate warehouse; and many buyers know exactly which brand-name product they want, so you'd better be prepared to compete either by offering the best selection, by offering low-price alternatives to the name brands, or by cutting prices on the national brands. (But the image most people have of liquor stores is more sedate than their idea of electronics stores, with their strident ads and insistence that they can beat any price, however low, offered by the competition.)

| | |
|---|---|
| CIRCUIT CITY STORES, INC. | |
| Alan Wurtzel, chairman | $402,502 |
| Richard Sharp, president/CEO | $241,102 |
| THE GOOD GUYS! INC. | |
| Ronald Unkefer, chairman | $391,667, voluntarily reduced to $250,000 |
| NEWMARK & LEWIS, INC. | |
| Richard D. Lewis, president and treasurer | $375,858 |
| Warren G. Hyman, chairman and secretary | $365,728 |

But electronic goods are durable goods. After all, people drink up the Scotch and buy a new bottle, but once people have a TV, they may not buy another one for years. No matter how amazing the improvements in consumer electronics products (and they have been sensational), some consumers will simply hang on to their old phonographs instead of buying CD players, will resist buying home computers, and will happily watch twelve-inch black-and-white TVs even though forty-one-inch color sets with Dolby sound are available.

A "mature market" is the business term used when just about every potential buyer has one of the item whose market is being analyzed. That's what happened to VCRs and CD players, the electronics industry's last two really big innovative products for the home market. Factory sales (sales from manufacturers to distributors and retailers) went up 18 percent from 1984 to 1985 and another 14 percent in 1986, but they were just about level in 1987, with a 2 percent increase over 1986.

## STORAGE

For electronics stores, the problem of storage is especially acute, since TV sets, VCRs, turntables, and the like come packed in cartons about the size of Central America. In big cities and affluent suburbs, where rents are highest, customers also demand the widest range of merchandise, so it's difficult or impossible to cut back on storage space.

The effect of these factors is to make survival easier for chains and franchises than for single stores. So much capital must be tied up in inventory and paid out in rent, and price competition can be so vicious, that the single store is at a great competitive disadvantage.

Of course, not every chain survives, either. In early 1987, Stereo Village, an Atlanta-based chain of twenty-five stores, filed for Chapter 11 protection after nine years of operation. The chain lost $1.2 million for its quarter ending September 30, 1986; the losses were blamed on weak internal corporate controls on spending and on overly generous promotions that may have increased sales but that definitely cut into gross margin. In the spring of the same year, the six-store chain Luskin's, Inc., in Florida did the same. CMC Electronics, Inc. (St. Louis) is a more recent casualty.

In the mid-1980s, it looked as if even electronics chains would be swept away by gigantic (30,000 square foot) superstores. But superstores became like brontosauruses: huge, unwieldy, and fighting to the death for territory. Only one chain—Circuit City Stores—really did well with superstores. Newmark & Lewis, Best Buy, Fretter, Federated Group, and Crazy Eddie all either had disappointing results or lost money on their superstores.

## STAYING SECURE

Electronics retailers must also resolve tremendous security problems. There usually isn't much cash in the register, so stickups aren't too big of a problem. Shoplifting is fairly easily controlled by keeping only a single sample on display (attached to the shelf with a cable) and by fetching the actual merchandise to be sold from the stockroom. Small items, like blank videotapes ($913,686,000 worth sold in 1984—goodness knows how many stolen), can be kept behind the cash register where the clerk can keep an eye on them.

The real threats are burglary (if burglars can make money stealing cassette recorders from people's houses, they can certainly make money boosting brand-new ones from stores), employee theft, truck drivers who let a few units "fall off the truck" in each delivery, and employees at the manufacturer who earn a little extra by selling the contents of cartons and then shipping out empty boxes filled with newspaper.

## FOREIGN AFFAIRS

Electronics retailers are particularly subject to the delicate trade relationship between Japan and the United States. Nearly all consumer electronics are imported, mostly from Japan, and many from Korea. A stronger yen and weaker dollar mean higher prices, which can depress sales.

For many retailers, the last five years have been gorgeous ones (with an annual sales growth of 10 percent or more)—thanks, in large part, to sales of Japanese-made VCRs. But today, with this market having matured, the Electronic Industries Association (EIA) expects that 1988 sales will be only 5 percent above 1987 levels (expected to be about $30.04 billion overall—with more than $5 billion coming from VCRs).

The EIA projected 1987 sales like this: $13.3 billion for video products—about half of that in color television sets with an average price of $333; $5.4 billion in VCRs, averaging $315 apiece; $1.6 billion in video "camcorders" (cameras compatible with VCRs) at an average price of $1,000.

The audio segment of the market was projected to be $7.4 billion, with portable, separate, and system players each commanding 19 percent of audio sales; CD players were expected to bring in $420 million. The biggest part of the audio market comes from car stereos and tape players ($2.8 billion, or 37 percent of the audio market), maybe because these get stolen so often that every car owner is a continuing market.

Consumers were expected to spend $4.57 billion on information and communication products: most of that will be for home computers ($2.9 billion), the rest for telephones ($705 million for the kind with the cords, $310 million for cordless), and about $400 million on answering machines.

## PRICE-CUTTING PROBLEMS

Where will we buy these items? It's less and less likely that we'll go to department stores, which have difficulty matching discounters' prices and meeting inventory requirements. It's also less and less likely that there'll even be a mom-and-pop store for us to visit, for the reasons detailed above. Probably we'll end up at a chain store or at one of the surviving superstores that's low on both prices and amenities. It's also likely that the store will sell both consumer electronics and major appliances such as refrigerators and dishwashers, with a probable division of about 80 percent consumer electronics and 20 percent appliances.

This pattern holds for Circuit City Stores, which has seventy-one stores in eleven states, Highland Superstores, with fifty-three locations in the Midwest and West, and Audio/Video Affiliates, Inc., with seventy-eight stores in fifteen states. However, the thirty-four Crazy Eddie stores on the Eastern seaboard sell only consumer electronics; so do the eighty-four Mid-Atlantic Wall to Wall Sound & Video stores, and the fourteen The Goods Guys! stores in and near San Francisco.

But even the deepest discounters are crying the blues now (or playing the blues on CD players). To stay competitive, they must continually open new stores (with correspondingly high costs of equipping the new location, advertising its presence, and probably throwing a super-duper sale to celebrate). They must also get involved in price wars, offering rock-bottom prices and claiming they can beat the competitors' prices time after time.

The end result can be high sales: Newmark & Lewis, for instance, with thirty-five stores in New York and Connecticut, had 1986 net sales of

$141,559,934, but its net income was only $3,811,291. By 1987, it had expanded to forty-four stores and sales were up thirty percent—but net income was down a catastrophic 93 percent. Florida's Sound Advice, Inc., sold more than $18 million worth in its fourteen stores in the last six months of 1986, but managed net income of less than $1 million.

After a while, price cutting simply becomes suicidal. Electronics chains are experimenting with other ways to compete: better training for sales personnel, for instance, or extended warranties and service contracts customers can buy for a fee. (Fundamentally, warranty service is the responsibility of the manufacturer, but for their own and the customers' convenience, manufacturers often contract with major dealers to handle service through retail stores. Availability of repairs and extended warranties are factors in choosing where to buy big-ticket items.) The key to success in selling twenty-first-century products could be old-fashioned service.

In April 1988, *Forbes* magazine profiled Circuit City, finding that good store design and efficient management contribute heavily to the chain's success. Customers entering the stores usually see both well-stocked warehouse-style shelves (hinting at large supplies of discounted merchandise) and a visible service department (reassuring customers that repairs are readily available). The most popular items (TVs and VCRs) are located toward the back of the store, so customers must pass a display of stereo components. On the way to the cash registers, the customer must pass large home appliances like refrigerators and washers and dryers; impulse items like blank tapes for the new VCR are right near the register. This layout resembles that of a supermarket, where customers have to pass the meat and frozen foods to get bread and milk, and where the checkout counter gives them a last chance for impulse magazine and snack purchases.

# 45

# Computers and Software

(Sorry, no statistics: the home-computer industry is too new for the Department of Commerce to have analyzed it yet.)

In the early 1980s, it was confidently predicted that paper would vanish from our offices and that every household would have its computer (or computers). As we all know, there still is *plenty* of paper in offices. As for home computers, well, computer games went out of fashion, and no one in his or her right mind would use a home computer to organize the recipe file (a boneheaded idea regularly mentioned as a great reason to buy a computer). But there's still a legitimate need for kids' computers for homework and personal exploration of computing; and many people use computers at home in their own businesses or as part of a job outside the home.

In short, not that many people need home computers, although many people want them. The problem is that this is a fairly mature market. That is, many of the potential buyers already have computers, in good operating condition even if they're not the latest and most advanced. It's tough for the 4,500 computer stores in the United States to convince computer owners to replace their hardware with newer models; they're more likely to upgrade by adding additional peripherals or add-on boards, or by buying better software. According to Future Computing, Inc., U.S.

personal computer sales in 1983 were about $7 billion. Sales peaked in 1984, at more than $7.5 billion, dipped in 1985 to just about 1983 levels, and took off again in 1986, to just under $8 billion with projected 1987 sales of over $9 billion. As you can see, American consumers spend a lot more on Big Macs than they do on Big Blue (IBM's nickname).

Buying lots of computers—even at wholesale—is expensive, so computer stores need a lot of capital. To become a ComputerLand franchisee, you'd need capital of at least $250,000, including a $75,000 initial franchise fee; opening an Entre Computer Center costs at least $300,000, with a $40,000 minimum franchise fee. Once the doors open, a particular computer can sit around in inventory for a long, long time, so the capital will be tied up for a while.

It's also helpful to have a well-trained, articulate sales force who can explain computers to nervous first-time buyers or who can swap technical specifications with a buyer with cash in hand to upgrade an existing system. That means that computer stores either have to maintain heavy payroll costs or lose sales to stores with a better-trained sales force. About the only way a computer store can succeed without technologically knowledgeable sales people is to be the only computer store for miles around— or to slash prices so much that the bargains are irresistible.

It's a lot easier for a heavily capitalized chain of stores (or a franchise operation) to meet these marketing challenges and to run enough advertising to create a corporate image. That's why personal computer sales are dominated by chains such as Tandy Corporation (Radio Shack), ComputerLand, and The Computer Factory, Inc. But merely being a chain doesn't guarantee high profits: in 1987, MBI, Inc., shut down over one-third of its stores (thirteen out of thirty-three) and the troubled megamerchandiser Sears, Roebuck & Company boarded up forty-one of its one hundred computer stores.

## THE CHAINS

For its fiscal year ended June 30, 1986, Tandy sold nearly $950 million worth of computers (40 percent of them home computers, most of the rest designed for small businesses or schools) through its chain of 283 specialized computer centers and 6,700 Radio Shack electronics stores. For 1986, CEO John V. Roach, heading up a company with 35,500 employees, earned $609,000 in salary and bonus and $64,000 in deferred compensation; in that year, Tandy sold $3.655 billion of various products (Tandy makes and sells a wide range of electronic and related products) and kept profits of $197.7 million.

Tandy had an unusual plan for compensating store managers: there were lots of profit-sharing possibilities and stock options, but managers also got charged with unsold inventory and shoplifting losses. In a slow year, computer-store managers could see their checks reduced from about $200,000 to less than $50,000. That led to high turnover in managers. So did Tandy's low pay for sales trainees ($12,000 base salary) and technicians who hook up computer systems and networks ($18,000 starting salary). To motivate its personnel, Tandy switched gears by increasing commissions for salespeople to 8 percent from 5 percent, and by guaranteeing some experienced sales pros $80,000 a year to sell computers to major corporations.

For the first quarter of 1987, Computer Factory, Inc., had sales of $41 million (for the corresponding quarter a year earlier, sales had been only $22 million), but its profit margin after tax was a slender 3.2 percent (still much better than the razor-thin 1.8 percent the year before). Entre and Microage (both aimed at the business market) both lost money in 1987's first quarter.

Computer Factory's margins suffered because of a price war with Exel computer stores, a particularly bitter war because Exel is outgunned: it has six stores in the New York area, and Computer Factory has forty-five in New York, New Jersey, other states, and Washington, D.C., and is expanding in Philadelphia and Boston. Computer Factory is joining the trend toward superstores in electronic products. Although its average store is about 3,000 square feet, its newest stores are more than 5,000 square feet.

Early 1987 was a time of transition for ComputerLand Corporation also; the 800 stores in its $1.45 billion chain were purchased from their founder by a group of private investors. Like most computer stores, ComputerLand hoped to move from selling computers out of stores to maintaining a sales force that would call directly on lucrative corporate clients. Because ComputerLand is also a franchisor, much of its revenue comes from franchise fees, which average 5.6 percent per month of the franchisee's gross sales.

## BIG BLUE OR CLONE?

Dealers must decide whether to sell IBM products—and if so, whether to deal only with the three authorized distributors who sell IBM goods on the up-and-up to about 2,200 retailers or whether to enter the gray market (IBM products purchased outside normal distribution channels—e.g., computers exported from the United States to another country, re-imported from a distributor in another country).

IBM retailers have to meet sales quotas, submit a business plan, and send employees for special training in order to get the most advanced IBM models. When they do, they must pay for the merchandise within thirty days, which can create a cash-flow bind if the expensive systems move slowly. If the retailer succumbs to the temptation to buy gray-market goods, IBM will instruct its authorized dealers to stop selling to the retailer—but the extra profits may still prove worthwhile.

Then again, the retailer can sell "clones" (machines that resemble those made by IBM but that are made by other manufacturers), sacrificing the name recognition and higher retail price of IBM products in order to earn higher profit margins. Besides, IBM tends to sell "loaded" models (computers with most of the features already built in). Clones tend to aim for the low-price end of the market, selling "stripped" models with a low sticker price. That not only attracts buyers but gives retailers a chance to earn high profits by selling upgraded equipment and servicing.

## SOFTWARE SALES

Another big question for the computer retailer is whether to sell software, which is projected to be a $2.8 billion market in 1987. Some retailers don't want to bother because programs can be updated so fast that their inventory becomes obsolete before they can put it on the shelves. They also face strong competition from discounters, especially mail-order operations: once a customer knows he wants a particular program, it's hard to make him buy it from a retailer instead of sending a check to a discounter unless the retailer specializes in service or provides guidance about the best programs to purchase. Computer retailers also face competition from bookstore chains, some of which discount software heavily.

Computer retailers who do stock software usually carry between thirty and one hundred titles, each of which may be available in formats for many computer models. The margin on software sales is an attractive 20 to 30 percent. Home computer owners often buy low-priced software, perhaps $9.95 to $39 for entertainment, home business, and self-improvement software. Software publishers often have "super-discount" lines, selling for around $10, for sale at high-volume discount stores such as K Mart, with more expensive software sold by retailers.

Some stores sell nothing but software: Egghead has one hundred twenty stores, a company mascot who looks like Albert Einstein, and regular "Eggzhibitions" (aka software shows); fiscal 1988 sales were $201,096,000. Babbage's, Inc., has seventy-four stores and 1988 net sales of $29.3 million. Both chains prefer shopping center and mall locations. Heavy competition among software publishers (to offer cheaper, yet better, programs for popular uses) and among stores will work to the software consumer's benefit.

# 46

# Camera Stores

Number of establishments:   4,003
Total receipts:             $1.88 billion
Average net sales:          $470,700
Number of employees:        21,300
Total payroll:              $224.8 billion
                                (Department of Commerce, '82)

Camera stores, of course, focus (get it?) on selling photographic equipment: cameras, lenses, film, accessories like camera bags and "changing bags" (little hoods that provide darkness for changing rolls of film), tripods, and developing equipment. However, the independent camera store, like the independent bookstore or appliance store, faces formidable competition from large-scale discounters. (As a matter of fact, one of the largest electronics discounters, New York's 47th Street Photo, began as a camera store, then branched out to stereo equipment, photocopiers, and video equipment.)

One way for the independent store to survive is to target the knowledgeable professional or very, very serious amateur photographer, providing only the best equipment and salespeople who know which $500 lens to choose. Or the store can motivate sales by permitting trade-ins: according to the Photo Marketing Association International in January 1987, four out of five camera stores take trade-ins, usually giving credit for one-quarter to one-half of the resale value of the camera. (Who buys used cameras? Students, infrequent users, people who want a second camera but don't want it enough to pay full price.)

Another way is to offer a variety of related services (photo developing) or unrelated products (television sets, blank videotapes) to increase revenues and bring in customers who might also buy camera equipment.

That's the solution that Hudson Camera has pursued for thirty-seven years in a downtown Jersey City that's seen plenty of changes in that time. The small store (about 20-by-75 feet, two-thirds of it display space, the rest a crowded stockroom) gets about 25 percent of its revenue from photo processing: it deals with both Kodak and a custom lab. It employs six full-timers and one part-time worker. Business is fairly steady through the year but picks up around Christmastime since cameras, accessories, and video camcorders are common (if luxurious) Christmas gifts. (About 40 percent of all cameras sold are given as gifts; but the most popular gift items are the under-$50 disc cameras and instant cameras that develop their own film, not the 35mm cameras preferred by professionals and serious hobbyists.)

Hudson Camera gets its inventory from at least twenty sources, both manufacturers and distributors, but it uses only one hard-and-fast rule when determining which source it'll buy from: no gray-market goods. It feels that selling gray-market goods is a disservice to customers.

Among the most popular gray-market goods are 35mm cameras, and customers willing to forego warranty protection can get substantial savings: in 1986, for instance, a Hasselblad 150 F4CF lens imported through authorized channels cost over $1,000 while the same gray-market lens could be purchased at 47th Street Photo for $849. Three manufacturers (Minolta, Nikon, and Ricoh) have snapped up about 60 percent of the market for reflex cameras. Nikon U.S.A. sells to dealers at a markup of about 20 percent over Nikon's own cost, which covers advertising, translating the instructions into English, and providing repairs under warranty.

## CONSUMER TIP

If you want to buy a used camera, there are blue books for used cameras just as there are for used cars, showing the value of various models in a range of conditions.

A gray marketer can sell at 50 percent of the manufacturer's suggested list price, mark the merchandise up a mere 10 percent over cost, and still earn a 2.5 percent margin because he avoids many of the authorized importer's expenses.

## WHO BUYS WHAT?

*Chain Store Age* researched male and female habits in buying cameras and film. About 60 percent of the cameras sold are 35mm, and men make 57 percent of the decisions to buy these cameras. Women make 58 percent of the decisions to buy instant cameras and 68 percent of the buying decisions for disc cameras. And new parents buy a *lot* of cameras and film: an average of $220 worth in the year after the baby's birth. That's twice as much as they spend on toys for the tot—the largest nonessential expense for babies.

# 47

# Record Stores

| | |
|---|---|
| Number of establishments: | 4,420 |
| Total receipts: | $1.9 billion |
| Average net sales: | $430,600 |
| Number of employees: | 25,800 |
| Total payroll: | $192,200,000 |

(Department of Commerce, '82)

The usual pattern in an industry is for sales to grow and grow until the market matures or until the product itself has been superseded by something newer and better (or, at least, more fashionable).

Record stores face both those problems. For many years, records provided the only way to hear music short of going to a concert or sitting down at the cello yourself. Then radio struck a blow at record sales (why pay for records when you could hear music free on the radio?) Yet radio also helped record sales by creating a demand for hit records. Besides, the record player was still the only way to hear the music *you* chose, when you wanted to hear it.

Alas, then came the cassette player, the eight-track tape player, music videos on TV and music videos (or any kind of video you wanted to watch) on your VCR, and the stereo TV, with its superb sound quality. The golden year for U.S.-recorded long-playing records was 1978, with sales of $2,473,300,000 (more than 725 million records)—about three times the 1986 figure. However, the recording industry estimates that the LP has a useful life of at least ten more years: plenty of record buyers want to keep their old turntables rotating.

The total number of units of recorded music shipped in 1987 (706.8 million LPs, CDs, and tapes) was 14 percent higher than the 1986 figure. The total list price for all was more than $5.5 billion, but there's an element of fiction in list prices for recorded music: it's very common for retailers to charge less than the inflated "list" prices in order to make customers think they're getting a bargain.

The compact disc (CD) player helped recorded-music sales a lot. Not only did the CD players bring some very merry Christmases to retailers of electronic products, but by 1986 three million CD players were in use, and $700 million worth of CDs were sold per year. According to the mega-record-chain Tower Records (whose forty-two stores sell about 3 percent of America's record purchases), 50 percent of CDs sold are classical; 20 percent, popular; and the rest, jazz, ethnic, show tunes, and other categories.

Californian Ed Dempsey opened a small (1,200 square foot) store called the CD Warehouse in 1984 because he never could find enough CDs at the record stores he patronized. At first, the store turned over its inventory twelve times a year, with sales of $50,000 a month. For Christmas 1985, sales and inventory turns doubled, and 1987 sales were estimated at $650,000 or more, with an inventory of 25,000 discs and 5,000 titles, and plans afoot for franchising fifteen units. The store specializes in service, such as offering a CD "jukebox" so customers can choose from sixty hit titles before buying. (This is an old idea brought back to life: record stores always used to have listening rooms.) The store also buys back used CDs (for $5) and sells them (for $10), just in case the buyer decides he made a mistake with the record (or in case it was an undesired gift).

To stay healthy, most record stores are combining sales of records and audiotapes with something else: maybe electronic equipment (or vice versa: an electronics store can sell records). A common combination is records and video. However, videotapes can carry discouragingly high prices; and if the store wants to get into the highly competitive tape-rental business, it must learn an entirely new way of doing business (see page 301).

Another common combination is records and tapes, and a concert-ticket service; or prerecorded music, and blank videotapes, audiotapes, and maybe even computer discs and software. The store's image and desired customers determine the kind of business problems it'll have. Sales of Top 40 hits can be brisk—but ordering must be pinpoint accurate or the store will either lose sales that can never be replaced (because by the time a reorder is shipped the customers won't want the record anymore) or be awash in unsaleable copies of a record now as cold and stale as yesterday's french fries. Sure, the records and tapes can be shipped back to the manufacturer for credit (giving rise to the statement that such-and-such an album "shipped gold" (sold $1 million worth of records) and was "returned platinum" (record buyers were a lot less enthusiastic about it than record stores). But returns are a headache: the store's inventory records must be corrected, the unwanted items sent back, and loads of bookkeeping tasks handled.

In contrast, lovers of original-cast Broadway albums, admirers of a particular vocalist, or classical music fans often treasure recordings of long-ago performances; discs and tapes can be kept in stock indefinitely for them. But there are a lot more rock, hip-hop, and pop fans than symphony or opera lovers, so most stores must either sell a broad spectrum of music, or restrict their sales to a tight playlist of hits.

Which leads us to the new technology that could be the last nail in the record store's coffin: the Digital Audio Tape Recorder (DAT). Ever since tape recorders have been available, it's been possible for listeners to make taped copies of borrowed records or to tape music at a concert or from the radio. But until the DAT, the best reproduction of sound came from the digital sound of compact discs.

The DAT makes it possible to make perfect copies of compact discs; in other words, as long as there's one CD in a neighborhood, the owner's friends can borrow and copy it onto a blank DAT tape (or buy a prerecorded DAT cassette for about $8) instead of buying another copy of the CD for $12 to $15. The record store would rather sell the CD but will settle philosophically for selling the tape; the record company, however, will be left out in the cold. It's estimated that home taping already results in $1.5 billion a year in lost record sales. If the recording industry slumps and if no records are produced, there'll be nothing to tape.

It's up to Congress now to decide whether to impose a heavy tariff on DAT players unless they have a "spoiler" microchip that prevents them from copying recorded music. It's also up to the Japanese manufacturers of components (no American firm makes DAT players) to decide whether to make DAT players that lack copying capacity just to suit the convenience of record publishers.

# 48

# Music Stores

| | |
|---|---|
| Number of establishments: | 9,284 |
| Total receipts: | $3.7 billion |
| Average net sales: | $300,000 |
| Number of employees: | 53,300 |
| Total payroll: | $487 million |

(Department of Commerce, '82)

The glory days for music stores were in the beginning of this century. The nation was prosperous enough to put a piano, if not in every parlor, in a high proportion of them. Innocent amusements such as marching bands, tea dances, and church choirs flourished. Yet, thanks to vaudeville, touring theater companies, and industrious traveling "song pluggers," the demand for sheet music of a hit song was strong enough to make today's recording artists jealous.

At the end of the 1980s, playing the piano (or harp, or violin) is no longer considered an essential accomplishment for every young lady—and there are plenty of forms of family entertainment other than a musicale provided by family members. Still and all, there are millions of professional and amateur musicians, ranging from kids dragooned into clarinet lessons, to teenagers making the walls of the family split-level vibrate with their amplified guitars, to professional oboists in the philharmonic or on Broadway. According to the National Association of Music Merchants, $290 million worth of sheet music was sold in 1986, most of it to music students.

Dun & Bradstreet's survey of 1,276 music stores showed average 1987 net sales of $66,403. Their gross profit was 36.8 percent of net sales, which is fairly low compared to other businesses. Return on sales was also low, at 1.1 to 9.5 percent, as was return on assets, at 2.1 to 14.8 percent.

Gene Tupper, the leading salesman at Steinway & Sons main store in Manhattan, was profiled by the *New York Times* ("Sales Virtuoso Gene Tupper: Perfecting the Art of Selling a Steinway," July 12, 1987) as 1986's leading salesperson in the retail music industry. His more than $2.6 million in sales is a figure that many music stores would consider a pretty decent year all by itself. His average sale was $20,000; Steinway uprights are available from $6,280, and concert grands can cost $45,600. In 1986, 166,555 pianos (about half grands, half uprights) were sold overall, for a total of $619.7 million. Steinway makes about 5,000 pianos a year; Baldwin, 35,000; and Yamaha, 200,000.

A piano, especially a superb concert instrument, is obviously not an impulse purchase, so how do customers make the decision to buy? Serious musicians have their own preferences about the kind of sound and action they prefer, and they take recommendations of fellow artists, piano teachers, conservatory faculty, and, in the end, buy the piano closest to their dreams that they can afford. Parents who just want a piano in the house because they think every kid should have piano lessons also listen to piano teachers but may devote more attention than the pros do to which piano fits in best with their decor. They're the group most receptive to a pitch from a knowledgeable salesperson.

The Steinway salesmen take turns with walk-in customers until each has had an equal number of prospects—equality is important because they work entirely on commission, and a piano sale can net a $1,200 commission. But the top salesmen don't rely on walk-in trade: they keep past customers on their mailing lists, send them literature about new products, and go to great pains (and some expense) to cultivate relationships with piano teachers. Teachers sometimes get a 1 to 2 percent commission when they refer a student who buys a piano; or they may get a discount on pianos or free piano benches.

It's hard to imagine a world without Mozart or Beethoven, so traditional instruments will always have a place. Many young musicians (or kids who like to make a lot of noise) prefer synthesizers, electronic pianos, and electric violins, but that takes us out of the realm of music stores and into that of electronics stores (see page 190).

# 49

# Bookstores

Number of establishments:  9,355
Total receipts:            $3.13 billion
Average net sales:         $334,900
Number of employees:       58,100
Total payroll:             $400.8 million

(Department of Commerce, '82)

Whatever happened to the good old bookstores of the past that reflected the personal stamp of an owner who knew everything about books and had a rich trove of reminiscences about Sherwood Anderson and Theodore Dreiser? We'll tell you what happened: many of these seasoned bookmen were better raconteurs than they were businessmen—and their customers, who were more addicted to browsing than to book-buying, fled eagerly to discount stores when they began to sell cut-price books. Although we mourn the knowledgeable clerks who have been replaced by gum-chewing teenagers who direct requests for *"Less Misérables"* to the Psychology and Self-Improvement section, we're glad that books are being made more available, at lower prices. (Where did you buy this copy—at Waldenbooks? B. Dalton? Crown Books?)

The impact of the domination of the big bookstore chains on publishers' lists of books is ambiguous. To a certain extent, the chains encourage the "blockbuster syndrome" by stocking up on best-sellers, which will move quickly. However, a decent-sized chain bookstore is going to have plenty of room left once it sets up the displays of the latest Stephen King, Tom Clancy, James Michener, and Danielle Steel novels, and the latest Garfield the Cat books; and the chain management wants customers to buy eight or eleven more items once they've bought the best-sellers. Besides, the chains often have a comfortable profit cushion and can afford to take chances with less-proven titles. An independent bookseller, operating perilously close to the break-even point, may not be able to do this. Sometimes the book chains believe in a particular book and turn it into a success by discounting it heavily (the bookstore, not the manufacturer, decides the book's retail price), giving it a favorable display, or featuring it in the book chain's catalogue.

The clear trends in bookselling are toward chain operations instead of small independent stores; toward discounting; and toward combining sales of books with other items—magazines, games, software, and audio- and videocassettes. However, even operating a chain of bookstores does not ensure automatic success. Brentano's, a New York chain of bookstores, went under several years ago; and B. Dalton now belongs to Barnes & Noble, which spent about $300 million to make the acquisition. Together, Barnes & Noble and Dalton have 995 stores and sold $850 million of books and other stuff in 1986.

"And other stuff" is crucial—and controversial. The new strategy for Dalton calls for concentrating on books rather than on gifts, games, or tapes. However, Dalton has one hundred Software etc. stores, some of them units in bookstores, some of them separate stores selling computer books, programs, and discs (including Dana's favorite brand of floppy disc—an unsolicited testimonial). The new owners have closed down thirty B. Dalton stores and fired twenty employees—including fourteen buyers—as part of an efficiency drive that includes simplifying the buying procedure. Dalton used to have individual buyers for categories of books (for example, history or self-help); now the Barnes & Noble/Dalton chain will deal with a publisher's entire line together.

The 1,130-store Waldenbooks chain (part of the K Mart empire), with 1986 sales of $650 million, disagrees, finding that a combination of discounting and stocking video and audio merchandise suits their clientele better. Waldenbooks is also opening Waldenkids stores that sell educational toys and games in addition to books. Kids get "visa" stamps for their "passport to adventure" with each purchase; the stamps can be turned in for a gift watch. The stores are so attractive, with their puppet shows and bright primary colors, that parents tend to use the stores as informal child-care centers while they browse the rest of the mall.

When it comes to conventional adult books, however, Harry Hoffman, president of Waldenbooks, says that his company has gone too far in discounting and will now discount best-sellers by 15 to 20 percent—not the 1986 levels of 25 to 35 percent. Waldenbooks used to have separate stores selling only discounted books, but those have been closed. Despite Waldenbooks' recantation, at least some stores stick with deep discounting. Crown Books, for example, boosted its discount on best-sellers to 40 percent in 1987, up from 35 percent in 1985.

The 150-store Crown chain is also involved in several suits in California's federal court. A number of independent bookstores joined in the Northern California Booksellers Association brought an antitrust suit against publishers, challenging their practice of giving chain stores an additional 4 percent discount on the price they pay for mass-market paperbacks. (Bookstores usually pay trade-book publishers the list price of the books, less 40 percent; textbooks publishers get a higher percentage of the books' cover price; very large orders may be priced lower.) The association claims that this practice violates the federal Robinson-Patman Act, which makes it illegal to harm competition by practicing price discrimination against certain retailers.

Crown Books countersued, charging that eliminating the practice would raise book prices and harm consumers. The publishers, in turn, said that the price difference was a rational one because the costs of selling to a chain are lower than those of dealing with numerous, widespread independent bookstores.

The eventual outcome of the suit (which began in March 1987 and so will be around for a while) may affect the way publishers and bookstores deal with inventory. Unlike most store owners, who are stuck with inventory once they buy it (unless it's defective, in which case it can be sent back to the manufacturer), bookstore owners (and record-store owners) can return unsold inventory for full credit at any time. That makes it easy for publishers' reps to persuade stores to take a lot of copies of promising titles while at the same time it makes it tough for bookstores, who need extra space and must keep track of what's selling and what should be shipped back to the publisher. One possible outcome of the suit would be for other publishers to follow the system used by New American Library, where stores are penalized for inefficient ordering because they can't return unsold books for full credit, but all stores get the same discount.

The superstore—that is, a huge store with an exceptionally broad selection of merchandise and very deep discounts—is a phenomenon in many kinds of retail businesses: Toys 'R' Us is a toy superstore; Drug Emporium, Inc., is a health and beauty aid superstore. Texan Gary E. Hoover is trying to bring the superstore to bookselling, with his twenty Bookstop stores, which carry 40,000 titles (the average bookstore carries about 12,000) and discount all books, not just best-sellers. Bookstop depends on computers for a sophisticated inventory-control system. In 1986 sales were a very healthy $26 million, but the company lost $100,000 (because of the heavy start-up costs).

## WHAT AND WHERE TO ORDER

There's no shortage of books available to booksellers; the listings of books in print run to several volumes of minuscule type. There are some reliable items that nearly every bookstore must keep in stock at all times: Bibles, reference books such as dictionaries and atlases, at least a few coffee-table books earmarked for gift purchases, some detective stories, some cookbooks. A policy decision has to be made: stock a lot of different titles or only a few reliable sellers? The fewer titles in stock, the less appealing the store is to browsers, and the less likely it is that avid readers will make a special trip.

After that, it's up to the bookstore to select a mix of titles reflecting the image it wants to project: best-sellers at low prices? scholarly books? everything ever published about fly fishing? books appealing to an ethnic group, a geographical area, a particular hobby or life-style? Then the bookstore must decide how many copies of each title to order. That's a complex decision because there may be a minimum order level set by the publisher, or the discount level may fluctuate with the size of the order, giving booksellers an incentive to risk ordering too many instead of losing sales when books are unavailable. But that isn't a perfect solution either. Over-ordering means that books that don't sell take up expensive floor space that could be used for books that *do* sell and tie up the store owner's capital. Even returning the books for credit is a time-consuming, labor-intensive task—and the bookstore pays the postage.

Booksellers have several ways to purchase their stock. The major chains, in effect, sit down with the publishers and have "summit meetings" to set the chains' purchasing policies for the ordering period. Originally, most of the publishing action came in the publishers' "Fall lists," targeted at Christmas sales; now books are published pretty much year-round for the excellent reason that most readers are book junkies who read year-round.

Smaller, but still substantial, bookstores get visits from publishers' representatives. Depending on the size of the publisher and the bookstore, the rep could work for a single publisher or for a group of smaller publishing houses. If the bookstore is too small or too far out of the way to rate a visit from the rep, or if the bookseller doesn't want to take the time to listen to the sales talk, books can be ordered directly from the publisher's catalogue (although there may be a minimum order, or a minimum number of copies of a particular title that must be ordered if the store wants to stock that particular book).

Booksellers can also buy from wholesalers. The wholesalers have to make a profit, of course, so the books are a little more expensive, and orders can take longer to arrive, but the wholesaler offers the convenience of placing a single order for books from a number of publishers.


## REMAINDERS

It would be really tough to run a profitable clothing store if the city government let people borrow all the clothes they wanted from a municipal clothing store. Bookstores face similar competition, from public libraries. (At least the libraries let customers "try on" books that they may later purchase from bookstores.)

Booksellers face another unique problem: they're competing with their own merchandise. In a typical chain bookstore, for instance, the same book may be available at three different price levels: as a hardcover (probably discounted from the full price), as a remaindered hardcover (way below full price, after the book has gone out of print), and as a paperback. Sometimes bookstores create their own remainders, by slashing prices to induce sales of books that they don't want to send back to the publisher or of books kept so long that returns are no longer permitted. But usually remainders are books that the publisher decides can no longer be sold at full price. Either the books are sold to booksellers at a special low price, or they're sold to wholesalers at *really* low prices, and then sold to bookstores.

By the time the public gets tired of it, a particular book, or excerpts of a book, may have appeared serialized in one or more magazines. With luck, the book will be made into a hit movie or miniseries, making it possible for the publisher to reissue it with a new cover (and, no doubt, a higher price); maybe the store will even be able to sell an audiocassette of the book, with a well-known star reading it, or a videocassette.

Videocassettes supplement bookstore operations, but they don't really serve the same market as books. People who like to read insist on reading, whether or not they also like to watch TV, go to the movies, or rent movies for their VCRs. No matter how many electronic media appear, there'll always be a place for books. You can't watch videos on the subway or in the bathtub (unless you have an unusually well-equipped bathroom); and an audiotape can't replace the picture book lovingly read to a sleepy child.

# 50

# Card Shops

Sometime when you're really bored, consider the lot in life of the well-brought-up nineteenth-century lady. Of course, she didn't have a job. If she had children, the nanny took care of them; the maids cleaned the house. Her days were spent in the family carriage, paying calls on the ladies of similarly impeccable family. If the other ladies were out paying calls themselves or lying down with a headache, a bottle of laudanum, or the gamekeeper, the visitors would "leave their cards": small pasteboard cards engraved with their names. They could leave implied, but well understood, messages by bending the corners of the cards in certain ways ("we're going on a trip"; "greetings from the ladies of our household to your household"; "greetings from the gentlemen and ladies of our household to your household"). No doubt they often wrote a few personal words on the card.

The sending of Christmas cards, long a part of German tradition, was adopted in England in the nineteenth century, as a result of Queen Victoria's happy marriage to a German prince. English customs seemed very elegant to Americans, who seized on this habit enthusiastically. Responding to the demand for Christmas cards, printers began to make cards available, with either a religious scene or one of hospitable Christmas cheer.

Today, in the United States, there are eight hundred greeting card companies, which offer cards for every imaginable holiday and for a person in any imaginable relationship to you, and in any condition or state of mind. You can get cards that celebrate Chanukah, saints' days, your dog's birthday, and probably even your grandfather's third marriage. Americans—by and large, that means American women, since nine-tenths of cards are bought by women—buy $3.6 billion worth of cards a year. And, by and large, although there are eight hundred card companies, that means cards sold by the Big Three card publishers: Hallmark (with about 40 percent of the market), American Greetings (with some 30 percent), and, way behind, Gibson Greetings (with 10 percent). The other 797 publishers divide the remaining 20 percent of the market.

Therefore, the card store owner has a number of problems: staying on the good side of the major card publishers (if, in fact, the store is not owned or franchised by a card publisher); choosing cards from the minor publishers to suit the market (whether it be senior citizens, black professionals, people who speak Portuguese, or those with a mordant sense of humor); negotiating favorable terms with publishers (a few publishers will accept returns of unsold cards—like unsold books—but most insist that, once a store has bought cards, it's stuck with them). The sales of "alternative" greeting cards (those aimed at specific ethnic groups, or with more sophistication than the average card) are growing at about 25 percent a year. Traditional card sales are growing at only 8 percent a year, so card store owners have to keep up.

The biggest problem for card stores, though, is the fact that many other types of stores sell greeting cards and can use them as loss leaders for their other lines of merchandise.

Independent card stores and gift shops sell about 35 percent of all cards, dividing the rest of the sales with supermarkets (10.5 percent of sales), chain drugstores (33 percent of sales), other drugstores, bookstores, and department stores. A really large supermarket, or discount store, can have as much display space for cards, and as many or more different cards on display, as an independent card store.

Card shops fight back by offering a selection better tailored to the individual customers; by locating in convenient mall locations, or near offices, to attract busy shoppers; and by offering other merchandise. Giftwrap and gift boxes are a natural combination with cards as well as a growing market ($700 to $800 million a year). Sales of giftwrap are growing by only 5 to 8 percent a year (with the typical price about $2 a roll); sales of more elaborate bags, boxes, and totes are growing by 20 percent a year or more, with typically higher prices ($4.50, for example). Clearly customers are buying elaborate boxes and bags to jazz up somewhat modest gifts. That's terrific for the store owner because the wrappings aren't perishable and don't take up all that much room. However, the business is highly seasonal: about 70 percent of wrappings are bought at Christmastime, which leaves the card shop owner with a long face in July.

Card shops can also stock candy (a natural birthday, Christmas, or anniversary gift), stationery items, and party goods (paper hats, decorations, party favors). A new trend is to have an in-store computer system for personalizing greeting cards (you can, for example, get a Hallmark card with the Peanuts gang addressing you—or the recipient of the card—by name), printing T-shirts and posters, or both. Perhaps it's a wistful attempt to bring a personal touch to the electronic world of pixels and data banks.

# 51

# Gift Shops

| | |
|---|---|
| Number of establishments: | 22,311 |
| Total receipts: | $4.61 billion |
| Average net sales: | $270,000 |
| Number of employees: | 109,600 |
| Total payroll: | — |

(Department of Commerce, '82)

Gift shops are a very American phenomenon. Of course, people in other countries give gifts, but the United States is probably the world capital of things that exist specifically to be given as gifts. A place defined as a "gift shop" can be an exquisite gallery of craft objects that serve a useful function or a hilarious collection of plastic objects that glow in the dark, sequinned fake fruit, and hats that hold beer cans; it's a function of the tastes of the store owners and of their customers.

Gift shops depend heavily on passersby; many of their items are impulse purchases, something in the window that teases a buyer's attention or reminds him that a birthday is coming up. So a location with heavy foot traffic is imperative. There's a symbiosis between gift shops and malls: malls are great locations for gift shops because they generate heavy foot traffic; gift shops in turn are ideal mall tenants because they don't take up much space or attract a rowdy crowd. They also tend to ring up enough small sales to make their monthly rent payments secure, unlike an art gallery or foreign-car dealership that can go a long, long time between major sales.

Probably the biggest problems for owners are the very seasonal nature of the business (it's oriented to holidays—especially Christmas), which leads to "bumps" in cash flow, and the difficulties of choosing and controlling inventory. (Small gift items are particularly easy for shoplifters to steal.) Chain operations and franchises can address these problems by suggesting which items to stock (and can also purchase them in bulk and deal with shipping) and how to display them for maximum sales effectiveness.

For instance, Spencer Gifts (owned by entertainment giant MCA, Inc.) owns 440 Spencer Gifts stores, six high-end A2Z stores, and 95 Intrigue jewelry stores and kiosks in malls. In 1985, the chain brought in volume of almost $500 million. Intrigue stores are small (600 to 1,000 square feet) and profitable, realizing sales of $482 per square foot in 1986. The kiosks—little booths in malls—are even smaller (144 to 300 square feet) but generate stunning volume: $1,311 per square foot. Spencer Gift stores, which are larger, having an average of 2,500 square feet, typically enjoyed yearly sales of $200 a square foot; A2Z stores are significantly larger still, at 3,500 square feet, and had first-year sales of close to $300 a square foot.

Spencer specializes in "concept retailing," based on "Monday Morning Quarterback Club" meetings with buyers, merchandisers, and operations executives. At the meetings, buyers discuss the best items they've gotten from vendors or special items they've designed for production by the vendors. Then the people at the meeting decide, using information from an IBM interactive computer system, the best way to display the new items in conjunction with other items in stock.

Kirkland's, headquartered in Jackson, Tennessee, is a smaller chain, with twenty-three stores in the Southwest—all of them in major shopping malls. The average store has 6,000 SKUs, and an inventory costing about $180,000 and retailing for nearly twice that (the usual markup is either 40 percent or "keystone," meaning the retail price is twice the wholesale price). Of course, during the fall (pre-Christmas shopping season), the shelves are much fuller. Many of Kirkland's shops sell over $1 million a year.

## FRANCHISING

Franchising is also strong in gift sales. Many people who open gift shops have never owned a business before, so they're grateful for help with displays, marketing, and bookkeeping. Starting up a gift franchise can cost anywhere from $13,000 to over $200,000, and monthly fees can range from 2 to 7 percent of sales. For instance, if you'd like a Balloon Age franchise (which specializes in delivering balloons for special occasions and corporate promotions, but which also sells plush toys, stationery, and cards), you'll probably need a 750- to 1,000-square-foot mall location and about $20,000. If you want a Wicks'n'Sticks store (candles, of course), you'll need to pay $35,000 as an initial franchise fee, and the start-up will cost about $135,000 to 200,000. One Long Island franchisee has six Wicks'n'Sticks stores and averages volume of $235,000 in the first year after a store opens, $325,000 subsequently. To join Dial-a-Gift's 500 dealers and affiliate dealers would take the $7,495 (of all odd amounts!) initial franchise fee, a total of $13,000 to $15,000 in start-up costs, a monthly royalty of 2 percent of gross sales, and $100 a month for national advertising.

## AN INDEPENDENT VIEW

However, there are many independent gift shops. In tourist areas such as Provincetown, Massachusetts, they serve dual functions of furnishing outlets for local artisans and contributing to the distinctive atmosphere of the town. In cities, they appeal to distinctive local sensibilities; again, they offer a market for craftsworkers who would otherwise be dependent on craft shows and street fairs to make sales.

Another symbiosis is at work here: gift shops take over the job of marketing crafts, giving the creator more time to work at the kiln, loom, or jeweler's bench. But craft items are often consigned (that is, the gift shop owner doesn't buy them—or pay for them—until a customer has purchased the item) rather than sold outright to the shop. That limits the amount of capital that the owner needs to tie up. If the store stocks mass-manufactured items rather than handicrafts, the goods will probably have to be paid for in advance and probably can't be returned to the manufacturer if they don't sell.

Last fall, Dana bought a beautiful little pearl-and-garnet ring at Betty Murray's (on Jersey Avenue in Jersey City), then interviewed the owner (checkbook journalism at its most sordid). The 750-square-foot shop, which has additional storage space in the basement, is located on a yup-and-coming street in an area undergoing gentrification.

The store (or emporium, or gallery . . . the proprietor is not sure quite what to call it) currently specializes in handcrafted jewelry, much of it made by local artisans. Earrings are by far the best-selling jewelry items. Ms. Murray also sells art pottery, soft sculpture, and a burgeoning line of items for kids; when store sales are slow, she does custom framing, which, she says, "saves her bacon": the markup is low, but payment is immediate—unlike a beautiful piece of art pottery, which gives tone to the store but which can take months to sell.

Ms. Murray handles much of the store management and selling herself, supplemented by part-timers when she's out acquiring new merchandise or handling other aspects of the business or when gift sales are strongest: Christmas, spring graduations, Mother's Day, and June weddings.

# 52

# Jewelry Stores

| Number of establishments: | 22,786 (According to *Jewelers Circular-Keystone,* 32,346 retailers—not all limited to jewelry—sold jewelry in 1986.) |
| --- | --- |
| Total receipts: | $8.35 billion |
| Average net sales: | $366,500 |
| Number of employees: | $132,300 |
| Total payroll: | $1.43 billion |

(Department of Commerce, '82)

In many ways, the jewelry business is an unusually tough one. (Of course, there's jewelry and jewelry—we're talking about gemstone and precious-metal jewelry, not $2.00 vinyl earrings.) Payroll absorbs a high percentage of sales: 17.2 percent, according to the Department of Commerce; 20 percent, according to the trade journal *Jewelers Circular-Keystone.*

The jeweler (whether he just retails jewelry or manufactures it as well) needs a very, very expensive inventory of finished pieces, precious metals, and gemstones. The jeweler is also at the mercy of fluctuating prices for the raw materials, especially when gold attracts the attention of investors as well as jewelry buyers (and dentists). It's not uncommon for

219

a jeweler to order a lot of merchandise when gold and diamond prices are high, then try to sell it when prices have collapsed, providing the unattractive choices of cutting prices to current levels and losing money or hanging on to the inventory until prices rebound (if they ever do), making no profit on the items.

Lots of people want jewelry, but nobody needs it. Buyers may turn to jewelry when they're disappointed in other investments or may build up a portfolio of good jewelry gradually, but very few people can afford to buy hundreds or thousands of dollars' worth of jewelry on impulse.

It's a highly seasonal business, but fortunately there are a number of holidays and occasions on which gifts of jewelry are popular: Christmas, of course, and Mother's Day, and the rush for rings for June weddings, and watches, fountain pens, and charm bracelets for graduates. Also fortunately for the jewelry business, birthdays occur all year long. Fashion moves much faster in clothing than in jewelry, but there are fashions in jewelry as well, and a retailer can get caught with thousands of dollars' worth of merchandise that just looks embarrassingly old and tired, but not old enough yet to rate a revival (like the Duchess of Windsor's 1940s jewelry collection).

Dun & Bradstreet's 1987 survey of 1,762 jewelry stores showed that gross profit averaged 45.5 percent of sales, above average for retailing as a whole. Net profit after tax was also strong, at 7.0 percent. The range of return on sales was 1.4 to 13.5 percent; return on assets ranged from 1.6 to 15.4 percent.

## BAD DEBTS AND BAD GUYS

It's common for jewelers—especially chain stores such as the 428-unit Kay Jewelers, Inc.—to make sales on credit. That gives them the potential to earn high interest, but it also exposes them to a significant risk of bad debts. Half of Kay Jewelers' $234 million sales are on credit, but in 1985, Kay had to write off nearly 4 percent of sales as bad debts, twice as much as in 1982.

Nor is Kay the only company to suffer this problem. Barry Jewelers sold more than two-thirds of its merchandise on credit, but in 1986 it had to wave bye-bye to more than $2 million in bad debts—more than 3 percent of its sales. Gordon Jewelry Corporation had to treat nearly 15 percent of its accounts receivable as either doubtful or uncollectable.

The jewelry retailer's security problems are hideous—a jewelry store filled with expensive watches, gold and silver, and gemstones is a natural target for burglars, and those items and the cash in the till are natural targets for robbers. To qualify for a "block" insurance policy, a jewelry store must have a fireproof safe and an effective electronic alarm system—all of which costs at least $5,000 to install. Jewelry stores can protect themselves by wiring up elaborate security systems, hiring guards, and keeping the front door locked, to be opened only when a reputable-looking potential customer rings. Some stores even require customers to make an appointment or refuse to open the door to men at all. But all these strategies cost money; the last few can drive away disreputable-looking but nevertheless honest (and cash-rich) buyers.

## WHO BUYS WHAT?

It's true that nearly all the robbers are male, but then so are many potential buyers. According to a survey in the April 1987 issue of the trade magazine *Jewelers Circular-Keystone,* men bought a little over half the diamond jewelry sold in 1986 but they paid far more on the average than women diamond buyers did. Furthermore, they were far more likely to shop at jewelry stores than women, who often went to department stores, discount stores, or bought jewelry by mail order.

Women bought the majority of gold jewelry, fine watches, and jewelry with colored gemstones (and five times as much costume jewelry as men did); but, in most categories, they paid less than men and were less likely to shop in jewelry stores. (Women paid more for watches than men—perhaps because they were buying expensive watches as Christmas, anniversary, or graduation gifts for men.)

Only about one-third of purchases of colored stones (precious and semiprecious stones such as emeralds, sapphires, and amethysts) are made in jewelry stores; the rest are made in department stores, discount stores, through mail-order retailers, and through home shopping. Although

## TRADE TALK

An "upstairs" jeweler is a small discount operation, usually literally "upstairs" in an office building, rather than poised in a retail storefront or high-rent shopping mall. While a typical mall rent might be $20 (or more) a square foot, and 3.7 percent of gross sales a month (see page 137 for more about malls), the "upstairs" jewelery store may be paying only $10 a square foot in rent. It can cut prices because its security problems are smaller (though far from nonexistent), it attracts its customers by word-of-mouth (which cuts the ad budget; major retail chains can spend 5 to 10 percent of their gross income on advertising), and it can maintain a smaller inventory. Of course, if you want a more unusual piece of jewelry, you'll be happier at a larger operation, with a wider selection.

# CONSUMER TIPS

▶ If you've taken a bath in the stock market, don't think that you can make your way back to fame and fortune by "investing" in jewelry. Some people (very, very few of them novices or innocents) have made a lot of money speculating on precious metals and gemstones, but usually they're betting on price movements of commodities. The trouble with finished jewelry as an investment is that you tend to buy at retail prices; when you want to sell, you must usually sell at a lower price to a retailer or put the piece up for auction and pay the auction house's fees.

▶ There's a real danger of being defrauded when you buy fine jewelry. In 1982, for instance, Cartier made 200,000 watches—and crooks made 400,000 counterfeit "Cartier" watches for sale to unsuspecting marks. Before you buy expensive jewelry, find out how it's packaged and what it should cost. Real Rolexes, for instance, are sold in leather or needlepoint boxes, but, of course, it's cheaper for an unscrupulous jeweler to buy real (or real-looking) Rolex boxes than the Rolexes themselves. Once you know the normal retail price, you'll know if the bargain you're being offered is an implausible one. If a retailer pays half the normal retail price, how can he sell the watch to you for $200 less than that? He can't—unless he must raise cash; unless he somehow managed to acquire legitimate merchandise at unusually low wholesale prices; or unless there's something wrong with the merchandise, or his title to it.

Stones—especially colored stones—can be doctored to cover flaws or to resemble more expensive stones. Of course jewelers love to display diamonds on black velvet: it makes even off-color, flawed diamonds look great.

shoppers often look elsewhere for gemstones, jewelry stores can't afford to ignore these sales: the average jewelry store does 8 to 10 percent of its business in colored-stone jewelry. Industry experts suggest that the store's inventory of colored-stone merchandise should be divided into groups of about one-third each of moderately priced semiprecious stones (for impulse buys), better-quality pieces, and major gem pieces. If the store maintains the normal keystone markup, and if they estimate they'll sell $1,000 a month in colored-stone jewelry, with 1.5 merchandise turns a year, they'll need an inventory of $4,000—that is, they must have $8,000 in inventory at all times if inventory turns over 1.5 times a year, but the inventory costs only $4,000 to buy.

## MARKUPS AND DISCOUNTS

The typical jeweler charges a keystone markup, but the typical discounter marks up goods only 25 to 50 percent over his own cost. Furthermore, the discounter may have a lower wholesale cost, if he orders in huge quantities or buys closeout items.

# 53

# Sporting Goods Stores

Number of establishments:   20,152
Total receipts:   $7.51 billion
Average net sales:   $372,900
Number of employees:   106,200
Total payroll:   $925,300,000

(Department of Commerce, '82)

As the health club entry shows, Americans are Jocks Around the Clock. They're panting and puffing in aerobics classes (almost six million pairs of aerobics shoes were sold in 1985; total footwear sales for 1986 were $3.2 billion), lifting weights (2.7 million sets of barbells and 1.2 million multipurpose gym sets were sold in 1985), and working like galley slaves at rowing machines (1.8 million were purchased in 1985). They were also swinging their tennis racquets, schussing on their skis, and digging their cleats into the turf.

But is owning a sporting goods store a license to print money? Not really. For one thing, once a person buys a tennis racquet, he or she is probably out of the market at least until some fancy improved racquet, which may or may not win over the racquet owner, is developed. Sporting goods tend to be durable, not easily used up. So the equipment owner who gets tired of the sport or retires with a sprained ankle is likely to pass along the equipment to a friend or offer it up at a garage sale—eliminating another potential buyer from the market.

There are other difficulties for the traditional, independent sporting goods store: competition from franchises, warehouse clubs, department stores, general discount stores, and even supermarkets. It's also a heavily seasonal business. Sporting goods dealers do most of their buying in January and February, anticipating their merchandise needs for six to twelve months. Sweats have to be ordered a year in advance; orders for shoes and shorts take about six months. About a third of sporting goods sales are made either as back-to-school purchases (13 to 15 percent) or as Christmas gifts (13 to 20 percent). Naturally, outdoor sports are more seasonal than indoor ones: it's tough to sell water skis in the winter, or snow skis in the summer.

## RECENT TRENDS

Sporting goods dealers had a pretty good year in 1986: a survey by *Sporting Goods Dealer* magazine shows that 63 percent of those surveyed had a sales increase between 1985 and 1986; 60 percent reported a profit increase. In both cases, specialty dealers did better than full-line dealers. Sales stayed the same for 8 percent of respondents, and profits were stable for 11 percent of specialty dealers and 12 percent of full-line operations. The rest saw lower sales or profits or both in 1986.

However, there were dramatic differences among regions. In the Northeast, it was a fabulous year: 82 percent of dealers had increased profits; 9 percent had stable profits; and another 9 percent suffered losses. (Did every yuppie on Wall Street or Route 128 buy six new squash racquets and a home rowing machine?) Not so shabby in the South Atlantic, either: profits were up for 67 percent of respondents, down for 23 percent. But away from the eastern seaboard, the picture was darker. In the North Central region, profits were up for only 58 percent of dealers, down for 28 percent, and the same as 1985 for 14 percent. Out West, profits rose for 57 percent of dealers but sank for 33 percent. The hardest-hit region was the South Central (probably because of the oil patch's economic woes). There, only 40 percent of stores saw higher profits while 46 percent experienced a decline.

The most successful products were licensed: those bearing a team or celebrity name, or even a well-known logo such as Reebok. It was also a great year for sweat clothes, fishing tackle, aerobic shoes and cleats, and shoes for exercise walking. However, sales of running shoes were disappointing, and tennis equipment and clothing were in the doldrums.

According to the National Sporting Goods Association, total 1986 sales for all athletic equipment, shoes, and clothing were $16.6 billion. Here's how it breaks down:

**1986 Sporting Goods Sales**

| | |
|---|---|
| Athletic equipment: | $9.5 billion |
| Recreational transportation (bicycles, snowmobiles, etc.): | $30.6 billion |
| Athletic shoes: | $3.2 billion |
| Clothing: | $3.9 billion |
| Exercise equipment: | $1.2 billion |

The relatively high clothing figure may show a certain degree of hypocrisy in our national pursuit of physical excellence. You can wear a jogging suit (even one with a fashionable logo or an endorsement by a leading athlete) while you're slumped on the couch eating Deep-Fried Lardies.

However, when it comes to sporting equipment, outdoor sports were definitely the leaders in 1986. The largest single category in the National Sporting Goods Association's survey was firearms and hunting equipment ($1.7 billion in 1986 sales). (Well, maybe some people wanted them for indoor sports.) Sales of camping equipment went up 15.5 percent; fishing tackle reeled in a 13.5 percent increase; and golfers bought 11 percent more in 1986 than in 1985.

## RUNNING THE STORE

The cornerstone of sporting goods decoration is the "slat wall": the 40 to 50 foot wall covered with horizontal planks that support shelving. The slat wall can display up to 450 SKUs, including footwear and small items of equipment and paraphernalia as well.

Fifteen hundred square feet is a typical size for a sporting goods store, although if the inventory is large and rents are low stores can be almost ten times that size. For instance, Andy Anderson's Sporting Goods, in Oklahoma City, is 12,000 square feet; for a store that size, electricity alone costs almost $35 a day (3 percent of the store's operating costs).

## FRANCHISES, CHAINS, AND WAREHOUSE CLUBS

Because the sporting goods business calls for a lot of inventory and is plagued by up-and-down seasonal sales and changes in demand, the independent dealer's life can be tough. One response is to specialize, becoming a store that sells everything for fishing (but nothing else), or nothing but footwear, or racquet sports paraphernalia only. Inevitably, another trend is toward chains, franchises, and warehouse clubs.

Herman's Sporting Goods, Inc. (which is now owned by a British company) is "the closest thing we have to a national chain," as James Faltinek, president of the National Sporting Goods Association, told *Crain's New York Business* ("Herman's New Lineup Bolsters Growth," August 10, 1987). Herman's owns two hundred stores in twenty-seven states and scores hearty annual sales of $265 per square foot. The staffers aren't necessarily experts on sporting goods, and regional chains may offer better value. But Herman's has the budget for extensive advertising.

Independent store owners can join one of the six hundred authorized dealers of Sport-It, which sells products wholesale to retailers. It costs $1,500 plus $25 a month to join up; there are no royalties.

Retailers who prefer franchising can open a 1,500-square-foot Sport-About full-service franchise for about $50,000 or $60,000. In return for a $15,000 franchise fee and a monthly royalty of 4 percent of gross sales, Sport-About provides training, central warehousing, and shipping to its franchisees. Opening a 2,000- to 6,000-square-foot Sport Shack probably costs at least $125,000, including the $17,500 franchise fee (which includes training, help with setting up the store, central ordering, and marketing help). The monthly fees are 4 percent for royalties and 2 percent for advertising. Fleet Feet estimates that it takes $64,000 to open a franchised running shoe store; the franchise fee is $10,000, and the monthly royalty ranges from 1 to 4 percent, depending on sales volume.

For a while there, it looked as if sporting goods sales would shift to extra-large warehouse outlets (say, 8,000 to 15,000 square feet) run by established chains and used to discount their slow-selling merchandise. However, many experienced merchandisers have been disappointed— maybe the traditional method of setting up discount tables in regular stores at higher-traffic locations is more productive.

If the trends hold, then, you're likely to buy your future trout flies, aerobic walking shoes, and name-brand sweatsuits from a chain store or franchise operation rather than from a full-line retailer with a single store.

# 54

# Toy Stores

| | |
|---|---|
| Number of establishments: | 7,691 ("toy/hobby shops") |
| Total receipts: | $3.23 billion |
| Average net sales: | $420,900 |
| Number of employees: | 46,100 |
| Total payroll: | $435 million |

(Department of Commerce, '82)

Ho, ho, ho! In 1977, the average kid got an average of $65 worth of toys; by 1984, the average had climbed to $168; and the industry as a whole reached $12 billion proportions by 1987. Toymakers and retailers enjoyed magical years in 1984 and 1985, flush with success from super-hit toys like Cabbage Patch Dolls, Pound Puppies, Transformers, and Masters of the Universe. In those wonderful days (for the sellers, anyhow), buyers would do almost anything to get hold of the hit toys. Today, sellers are actually offering cash rebates on Cabbage Patch Dolls. Manufacturers are letting toy stores buy their Christmas goods in March and pay for them at Christmastime.

But 1986 was slow. Parents bought 934,839,000 toy items—$5,266,760,000 worth, an average of $6.60 per toy (less than one-quarter from toy stores; the rest from discount or department stores, or even from drugstores and supermarkets). Grandparents spent a little less, about $5.39, and bought 375,291,000 items for a total of $1,798,442,000. They were even less likely to patronize toy stores—only 13.6 percent of their purchases and 19.7 percent of their toy dollars involved toy stores rather than other outlets.

Even before the stock market crash (which depressed the market in toys yuppies buy for themselves, as well as those they purchase for their baby-boomlet offspring), 1987 was nothing to write home about, either. The timing of the crash wasn't too great for anybody (except short sellers and brokers who managed to hang on to their jobs), but it was awful for toy stores. The crash came in October, just as toy buying heats up (in the late 1980s, about 58 percent of toy sales come during the Christmas season). Things might have been worse: traditionally, until the mid-1970s, more than two-thirds of all toy sales were made between Thanksgiving and Christmas.

## WHO BUYS TOYS?

Sure, some kids save up their allowance and truck down to the toy store for just the plastic brontosaurus, Barbie couture outfit, or action figure they want. But, by and large, toy purchases are made by adults—typically, either parents or grandparents (who, together, make up two-thirds of the toy market) or other relatives and family friends. More than 90 percent of toys, games, hobbies, and craft items are bought for preteens and young teenagers, and nearly 95 percent of purchases are made by people over eighteen.

Parents and grandparents have somewhat different toy-buying habits. Parents buy more toys and bicycles than grandparents. They also spend more than grandparents. Parents spent an average of $15.60 on baby dolls, $9.32 on soft plush toys, and $7.85 on robots and accessories, while on those same items grandparents paid an average of $12.36, $9.32, and $7.60, respectively. Parents and grandparents also have different preferences as to where to buy toys. Parents did about a quarter (23.62 percent) of toy buying in toy stores, about a third (31.71 percent) in discount stores, 16.24 percent in department stores, and 7.58 percent in catalog showrooms. Grandparents, on the other hand, left only 19.66 percent of their toy dollar at the toy store and were somewhat more likely to go to discount stores (32.7 percent of spending) and catalog showrooms (8.27 percent of spending) than parents were.

Just because most toy spending is for kids doesn't mean that adults never buy toys for themselves (and we don't mean a Porsche to cheer up a mid-life-crisis sufferer). Chicago's two Eclectricity stores sell eight hundred products, with an average sale of $70 worth of "adult toys": board games (either sophisticated or salacious), complex jigsaw puzzles, and strategy games from many cultures. The product mix is 25 percent toys and games, 25 percent gifts, 25 percent design items, 15 percent electronic items, and 10 percent fitness-oriented merchandise.

## TURNAROUND 'R' THEM

The undisputed industry leader is Toys "R" Us, Inc., which made a dramatic rebound from Chapter 11 to the top of the heap. In 1988 Toys "R" Us sales were $3.13 billion, with net earnings of $203.9 million. The company was ranked as the 115th largest of *Business Week*'s Top 1000 corporations, with a market value of $4.541 billion (in April 1988), assets of $2,343 million, a return on investment of 18.4 percent, and a return on equity of 20.9 percent.

In 1987, Toys "R" Us had over 32,700 employees, undoubtedly the best-paid of whom was CEO Charles Lazarus, the 33rd-highest earner of 1986 with total compensation of over $3 million. The company had 313 toy stores and seventy-four Kids "R" Us clothing stores. The chain is a pioneer in introducing UPC scanners (the ones that check bar codes, like the ones in your supermarket); it was willing to devote $30 million to this purpose, to reach the goal of "no baskets left"—that is, no potential buyers who abandon a basket of unbought toys because they don't want to wait for a long checkout line to shorten.

## OTHER MAJOR PLAYERS

Although no other toy store measures up to Toys "R" Us, there are many other major toy chains and successful independents. Child World/Children's Palace, for example, has 134 stores in twenty-eight states. Its sales were up 22.5 percent in fiscal 1986, reaching $628.8 million and yielding a net income of $10.9 million (up from $9.4 million in the preceding year)—a degree of prosperity that made it possible to add fifteen new stores in 1987.

Franchising is strong in the toy business. There are fifty-six Chad's Rainbow stores throughout the country. The founder considers 1,700 square feet the ideal size for the franchise. Franchisees get to choose which toys to stock, averaging 15,000 SKUs. The first, tiny store (500 square feet) paid only $298 a month rent and grossed $160,000. Franchised stores in strip shopping centers average a first-year gross of $200,000—and stores in malls do even better, averaging sales of $500,000.

Single stores and minichains can also do well. Play Pen has one

6,600-square-foot store in Jackson, Mississippi, stocked from a 16,500-square-foot warehouse. In 1984 and 1985, the store grossed $1.3 million. Toby's Toys also has a store in Jackson, and one in Montgomery, Alabama. The 32,000-square-foot stores carry 12,000 SKUs, and the stuffed toy display carries 600 cuddly toys in 200 SKUs. It takes twenty employees to run each store, even though they're designed for maximum self-service.

## FUTURE FUN

Sales of educational toys that swear up and down your kid will get into Harvard seventeen years from now will no doubt continue strong. So will toys that let little boys feel omnipotent. Manufacturers are betting on electronic toys that interact with TV programs, but either market forces or an FCC crackdown on product-related kid-vid could KO *that* idea. (Whether it's natural to the species or conditioned by society, little girls don't seem very interested in war toys. Boys do like dolls—as long as they're either called action figures, made to look like animals or aliens instead of people, or promoted as a way for the Alan Aldas of the future to get in touch with their feelings.)

The 1987 Dun & Bradstreet survey of 679 toy stores showed gross profits of 35.1 percent of sales (lower than many other types of retail business). Net profit after tax was a slightly below average to average 4.4 percent of net sales. The range of return on sales was very wide: anywhere from 0.5 to 10.3 percent. A similar disparity was shown in the return on assets of the various stores: anywhere from 2.2 to 18.8 percent.

Toy sales depend in large part on the number of kids around in any given year. Birth rates are far lower than they were thirty years ago, so there are fewer potential customers; however, there are plenty of prosperous, indulged eldest or only children. And, according to business commentator David Owen, the more divorces there are, the more indulgent grandparents each kid has. First-borns get the most, and the most expensive, toys; the younger kids in the family often have discount purchases or hand-me-downs fobbed off on them.

Toy manufacturers and retailers are waiting, desperately, for a hot new toy to replace the waning appeal of Masters of the Universe and Cabbage Patch Kids. Maybe the stork will bring one.

# 55

# Florists

Number of establishments:   22,393
Total receipts:             $3.42 billion
Average net sales:          $152,600
Number of employees:        103,800
Total payroll:              $711 million

(Department of Commerce, '82)

In an urban area, there will always be reminders of the country: street vendors with bunches of flowers, stands near the bus stop or subway station blazing with colorful bundles wrapped in cones of paper. However, retail flower sales are only—well, not the tip of the iceberg; perhaps we should say the bud, with much of the plant underground or taking the form of sturdy stems. Seventy-five percent of flower sales are for "occasions": weddings, funerals, gifts to hospitalized friends, and anniversaries.

Sure, people buy flowers on impulse, bring them along when they're invited to dinner, or use them as a sentimental remembrance for spouse or friend. But Americans are far less flower-conscious than Europeans, who buy an average of $20 worth of flowers a year—double the American average. Still, that adds up to $7 billion a year in U.S. sales of flowers, houseplants, and bulbs for planting. The Department of Commerce's 1982 survey found that florist shops in Alaska had the highest average sales ($218,000 a year); South Carolina florists managed only $103,000—which can probably be explained by the comparative difficulty of growing one's own flowers in the two states, as well as by Alaska's high cost of living.

But businesses also buy flowers, to decorate restaurant tables or furniture showrooms or as goodwill gestures from one business to another. We spoke to Rick Crawford of Jersey City's Horizon floral shop, who says that only 40 percent of his business is individual, including sales from his subway stand; 60 percent is commercial ("catering" flowers for parties, or supplying law firms, public relations firms, and other businesses that need fresh flowers for the image they want to present). He says that commercial sales "make up for the hot days when everybody is at the beach." It's very much a special-occasion business. Fluctuations are less seasonal than keyed to holidays, with Christmas inspiring many people to buy flowers, flower arrangements, and potted poinsettias, and Valentine's Day and Mother's Day the two peaks of the year. Mr. Crawford gets most of his flowers—usually fifty to sixty kinds—from the New York wholesale flower market, with a few from New Jersey farms. (Mr. Crawford tips us that exotics are in, but carnations and spider mums are way out.)

Flowers are usually "ranched" on large farms, some in rural and suburban areas of the United States (suburban, because the markets are in major cities, and it cuts costs if the flowers don't have to be transported too far). However, a great many flowers are airfreighted into this country from low-wage countries in Central and South America that have long growing seasons. Luxury flowers are imported from Holland and other European countries.

## INDEPENDENTS AND FRANCHISES

It doesn't take much capital to open a flower shop: all you need is a small store, a few refrigerators, and a couple of days' worth of posies. You don't have to invest much in inventory, but you do need to run to the flower markets daily. That's one reason why florists' personnel costs—20.8 percent of sales—are higher than average. Someone has to keep the store open when the buyer is at the market, and someone has to unload the flowers. The florists surveyed by Dun & Bradstreet in 1988 achieved gross 1987 profits averaging 49.2 percent of net sales (above average), and net profit after tax of 4.8 percent (a little above average).

There are some franchises in the flower business, but it's pretty easy for independents to get started (especially if they have good contacts with caterers, funeral homes, or halls that are rented for weddings). Retail sales depend heavily on walk-in trade, so it's crucial for a store with substantial retail business to have a good location, which usually means high rent.

Conroy's, Inc., a chain of seventy-four franchised shops in the Southwest, belongs to Meldridge, Inc., a $40 million-a-year company that also handles wholesale flower distribution and sales and development of new varieties of flower bulbs. Flowerama, which is nationwide, has thirteen company-owned franchise shops and seventy-seven under individual ownership; the cost of the franchise is $17,500, and franchisees pay 5.6 percent monthly as a franchise fee, with no advertising fee.

# 56

# Hardware Stores

| | |
|---|---|
| Number of establishments: | 19,870 |
| Total receipts: | $8.33 billion |
| Average net sales: | $420,500 |
| Number of employees: | 126,900 |
| Total payroll: | $1.25 billion |

(Department of Commerce, '82)

"You can always tell a man who owns a house," said humorist Kin Hubbard. "He's the fella who's always just coming out of the hardware store." For homeowners and apartment-dwellers alike, there's a constant parade of chores around the home and garden: fix that leaky faucet, paint that wall, plant those tulip bulbs, change those light bulbs. In January 1987, hardware store sales were $933 million, much higher than January 1986 sales, which were $853 million.

The business has been growing steadily: in 1980, total sales of hardware stores, "home centers" (larger stores that sell lumber, perhaps kitchen cabinets and bathroom fixtures, and some decorating items in addition to traditional hardware items), and lumber yards were $38.1 billion. Total sales in 1985 from these stores were $60 billion, an

**Where the Money Went**

| | |
|---|---|
| (1) Cost of operations: | 67.2% |
| (2) Officers' compensation: | 4.1% |
| (3) Pensions and benefits: | 0.9% |
| (4) Rent: | 2.4% |
| (5) Repairs: | 0.4% |
| (6) Depreciation, depletion, and amortization: | 1.2% |
| (7) Interest: | 1.0% |
| (8) Bad debts: | 0.2% |
| (9) Advertising: | 1.8% |
| (10) State, local taxes: | 2.2% |
| (11) Other expenses: | 17.2% |
| (12) Net profit before tax: | 1.4% |

(Troy, '83–'84)

increase far greater than the rate of inflation. Projected sales for 1990 are $99 billion. The vast sales increase is probably related to the very high mortgage rates of the early 1980s. People who can't afford to buy a new house will fix up the old one; and people who can't afford to hire contractors will, whether enthusiastically or reluctantly, develop their skills as do-it-yourselfers.

Hardware store profits are close to the average for American retailing. The 1987 D & B survey showed gross profits averaging 33.5 percent of net sales, and net profit after tax of 3.8 percent.

Traditional hardware stores usually turn over their inventory 2.5 to 2.7 times a year; home centers average 3.8 "turns." The difference could be due to the fact that home centers tend to be newer, larger, and better capitalized, which means they can afford more advertising and market research, attracting new customers and keeping them on top of sales trends. Hardware stores can be run by the fifth generation of crotchety old guys who *know* what their customers should buy, dammit.

The two types of store attract a slightly different clientele. Home centers combine hardware with complementary merchandise, and their lower cost of goods sold (huge orders from wholesalers and manufacturers mean big discounts) is sometimes passed on to the customers. The traditional hardware store offers neighborhood convenience (home centers tend to be located, with other large stores such as appliance discounters, at Route Something or Exit Whatzis, not the Elegant Plaza Mall), the chance of finding that specialized piece of hardware that few customers ever need but for which no substitute exists, and often have knowledgeable woodworkers and homecrafters instead of teenage clerks earning the minimum wage to ring up bubble packs of nails on computerized cash registers.

Hardware stores of both types tend to be fairly large. For instance, Max's in Quincy, Massachusetts, described as "An Old-Fashioned Modern Business" by the trade magazine *Hardware Age* (April 1987), is one of a minichain of five stores owned by a single family. The flagship store has 4,500 square feet of selling space and 3,200 square feet of storage; the five stores sell $8 million worth of hardware a year.

A larger chain, Michigan's ACO, Inc., grew to fifty-nine stores (and annual sales of $88 million) by adding six new ones, averaging 10,000 square feet each. Each of the stores stocks 18,000 SKUs—about $500,000 worth of inventory—and sells $1.5 to $1.7 million a year. Five percent of sales is budgeted for advertising.

Although old-fashioned tinkering is losing ground (appliances come in sealed cabinets, so you can't fool around to see if you can get a baulky CD player or microwave oven going again—you either have to get a professional repairman, or start over again with a new gadget), there's an ever-expanding market for home repairs and improvements. Housing starts are low, which means that few people can live in newly built houses (and even newly built houses can need repairs, or just a new set of bookshelves). That means that there's a huge market for the bookshelf standards, drain snakes, and picture hooks, not to mention the power tools, sandpaper, and varnish that help trim and refurbish homes.

# RETAIL RAP: Inventory and Turnover

As we've seen on page 53, it's a subtle philosophical question whether a business is making any money or not. The answer depends on accounting systems, tax laws (you can't just pick any old accounting system you want), and even whether the business owners *want* to make any money (some juicy tax losses could come in handy). Oh, yeah. It also depends on facts—how much the business sells; how much it paid for the goods it sold; how high the other expenses were; and how many items walked out the door without a preliminary stop at the cash register (see page 284).

No business has much hope of making these determinations unless it understands its inventory, which is the stuff it buys or makes to resell to the public, and its turnover, which is the number of times each year it must replace its inventory (it certainly can't afford to have the same stuff sitting around in the stockroom for years on end).

Theoretically, businesses *must* take inventory once a year to keep the IRS satisfied. The better practice is to take inventory once a month. The old-fashioned, low-tech way is to go around and *count* everything: 226 boxes of #2 pencils—check; 193 Transformers loose-leaf binders—check; and so on into the night.

The new-fashioned, high-tech way is to stick a computerized label on every item in the store; the computerized cash register will then automatically subtract it from the inventory, and perhaps even contact the manufacturer's computer and reorder if the item is on the "reorder" list instead of the "Hallelujah, some sucker finally bought it" list. This is a wonderful advance, except on the occasions when the label has peeled off, the computer is down, the person working the cash register doesn't know how to handle it, or the item has been shoplifted or stolen by an employee, instead of purchased.

Inventory is usually tracked by "SKUs" (Stock Keeping Units). An SKU is one size, in one color and style. So if a boutique has periwinkle blue Pringle cashmere sweaters in sizes 4 to 14, it has six SKUs. If it has the same style, in the same sizes, in celadon green, that would be six more SKUs. As you can imagine, stores typically carry thousands of SKUs. It's worth the trouble to manage them separately because it then becomes possible to determine which SKUs are selling well and should be reordered and which are less successful or an outright flop.

## THIRTEEN FIGURES

Stores compute thirteen inventory figures a year: twelve "FOM" (First of the Month) inventories and an end-of-the-year figure. They don't necessarily

238

count everything (take "physical inventory") each month; they use "book inventory" for most months. In other words, they adjust the inventory records in light of the sales records, merchandise returned to the vendor, and markdowns (items sold at 10, 15, 20, or whatever percent off to get them out of the store before they become a permanent fixture), which reduce the inventory, and the new merchandise and markups (percentage added to the wholesale price), which increase it.

## STOCK TURNS

Stores calculate their turnover ("stock turns") by adding the FOM inventory for each month to the end-of-year inventory, then computing an average by dividing by 13. Turnover equals total sales divided by the average.

Remember the guy who was selling pencils on the street, and a potential customer asked how much they were? The salesman said, "A million dollars each." Startled, he asked, "You won't sell many pencils that way, will you?" The reply was, "I only have to sell one!" For some businesses, the merchandise is so expensive, or the markup so colossal, that turnover is not a pressing question. But where the profit margin is low, or the merchandise itself is perishable, then a successful business *must* turn over the merchandise.

Supermarkets (see page 89) have razor-thin profit margins, but the average supermarket has sixty-two inventory turns a year in some departments, and 122 a year in others. (Then there was the other fella who complacently told his business partner that they were losing a dollar on every item of merchandise they sold—but making it up on volume.)

Successful retailing involves judgment, not just routine. A clothing store may find that a particular line of fall sweaters is very successful, yet will not reorder them because it's time to clear out the fall merchandise and stock the heavy winter clothing and the cruisewear.

The initial ordering decision is a very tough one. A store has only limited amounts of both money to buy merchandise (the "open-to-buy" figure) and storage and display space. A successful store has to keep inventory "lean and mean"; ideally, each item should run out just as its replacement is delivered. If customers can be diverted to other merchandise in the store, it may even be worth running out of some items: for instance, if the customer wants a Father's Day present, a shirt and tie may do just as well as the out-of-stock robe.

However, there are situations in which a retailer will "stock up" or even risk over-ordering an item. If it is a high-demand, low-supply item, the retailer may place a large order to avoid finding out that the item is unavailable later on. It may be a fad item, where sales are "now or never," so the retailer buys the items and takes the profits quickly, recognizing that some of the merchandise may be unsaleable as the next fad takes over. Or just the opposite may be true: the item may be a perennial, one that can be kept in stock and brought out later, sure to sell eventually. (It's not a tragedy for a bookstore to have too many copies of a dictionary, but a book of this season's sports statistics won't be worth much next season.)

The speed of reorders is also an important factor. The "just in time" system, popular in Japan, allows a company to develop a network of relationships with suppliers who will furnish replacement merchandise almost immediately. If retailers can achieve such a relationship (even at the cost of paying higher prices for the goods), then they can reduce their initial orders of merchandise and reorder what they need. But it can take weeks, or even months, to get certain merchandise such as items that are in such hot demand that production can't keep up (for example, Cabbage Patch Dolls when they were first introduced); items that must be crafted specially; and some imports.

## MARKUPS AND MARKDOWNS

Of course, stores can't make a policy of selling merchandise for less than what it cost them to buy it. In fact, to cover the cost of doing business and to make a profit, they must "mark up" the merchandise. Usually, a business will set a policy for markups. For instance, a "keystone" markup is exactly twice the wholesale cost of the goods: something purchased for $50 will be sold for $100.

Manufacturers compute their markups by starting from the cost of production and moving up; retailers compute theirs by moving down from retail price. A retailer's "markup," also called a "margin," can be expressed either in numbers (the retail price minus the wholesale price of the merchandise) or as a percentage (usually a percentage of the retail price). In mathematical terms, markup on cost equals the selling price minus the wholesale cost, divided by the wholesale cost; margin on selling price equals selling price minus wholesale cost, divided by the retail price.

Markdowns are taken when a retail price is reduced—usually to sell a slow-moving item, but sometimes to inspire customers to enter the store in search of wild bargains. In the latter case, the item is called a "loss leader." The claim that merchandise is being sold below the retailer's cost is unlikely, but possible.

If an item really won't budge, it either takes up space on the selling floor that could be used for a more profitable item or gathers dust in a stockroom or warehouse (the space in both of which has to be paid for). (Retailers can return defective merchandise and certain exceptional kinds of merchandise such as items sold on consignment, books, records, and tapes—but the usual rule is that a manufacturer's or distributor's sales to retailers are final.) The retailer's choices are to slash the price and earn *something* on the item; "close it out" and sell it to a liquidator, in which case it will eventually turn up in Filenes Basement or a "job lot" store; or donate it to charity—if anybody wants it—and take a tax deduction.

Inventory, then, is in constant transition: new items are delivered, merchandise is sold or otherwise disposed of. The retailer's job is to predict what customers will want, and the combination of price, store decor, service, selection, and exclusivity that will impel them to purchase it at the retailer's store(s) and not from competitors. If a retailer promotes his store on the basis of either its wide selection of merchandise or its convenience for one-stop shopping, then being out of stock on a popular item is devastating. But if the retailer stresses a boutique approach and an elegant selection of merchandise, the customer can be made to feel like a peasant for wanting the unavailable item in the first place.

PART **E**

# Getting Around

# 57

# Car Dealers

|  | New Car Dealers | Used Car Dealers |
|---|---|---|
| Number of establishments: | 79,647 | 11,421 |
| Total receipts: | $184.47 billion | $6.27 billion |
| Average net sales: | $2.316 million | $549,200 |
| Number of employees: | 1,015,000 | 36,103,000 |
| Total payroll: | $16.43 billion | $449 million |

(Department of Commerce, '82)

In the 1950s and 1960s, owning a dealership for a major automobile make was pretty close to owning a private mint. The spacious lot stretched out over low-cost suburban land, and every year, when the eagerly awaited new models came in, the faithful customers would exchange one large, plush American car for the latest replacement. New cars were easily affordable for most people; and the trade-ins provided an endless stream of used cars in cream-puff condition for those who couldn't afford a new land yacht. And if the car dealer needed credit to finance the new year's inventory for the brief time until its sale, well, the bank would open the tap and loans at 2, 3, or maybe 5 percent would flow out.

245

**Where the Money Came From**

| | |
|---|---|
| (1) Sales of new cars: | 67.61% |
| (2) Sales of used cars: | 19.04% |
| (3) Parts and service: | 13.35% |

(Nat'l Ass'n of Automobile Dealers, '85)

**Where the Money Went ("Motor Vehicle Dealers")**

| | |
|---|---|
| (1) Cost of operations: | 87.4% |
| (2) Officers' compensation: | 1.1% |
| (3) Pensions and benefits: | 0.4% |
| (4) Rent: | 0.6% |
| (5) Repairs: | 0.2% |
| (6) Depreciation, depletion, amortization: | 1.0% |
| (7) Interest: | 1.0% |
| (8) Bad debts: | 0.1% |
| (9) Advertising: | 1.0% |
| (10) State, local taxes: | 0.8% |
| (11) Other expenses: | 7.2% |
| (12) Net profit before tax: | Not disclosed |

(Troy, '84–'85)

Then the mint chipped, so to speak. Suddenly the land under the cars seemed a lot more valuable underneath a shopping mall. The banks wanted well into the double digits to finance inventory, which had a way of hanging around the lot much longer. Buyers were searching for fuel-efficient cars, then hanging onto them for years and years, or buying used cars instead of new ones, in part because a new car cost at least half a year's salary for many people. And, suddenly, American cars had fearsome competition, even from countries like Korea and Yugoslavia, not previously known for their automotive engineering.

The number of domestic-car dealers began to drop. As of January 1, 1987, there were 20,405 outlets for domestic cars (258 closed in 1986; 229 closed in 1985). Chrysler gained twenty dealerships in 1986, and Volkswagen picked up one, but there were seventy-two fewer dealers for AMC/Renault cars, fifty-seven fewer for Ford Motor Company, and 150 fewer for General Motors Corporation.

However, the number of outlets for imports went up: on January 1, 1986, you could buy an imported car at any of 24,823 places. A year later that number had risen to 25,156, nearly all of which carried both imported and domestic cars (only 4,751 stuck to imports).

To put it charitably, auto dealers were prepared for their custom- ers' requests: on February 1, 1987, dealers' current inventories and vehi- cles being shipped to dealers added up to 1,734,299 vehicles—enough to meet the needs of 105 selling days; that is, they could do a roaring business for over three months without having a single additional car delivered. That was tragic news for car dealers who were used to turning over inventory rapidly or even having to turn down would-be buyers of popular car models.

Still, it's not exactly curtains for the $260 billion auto-retailing indus- try. (Recreational vehicles alone bring in $7 billion, or 379,500 vehicles— and, as an industry executive points out, "Nobody really needs an RV.") Each year, 15 million Americans buy a car or truck. In 1985, average sales per dealer were estimated by the National Automobile Dealers at $10.5 million. The management consultants Booz, Allen reported that the typical new American car retails for $11,333—and brings in a pretax profit for the dealer of $1,500 or so. The dealer probably paid about $7,900 for the car itself, $470 for delivery from the manufacturer, and $360 for marketing costs and overhead.

The Department of Commerce estimates that the average price of domestic cars sold in 1986 was $12,540; for foreign cars, the average was $14,044. Price rises are forecast for 1987 ($13,113 for domestic cars, $14,329 for foreign cars) and 1988 ($13,899 for domestic cars, $14,902 for foreign cars). The increases are due in part to Detroit's tendency to send cars out of the factory "loaded"—with plenty of what used to be options as standard equipment, which naturally raises the prices. That means more profit for the manufacturers but more trouble for the deal- ers, who have to convince baulky customers to pay for the plusher models.

The Hertz Corporation says that the average used car sold in 1986 cost $5,833, had notched 41,140 miles in its four-and-one-half-year life, and had another five-and-one-half years to go before its retirement. Forty-five percent of used cars were bought from new-car dealers; the rest, from used-car dealers or directly from the previous owner. Al- together, 16.5 million used cars were sold in 1986, for a total of $96.4 billion.

How many cars does a dealer sell? That depends on the kind of car: Honda outlets each averaged 640 sales—twice as many as Chevrolet out- lets, with 331, and Ford dealerships, with 295. Chrysler lagged far behind, with an average of 124 sales per dealership; American (before its acquisi- tion by Chrysler) averaged an even lower 87 per dealership. But the largest domestic-car franchise in the United States, Dale Oldsmobile (in the Bronx, of all places) sold 26,565 cars for a total of $379 million. However, only 1,850 of those were retail sales to plain old ordinary customers; the rest were sales of fleets of automobiles to corporations.

## SUPERDEALERS

Dale Oldsmobile is a "superdealer": one of 250 or so dealers who already have 15 to 20 percent of car sales locked up—and may wrest 30 percent of sales from the mom-and-pop dealers by 1990. The superdealers usually sell a number of different brands of car and truck and may operate in several states. The number-one superdealer, Potamkin, sold 66,000 vehicles of fourteen brands in 1986 ($800 million in sales; the 1987 figure was $856 million), although it took thirty-three outlets in five states to do it. Superdealers achieve hefty sales and healthy profit margins by operating efficiently—and by cutting a good deal with manufacturers eager to sell large numbers of cars to volume operations.

Wall Street is getting excited about a new kind of stock offering: giant auto dealers becoming public corporations and selling their stock to investors. As of May 1988, a couple of these initial public offerings were in the works, and many more were under consideration. Why didn't it happen before? Because the once-mighty U.S. auto manufacturers squashed any attempts by their franchised dealers to earn money in any other way than by selling lots more American cars. Today, the manufacturers are a lot less powerful and are just happy to sell their inventory any which way they can.

A well-managed, successful superdealership could be an excellent investment for a stockholder. Consumers could also benefit if new capital allows dealers to improve their service facilities; and dealers can surely benefit if they get loads and loads of money when the public buys their stock. But consumers could also lose out if dealers become remote managers, not hands-on sellers and servicers, or if they worry more about today's stock price than long-term customer satisfaction.

## INCENTIVES AND INDUCEMENTS

Auto manufacturers never used to offer "incentives"—cash rebates or low-cost financing. They didn't have to. Today, incentives are common, but the law of diminishing returns has set in. [The manufacturer encourages dealers to buy certain models by cutting the price the dealers must pay for these models in the hope that, as the *Wall Street Journal* ("Car Sales Slid in 1st 10 Days of This Month," November 16, 1987) delicately put it, the manufacturers will pass along some or all of the saving to the car buyers, who, cheered by the lower price, will buy the car.]

Consumers understand that incentives are offered only on the cars that are slow sellers, not on the models they really want. They also know that

## CONSUMER TIP

In September 1987, the Center for Auto Safety reported that at least five manufacturers (GM, Ford, Chrysler, American Honda, and Toyota U.S.A.) maintained secret warranty programs covering at least thirty million 1980–1986 vehicles— that is, the manufacturers were aware of problems with these cars and agreed to pick up the cost of repair if the car owner bellowed loudly enough—but potential buyers were not advised of the problem or the availability of the warranty programs. Always ask the dealer if a service bulletin has been sent about the particular problem that troubles your car; you may be entitled to free or reduced-price repairs.

the sticker price quoted for any car is only the opening bid in a round of negotiations; dealers will cut prices when they get sick of seeing expensive inventory take up space on the lot. And make no mistake, the inventory is expensive: there was a $458.66 increase in the manufacturers' list price for the eighteen makes tracked by the Department of Labor for the period 1987–1988, and the price to dealers rose $399.01. According to DOL, approximately 54 percent of the price increase came from quality improvements such as extra equipment, better rustproofing, and better warranties.

## CONSUMER TIP

Nearly all states have "lemon laws" to help aggrieved consumers get refunds or replacements for new cars that are not just lousy but unfixable. A growing trend is for states to require used cars to be sold with warranties, not just "as is," which protects the buyers of used lemons. Rhode Island, Connecticut, New York, Massachusetts, Minnesota, and the District of Columbia have these laws; they vary as to which vehicles are covered (it depends on the car's selling price and the number of miles it racked up in its previous life).

---

## CONSUMER TIP

Most auto manufacturers survey customers (and perform fol-low-up surveys) to find out if they're satisfied with dealer performance; a bad "report card" can mean that a dealer's franchise is cancelled or that a foreign maker refuses to let the dealer sell its cars. Dealers, in turn, say that customers would be more satisfied if manufacturers made better cars.

Don't just toss the rating form into the trash. Your response could be helpful to other buyers or could pull a lagging dealer into line. By the way, if you get a box of candy or a tin of cookies from your dealer, that's a hint that rating forms are on the way, and he hopes a few sessions of con-tented munching will improve your feelings about him.

---

### SERVICE

That brings us to the question of service. According to a Harris Poll commissioned by *Business Week,* about one-third (32 percent) of respondents said that dealers offered the best quality of service (28 percent opted for garages, 15 percent for specialty retailers; and only 7 percent chose gas stations). However, garages got the vote for best value in service (31 percent as compared to 21 percent for dealers). Garages also won out when it comes to honesty (32 percent as compared to 25 percent for dealers) and caring about customers (32 percent as compared to 29 percent for dealers). So, it seems that drivers like the service they get from car dealers, but not the way in which it's delivered. In 1986, according to *Automotive News,* car dealers' gross profit on labor, parts, and accessories was up 7.1 percent over 1985 levels, even though the number of repair orders written was about the same (down 0.1 percent); total billing for labor was up 8.6 percent; and sales of shop parts were up 6.6 percent.

### PROFITABILITY AND RETURNS

Maybe you'll feel a little more charitable toward the dealer when you realize that the 2,120 auto dealerships responding to the 1986 Dun & Bradstreet survey had an achingly small average gross profit of 13 percent. (Remember, many of the industries discussed in this book have average gross profits higher than 50 percent of sales.) Net profit after tax averaged 2.2 percent, which is also on the low side. The 859 used-car dealers in the survey did a lot better, with an average gross profit of 23.2 percent of sales and an average net profit after tax of 5.0 percent.

The Department of Commerce's 1982 census showed that the average pay of employees of auto dealers was well above the average for other businesses: $12,453 for used-car dealers' employees and $16,059 for those involved in selling new cars. But payroll represented a low percentage of sales: only 8.9 percent for new-car dealerships and 7.2 percent for used-car dealerships. Rent and inventory maintenance are so expensive that they make even relatively high salaries a small component in the calculations.

# 58

# Gas Stations

| | |
|---|---|
| Number of establishments: | 116,188 |
| Total receipts: | $94.7 billion |
| Average net sales: | $815,200 |
| Number of employees: | 603,800 |
| Total payroll: | $4.768 billion |

(Department of Commerce, '82)

Imagine the courage it must have taken to install a fuel tank and gas pumps early in the century. There were no superhighways, no drive-in restaurants or bank-teller windows. Nobody could be sure that the automobile, that smelly, smoky, newfangled contraption, would stay around long enough to make the investment worthwhile.

In the long run, the investment did prove worthwhile, but the gas station business has seen some tough times. Low oil prices in the 1950s and 1960s were heaven on earth for drivers who could cruise for hours in a land chariot for a buck's worth of gas but lousy for the gas stations that had to compete for every penny. In order to attract drivers, gas stations had to provide free service from attentive gas jockeys, engage in constant, suicidal price wars, and offer everything from sets of glasses to steak knives with a fill-up.

## Where the Money Went ("Gasoline Service Stations")

| | |
|---|---|
| (1) Cost of operations: | 86.3% |
| (2) Officers' compensation: | 1.2% |
| (3) Pensions and benefits: | 0.2% |
| (4) Rent: | 1.1% |
| (5) Repairs: | 0.3% |
| (6) Depreciation, depletion, amortization: | 0.9% |
| (7) Interest: | 0.4% |
| (8) Bad debts: | 0.2% |
| (9) Advertising: | 0.2% |
| (10) State, local taxes: | 1.7% |
| (11) Other expenses: | 7.4% |
| (12) Net profit before tax: | 0.1% |

(Troy, '84–'85)

Gas is a perfect example of a "commodity": a uniform product that must be sold on the basis of price because, while people will fight to the death on the relative merits of Coke and Pepsi or Gloria Vanderbilt and Guess jeans, hardly anybody really cares about the brand name of gas as long as it has the right octane rating.

That's one reason why premiums are important (especially premiums issued in a series; a driver might come back to get #244 in the Heroes of the NFL Juice Glass series) and one reason why gasoline credit cards are a great idea. People tend to buy more on credit, given the normal human belief that the bill will never come. And people have a good reason to drive a little further to the station where they can pay by credit card, instead of the one where they'll have to produce cash on the spot for the gas. Last but not least, the credit cards help the gas station with a perpetual problem: the presence of lots of cash in a lonely gas station is a tremendous temptation to robbers. A heap of credit card receipts just doesn't have the same allure.

With the infamous events of the 1970s—oil shortages, high prices, even a short interval of rationing—suddenly gas stations had the entire supply of an expensive, precious, and hard-to-find good. Not only did prices rise but service contracted. Customers no longer got a free oil check, windshield cleaning, and a new supply of road maps; they were often expected to pump their own gas and pay for it with a credit card, whether they wanted to or not.

Eventually, a new equilibrium was established. Oil prices came down, supplies went up. Yet demand went down, because many drivers switched to frugal subcompacts; even big cars lessened their appetite for gas. Rents went up: a gas station has to be fairly large to give cars the chance to turn around. In a crowded urban area, where the space could be used for three Benettons and a cookie store, or on a busy highway, where the space could accommodate a fast-food restaurant, rents will naturally be at a premium.

By November 1987, according to the *New York Times,* gas stations were back to offering premiums to boost gasoline consumption, which was 2.5 percent higher than 1986—encouraging, but nothing to write home about. Furthermore, dealers were operating on nostalgic profit margins: nostalgic, because they weren't any higher than thirty years earlier while costs were much higher. (Dun & Bradstreet's 1987 figures show gross profit for the 1,582 gas stations surveyed to be 21.5 percent of sales—one of the lowest figures in the entire survey; net profit after tax, however, was 3.1 percent—not too bad, in context.)

Ron Clancy, a Texaco dealer interviewed by the *Times,* sold unleaded premium gas for twelve cents a gallon more than he paid for it. However, that represented only 30 percent of his sales; half the sales came from unleaded regular, at a mighty slim five cents per gallon over cost. His inventory of gasoline now costs $10,000, which means he has to borrow more to maintain his inventory than when it cost $1,500 to stock up—and interest rates are higher. Furthermore, he has to pay $6 an hour to his employees (triple what they used to make) and now must spend $100 to $150 a year to replace gas pump nozzles that Texaco used to provide free. It's not easy work, either; gas has to be pumped in rainstorms, snowstorms, and heat waves, not just in clement weather.

Gas stations face strong competition from discount stores on certain items (such as motor oil and automotive accessories). They also face strong competition from convenience stores, which often sell gas at a loss, if necessary, as a way to entice customers inside to buy high-markup food items.

Some chains of gas stations are trying the opposite strategy. For example, ARCO (the new name for Atlantic Richfield Co.) now has almost six hundred service stations combined with franchised convenience stores called AM/PM, which are open twenty-four hours a day and sell grocery staples and fast foods in addition to gas. ARCO gets only 11 percent of the convenience-store sales, but AM/PM's 1986 sales were $240 million and its revenue in 1990 is predicted to top $1 billion, so it's a promising start. Since many retailers are finding success by combining several products (books and tapes and videocassettes) or by combining products and services (health clubs that sell athletic equipment and sports clothing), perhaps gas stations and convenience stores will be another profitable combination.

# 59

# Auto Repair and Service

| | |
|---|---|
| Number of establishments: | 179,093 (108,543 "general automotive repair shops"; 40,778 "top and body repair shops"; 28,772 "other automotive repair shops") |
| Total receipts: | $20.41 billion ($8.9 billion general; $5.3 billion top and body; $6 billion other) |
| Average net sales: | $113,900 |
| | (Department of Commerce, '82) |

Servicing cars (in case of defect or accident) and providing "aftercare" (taking routine care of them once they roll off the dealer's lot) is a $104 billion market. Dealers handle about one-third of service needs (after all, they have a lock on warranty repairs), and independent auto shops handle another third—including most of the nonwarranty work. The remaining third is split up among gas stations, specialty shops—Ferraris "R" Us, so to speak—and Sears and other mass merchandisers.

In a Harris poll about customer perception of automotive service commissioned by *Business Week,* dealers and garages were the clear winners over tire dealers, specialty shops, and gas stations. (Although gas

**Where the Money Went ("Auto Repair and Services")**

| | | |
|---|---|---|
| (1) Cost of operations: | 51.6% | |
| (2) Officers' compensation: | 4.7% | |
| (3) Pensions and benefits: | 1.3% | |
| (4) Rent: | 3.9% | |
| (5) Repairs: | 1.2% | |
| (6) Depreciation, depletion, amortization: | 9.2% | (all that equipment, y'know) |
| (7) Interest: | 3.5% | |
| (8) Bad debts: | 0.4% | |
| (9) Advertising: | 1.2% | |
| (10) State, local taxes: | 3.4% | |
| (11) Other expenses: | 20.2% | |
| (12) Net profit before tax: | Not disclosed | |

(Troy, '83–'84)

stations used to be a top choice for service, fewer and fewer now provide anything except self-service gas pumps.) More than a quarter of those surveyed (28 percent) said that garages provided the best service—slightly behind the figure for dealers (32%). However, garages were way ahead, in customers' eyes, when it comes to value, honesty, and caring about customers. The consulting firm Temple, Barker & Sloane found that customers believe that independent service organizations charge less than car dealers (though, in fact, prices are about equal).

For the car that has everything—a lousy transmission, faulty electrical wiring, bad alignment—auto service malls are springing up, mostly in the Sun Belt. There are already two hundred of these single-purpose malls, usually in the range of 10,000 to 45,000 square feet, and with five to twenty auto shops. The "anchor" tenant is usually a tune-up shop, a shop that handles lubes and oil changes, or a car wash. The tenants typically pay $10 to $18 a square foot in rent, which is a good deal for them because city rents are usually much higher. The auto mall is also a good deal for its developer because the malls cost only about $30 a square foot to build, for a total investment of $70 to $90 a square foot; a 16 to 20 percent return on the developer's investment is common. (See page 137 for more about the conventional types of shopping mall.)

Some enterprising auto technicians are even beginning to *deliver* auto repair services: Wisconsin's Freedom Tire will deliver tires and put them on the customer's car, wherever it happens to be. Freedom can charge a bit less than conventional tire stores because it doesn't have to pay rent or other retail overheads. The same is true of Colorado's Express Lube Corporation and Minnesota's Novus, Inc., which travels to repair windshields.

## FRANCHISE HEAVEN

Express Lube and Novus, like many auto-repair and service businesses, are franchises. When a confused driver hears an ominous clunk or rattle in the car, he or she probably doesn't know what causes it or how to fix it—and probably wants to find a skilled repairer right away. If the driver sees commercials for a particular franchise week in and week out, it's likely to be his or her first stop when car trouble arrives; if the franchise does a good job, it'll gain repeat business and word-of-mouth recommendations.

Midas Muffler is one of the best-known franchises, with over 1,500 shops nationwide. A would-be muffler shop operator needs about $142,000, including a $10,000 initial franchise fee, to align with Midas Muffler; there's a monthly 5 percent royalty and 5 percent advertising fee once the business is up and running. The four hundred or so Meineke Discount Muffler shops require a higher initial franchise fee ($20,000) and at least $75,000 in capital; monthly fees are 7 percent and a 1 percent advertising fee.

A Novus windshield repair franchise costs about $1,400 to $6,700 to get started, including a franchise fee that varies from $600 to $2,900. If you do decide to join its 550 franchisees, you'll have to pay a monthly 6 percent royalty but no other fees. But if you'd rather become a Freedom Tire franchisee, be prepared to pony up $144,500, which Monte Tobin, the company's founder, claims is far less than it would cost to open a tire store at a fixed location.

Other popular franchises are AAMCO transmission shops and MAACO auto painting (no relation), and the various companies that lubricate cars: Jiffy Lube, Laser Lube, McQuick's Oilube, and Express Lube, for instance. Pampered cars go to Steve's Detailing, which has fourteen franchises and five company-owned locations, or to Wax Man, where they are gone over figuratively with a fine-tooth comb and literally with Q-Tips and lambswool until they're gleaming inside and out. Detailing a car costs at least a hundred bucks, maybe two hundred; it's already a $500-million-a-year business, with projected growth to $2.5 billion in 1995.

All sectors of the automobile aftermarket are likely to grow. People are buying more expensive cars and keeping them longer, well past the warranty period, which creates a need for service. Dual-income couples have more disposable income but less time to tinker with the car or even to take it to the shop, which creates a need for at-home service or for quicker and more convenient ways to get the car repaired or serviced.

There's a tremendous amount of competition in the auto-repair field—175,000 shops, according to a 1982 Department of Commerce survey. (That's good for consumers because they are likely to have a repair shop close to their homes or offices, but it can also be bad for consumers, if too many of the shops are fly-by-nights that provide poor service until customers catch on and the shop closes.) The 1986 Dun & Bradstreet survey of 1,385 shops found that the industry was nonetheless a fairly profitable one, with gross profits of 40.6 percent of net sales and after-tax net profit of 6.2 percent. Figures for top and body shops were similar, with a gross profit level of 40.4 percent of sales and net profit after tax of 6.7 percent.

# 60

# Car Rentals

| | |
|---|---|
| Number of establishments: | 9,024 |
| Total receipts: | $9.6 billion |
| Average net sales: | $1,068,000 |

(Department of Commerce, '82)

The Avis car-rental firm made advertising history with its campaign, "We're #2, but we try harder." Before that, all advertisers claimed to be #1, whether or not it was true in any commonly accepted sense. Avis has also made corporate history by bouncing back and forth from owner to owner like a basketball. The firm was started in 1946, with rental units at the Detroit and Miami airports (as we'll see, there's an intimate connection between the car-rental business and airports). In 1977, Norton Simon, Inc., bought Avis; then Esmark, Inc., bought Norton Simon, so Avis went along. In 1984, Beatrice bought Esmark, and in 1986 Beatrice "went private" and Avis was sold again, this time to a group led by Wesray Capital Corporation. Guess what—it was sold *again* in 1987, to Avis' own Employee Stock Ownership Plan, for $750 million in cash plus the assumption of about $1 billion in debt (mostly incurred to buy cars). Avis lost money in 1982–1984, but by 1987 it had sales of about $900 million and pretax earnings of 10 percent from its 1,200 company-owned and 2,300 franchised locations.

Meanwhile, the industry leader, Hertz, became part of the Allegis Corporation travel empire (along with United Airlines) and was sold in the fall of 1987, when Allegis was unwound.

Apart from these corporate machinations, 1987 was a pretty good year for car rentals, with rental fees up 10 percent but costs up only 7 percent. Revenues for the whole industry were up 20.3 percent (totalling $6.5 billion). In fact, Hertz's operating profits nearly tripled from 1986 to 1987; Budget Rent-a-Car, another leading rental firm (twelve company-owned and 1,000 franchised units) nearly doubled its net profits in the first half of 1987 over 1986 levels.

However, although the Big Four (Hertz, Avis, Budget, and National, the last of which has almost a thousand units, two-thirds owned by franchisees) collectively get 90 percent of the car-rental business, they face plenty of competition from smaller, not necessarily nationwide, firms. The Big Four get two-thirds of their business from corporate accounts; the competitors try to appeal to individual renters by cutting prices—in some instances to 30 percent less than those charged by Hertz.

Hertz has the largest fleet of cars (160,000) and owns nearly all of them; the rest of the Big Four own at least two-thirds of their cars and lease the rest. That was a great move before the 1986 tax reform act, when there were enormous tax incentives to own the vehicles. After 1986, though, the smaller rental firms, which either lease their cars or have franchisees buy them, were in a better position because of tax factors.

In the car-rental business, "small" doesn't always mean minuscule: Miami-based Alamo Rent-a-Car has 60,000 cars available at its 65 rental locations. Dollar Rent-a-Car of Los Angeles has fewer cars (46,000) but a lot more places to rent them: 450 locations. General Rent-a-Car, also centered in Miami, has only 33 rental locations but a healthy 20,000 cars, and Tulsa's Thrifty Rent-a-Car has 24,000 cars and a hefty 360 locations.

## AIRPORT OR NOT?

One of the most important decisions a rental company must make is whether to locate at an airport. The Big Four companies get the first crack at travelers who want to arrange car rentals as soon as they hit the airport, but they must pay for space at the airport and parking fees, and turn over about 10 percent of their revenues to the airport. Airports, in turn, can earn up to 30 percent of their own revenue from the big guys in auto rental. The smaller rental companies avoid this by maintaining a bus fleet to drive potential customers to their off-airport locations. However, the airports are getting wise and are beginning to impose fees on off-airport rentals, too. A federal court has invalidated such fees at Sarasota Airport, and the Palm Beach charge is now the subject of litigation.

---

## CONSUMER TIP

Before you pay for the waiver, check your own auto insurance policy. Many of them have a "DOC" (Drive Other Cars) provision that protects you if you're involved in a collision in a rental car. If you travel frequently, it might pay to beef up your auto insurance policy to get or increase this coverage.

---

## WAIVER OR NOT?

It's tough to figure out which car rental is the cheapest unless you have a mainframe computer and a degree in statistics. There's the matter of whether you qualify for a corporate rate, a discount rate based on fre-quent-flier miles, or one offered by your professional organization or even your telephone company. But the daily or weekly charge is only the beginning. Depending on the company, there may or may not be mileage charges (or charges beginning after a certain number of "free" miles), gas charges, drop-off charges, and a charge for dropping off the car someplace other than the place you picked it up.

Then there's the vexing question of the collision damage waiver—that is, if you rent a car, the car-rental company makes a simple offer: either you pony up $9 or $10 a day for a collision damage waiver, or you agree to pay either the first $3,000 in damage caused to the car if it's damaged in a collision during your rental or *all* the damage, with no limit, depending on company policy. Consumer advocates are angered by this practice because rental fleets naturally have auto insurance and are in a position not only to bargain for the best possible insurance premiums but to either set up their own repair shops or make a good deal on the volume of auto repairs they generate. Anyway, the rental fee should include all the company's cost of doing business, including paying insurance premi-ums—you don't have to pay a "pressing machine damage waiver" every time you get your shirts laundered or a "kitchen fire damage waiver" every time you order a restaurant meal.

Selling the waiver puts the rental company in the position of selling a kind of insurance—without an insurance license. Consumer groups and state regulators are trying to require licensure (and disclosure to consum-ers). However, so far California and New York courts have said that no license is required to sell the collision waivers.

# 61

# Limousine Services

Faster than a speeding subway (well, sometimes), more elegant than a taxi . . . it's a bird, it's a plane, it's a rented limousine. For those who want to make an impression when they arrive (but not a flawless one: the real snobs can see from the license plate that the limousine is rented, not the property of the arriviste), the "limo"—especially the stretch limo—is the only way to travel. Besides, it's so practical: it holds plenty of luggage.

No doubt because it contains so many people who are hungrier for status than their assets will permit, the New York area is the leading consumer of limousines: there are 9,000 of them plying for hire in an area with 17.5 million people. Chicago is next, with a mere 1,600 limousines to serve 8 million people. The Los Angeles area has 11.5 million people, served by only 1,200 rental limos—no doubt because anyone who is anybody either has his own or drives a sports car. Boston, with 1,000 limousines serving a population of 4 million, is the fourth-largest market.

## THE FLEET'S IN

Overall, there are about 45,000 limousines in the United States. Eight out of ten of them are livery cars; the remaining 19 percent are pri-

## TRADE TALK

A "black car" is a limo or sedan that cruises the airports to pick up passengers without reservations.

vately owned or part of corporate fleets. Readers of the trade magazine *Limousine & Chauffeur* deploy a fleet that's about two-thirds limousines (40 percent are stretch limos; 22 percent are plain old ordinary "formal limousines," defined as limousines "without entertainment amenities"— no bar, no VCR, no color TV. Tsk tsk!), 20 percent sedans (also called "town cars," frequently used for airport runs), 11 percent vans, and 7 percent buses.

The services' average hourly rates are about $45 for stretch limousines, $35 for formal limousines, and $30 for sedans (rates are somewhat higher in the western than in the eastern United States). It costs the fleet about eighty-nine cents a mile to operate a limousine. To purchase a limousine, you can pay anywhere from $16,000 for a used one to about $31,000 and way up (because the sky's the limit for interior amenities) for a new one.

Eastern limousine services employ an average of 8.4 full-time and 8.2 part-time chauffeurs—far more than the western average of 3 full- and 3.5 part-time chauffeurs. About half (55 percent) of limousine services "farm out" business: that is, they pass on orders to other companies and split the fee.

Usually, potential customers telephone the limousine service; the service's dispatcher communicates with the drivers by means of two-way radio. The chauffeur makes up a written trip sheet giving the customer's name and special requirements, the time and length of the trip, and the payment method. Depending on the service and the area, business can be almost entirely corporate or split between corporate, airport, and wedding business. Many limousine services have an arrangement with a hotel or casino that includes in its rates limousine service for guests. The agree-

## TRADE TALK

A stretch limousine is one that's been cut in half and extended; it usually carries a bar, probably a TV, and a moonroof (since hardly anybody goes anyplace by limousine during the daytime). A single-cut stretch is sawed in half behind the driver's seat; a double-cut, extra-long limousine is sliced into three parts (usually behind each door) and reassembled. A double divider limousine has both a glass window and a solid partition between the passengers and the driver.

ments usually last for two years; the hotel gets a 15 to 20 percent commission on further business booked through the hotel.

SNOB TIP: Among the truly upper crust, a limousine is referred to simply as a "car," and the person in the natty little cap (89 percent of limo drivers are men) is the "driver"—calling him or her a "chauffeur" implies that you hired him or her for the day, whereas "driver" implies a permanent employee.

# 62

# Travel Agencies

| | |
|---|---|
| Number of establishments: | 28,416 |
| Total receipts: | $4.24 billion |
| Average net sales: | $149,365,000 |
| Number of employees: | 111,700 |
| Total payroll: | $1.411 million |

(Department of Commerce, '82)

Planning a vacation or business trip can be a vast, multivariable math problem. Finding out which airlines fly to the destination is pretty simple; so is finding out the alleged times of departure and arrival for the flight. The problem is that scheduled times include a proportion of wishful thinking—a problem that becomes more serious when the traveler has to make a connecting flight. Add in the questions of finding the lowest fare available, the fare that permits the largest refund if the traveler must reschedule the flight, and the flight that gives the traveler the largest number of frequent-flier miles and bonuses (or the flight that can be used to take advantage of the frequent-flier miles already accumulated), and you'll understand why travel agents can be a godsend—especially since they often make it possible for the harried traveler to arrange hotel rooms and

Where the Money Went

| | |
|---|---|
| (1) Salary: | 47.3% |
| (2) Other employee costs (pensions, etc.): | 5.6% |
| (3) Education: | 1.6% |
| (4) Computerized reservation systems: | 5.35% |
| (5) Advertising and promotion: | 5.0% |
| (6) Communications: | 4.2% |
| (7) Postage, travel and entertainment, business automobiles: | 3.1% |
| (8) Dues, subscriptions, and supplies: | 3.9% |
| (9) Insurance: | 1.1% |
| (10) Professional fees (lawyers, accountants, etc.): | 1.2% |
| (11) Rent, occupancy costs: | 6.9% |
| (12) Depreciation: | 2.6% |
| (13) Other operating costs: | 12.2% |

(American Society of Travel Agents, '84)

rental cars at the same time, and even pick up a ticket and boarding pass, saving precious minutes at the airport. Travel agents do all this, apparently without charging a cent to travelers. This is neither a miracle nor great charity, because the travel agents receive commissions from airlines, railroads, hotels, and so on. Paying these commissions is a cost of doing business for airlines and the rest; fares and hotel rates include the cost of commissions.

According to a survey undertaken by ASTA (the American Society of Travel Agents) in 1985, 70 percent of agency revenues comes from domestic flights and 30 percent from flights outside the United States. Vacation and group/incentive travel account for about two-thirds of revenues; business travel, the other third. A little more than half of agency owners are women (54.7 percent), and the work force is overwhelmingly female: 79.6 percent of non-owner-managers and 84.4 percent of employed travel agents are women. Nearly all travel agency owners, managers, and employees are white (approximately 90 percent or more in each category).

Employed travel agents usually get a salary only; outside salespeople, who count as "independent contractors" for tax purposes, usually get commissions only. The distinction is a little like that between attorneys who are on the payroll of a particular company and private practice attorneys, who get fees from clients instead of a steady salary. Nearly all the agencies surveyed paid part or all of the cost of employees' vacations (88.0 percent) and family trips (82.3 percent) but hardly any provided retirement plans (9.2 percent). (This is probably because employed travel agents frequently move from agency to agency or take time off for family responsibilities; few of them stay in one place long enough to accrue pension benefits anyway.) Health insurance (64.6 percent) and bonuses (59.7 percent) were common; life insurance (39.0 percent), disability in-

## CONSUMER TIPS

▶ If your local travel agency is under new management, watch out. It could have been taken over by "bustout" operators who buy travel agencies just to get their supply of blank tickets, which are worth as much as $850 each and can be sold on the black market. (The bustout operator has no intention of functioning as a legitimate travel agent, only of grabbing the blank tickets. But he doesn't mind collecting money from credulous customers who come back later for their tickets only to find that the bustout operation has disappeared. Make sure you get your tickets when you pay; and find out what the agency and agency operator's business background are before you entrust your money to them.)

▶ If you have to travel between one "hub" city (that is, a city in which airlines concentrate their operations) and another, it may be cheaper to buy a ticket for a flight to a city further than your destination, but which stops in your destination city, than to travel directly to your destination. For example, if you have to get from Newark to Atlanta, it might pay to buy a ticket on a flight to Houston that stops in Atlanta. Once the plane stops for the "connecting flight," just get off and throw away the ticket to the next destination. (Airline tickets are nontransferable, so you're not allowed to sell it to someone else.)

▶ Travel agents make payments to airlines only once a week, on Tuesdays. That creates a loophole on Wednesdays through Mondays: if a valued customer has to cancel a non-refundable airline ticket on one of those days, the travel agency can void the ticket because it hasn't paid for it yet and so doesn't have to seek a refund from the airline and encounter cancellation penalties. Agencies bend the rules when they do this, but they may go out on a limb for a frequent customer.

surance (21.2 percent), profit sharing (17.9 percent), and dental insurance (17.0 percent) were less so.

It's not that well paid a business, as you can see from the following table:

|  | Agency Owners | Employed Agents |
|---|---|---|
| *Pay per month:* | | |
| Less than $800 | 0 | 15.3% |
| $800–999 | 0 | 27.3% |
| $1,000–1,499 | 22.6% | 43.5% |
| $1,500–1,999 | 20.0% | 11.5% |
| $2,000–2,999 | 17.9% | 2.3% |
| More than $3,000 | 15.1% | 0 |

Another survey of travel agents, by Robert Morris Associates in 1985, found that operating profit averaged 4.2 percent of net sales in 1984–1985. That was way up from the dismal 2.8 percent the year before but below the miraculous year of 1981–1982, when operating profit averaged 8.4 percent. Why was 1981–1982 such a great year? Because airlines charged into the deregulation era and offered tremendous incentives to agents to steer agency clients their way instead of to one of the competitors.

Profits sagged in 1983–1984 because agencies had to spend a lot on computerized reservation systems. Apollo (United Airlines) and Sabre (American Airlines) computerized systems were by far the most popular, with about one-third of agencies having terminals in each system. Airlines will invest flattery, service improvements, and even cash incentives to get travel agents to use their reservation system because Airline A must pay Airline B whenever a passenger on Airline A gets his or her ticket through Airline B's reservation system. In a highly competitive, deregulated environment, those few bucks could mean the difference between a profitable airline trip and one that the airline loses money on.

All of the survey respondents grossed over $1 million in 1984, but only 3.1 percent grossed over $20 million. About 60 percent grossed $4 million or less. Pretax profit in 1984–1985 was 2.9 percent of sales, once various nonoperating expenses had been met.

# 63

# Airlines

In the 1930s, air travel was rare, expensive, and glamorous. The first airline stewardesses were trained nurses in case the passengers succumbed to the terrors of the exotic aviation experience and fainted, panicked, or became ill.

Today, air travel has all the glamor (and all the thrills) of riding a ramshackle World War II vintage local bus over the narrow, winding roads of the Bolivian Andes (though it is very unlikely that there will be any cages of live chickens tied to the top of the airplane). Air travel is sometimes inexpensive—*if* you happen to want to travel from one airline hub to another and *if* several airlines are competing for your business by engaging in a fare war. But if you want to travel to an unpopular destination or one served by only one airline, expect to have to make several stops or to change planes, and expect to pay monopoly prices for the privilege.

Everybody wants the convenience of an airport a few minutes from home or the office, but no one wants to live or work near a noisy airport that's the center of a perpetual traffic jam. Even if it were easy to get permission to build a new airport, it's hard to find a vast tract of land near a city at an even vaguely affordable price. Land that could be turned into an airport is probably far more valuable as real estate for homes, offices, or industrial parks.

**Market Share, 1987 (Travel within the United States)**

| | |
|---|---|
| (1) Texas Air Corporation (which owns Continental and Eastern): | 19% |
| (2) United Air Lines, Inc.: | 16.9% |
| (3) American: | 13.8% |
| (4) Delta Air Lines, Inc.: | 12.2% |
| (5) Northwest: | 10.3% |
| (6) USAir, Inc., Trans World Airlines, Inc. (TWA), and Pan Am Corporation: | 18.8% |
| (7) All others: | 6% |

*(Business Week,* March 16, 1987; *New York Times,* September 9, 1987)

**Where the Money Goes**

| | |
|---|---|
| (1) Cost of operations: | 47.7% |
| (2) Officers' compensation: | 0.4% |
| (3) Pensions and benefits: | 3.5% |
| (4) Rent: | 6.7% |
| (5) Repairs: | 2.6% |
| (6) Depreciation, depletion, amortization: | 6.8% |
| (7) Interest: | 3.4% |
| (8) Bad debts: | 0.3% |
| (9) Advertising: | 1.7% |
| (10) State, local taxes: | 2.7% |
| (11) Other expenses: | 28.4% |
| (12) Net profit before tax: | Not disclosed |

(Troy, '84–'85)

**Top Earners, 1986**

| | Salary, Bonus | Deferred Comp. | Total |
|---|---|---|---|
| R. L. Crandall, AMR (the parent company of American Airlines) | $835,000 | $337,000 | $1,172,000 |
| D. C. Garrett, Jr. (Delta) | $529,000 | $352,000 | $881,000 |
| E. I. Colodny, USAir Group, Inc. | $604,000 | $114,000 | $718,000 |
| F. Lorenzo, Texas Air | $474,000 | $11,000 | $485,000 |

Add to this problem an ever-increasing amount of air traffic, an overburdened air traffic control system, the problem of preventing hijacking and other forms of terrorism, and the need to fill airplane gas tanks with large amounts of expensive fuel (when the price of aviation fuel goes up a penny, the industry has to pay an additional $115 million to gas up its fleet—and it doesn't even get a set of glasses from the gas station), and the average air traveler's gripes are easy to explain. It's far too simplistic to attribute all the problems to deregulation or to condemn airline management as incompetent SOB's. But whatever the reasons, many travelers find flying a miserable experience.

## THE PROFIT SQUEEZE

The airline industry is enormous. If you consider all the airlines as a single industry, the composite would rank #28 in *Business Week*'s Top 1000 corporations, with assets of $47.93 billion and an overall market value of $14.91 billion. (The smaller market value shows that investors are chary of airline stocks.) In 1987, the industry had sales of $46.88 billion but profits of only $58.5 million. That made its margin 2.8 percent for 1987.

The major airlines take in huge amounts of money but operate on profit margins as skinny as a Seventh Avenue fashion model. For instance, in 1987 Allegis (parent company of United Air Lines) scored sales of $8 billion ($8,293,000,000, to be exact) but actually *lost* $4.2 million. (Well, they had 87,000 employees on the payroll, and CEO Richard Ferris earned $583,000.) Things were a lot tougher for Pan Am, which had quite healthy sales of $3,038,000,000—and a loss of $462.8 million. You'll be glad to know that CEO C. Edward Acker still managed to be the 470th-best-paid CEO, earning $520,000 in total compensation. Maybe the airline would have lost a lot *more* money in less skillful hands.

For airlines, profits can be fly-by-night (sorry, we couldn't resist). In the fourth quarter of 1986, the airline industry as a whole operated at a profit margin of 2.8 percent, with overall sales of $9.2 billion and profits of $260 million. But by the first quarter of 1987, sales were down to $7.9 billion. In part, this was expected—Thanksgiving and Christmas bookings happen only once a year, and January and February weather discourages impulsive plane journeys. But the profits had evaporated, leaving a $44.9 million loss for the industry overall, thus making it impossible to calculate profit margins.

Individual airlines also suffered in this pocket of turbulence. For instance, Delta Air Lines had a generous profit margin of 10.5 percent in the fourth quarter of 1986—and a measly one of 1.8 percent in the first quarter of 1987. Piedmont, a smaller airline, had a smallish profit margin of 3.4 percent in the fourth quarter of 1986, which diminished to 1.2 percent in the first quarter of 1987. We bracket these two airlines together because they were the only ones among those listed in *Business Week*'s Corporate Scoreboard to earn a profit in the first quarter of 1987. TWA swooped from a 9.9 percent margin, sales of $856.9 million, and hefty profits of $85.0 million to a loss of $54.8 million on nearly identical sales ($824 million).

## BILLS OF FARE

Airlines can't do much to make people buy tickets, although they can try to make air travel in general seem attractive, with ads showing glorious beaches or Big Ben, and to motivate travelers to choose their airline over the competitors by claiming better service or offering additional comforts or frequent flier miles to customers.

Another thing that airlines can do is change their fares. The decision is far from a simple one: higher fares, of course, mean more income—but perhaps at the expense of the all-important "passenger miles," "load factors," and "yield" that determine airline success.

Within the United States, airlines depend on business travelers for both volume and profit. Except for people rushing to Granny's bedside after she's had a heart attack, people traveling for personal reasons can usually reschedule the trip or decide to drive to Yellowstone Park or Disney World, to take the train, or even to go somewhere else entirely. But business travelers don't have that luxury: they *must* go to the Topeka plant to figure out what's wrong, or go to Denver to meet with a potential new client, or go to San Francisco for the annual sales meeting.

That means that airlines treat business travelers entirely differently from tourists and pleasure-trippers. When a million-dollar deal hangs in the balance, a $200 plane ticket seems pretty unimportant—especially

## TRADE TALK

*Passenger miles* are computed by multiplying the number of paying passengers by the length of their journeys. *Load factors* measure the ratio of paying passengers to empty seats on a flight; the industry average is about 60 percent. *Yield,* which averages 11.26 cents for flights within the United States, is the amount earned for each mile a passenger flies.

In 1986, for instance, Continental had an above-average load factor of 63.2 percent—but it needed a 62.5% figure to break even. The average passenger rode Continental for a little more than 1,000 miles, at an average yield of 8.66 cents per passenger-mile—and costs of 5.95 cents per seat-mile. (Costs are measured by seat-mile because the costs are incurred whether or not anyone is actually sitting in the seat.) The airline had revenues of a little over $2 billion but operating expenses of $1.87 billion, leaving operating income of only $143.2 million and a decidedly modest net income of $17.9 million, which is, no doubt, why Continental is now part of Texas Air.

since the person taking the plane trip isn't the one paying for it. (A constant source of irritation to the IRS is the fact that the business traveler usually gets to keep the frequent-flier bonuses for himself or herself even though the company paid for the ticket. The IRS constantly proposes that business travelers be taxed on the value of the airline ticket to Hawaii that those bonuses eventually "buy" for him. Congress never listens.)

As a special accommodation to those travelers (or companies) unwilling to spend the first-class fare, many airlines offer a business-class fare between regular coach fare and first-class fare, offering more amenities than the one but less luxury than the other.

The need for business travel often emerges suddenly, with an unexpected business opportunity or the need to deal with a crisis at a distant office. That means that business travelers nearly always pay full fare because they can't book far enough in advance to qualify for low "max-saver," "super-saver," or "ultra-saver" fares. Furthermore, they often return home on the same day, or a day or two later, so they don't qualify for the reduced fares that require the traveler to stay at least seven days, or over a weekend, at the destination (or rather, the restriction exists precisely so that business travelers won't qualify).

Airlines can always fill seats with vacationers during the summer and for major holidays and with college students at the beginning and end of each college term, so coach fares are highest at these times. If an airline wants to touch off a fare war, it's likely to make its first move right after Labor Day when traffic declines and customers can be tempted to take another plane trip only if fares are attractively low.

Fare wars are funny things. Sometimes an established airline will make a daring move to cut fares, hoping to improve its market share either temporarily (until the other airlines follow suit) or permanently (if they never do). Or the airline may have the explicit intention of driving other, less solvent airlines off a particular route or out of business; to do this, an airline may be willing to cut the fare so low that it loses money on a particular run in order to deprive competitors of passengers or revenue. Every once in a while an outsider will make an even more daring move and set up a cut-price airline, but as Laker and People Express have already proved, that strategy is unlikely to succeed in the long run. In 1987, the new kid on the block was Tempe-based America West Airlines, Inc.; it'll be interesting to see if it can sustain its growth in revenues and passenger miles while maintaining low costs (6.2 cents per seat-mile—way below the industry average of 7.4 cents), low fares, and comparatively high salaries for personnel.

Airlines also manipulate fares in the other direction: a pioneer will cautiously raise fares or tighten up the restrictions on discount fares, hoping to earn extra income at least until competitive pressure forces fares down again. Several attempts have been made to have "all-frills," luxury service for business travelers; Midway, Air One, and Regent Air all failed with this strategy.

## LABOR WOES

Airlines have to spend a lot of money not only on "equipment" (which is what they say instead of "airplanes"), but also on fuel—and there's not much they can do about either. They can control the cost of food and beverages (which is one reason why airplane food is so awful—but even Escoffier couldn't serve terrific meals to a planeload of people at once with nothing but a microwave oven to heat them up). For the record, in the third quarter of 1987, Pan Am spent the most on its average meals and beverage—$6.54 a passenger, and USAir spent the least—$1.93; the industry average was $4.21. USAir says it wasn't really chintzy because its short-hop flights get snacks, not full meals, and because it uses good management techniques such as owning its own ice machines, instead of buying ice, to save money.

Airlines can also control labor costs, but it's a difficult and delicate process. You can't entrust a planeload of passengers to anyone with a pair of aviator glasses and a learner's permit. If there are plenty of fully qualified pilots looking for work, an airline can offer salaries below the industry norm (especially if its work force is nonunionized, or if the airline has gone through a bankruptcy process, which cancels union contracts). However, that means that the pilots will quit at the first job opening at a higher salary—and it also means that they'll be less than willing to work extra hours if a crew is needed for a rescheduled flight. An airline can take off without headsets for the movie and without blankets to clutter up the overhead luggage bins, but it can't take off without the cabin crew required by law.

It's a lot easier to hire a new cabin attendant than a new pilot because the initial qualifications are much lower and because plenty of people want what is perceived to be a glamorous job with lots of travel. (American Airlines gets eighteen applications for each flight attendant job opening.) But a job as steward, stewardess, purser, or ticket agent is frequently low paying: the base rate for members of the flight attendant's union is less than $12,000 a year.

Most airlines have a two-tier wage scale for flight attendants: that is, those hired after 1983 have a lower wage scale and earn about one-third less at each step on the wage scale than those hired earlier. (Wage increases stop after five years for both tiers.) The lower-paid "B-Scale" attendants at American earned an average of $14,728 in 1986—less than half the average A-Scale wage of $33,530.

Lower salaries mean dissatisfaction and a great exodus out of the

## CONSUMER TIP

Don't assume that you'll be able to buy a ticket at the advertised low-low-low fare for your destination. Most airlines severely limit the number of seats available at the lowest price and load on restrictions (how far in advance you must buy your ticket, how much you must forfeit if you cancel, how long you must stay at your destination). Often, it takes a travel agent, if not a psychic, to figure out the best route and price to fit your travel plans.

airline job market altogether. The airlines can quickly train replacements, but airlines depend heavily on their image of friendly, cooperative, well-informed service workers. An unsure or surly flight attendant or reservation clerk can motivate a traveler to book his next flight on another airline, which nullifies any advantage the airline gains by lowering labor costs.

Sophisticated computerized reservation systems help airline profits in several ways. First of all, some of the largest systems are run by the airlines themselves, such as the Sabre system run by AMR (which owns American Airlines). The Sabre system brings in less than 7 percent of AMR's revenues but close to one-third of its operating profit.

Second, travelers tend to book on the first airline offering a convenient flight to appear on the computer screen—an obvious advantage for the airline that runs the system and so big a disadvantage for others that small airlines often set up "two-letter-code" deals with major airlines; that is, a small commuter airline's planes may be listed on the computer system by the same two-letter code as a larger, better-known airline.

By the way, computerized registration systems also contribute to airline delays because airlines have a real incentive to schedule a plane at popular hours (to attract travelers or to at least keep the airline's name before their eyes) even if there isn't a snowball's chance in hell that a plane can take off at that hour. And the reservation system often lists flights with the shortest scheduled time first, which penalizes the more candid

## TRADE TALK

The "Q" fare is the deepest discount; a fare code beginning with "Y" is probably for a full-price coach seat. These codes appear on the ticket.

airlines. For example, one airline may claim that a particular flight takes three hours; another airline claims that it takes two hours and forty-five minutes. The second airline's flight would be listed first on the computer—even if the flight has never, in its history, taken less than three hours and fifteen minutes.

Remember that advertised fares are usually based on round-trip purchases, so you may have to pay more for a one-way ticket. There may also be surcharges for flying into or out of certain particularly busy airports.

Shortly before Elizabeth Dole, the former Secretary of Transportation, left to help with her husband's unsuccessful presidential campaign, she implemented a ruling that will increase the amount of information available to airline passengers from 1988 onward. The ruling obligates airlines to release information about their flight delays (although some delays are genuinely caused by bad weather or by the order of air traffic control, others are caused by airlines that, in their efforts to advertise planes "on the hour" or "more flights to Wherever than Anybody Else," promulgate a schedule heavily laced with fiction, or at least wishful thinking). It also gives consumers a right to see comparisons of the fourteen largest airlines' baggage-handling performances. The ratings are updated monthly and are usually reported in newspapers' business sections.

Although the regulation doesn't cover safety factors, newspapers cover this beat carefully. For instance, in May 1988, the Federal Aviation Administration (FAA) released documents relating to proposed fines of $6.5 million that the FAA claimed from fifteen airlines for safety and security violations, including failing to spot "weapons" concealed in baggage by FAA inspectors; flying without the required vapor-seal wing covers; and failing to make required engine inspections. Most of the fines ($1.26 million and $1.16 million, respectively) were sought against United and Hawaiian airlines; in 1987, Eastern Air Lines, Inc., alone paid $9.5 million in fines to the FAA as a result of charges of unsafe operation.

The forecast for the rest of the century: continuing trouble in the airline industry. There'll be no shortage of passengers—quite the contrary!—but airport facilities and air traffic control are stretched to their limits, and it's almost impossible to build new facilities. Ironically, the fact that the United States hasn't been in an air war for a while limits the availability of the best pilots, those with combat training. Airlines (and other carriers, such as railroads and trucking lines) also face ever-increasing drug problems. Lower fares cut into profits; higher fares cut into passenger traffic. It's comparatively easy to assemble an empire, as Frank Lorenzo has done by acquiring troubled airlines, but tough to run it at a profit.

# 64

# Cruise Lines

Between the nineteenth century and the rise of commercial aviation in the 1930s (see page 269 for more about airlines), the great cruise ships combined practicality (no matter how rich you were, you couldn't walk or drive to Europe or the Far East from the United States) with the utmost luxury—at least in first class. Accommodations for second-class and steerage passengers were considerably less attractive.

Once there were regularly scheduled airlines, it became impractical to make a business trip by ocean liner. At first, the airlines also captured the tourist trade because of the novelty and (believe it or not) luxury that the early commercial airlines provided their upper-crust passengers.

Today, though, cruise lines are making a comeback. A cruise ship combines travel with the amenities of a floating hotel, the restfulness of watching the waves lap against the bows, the fun of shuffleboard, the possibility of a shipboard romance, and the virtual certainty of pigging out on three lavish meals a day, bouillon on deck, and a midnight buffet.

Usually, ships cruise the Caribbean, though it's also possible to sail to Alaska, Europe (and, perhaps, fly back on the Concorde), or around the world. Most cruises promise blissful leisure, but some offer lectures by experts, tournament-level bridge, or other special interests. There are even a few "spa cruises," featuring exercise classes and slenderizing gourmet menus, but that seems like a shame.

In the first half of 1986, the twenty-six members of the Cruise Line Industry Association deployed eighty-one ships and carried 1.1 million passengers, a 15 percent increase from the previous year. The winter is the peak cruise season, as travelers seek someplace balmy. Miami is a leading point of embarkation, with 1.3 million departures in 1986; other Florida ports accounted for more than 770,000 more departures. Overall, the cruise industry takes in an estimated $5 billion in revenue. New ships (perhaps an oversupply) are being built, with a 26 percent greater capacity (15,000 more berths) scheduled by 1990.

If you'd like to buy your own 2,600-passenger cruise ship like Carnival's new companion to its *Sovereign of the Seas,* it'll cost you about $200 million.

The largest cruise line is Carnival Cruise Lines, Inc., which has seven cruise ships (and carries 20 percent of U.S. cruise passengers—an estimated 550,000 in 1987) and a casino and hotel in Nassau. Carnival's innovation was to offer popular, and popularly priced, cruises, whereas traditional cruise lines were for, umm, the carriage trade. It's the only cruise line to advertise on network television—to the tune of $60 million over a three-year period. Carnival is organized as a Panamanian corporation, sparing it the minor inconvenience of paying U.S. taxes, so its profit in 1986 was $97.7 million on $420.8 million in revenues, an operating profit of 24 percent. (Registration under a "flag of convenience" offered by a cooperative nation such as Liberia is common for both cargo and passenger ships.) Even in its worst recent year (1984), Carnival managed operating profits of 16 percent of revenues—buoyed, no doubt, by the success of the TV show "The Love Boat" and the on-board gambling casinos. Other cruise lines have more modest, but still decent, profit margins of around 10 to 15 percent.

About five percent of Americans have taken a cruise. The industry chooses to regard this as a splendid indication that there's plenty of room for expansion, rather than a sign that nobody much wants their services. The American Association of Travel Agents confirms that cruise travel is the fastest-growing segment of the travel industry, with 10 percent annual growth. It can be an addictive way to vacation: on some ships, half or even three-quarters of their passengers are satisfied customers who have enjoyed other cruises in the past.

# 65

# Hotels

| | |
|---|---|
| Number of establishments: | 11,510 (There were also 36,061 motels and tourist courts.) |
| Total receipts: | $22.20 billion ($10.46 billion motel/tourist courts) |
| Average net sales: | $1,929,000 ($290,253 motel/tourist courts) |
| Number of employees: | 707,200 |
| Total payroll: | $6.647 million |

(Department of Commerce, '82)

Although you may think of hotels as places to stay on vacation, the hotel business concentrates on the business traveler.

A recent new focus in the hotel business is the woman business traveler. Hotels are providing better security, lighter restaurant and room-service menus, and even ironing boards and hangers that won't mutilate skirts. Hotels are also appealing to fitness-minded travelers of all kinds by providing maps of local jogging areas or even by opening in-hotel workout facilities.

The increase in the number of women traveling on business is one reason why the "all-suite" hotel (which provides all guests with a bedroom

279

**Where the Money Comes From (Hotels with 25 or More Rooms)**

| | |
|---|---|
| (1) Room rentals: | 49.81% |
| (2) Food, soft drinks: | 20.56% |
| (3) Bar sales: | 8.65% |
| (4) Other (renting space for meetings and trade shows; sales of merchandise such as newspapers and souvenirs): | 20.98% |

(Department of Commerce, '82)

**Where the Money Comes From (Motels)**

| | |
|---|---|
| (1) Room rentals: | 80.65% |
| (2) Food, soft drinks: | 11.35% |
| (3) Bar sales: | 4.3% |
| (4) Other (gas and oil; bottled liquor; other merchandise): | 3.7% |

(Department of Commerce, '82)

**Where the Money Goes (All Hotels; Before Federal Taxes)**

| | |
|---|---|
| (1) Cost of operations: | 47.6% |
| (2) Officers' compensation: | 1.8% |
| (3) Pensions and Benefits: | 1.3% |
| (4) Rent: | 4.3% |
| (5) Repairs: | 2.1% |
| (6) Depreciation, Depletion, Amortization: | 6.3% |
| (7) Interest: | 6.1% |
| (8) Bad Debts: | 0.5% |
| (9) Advertising: | 2.1% |
| (10) State, Local Taxes: | 4.7% |
| (11) Other Expenses: | 27.9% |
| (12) Net Profit Before Tax: | — |

(Troy, '83–'84)

and living room, and perhaps a kitchenette) is a growing segment of the hotel industry. The suite gives business travelers a chance to hold a meeting in the hotel suite without suggesting bedroom hanky-panky. Today, only about 2 percent of the nation's 2.75 million hotel rooms are "all-suite," but 22 percent of business travelers have stayed in one.

Close to 3 million (91,000 built in 1986, 50,000 to 55,000 more under construction in 1987) is a lot of hotel rooms and one reason why the hotel industry is singing the blues. (Why risk red ink by building even more

---

**CONSUMER TIP**

Because hotels cater to the business traveler, you may be able to get a very good deal on weekend stays at some of the best hotels in the country, which sometimes offer especially attractive rates to fill rooms that would otherwise go empty when the business travelers go home for the weekend. Find out if the hotel offers discounts to frequent guests or coordinates with a frequent-flier program in which you participate.

---

hotel rooms? For tax reasons—but the Tax Code of 1986 makes this less attractive, another good reason for the slowdown.) On an average night, about two-thirds of those rooms are occupied; the rule of thumb is that a hotel needs 62 to 63 percent occupancy to turn a profit. Travelers pay an average rate of $53.81 per room in full-service hotels (although $150 to $200 a night is a common charge in a luxury hotel), $29.09 in economy hotels.

About one out of every seven rooms is an economy room—the fastest-growing segment in the market, according to the authoritative consulting firm Laventhol & Horwath. In 1970, there were only 10 major economy chains, which owned 250 hotels and 20,000 rooms; in 1986, there were sixty-five such chains, which owned 3,300 hotels and 380,000 rooms.

One reason for the expansion is that travelers are looking for bargains; another is that hotel owners are looking for profits. In 1986, for example, the average full-service hotel room took in $20,117 per year, about three times as much as an economy room ($7,096). However, the average payroll per room was $9,449 for a full-service room but only $1,487 for an economy room. In fact, the average full-service hotel lost money when its pretax income was divided by sales, but the average economy hotel's pretax income was a healthy 5.7 percent of sales.

Dun & Bradstreet's 1986 survey of 1,912 hotels shows that those in the top quarter had a return on sales of 13.6 percent; those in the middle had a return on sales of 6.0 percent; and those in the bottom quarter had a tiny 0.1 percent return on sales.

## TRADE TALK

A hotel's "rack rate" is its basic, no-discount rate; to sound knowing, ask if discounts from the rack rate are available.

This is not to say that running a full-service or even a luxury hotel is always a passport to poverty, as you can see by these figures for Marriott and Hilton:

|  | Marriott Corporation | Hilton Hotels Corporation |
|---|---|---|
| Position in *Business Week*'s Top 1000 for the year 1987: | 133 | 258 |
| Market value | $3.965 billion | $2.199 billion |
| Assets | $5.371 billion | $1.424 billion |
| Sales | $6.522 billion | $844 billion |
| Profits | $223.0 million | $139.9 million |

(In the spring of 1988, Marriott planned to enter a new market segment—the fast-growing, but highly competitive, "no-frills" motel industry—by investing $500 million over five years to build 100 Fairfield Inns with rooms renting for between $29.95 and $35 a night.)

These two giants aren't the only major players in the hotel industry. The Pritzker family owns Hyatt Hotels, which owns or operates eighty-four hotels in North America and gathers revenues of about $1.7 billion a year. Hyatt plans to spend $1.5 billion or so to carry out its five-year plan to build a dozen luxury resorts (at a cost of $150,000 to $200,000 per room) and to spend $750 milion to build forty small hotels (at a more modest $70,000 to $85,000 per room). The gamble is likely to pay off; although Hyatt spends 50 percent more than the industry average to open a new resort, the resort hotels average 78 percent occupancy—way above the usual occupancy rates.

## SAY AMENITIES, SOMEBODY

Furnishing a hotel room can cost anywhere from $2,700 (for an economy package of furniture, wallpaper, carpet, linens, and lamps) to . . . well, the sky's the limit. The Portman–San Francisco ultraluxury hotel features free limousine service, a valet for every seven rooms, and a three-phone system in every room, with the capacity to take messages; the Hyatt Regency in Scottsdale has a water garden with ten pools, a man-made beach, twenty-eight fountains, and forty-seven waterfalls.

In order to attract guests, hotels provide amenities, on which they spend anything from seventeen cents per room for a tiny bottle of shampoo to $15 per room per night for an elaborate selection of designer body-pampering products. (One Montreal hotel discreetly includes a condom.) Providing HBO or Showtime costs about $4 to $6 per room monthly, depending on the number of rooms, programs available, and the maintenance contract. An increasing number of hotels provide in-room VCRs and cassette rentals, either by taking on the task themselves or by contracting with an outside supplier.

Experienced hotel guests are blasé about chocolates left on their pillows as a bedtime snack, so some hotels substitute chic chocolate chip cookies. For the ultimate touch of home, Anderson House (in Minnesota) maintains a supply of cats that can be sent to keep homesick, or merely cat-loving, guests company during their stays.

## RETAIL RAP: Don't Steal This Book: Shoplifting and Security

Department stores, mass merchandisers, and specialty stores are fighting a losing battle: although they're spending more for security each year, they can't stem the tide of theft. In 1985, for instance, theft cost retailers $1.3 billion—the equivalent of 1.8 percent of sales—despite their spending $255 million on various security measures (15 percent more than in 1984). Department stores spent the most on security, paying 0.5 percent of sales; mass merchandisers spent a little more than 0.33 percent of sales; and specialty stores a little more than 0.25 percent of sales. (One advantage that malls give their tenants is a mall-wide security force of patrolling guards; the mall may also be built with a central video security system. The costs for such security measures are shared by all the mall tenants. An independent store located outside a mall probably finds it hard to afford comparable security.)

Although theft losses from shoplifting were high—31 percent of the "inventory shrinkage" was due to this—42 percent was due to employee theft, 23 percent was caused by errors in bookkeeping, and 4 percent was stolen at the vendor level before the merchandise ever got to the store.

Most of the security budget went to the low-tech area of payroll: 24 percent of this budget was used to hire guards; 24 percent, to hire other security staff (such as the people who watch screens showing a video picture of the sales floor or dressing room). However, the typical budget reflected modern technology: 9 percent went for electronic tags, and 5 percent for other electronic equipment.

Although significant losses are caused by casual shoplifters seeking thrills as well as merchandise and by addicts who steal to buy drugs, the biggest problems are store break-ins and professional shoplifting teams, some of whom make the teamwork of Rogers and Astaire look positively amateurish. In the team routine, one shoplifter distracts the clerk or security worker, while the other actually makes away with the goods.

Theft losses set up an unhealthy cycle: shopkeepers raise prices to compensate for theft, which leads some to believe that they're entitled to "help themselves" to merchandise, either because they want to protest high prices or because they believe that the merchant is cynically exploiting the situation by raising prices even higher than actual losses require. Honest merchants, and honest customers, suffer.

# Leisure

# 66

# Television: Networks, Affiliates, and Syndicators

NBC didn't appear on the *Business Week* list, not because it was destitute (far from it—it was the top-rated network and had the highest operating profits—over $400 million in 1986, as compared to a little under $350 million for ABC and about $250 million for CBS), but because it's part of General Electric.

It's said that a hen is just an egg's way of making another egg. On television, a program is just a way of getting you to watch commercials, so advertisers will pay a lot to put their messages before you. In one sense, the process is working: in the first half of 1987, six corporations each spent more than $100 million on network advertising. The champ, Procter & Gamble, spent $192.3 million; its sudsy rival, Unilever, spent $124.8 million. Philip Morris Companies, Inc., was second in advertising expenditure, at $181.2 million, followed by General Motors, at $129.9 million (no other car manufacturer came close). Kellogg Company spent $124.8 million to sell cereal, and McDonald's Corporation far outspent its fast-food rivals, with an ad budget of $105.4 million for those six months.

Networks aren't shy about charging for a commercial on a popular show: a thirty-second message on, for example, "The Cosby Show" costs $352,900; on "Family Ties," $258,000; and on "Miami Vice," $158,400. (By contrast, an affiliate station in New York typically gets around $15,000 to $25,000 to show a thirty-second commercial.)

|                                    | Capital Cities/ABC                      | CBS                                         |
|------------------------------------|-----------------------------------------|---------------------------------------------|
| Market value:                      | $5.962 billion                          | $3.924 billion                              |
| Assets:                            | $5.378 billion                          |                                             |
| 1987 sales:                        | 4.440 billion                           | 2.762 billion                               |
| 1987 profits:                      | 279.1   million                         | 136 million                                 |
| Return on invested capital         | 9.7%                                    | NA                                          |
| Return on common equity            | 13.2%                                   | 12.9%                                       |
| Chairman/<br>  CEO bonus and salary | $801,000 plus<br>148,000 shares stock | $1,181,000 plus<br>5,857,000 shares stock |

National advertisers used to devote two-thirds of their budget to TV spots; now they rely heavily on coupons and other consumer incentives and spend some of their TV dollars on cable and independent local stations rather than the networks. This change is due, in large part, to viewers' shifting away from network television to cable TV and videocassettes, and to their recording network programs without the commercials or playing back recorded programs and zipping through the commercials.

In April 1988, all three major networks found to their chagrin that viewership had dropped since April 1987: the prime-time audience for the networks was down 9 percent. Capital Cities/ABC, Inc., held on best, losing only 3 percent of its prime-time viewership; NBC lost 10 percent; and CBS took a 15 percent hit. The three networks' Saturday morning audience was down a striking 27 percent; late-night viewership declined 14 percent; and evening news viewing was down 5 percent. This was more than embarrassing, it was expensive: the networks had to give advertisers $100 million in free airtime to compensate for anticipated viewers who had not tuned in as promised.

## A NEW NETWORK?

Throughout most of commercial television's history, there have been three major networks. Lots of other network owners have tried to muscle in as the fourth television power. The latest contender, media mogul Rupert Murdoch, made an audacious try in April 1987 by budgeting an estimated $150 million to launch the Fox Broadcasting Company. By October, it was clear that the effort would have an uphill climb to success. Murdoch's plan was twofold: to target eighteen- to forty-nine-year-old viewers (advertisers' favorite audience) with adventure stories and situation comedies that tested the limit of raunchiness permitted on television, and to appeal to advertisers with extra-low rates of $30,000 for a thirty-second commercial. (The same commercial run during a movie or sports event on New York's independent Channel 9 would cost only $3,000.)

Fox's flagship show—a late-night talk show with Joan Rivers as host—was a resounding flop by May 1988. Fox was spending about the same amount as the other networks to buy new shows from producers (about $300,000 per half hour), taking in less revenue, and giving a more generous deal to its affiliates: they can sell three of the nine thirty-second commercials in each half hour themselves and keep the money.

The three major networks usually let affiliates keep 2.5 minutes per hour in prime-time programming; the network keeps the rest of the "inventory" (in the television business, commercials are as close to inventory as you get), with thirty seconds for network and station identification and promotions and program credits. Affiliates get to sell seven minutes an hour of commercial time on weekends and anywhere from four to twelve minutes on daytime television. That's why daytime dramas are called "soap operas"—there's an endless parade of ads, many of them for household cleaning products.

As explained above, networks buy programming so that they can attract advertisers; they do this by promising a certain audience. If the ratings show that the network failed to deliver the audience, the advertisers are entitled to "make-goods"—commercial freebies until the promised audience has been exposed to the commercial. Fox got into this position in the spring of 1987, which left it with less advertising time to sell and thus made its financial troubles even worse. In its first year of operation, the network lost $75 million, but managed to provide 10.5 hours of shows a week to 121 affiliates. Ratings in 1988 were weak—only 2.9 percent of all households with television watched Fox on Saturday nights. Sunday night did better, earning a 4.3 percent rating.

Still, Rupert Murdoch spent $1.7 billion to buy seven television stations and $250 million to start programming on the Fox network, so obviously he came to play. Murdoch's newspaper business had revenues of over $5 billion in 1987, so he can certainly afford to lose millions of dollars on his long-shot gamble that a fourth network can succeed.

## WHERE TV COMES FROM

To a limited extent, network television is "vertically integrated": the networks can and do produce some programs and can own some stations.

However, as a result of an antitrust consent decree issued in 1980, networks are allowed to produce only three of the twenty-two programs shown each week in prime time. The other nineteen must come from television studios such as Universal Pictures and Lorimar Telepictures Corporation (which supplied eleven of the sixty-six prime-time series in

## TRADE TALK

An "O and O" is a station owned and operated by a network.

the Fall 1987 season); such shows consume about 90 percent of the networks' prime-time budget. According to the terms of the consent decree, the networks can move up to producing five shows in 1990.

For the 1984–1985 season, production fees averaged $13,500 per minute; a sixty-minute "Hill Street Blues" episode cost about $925,000 to produce—a little more than "Dallas" or "Dynasty," each at $900,000 an hour. (Even that looks pretty anemic next to the all-time record of $3.1 million for a single particularly expensive, albeit award-winning, "Moonlighting" episode; a "normal" episode of that show cost $1.6 million.) "Cheers" and "Gimme a Break" cost a mere $375,000 per half hour, probably because these programs center around a single, indoor set, with little or no expensive location shooting or pricey car chases.

The networks produce their own news and sports programming, often at a loss. (A daily one-hour news show can cost $250,000 to produce—a lot less than a prime-time drama at $500,000 an hour, or action-adventure at $800,000 an hour, but more than the measly $100,000 for a half-hour daytime soap, or the truly parsimonious $30,000 for a half-hour game show.) But expensive or not, a respectable network *has* to have news shows, and sports programming is essential to attract advertisers who sell products attractive to male consumers. In the 1984–1985 season, "60 Minutes" cost $700,000 per show to produce, and "Monday Night Football" cost $2 million (but hey, it was at least two hours a pop).

Commercials during major sporting events don't go cheap: $116,200 for thirty seconds during the 1986 baseball playoffs, or $175,000 for a thirty-second spot during "Monday Night Football" (but only $33,000 to $36,100 for an ad of the same length during a college football game). That's why a player's action such as the 1987 NFL strike is so devastating. Not only is advertising revenue lost during the strike, not only do networks have to ante up expensive make-goods to advertisers who have already paid for advertising, but advertisers can give up on TV altogether and shift to radio or print ads, temporarily or permanently.

## SERIES STRUGGLES

Television shows are like salmon swimming upstream. Lots of them start out, but hardly any reach their goal. In an ordinary season, a total of approximately thirty pilots will be ordered by the three networks. Only half of them will get a regular series run—a commitment by the network to take thirteen initial episodes and an "option contract" permitting the network to buy four to six more seasons' worth of episodes at an increased price of 3 to 8 percent per season, which gives the network a chance to lock in a low price for a hit series. Many of the survivors will be dropped after a season or two, the options unexercised.

In a typical financing arrangement, the network pays one-third of the agreed-on fee when the filming or taping begins; another third when the episodes are completed; and the rest when the episodes are delivered and cleared by network censors.

For many years, television production provided a glamorous tax shelter for wealthy investors who could feel like movie moguls, write off tax losses, and collect profits that the shows were really making while they were losing money for tax-accounting purposes. In fact, the mysteries of accounting are so profound that the producers could make a lot of money, in real terms, and still tell their investors that the shows were losing money and that consequently no profits would be paid. (The producers include a lot of fees and overhead items—payable to the producers, of course—in the accounting statements; and they also take a lot of "reserves" against anticipated or vaguely possible events, all of which lessen the money "available" for the investors.)

Today, the tax incentives are much smaller, so producers are correspondingly more cautious: they want deals that make money, not just deals that generate tax benefits. However, an independent producer may be willing to gamble on an expensive series, perhaps even one that costs more than the network will pay per episode, because of the brass ring on the carousel: the possibility of the successful and very lucrative syndication of a hit show.

## THE SYNDICATES

No, we're not talking about the crime syndicates that Eliot Ness battled here, but television syndicators. The owners of television stations, after all, have to get their programming from somewhere. Much of it comes from the networks, and the affiliate station in an area will be able to show the network's new programming. However, for the times when network programming is unavailable or too expensive for the station's pocketbook (which, in turn, depends on its ad rates and success in attracting advertisers), the station must find other resources.

The station can originate its own programming—anything from a highly creative public affairs program to the owner of the station cavorting around in a Clarence the Clown suit. But it is more likely to buy the right to show a library of old movies (and show them and show them), perhaps with a local host or do the same thing with animated cartoons, or rerun old series that are "in syndication."

Usually, the syndicated shows are the big hits of the past (such as "I Love Lucy" or "The Odd Couple") because it takes four or five years to build up enough episodes for a long run, especially if the shows are to run five nights a week instead of the network's once-a-week schedule. Syndicators also make new episodes of former network shows and even produce their own shows: the new version of the 1960s hit "Star Trek," for instance, is a syndicated program.

In 1984, stations that were network affiliates spent $426 million on syndicated shows; independent stations spent $637 million. Syndicated shows are extremely attractive to network affiliates. If they preempt a network show and run a syndicated show instead, they must pay the syndicator for the program, but they can keep all the ad revenue instead of sharing it with the network. Syndicated shows are also attractive to independent stations, which often have a hard time appealing to advertisers because their ratings are low. New York's WWOR-TV (Channel 9), a perpetual loser in the ratings war, was willing to pay $365,000 per episode for "The Cosby Show" reruns when they became available in the fall of 1988.

The syndicator with the most clout is undoubtedly King World Productions, Inc., which handles the top three syndicated shows: "Wheel of Fortune," "Jeopardy," and "The Oprah Winfrey Show."

## NETWORKS AND AFFILIATES

A television station can be an expensive toy. In order to deliver mass audiences and keep ad rates high, networks need affiliates: stations that run their programming, get paid by the network for the service, and split advertising revenue with the network. (Networks are limited by law in the number of stations they can own.) A small, rural station may depend on the network for 30 percent of its revenues; a more popular station can get nearly all its money from advertising, with less than 5 percent coming from the network. Each station negotiates its own contract with the network, setting fees and the amount of commercial time that the affiliate can sell for its own purposes.

However, as explained above, it may be more profitable for the affiliate to "black out" the network programming (especially if the show is one of the network's less successful efforts) and substitute its own sports, movies, or syndicated programming. These programs may not only draw a bigger audience than the network show but allow the affiliate to keep whatever the advertisers pay for commercials on the program instead of sharing advertising revenue with the network.

In the 1960s and 1970s, speculators loved to buy and "flip" independent television stations, that is, sell them to someone else, making a big profit fueled by inflation and speculative fever. By the late 1980s, however, there had been a shakeout. Buyers were actually operating their stations, and not always making a go of it. Heavy borrowing, increasing program costs, and declining or stagnating ad revenues killed some stations by making it impossible for them to meet loan payments. Other stations recapitalized, shopped more carefully for programming, or cut personnel in order to survive. (In 1988 the average price for a network affiliate station dropped from $67.55 million in 1987 to $23.96 million.)

## THE MENACE OF THE PEOPLE METERS

If a tree falls in a forest with no one there to hear it, does it really fall? For advertisers, the answer to this ancient philosophical question is, "Hell, no": advertisers don't want to spend their dollars on a show that nobody watches. Furthermore, they want to advertise on a show that appeals to their intended clientele: for example, "Monday Night Football" is a more promising advertising vehicle for shaving cream than for nail polish.

Since 1950, most rating decisions (and corresponding ad rates) have been made based on information provided by the A. C. Nielsen Company. A television show's rating is based on the number of households watching it: one point represents almost 900,000 homes. A show's "share," on the other hand, represents the percentage of households watching television (instead of doing something else) that tuned in to that particular program. The top-rated "Cosby Show" has been measured as having a rating of 26 (26 × 886,000 households watching it) and a share of 45 (nearly half of the television viewers were tuned to it).

Nielsen, in turn, gets its information from homes whose television viewers fill out diaries about their television-watching habits. However, there are certain problems with this methodology: the results can be skewed by a viewer's desire to look good by reporting that he watched a prestigious program, not the junk he really tuned in to, and by his inability to remember what he viewed.

Theoretically, people are supposed to fill out the diaries as they watch TV, but, of course, human nature being what it is, the diaries tend to get filled out at the end of the week. Furthermore, many families participating in the surveys tend to think of filling out the survey as a household chore, so women do a disproportionate share of it. It's theorized that— accidentally or by design—women indicate less viewing of sports events than actually takes place.

The alternative is a people meter, which is a box attached to the television set in 4,000 homes used in the Nielsen sampling. Operated by a TV remote control, it's really an electronic diary, recording not only which programs were watched but who watched them. This information is crucial to advertisers who want to see if a particular show appeals to kids, to men aged eighteen to thirty-five, women over fifty, or whomever.

People meters are expected to reshape television programming, as networks schedule new shows and keep old shows that are intended to appeal to the yuppie viewer (and yuppie consumer), even if their ratings are somewhat disappointing. That's because a show with "people meter appeal" can deliver a lower "CPM" to advertisers. ("CPM" is cost per thousand consumers exposed to the advertiser's message.)

People meters will also reshape the financial standing of television stations by reinforcing the already considerable power of the advertisers. Most ad sales are made in the spring and summer, in preparation for the new fall season. As explained above, if the networks don't deliver the promised audience, they must provide make-goods; they'll also have to adjust their future price schedules to compensate. For example, to put a thirty-second commercial on "Miami Vice" costs $158,400. If an advertiser wants to reach women over eighteen and under fifty, their CPM, according to Nielsen diaries, is $21.74, but according to people meters, the CPM is only $19.17.

Why do advertisers bother to pay the huge ad prices that TV stations demand (especially considering the fact that many commercials are productions as sophisticated as feature films—and much more costly, on a per-minute basis)? They do it because, expensive as TV is, it can be the most cost-effective way to reach consumers. For instance, in 1983 the average CPM of television commercials was $5 while newspaper ads ranged from $10 to $20 CPM.

In short, television is a complex dance, involving producers, networks, independent and affiliate stations, and advertisers. If you like the results, but not the time they're shown, you can use your VCR (assuming you've bought one from an electronics store [see page 190] or department store [see page 141]) to "time shift." And if you don't like the results . . . well, you can always rent a tape from a video store (see page 301) or check out what's on cable (see page 295). If that, too, palls, maybe you can hang out at the mall (see page 137), go to a bookstore (see page 207), or pursue other recreational activities not treated in these pages.

# 67

# Cable TV

Cable TV started out as a way for isolated rural communities to get decent television reception. Today, it's a multibillion-dollar industry, with 40 million subscribers as of 1987 and 1987 estimated revenues of $11.8 billion: $10.4 billion from customer subscriptions and $1.4 billion from advertising. The advertising figure is ironic because the original appeal of cable TV was not just better reception on network channels, but programming unavailable on commercial TV and free from commercials.

Today, cable subscribers (depending on where they live, how local cable companies package their services, and how much the customer is willing to pay) can get a heady variety of movies; soap operas and sitcoms produced especially for cable; sports events; home shopping; programming in dozens of languages; and programs either too antiseptic (special channels for kids) or too dirty (a wild variety of pornographic films, call-ins, and talk shows) for regular broadcast TV. (Sometimes cable-originated programs move to broadcast television: Showtime's "It's Garry Shandling's Show" was picked up by Fox, and local stations carry WTBS' new version of "Leave it to Beaver"; Disney Channel viewers got the first crack at a "Winnie the Pooh" series later run on ABC.)

## CABLE HISTORY AND OPERATIONS

For the cable industry, 1980 and 1981 were years of explosive growth, with almost 6 million new subscribers added each year; then, between 1982 and 1986, growth slowed down to about 3.2 million new subscribers per year.

In 1983, a composite of the top thirty cable companies shows revenues of $3.45 billion, assets of nearly $7 billion, and pretax operating income of $626.5 million: an operating margin of 18.2 percent. The companies in the industry had dramatically different results. Capital Cities Communications (now part of ABC) had the slimmest margin, at 3.1 percent (revenue of $67 million, pretax operating income of just over $2 million), and Storer Cable Communications, Inc., had the highly impressive operating margin of 34.2 percent (pretax operating income of just under $100 million on revenues of $291.1 million). By 1984, 6,200 operating systems were in the cable market and had a total of 30 million subscribers, many of whom subscribed to a number of cable systems. Revenues in 1987 for the nation's 7,800 cable systems were $12 billion.

But for cable companies, the problem isn't getting subscribers, but keeping them. A 1983 survey conducted by the advertising agency Benton and Bowles showed that 17 percent of all current or former cable subscribers had cancelled at least one cable service that they paid for (the most common reason was that the programs were repeated too often; next most common, that the service just wasn't worth what it cost). Seven percent of cable subscribers bought four or more services; 10 percent bought three; and the rest bought only one or two.

The local cable service or operator receives programming from satellite dishes and transmits it to subscribers, whether or not there are actual cables laid in the ground or wires running overhead; the cable networks (for example, USA Network and Nickelodeon) provide the programming. Cable subscribers who pay a basic price get a package of broadcast TV and public service programs; for additional fees, they can subscribe to pay cable networks such as HBO, Showtime, the Disney Channel, or the Playboy Channel, or a combination.

In 1986, HBO was the largest pay cable network, with 15 million subscribers. Showtime had 5.4 million; Cinemax (owned by HBO) had 4.1 million; the Disney Channel had 3.2 million; the Movie Channel was trailing with 2.9 million subscribers; and the Playboy Channel lagged far behind, with 610,000 subscribers.

Until 1985, the movie networks had the enormous advantage of presenting almost-new movies to subscribers who would have to wait for years for those movies to appear (heavily cut and interrupted by commercials) on broadcast TV. But by 1985 the VCR was commonplace, and viewers could select their own movies without paying a monthly fee to a network that would choose movies for them. The cable networks' response was pay-per-view cable, where customers pay only for the events they watch (movies, sports events, concerts). The programs are sent out "scrambled"; the viewers order the programming in advance, by telephone, and the cable company decodes the signal through the subscriber's home decoder box.

## CABLE TODAY

By the beginning of 1987, over 48 percent of all households (more than 42 million homes) had cable TV: that represented a 4.1 percent increase over 1986 levels. More than 80 percent of households with TV sets had access to cable, if they wanted it. A surprising exception: New York City, parts of which weren't wired for cable TV until late 1987, for a number of murky reasons that were heavily influenced by political corruption. Nevertheless, the top cable market (judged by number of subscribers) in 1987 was the New York City metropolitan area, with 2,637,690 cable households; but that same market had a "penetration" of only 39.3 percent (that is, only 39.3 percent of households with TVs had cable). That leaves plenty of room for expansion. Judging by penetration percentages, Boston is the nation's #1 cable market, with 53.1 percent penetration (a little over 1 million households).

Cable subscribers could choose from forty-six networks such as MTV (owned by National Amusements, Inc.), ESPN (Capital Cities/ABC's all-sports, all-the-time network), and Cable News Network. In the years 1986 and 1987, deal mania raged in the cable industry, with mergers, sales, and takeovers of 456 cable companies. Want to buy a cable company? Expect to pay about $2,000 to 2,500 per subscriber.

Local cable systems carry anywhere from twenty-one to thirty-six channels, including five to six channels of normal broadcast programming, the rest either broadcast programming or programming exclusive to cable. Customers usually pay $2 to $8 per month for basic cable service; the total bill depends on how many other services they subscribe to and whether the cable networks are offering low-cost deals to motivate subscribers. A family of cable enthusiasts can easily spend $50 a month—a lot of money, but the equivalent of only a couple of family evenings at the local Thirty-Eight Plex Cinema.

Cable programming is transmitted by means of communications satellites; eight satellites are available to cable networks (and the hookup costs the networks up to $200,000 a month). But, just as there are elite and lower-class addresses, there are chic satellites and unpopular ones: most cable systems' dishes only pick up signals from three of the satellites. (There are also fashions in station numbering: the cable system decides which program is on which channel, and viewers are much more likely to watch stations numbered 1 through 16 than those in "Siberia," the higher channel numbers.)

## UP FROM CHICKEN NOODLE

There's no question that broadcast television is losing its dominance as viewers turn to cable, VCRs, pay-per-view, or simply to whatever they did for amusement before television was invented. And cable television news and sports programming is establishing a niche in reporting immediate happenings.

Cable News Network (which used to be called the Chicken Noodle Network because of its far-from-champagne budgets) broadcasts news around the clock (about 130 stories a day) to the 38.5 million U.S. households that can receive it. (Virtually all cable operators carry CNN and pay twenty-one cents to twenty-eight cents per subscriber per month for the privilege.) CNN also broadcasts in Europe to a quarter of a million homes (and even to the Kremlin, which bootlegs the signal from a satellite instead of paying the subscription fee; many Spanish hotels do the same thing).

The network has sixty-nine anchorpersons, a staff of 1,500 in eighteen bureaus, and a $100 million annual budget. The budget would be a lot higher if CNN were unionized; salaries range from $10,000 for eager young staffers to $70,000 on up into six figures for anchors. CNN correspondents get about $40,000 (and are on camera far more than their network counterparts—the trade-off is harder work for more exposure); network correspondents, about $150,000. Network anchors can earn millions of dollars a year.

CNN also sells commercials (so much for the cable-TV advantage of freedom from ad pitches): advertisers pay between $290 and $3,370 for a thirty-second ad, depending on the popularity of the time slot.

## CABLE SPORTS

The Entertainment and Sports Network (ESPN) lost money in 1982, 1983, and 1984, its programming replete with minor sporting events very few viewers wanted to watch. (A competitor—hardly the most objective source—described the network as "24 hours a day of underwater Australian wrist wrestling.") ESPN realized a tiny profit in 1985, but it took off in 1986, earning $40 million in operating profits, and nearly $60 million in operating profits in 1987 (on revenues of $140 million, 60 percent of which were derived from sale of advertising). By 1987, 42 million households (nearly half of the households that owned a television set) tuned in to ESPN, perhaps because its menu of sports had improved: it had exclusive rights to transmit live coverage of the America's Cup yacht races; it carried live coverage of the Stanley Cup playoffs; and, above all, it purchased (for $153 million) the rights to show three years of NFL Sunday night games.

ESPN anticipates earning a "modest" profit on the football games: say, $1 million or so. The cable network charges cable operators ten to eleven cents per month per subscriber for the "NFL package" of eight regular games, one preseason game, and the Pro Bowl; about 90 percent of operators who receive ESPN took this option, bringing in at least $140 million a year for the network. (ESPN can also earn money by selling the right to broadcast the games to broadcast-TV stations.) It may also motivate sports fans to sign up for cable just to watch the games.

ESPN, like CNN, is nonunion, which greatly reduces its costs. An hour of college football that costs a network at least $150,000 only costs ESPN $80,000; ESPN also pays about half as much as the unionized networks to produce a college basketball game.

Another spectator sport is expected to enrich cable networks: the 1988 presidential election. Demographics suggest that cable viewers are better educated, have a higher household income, and are more likely to vote than broadcast-TV viewers in general; that makes cable a natural forum for paid political announcements.

## THE CABLE FORECAST

In its earliest years, cable TV was heavily regulated. Subscription rates were subject to FCC control; so was the quality of the signal broadcast. Cable operators had to follow "must-carry" rules: they had to carry (and provide their subscribers access to) a basic package of broadcast television channels. For good or ill, the cable industry has been deregulated. Controls on subscription rates have been lifted, and the must-carry rules have been eliminated.

However, in the spring of 1988, the Supreme Court did uphold the set of FCC rules that permitted the FCC to set minimum technical standards for the quality of the picture broadcast to subscribers. This is not necessarily a victory for viewers: the decision means that states and cities aren't allowed to set their own, more stringent, rules, and the FCC's minimum standards don't require very much.

As a result of acquisitions (such as General Electric's ownership of NBC), vertical integration (such as cable systems producing their own programming), and interrelationships (such as large corporations owning an interest in broadcast and cable stations, movie and television production, and syndication), the entertainment business is coalescing. Borders are blurring: how do you describe a film funded by HBO that plays in a couple of movie theaters for a few days but lives out most of its life as a rental videocassette? What about a show that starts out on network TV, bombs, is picked up by cable, and becomes successful enough to interest broadcast TV in reruns of the cable shows or in new episodes? In the spring of 1988, another linkage seemed likely: NBC was negotiating to pay $21 million to buy the Tempo Television (12 million subscribers, concentrated in the southern United States) cable service from Telecommunications, Inc., a giant that reaches 20 percent of all cable subscribers. The purpose of the deal was to give NBC a foothold in cable broadcasting by operating information services dealing with sports and finance. But the deal fell through in June, and NBC decided to lease the prime-time hours for financial news programming instead of buying the station; tax reasons were cited for the change.

If current trends continue, it'll be almost impossible to trace the corporate connections among the companies that produce movies and television, those that show the product to the public, and those that distribute the videocassettes. About all you'll be able to say with certainty about the product is, "That's entertainment."

# 68

# Video Stores

| | |
|---|---|
| Number of specialized video stores: | approximately 25,000 |
| Number of other stores selling and renting videos (e.g., discount stores; department stores; supermarkets; bookstores): | approximately 45,000 |
| Total rentals of videocassettes: | $5.5 billion |
| Total sales of videocassettes: | $1 billion (Paul Kagan Associates, Cambridge Associates, CBS/Fox Video '87) |
| Average revenue for a video store: | $180,228 (down from 1986's average of $219,223) |
| | (*Video Store*, '87) |

In 1983, the wholesale price of a VCR was $470; by 1986, some models retailed for $200, and 47 percent of American households had VCRs. They could use them to "time shift" (record a program for later viewing), a harmless practice that the Supreme Court finally conceded was not a copyright violation. They could buy tapes, usually of Hollywood movies, and a surprisingly large number of people did so at $79.98 apiece. Many more bought tapes once the "normal" price dropped below $30. In fact, tape sales did a lot to dig the studios out of the hole they fell into by providing $2 million in studio revenues from the sale of more than 110 million tapes. All by itself, *Beverly Hills Cop* sold 1.2 million units at $29.95. Sports tapes represent only 3 percent of cassette sales and not even a blip on the screen in cassette rentals.

Which brings us to the third, and major, use of VCRs: to watch rented tapes. The number of rental shops usually hovers around 25,000: stores go bust, but new stores fill the gap. At first, most of them were mom-and-pop operations: a storefront with a few hastily carpentered shelves, holding copies of the few tapes that were then available. In the early 1980s, it was easy to get into the rental business. Just sign up a few hundred customers; charge an annual or "lifetime" membership fee (over $100 for the earliest "video clubs"; with time and competition, the fees sank or disappeared altogether); and use the membership fees and rental fees to buy new tapes.

During this start-up stage, video rentals cost $4 or $5 a night—a real bargain compared to the cost of paying for movie tickets, popcorn, parking, and perhaps a babysitter. At first, the movie studios priced their movies to encourage rentals: tapes often retailed for $79.95 but were sold to dealers at $52.

## SURVIVING THE SHAKEOUT

But a shakeout was inevitable. Novice VCR owners who wanted to rent at least one tape a night soon ran through the offerings at the local mom-and-pop store. Price wars ensued, forcing the standard price for rentals down to $2 a night, with ninety-nine-cent rentals, two-for-one deals, and discount coupons in common use. Studios made more and more movies available on videocassette (15,000 titles were available in mid-1985; 500 to 600 new titles, including "how-to" and other tapes, were added each month in 1988, which meant that stores needed more and more capital to keep restocking the shelves). More movies were available at lower prices to encourage "sell-through": purchases by home viewers. Paradoxically, some of the best-selling tapes were pornography (no doubt viewers were embarrassed to publicly rent the tapes) and kids' movies (kids love to watch their favorite movies over, and over, and over).

Stores also needed more and more sophisticated tracking mechanisms to find out what happened to 2,000 titles than to watch out for 125 movies. (A really large store can have as many as 6,500 titles, many in multiple copies, to cope with.)

Chains of video stores can cope with many of the problems better than Mom and Pop can. A chain can use its buying power to push down tape prices. If it's well capitalized, the chain can start a price war and complacently lose money by renting tapes for $1 or less until the competition either meets the price (and goes under) or loses most of its customers (and goes under). This logic can even lead to the amalgamation of chains, as in the May 1988 deal in which the 200-store Blockbuster Entertainment swapped $56 million of its stock for the 127-unit Major Video. The combined chain will be the nation's second largest, behind National Video.

For many local video stores, the final blow was the competition from huge corporations, most of them in other businesses entirely, which cleared off a few feet of shelf space for movie rentals. It's now possible to rent videos at K Mart discount stores, Pathmark supermarkets, and 7-Eleven convenience stores, often for as little as forty-nine cents a night, with no membership fee. According to Tom Adams, an industry analyst, convenience stores are doing much better in the video rental business than most specialized video stores.

Are you traveling on business and not tempted by the closed-circuit offerings on your hotel room's TV set? An increasing number of hotels provide VCRs and cassette rentals for their guests.

## DISTINCTIVE STRATEGIES

VCR owners are getting blasé. To tempt their jaded palates, rental stores have to offer something special. Sometimes it's a wider-than-usual selection or more innovative or artistic tapes.

The store can specialize in ethnic or foreign-language cassettes: Brooklyn's Uludag Video has the latest in Turkish cinema; Video 66 (in the same borough) has 500 Italian titles out of a total of 4,000 or so tapes. The foreign films, which usually cost $60 each, aren't always money-makers for the store, but stocking them may be worthwhile to help create an image of service to the community.

Or the cassettes might be available in a store the customer must enter anyway. American Home and Hardware (in Elkton, Maryland) rents cassettes for $1.90 a tape (ninety cents on Tuesdays, which is the slowest rental day), with 4,000 titles in stock, and up to twenty-five copies of hit titles. On a really good Saturday, the store will rent 1,000 tapes; first-year sales are estimated at between $300,000 and $400,000. The video department takes up 2,500 square feet in the store's basement; it employs two full-time and eight part-time workers.

A leading independent video rental chain, Erol's Video, had 1986 revenues above $147 million dollars from its 116 video clubs, which have a total of 450,000 members. Each store stocks up to 3,500 titles; unusually, no X-rated videos are carried, and R-rated tapes are kept in a separate "Mature Theme" section. Erol's pioneered the use of computerized bar codes to track video rentals. Like most stores, it keeps the actual rentable videos behind a sales counter; customers select empty boxes from the display shelves, and the salesperson grabs the corresponding video from the shelf. (Embarrassing mistakes are possible: Dana once rented a movie and got a series of ads running something like "Hi! I'm Kim! Call this number and my friends and I will perform totally perverted acts in exchange for a small fee, and we take Visa and MasterCard!" We wonder what would have happened if the same tape had been doled out to someone who rented *Bambi Meets Snow White* for the kids or *It's a Wonderful Life* for his in-laws.) Other stores have the customer present a tag or coupon for the video of their choice or have him give the code number assigned to the video.

However, some stores, like Los Angeles' Odyssey, 20/20, Nickelodeon, and the nationwide Blockbuster chain, are experimenting: they keep the actual videos on open shelves for customer selection. The advantages are more floor space, shorter lines at the cashier, and a spirit of "impulse buying" that increases rentals. Theft is curtailed (though not entirely prevented) by security devices such as alarm systems and metal tags on the cassettes that set off the alarm unless the clerk deactivates them.

## CASSETTE SALES

Some stores back into selling tapes. It makes good merchandising sense to have plenty of copies of a hit movie to rent. As the months pass and the movie is replaced on the charts by a newer hit, the store winds up with more copies than it needs, so why not sell the extras at a heavy discount? Another possibility is to sell the tape to a used-tape broker, for anything from a buck or two to $10, depending on the market for "previously viewed" copies of the tape.

Other stores decide to join 'em if they can't beat 'em, and try to capture some of the revenue that would otherwise be lost to home sales.

As of May 1987, the best-selling videocassette of all time was *Top Gun,* which sold 1.9 million units at $26.95 each (an unusually low price, made possible by the Diet Pepsi commercial at the beginning of each cassette), bringing in $30.7 million to Paramount, the studio that released the film. Jane Fonda's *Workout* is the #2 tape overall, with sales of 850,000 units at $59.95 apiece. *Ghostbusters* is next—800,000 sold at $79.95. The next two titles are almost tied: 1.4 million *Beverly Hills Cop* and 1.35 million *Indiana Jones and the Temple of Doom* cassettes, both retailing for $29.95, were sold. These four movies were hits; it's interesting to note that the VCR version of *Clue* (800,000 units sold at $39.95) is tied for #11—a movie that was a major-league flop in movie theaters.

Video Shack, a fifteen-store New York chain, combines sales and rentals. (Its Broadway store, with 20,000 square feet of sales space on two floors, and 50,000 copies of 10,000 titles, is all sales.) The stores specialize in flamboyant promotions (such as a "M.A.S.H. Bash," where the jeep from the Robert Altman movie was auctioned off; appearances by Mr. T. and a Playboy Playmate of the Month) and reserves floor space for manufacturers' displays: the manufacturers pay $12,000 a year for 100 square feet of display space, which they can use to display tapes, posters, cardboard stand-up figures—even a live salesperson. Video Shack also advertises heavily and sends postcards to its 45,000 customers.

The Video Shack chain belongs to RKO Warner Theatres Video Inc., which also owns Adventureland Video, a major chain (450 units) of franchised video stores, with estimated 1986 sales of $128,000 a store—$72.5 million overall. That's awfully impressive, except when compared to Video Shack sales of almost $1 million a store—70 percent of which is from sales, about the opposite experience of most rental-and-sale stores.

One vendor, Kartes Video Communications, advertised that it could supply "proven sell-through products" (that is, videocassettes that lots of people want to buy) with suggested retail prices of $14.95 to $19.95 and promised gross margins of up to 40 percent for the video store. The cassettes are sold "net 60" (that is, retailers have 60 days to pay for them); cassettes that are "wallflowers" after being on display for 120 days can be returned for full credit or exchanged for other cassettes.

The usual rule is that store owners must buy an inventory of tapes to rent or resell. National Video and New Video lease some of their tapes: they pay a certain amount per tape (New Video pays $8 for a one- or two-year lease), then share rental revenues with the tape manufacturer. That reduces the amount the store must spend on inventory (and keeps it from getting stuck with tapes that are no longer popular; they go back to the tape manufacturer when the lease is up); but, of course, it also reduces the amount of revenue that the store owner can keep.

The Beta format, which many consider technically superior to the VHS format, got trapped in a circle: the manufacturers of Beta machines refused to license their technology and so remained the only manufacturer of the machines. As a result, studios released more software in VHS than in the Beta format, which in turn influenced more consumers to buy VHS machines, so more software was made available for the more popular machines. Another "war of the formats" may be underway, as attempts are made to improve the fidelity of VHS cassettes. Videodiscs have been tried and have failed commercially, but they may make a triumphant return in the form of compact discs that carry both picture and digitally recorded sound. Video stores will have to decide whether or not to carry this new format. The wrong decision could doom the compact videodisc format, or even the videocassette stores.

# 69

# Movie Theaters

| | |
|---|---|
| Number of establishments: | 9,344 (7,215 conventional—capacity 5,123,677 patrons; 2,129 drive-ins—capacity 1,202,519 cars) |
| Total receipts: | $3.57 billion |
| Average net sales: | $382,700 |
| Number of employees: | 103,400 (92,203 conventional; 11,258 drive-ins) |
| Total payroll: | $566.6 million |
| | (Department of Commerce, '82) |

A movie theater sells dreams, good times, and the chance to laugh or gasp in terror with hundreds of other people. But, to stay in business, it had better sell popcorn and Raisinets as well. As you can see from the table on p. 308, refreshments account for almost a quarter of movie theater revenues; but, as you can imagine, it costs a lot less to produce a tub of popcorn than to buy the rights to show a film.

In the 1920s and 1930s, movie theaters served as community gathering places, palaces for the people, and sources of the most sophisticated form of mass entertainment then available. Somehow, even in the depths

### Where the Money Comes From (Conventional Theaters)

| | |
|---|---|
| (1) Admissions: | 80.92% |
| (2) Popcorn and other refreshments: | 18.18% |
| (3) Other: | 0.9% |

(Department of Commerce, '82)

### Where the Money Goes (Before Federal Taxes)

| | |
|---|---|
| (1) Cost of operations: | 35.2% |
| (2) Officers' compensation: | 1.3% |
| (3) Pensions and benefits: | 1.2% |
| (4) Rent: | 6.8% |
| (5) Repairs: | 1.8% |
| (6) Depreciation, Depletion, Amortization: | 5.0% |
| (7) Interest: | 3.2% |
| (8) Bad Debts: | 0.1% |
| (9) Advertising: | 3.5% |
| (10) State, Local Taxes: | 3.5% |
| (11) Other Expenses: | 39.3% |
| (12) Net Profit Before Tax: | — |

(Troy, '83–'84)

of the depression, millions of people managed to find a few coins for a weekly or twice-a-week escape to a place that revealed faraway landscapes and life-styles of impossible luxury. But for the movie business, it was all downhill from there.

During the 1940s, much of the potential audience was overseas, getting shot at; and in the 1950s, movie theaters suffered a crippling blow as television sets made their way into more and more homes, offering entertainment at no charge. Movie studios fought back by providing full-color, wide-screen spectacles more elaborate than the black-and-white, nine-inch screen could provide. Gradually, drive-ins began to fade away, as real estate prices made it more profitable to build something on that land than to use the space only during the warm months of the year. Then the movie theaters suffered further body blows: larger TVs, color TV, and at last, the worst of all: the VCR.

In 1984, for instance, there were 20,200 movie theater screens; if every seat had been filled at every show, theaters would have taken in a total of around $73 million a day, or $26.5 billion a year. But actual receipts for the year were only about $4 billion.

In 1986, gross profits for movie theaters slipped to $3.8 billion while those for videocassette rentals rose to $3.4 billion. This time, viewers could watch exactly the same movies that were shown in theaters a few months earlier. (In Mel Brooks's *Spaceballs,* when the villains get confused about strategy, they watch the cassette of *Spaceballs* for hints because, in Brooks's vision of the future, the cassette hits the rental stores before the movie is finished.) Cassette buyers can watch a movie as often as they can stand it, for one purchase price; renters can cram as many viewers as they like into the living room for a single rental fee.

However, movie theaters will never die. Some people will want to see brand-new instead of comparatively new movies: others want wide screens and Dolby sound. The conclusive argument is that the teenagers will always need to be with other teenagers, in a place that gives them enough privacy to fool around a little but that is public enough for them to avoid doing anything really frightening.

## WHERE DO MOVIES COME FROM?

Theater owners lease films from film distributors. The distributors initiate the process by sending out "bid letters" to the owners of theaters they think will find a ready audience for the film. Some films do best at art cinemas in college towns, others as the second half of a double bill at a drive-in.

There are three major ways in which "exhibitors" (movie theater owners, not flashers) make deals with distributors. Usually, the theater owner collects his "nut" (running expenses) first, then splits the box office gross with the distributor, on a sliding scale—usually with a specified "floor," or minimum dollar amount, that the theater owner is guaranteed in case the movie turns out to be another *Howard the Duck.*

Then there's the "four-wall" arrangement, which isn't handball although it may be hardball. The distributor pays the theater owner rent for the use of the "four walls" of the movie theater; the distributor then takes over all the expenses of the movie's engagement (usually including a lot of advertisements) and keeps all the ticket money.

Just the opposite arrangement may be used, with the theater owner paying a flat fee for the right to show the film during a certain time period and keeping all the ticket money—no matter how many, or how few, tickets are sold. This arrangement is most common late in a movie's run.

It's usually up to the theater owner to decide what ticket prices will be. The chain owned by Loew's Theatres, Inc., is usually the price leader, deciding when first-run prices will be bumped up. Other first-run theaters generally follow. There used to be well-defined "A," "B," and "C" circuits, but now there are a lot of first-run theaters and the occasional second-run or discount theater (some of which even go so far as to show double features!).

But sometimes theater owners want low ticket prices to fill the seats with plenty of potential popcorn-buyers (the operating margin on refreshments can be more than 50 percent; or the theater owner can trade the expenses and headaches of selling refreshments for a regular rent from a concessionaire), while the distributors press for higher ticket prices. If the movie is likely to attract a lot of kids, the distribution contract may suggest minimum admission prices.

## THE FUTURE (IF ANY) OF MOVIE THEATERS

The trends are clear: "plexes" (theaters built to hold two or more screens; or existing movie theaters converted to multiple-screen operation) and chains. In 1982, for instance, the Department of Commerce's census showed that about two-thirds of the theaters (5,474 out of 9,344) were single-screen theaters; 3,870 were multiscreen. But multiscreen theaters earned about two-thirds of the receipts ($2,456,212,000 for the multiplexes, $1,044,529,000 for single-screen theaters). For one thing, they had several screens to generate the receipts; for another, multiscreen theaters tend to be newer and in more affluent areas, so ticket prices can be higher.

Although it's not impossible for an independent movie theater to survive, it's very, very tough. The movie business as a whole is suffering; the chains, at least, have enough capital to wait it out until the next smash hit comes along. The chains can also afford more advertising and higher rents; they can even buy theaters outright or force landlords to moderate their demands for rent increases.

One way for independents to survive is by finding a "niche," a specialized audience that is not being served by the chains. For instance, an independent theater can be an ethnic theater, showing Russian, Indian, Italian, or other foreign films aimed at immigrants from that country. Or it can shown foreign art films that don't attract an audience large enough to displace "Rambo the Thirteenth, Part Nine" from a multiplex screen. Another possibility is the revival theater, showing older films on wide screens, with theatrical soundtracks, in the ratio at which they were meant to be projected. Serious cinema lovers will find this more attractive than watching the films on home video. The question is, though, whether enough serious cinema lovers will show up in time to rescue the revival theater from bankruptcy.

Because the movie theater business is so difficult (ever-increasing costs and decreasing audiences), the dominance of chains of movie theaters is likely to increase. For instance, Toronto's Cineplex Odeon Corporation is the largest player in the New York City area, which is the largest movie market in the country (175,000 seats, three hundred theaters); Cineplex Odeon owns over one hundred screens in the area.

The fact that most of the movie theater audience is somewhere between puberty and voting age naturally has an effect on the kind of movies that are made, many of which are about teenagers and provide just enough sex and violence to titillate the intended viewers without making it actually illegal to sell tickets to them. Another influence on filmmakers is the desire to pack films with special effects that are better appreciated on a wide screen.

However, lovers of the adult film (that is, films about adults or involving issues more subtle than the presence or absence of peepholes in the locker room) can take heart: the highest-grossing single-screen theater in the United States in 1986 was New York City's Paris Theater, which grossed more than $2 million by showing only films that appealed to adult viewers and many of which were foreign.

# Sports Teams

"When we say it's a game, you tell us it's a business," a disgruntled football player snarls at a team owner in *North Dallas Forty,* "and when we say it's a business, you tell us it's a game." Professional sports definitely fall into both categories. Dozens of men earn more than $1 million a year by tackling, skating, slam-dunking, or pitching in professional sports. And the team owners also have millions of dollars at stake—sometimes they profit, sometimes they cheerfully expend the millions for the pleasure of discussing strategy with coaches, firing managers, and palling around with athletes.

## Football

A major event of the 1987 sports season—and in the history of organized labor—was the NFL strike, which was a somewhat paradoxical event in American labor relations. Many commentators pointed out that there was something poignant, or funny, about a group of men with average salaries near or above $200,000 (the Houston Oilers were paid an average of

$162,033 in 1986; the Dallas Cowboys were the best-paid, at an average of $256,612) going on strike.

However, there's a wide disparity between the minimum salary ($50,000) and the more-than-a-million earned by the men at the top; football players have an average career of only 4.2 years, and when they leave, they are entitled to the decidedly modest pension of $9,000 a year, payable when they reach fifty-five.

Then there's the vexing question of free agency. Players want a more expansive right to negotiate with other team owners when their contracts expire; what they hope for is a nice cozy bidding war. Team owners say that any bidding wars would drive financially marginal teams out of existence because the owners would pay too much for players to make the team a little less marginal in terms of victories. Once a few teams scooped up all the best players, owners say, the game wouldn't be worth watching since the other teams wouldn't be able to compete effectively. The fans would lose the pleasure of seeing a great game, and the owners would lose the TV revenue of broadcasting a great game. As you can see, TV revenue is much more important to an owner than gate receipts.

Players respond to such charges by pointing out that, although baseball has had free agency for eleven years, the teams somehow manage to put on a show that entertains the fans.

As you remember, the players lost the NFL strike, decisively. In January 1988, federal judge David Doty let the team owners maintain restrictions on free agency until the negotiating impasse between players and owners could be resolved. The playing field then shifted to the National Labor Relations Board (NLRB); in April 1988, the NLRB held that the impasse was unresolvable. Union officials claimed a major victory because the NLRB dismissed the owners' allegation that the union had refused to negotiate in good faith. June 1988 saw the case back before Judge Doty, with a decision expected in July. Over five hundred football players are free agents, with contracts that expired in February; their contractual fate will depend to a great extent on the fiscal health of the owners.

But it's interesting that the owners won the strike in a way you might not have anticipated. It's true that fans hardly bothered to watch the games put on by the substitute scab teams fielded during the strike. For instance, the last games before the strike—on September 20, 1987—drew audiences of 693,263, more than twice as many fans as attended any of the games on strike-bound October 4, 11, or 18. The football-starved fans came roaring back on October 25, once the strike was over (after all, they needed something to take their minds off the stock market)—641,646 strong. (Only twelve games were played that day, instead of the normal thirteen, because the Vikings/Broncos contest was postponed as a result of the last World Series game.) It's interesting to note that some teams played to a capacity crowd (there were 53,497 Washington Redskins fans in a stadium that holds 55,750, for instance); other stadiums were half full, or less: the Los Angeles Raiders played to 52,735 spectators in a stadium seating 92,516, and Detroit's stadium, which can hold 80,638, attracted only 27,278 fans on the first post-strike Sunday.

But, according to the *Wall Street Journal* ("Broken Play: Labor Experts Fault Football Players' Strike Strategy," October 14, 1987), a typical NFL team earned $800,000 a week before the strike—and $921,000 a week during it. The TV and radio payments continued unabated. That would have been enough to sour network-NFL relations permanently had the NFL not agreed to pay the three major networks about $60 million to make up for the ad revenue and market share that the networks lost during the strike. (A sports fan who doesn't watch a scab football game doesn't watch the commercials during that game and presumably cuts back on consuming shaving cream, wine coolers, and other essentials of life.) This is not to say that the NFL wrote out a $60 million check. Instead, it paid $20 million and agreed to accept $20 million less in both 1987 and 1988 from the networks for rights to televise the post-strike games.

Obviously, ticket receipts, box rentals, and concession sales were lower during the strike (however, NFL teams share their ticket revenue, so the impact was evenly spread among all the teams). But most football players get paid by the game; and player-related costs dropped from $854,000 a week to a piffling $230,000.

As it happens, ten of the twenty-eight NFL teams raised their ticket prices for the 1987 season, usually by 10 to 12 percent; some other teams were undecided. Some teams, such as the Minnesota Vikings, maintain a single ticket price ($18); other teams, such as the Kansas City Chiefs, have complex ticket rates that depend on the seat placement and whether the ticket buyer is a student or a senior citizen.

The relationship between a team, its stadium, and the city in which the stadium is located is a complex one. (See page 321 for more about sports stadiums.) The Houston Oilers, not one of football's most glorious teams, have a lease on the Astrodome until 1988. The city of Houston would like them to hang around (it's estimated that there are more than a thousand Oiler-related jobs at stake and over $60 million a year enriching the local economy), although the fans might not miss them too much: season ticket sales keep going down. The Astrodome, which has 50,945 seats, is the smallest NFL stadium; local officials offered a $50 million refurbishing job, adding 10,000 new seats.

But Jacksonville, Florida, has an 80,000-seat auditorium, the Gator Bowl—and no NFL team. Jacksonville is offering a moving allowance and a share of stadium concessions and parking receipts to a team that will locate there. Given the reduced rent Jacksonville wants to charge, the Oilers could get the stadium almost rent-free—and Jacksonville will pledge ten years of sold-out games, which is worth $115 million. Why would a small city do all that? Precisely because it is a small city. The estimated $85 million a year that an NFL team would add to the economy would be welcome, and a major team would put Jacksonville on the map and in the consciousness of sports fans.

Summer 1987 saw the birth of a new sport, arena football, aimed at satisfying the ravening hunger of the football fan who can't wait until fall. Arena football is played with eight-man teams and a fifty-yard playing field; it's been called "watching football in a pinball machine." The $8.50 tickets are cheaper than NFL tickets, which average $10. Arena football is run by Arena Sports Ventures, and the four teams are subsidiaries of that company; the "owners" set policy, including the base salary for players ($25,000) and bonuses for winners.

The sport is the creation of James Foster, who was involved in the United States Football League (USFL), the failed rival to the NFL. He figures that the USFL's problem was its failure to control player salaries—and he doesn't plan to make that mistake again; he figures that it costs a mere $2 million to operate an arena football team for a year. Owning an NFL team costs ten times as much.

As for mighty television revenues, they haven't arrived yet, but ESPN, the cable TV sports network (see page 295 for more on cable TV), picks up the production costs of televising some arena football games and plans to split revenues with Arena Sports Ventures. The fast-food chain Hardee's Food Systems, Inc., shelled out $500,000 to sponsor two seasons of arena football; for its money, it will get to run twelve ads per televised game and be given the chance to use arena football players to entice sports fans to scarf down Hardee's sandwiches.

# Baseball

The usual definition of a millionaire is a fella who has a million dollars, no matter when he earned or accumulated it. That means that baseball teams have a respectable complement of millionaires. In fact, as of November 1987, fifty-seven baseball players earned $1 million a year or more. Maybe that's why they call it a baseball diamond. Five players (the Kansas City Royals' Dan Quisenberry and George Brett; the Boston Red Sox's Jim Rice; the Baltimore Orioles' Eddie Murray; and the New York Mets' Gary Carter) earned more than two million smackers. Steve Balboni, another member of Kansas City Royalty, earned the biggest bonus—$525,000, which is more than the salary of most major leaguers.

Since 1976 baseball has had a free agency system, which allows a player, once he has played for a team for six years and his contract with the club has expired, to offer his services to the highest bidder. Thirty-two players became eligible as free agents in 1985, joining thirty already eligible—yet by a curious "coincidence" (and after team owners had spent a hell of a lot of money bidding for top players) not one single player received a higher bid from another team. In September 1987, arbitrator Thomas T. Roberts ruled in favor of the Major League Baseball Players' Association, which had argued that the owners had acted collusively to frustrate the free agency process. As of November 1987, the penalty had not been set.

One thing the owners didn't have to worry about was an antitrust suit in federal court, charging them with obstructing interstate commerce and demanding "treble damages" (not ones in a high register, but damages triple the injury that can be proved). It's not that baseball isn't important enough—and it certainly involves interstate commerce—it's just that, as long as there have been antitrust laws, baseball teams (but not teams in other sports) have been exempt. Another cozy coincidence.

In 1987, most major league teams (twelve out of fourteen) stood pat on ticket prices; two raised ticket prices by a buck or so, but it's still a challenge to pay over $10 for a baseball ticket unless you insist on a luxury suite or skybox. You might say that, compared to football, baseball is the discount store of professional sports, cutting prices and relying on volume. In fact, baseball teams rely much more on ticket sales for revenue than football teams do. In 1982, for instance, football teams earned 34 percent of their $571 million revenues from gate receipts and 58 percent from TV and radio sales. Baseball teams, however, got the majority (54 percent) of their comparatively piffling $397 million in revenues from gate receipts; only 30 percent, or $119 million (only a little more than half of $195 million paid to football teams), came from radio and TV.

In 1987, according to *Broadcasting* magazine, broadcast rights for the twenty-six major league teams, twenty-four of which are based in the United States and two of which are based in Canada, brought in a total of $158 million. The Detroit Tigers had the best won-lost record (98–64), but far from the best broadcast record: rights to show their games brought in an even $6 million. The big winners in broadcasting were the two teams you might call the New York Bucks: the Mets, who won 92 and lost 70 games, earned $17 million, with the Yankees close behind, with an 89–73 record and $16.50 million in broadcast revenues. The cellar dwellers of Cleveland (61–101) earned a mere $3 million for broadcast rights, but the more adept San Francisco Giants didn't earn any more although they had a 90–72 record for the season.

The average salary for a major league player in 1987 was $412,454. The Royals had the highest average salary, at $555,275; the Pittsburgh Pirates were the big losers in this particular statistic, averaging a mere $160,980 in their pay envelopes.

Luckily for them, most baseball teams seemed to have strategies that promoted season ticket sales. Ten of the twelve National League teams had improved ticket sales in 1987 as compared to 1986, and the L.A. Dodgers (we remember when they were the Brooklyn Dodgers—so called because they allegedly dodged trolleys, a feature absent from the L.A. scene) had to put a cap on sales of season tickets.

Things weren't quite so good in the American League: half the teams had improved ticket sales, four held steady, and the White Sox and Twins were down. (The Yankees didn't comment on sales for either 1986 or 1987.) The bottom-ranked Seattle Mariners actually managed to increase their season ticket sales by, first of all, supporting a local home for disadvantaged kids (a good public relations move) and, second, by discounting the tickets by 18 percent—the deepest discount in pro baseball.

As of May 1987, the Mariners had sold 4,500 season tickets. That's a very significant number because the Mariners' contract with their stadium, the Kingdome, has an unusual escape clause: the team can pull up stakes and leave Seattle unless it gets 1.8 million fans or sells 12,000 season tickets—both falling into the category of "fat chance." The Mariners were likely to get a new owner in 1987 because the team's current owner, George Argyros, was forced to sell the team after he had treated himself to a $45 million shopping spree in buying the San Diego Padres. The Padres are a much better team, but no one is allowed to own two major league teams.

You'd think it would be curtains (or deep-six) for the Mariners, but plenty of cities want their own pro teams in all the major sports. However, baseball commissioner Peter Ueberroth takes a negative view of transfers of baseball franchises, which made the Seattle escape clause especially intriguing to cities in search of baseball teams of their very own.

Owning a baseball team is basically a rich guy's way of spending the entire summer in baseball camp. In 1982, the major league teams lost a total of $57.9 million. In the National League, only two teams managed to make a buck (Los Angeles, with a comparatively startling $7 million profit, and Atlanta, which was $1.5 million ahead of the game). Chicago ended up $8 million in the tank. In the American League, three teams made money, albeit in minimal amounts: Minnesota ended the season $100,000 ahead, and Detroit and Boston each earned $500,000. California and Toronto broke even, and the big loser was Texas, at $8 million in the red.

According to one owner, who was quoted in August 1987, "The best-run teams are very profitable businesses" ("Baseball Entrepreneurs Score in Bush Leagues," *New York Times,* August 24, 1987). No, he wasn't hallucinating, he was talking about minor league teams. He estimated that minor league teams have 10 to 20 percent profit margins. Attendance at minor league games is increasing, with more than 20 million fans expected for 1987 (compared to about 12.5 million in 1980). Of course, with a ticket price in the range of $3, that wouldn't mean prosperity if the costs weren't, uh, the polite word is rock-bottom. Players in the Empire State League (one of seventeen minor leagues) get a princely $350 a month while rental of a college field and dormitory expenses for the team each run about $50,000 a season; players collect foul balls because, after all, balls cost $30 a dozen.

The real source of profit, though, is the sale of the franchises themselves. (They're sort of like New York co-op apartments.) Buying a Triple-A minor league team can cost millions of dollars, and even a lower-ranked team can cost well into six figures.

# Basketball

Professional sports have always offered a way for talented members of minority groups to succeed. Right now, basketball is a sport in which black players are prominent (almost 80 percent of NBA players are black, as compared to about 40 percent in the NFL and about 25 percent of major league baseball players), and the dreams of many black kids center on basketball.

One reason is that while a halfway decent game of baseball or football calls for organized teams, uniforms, equipment, and a large, well-tended playing field, a full-scale basketball game requires only ten guys, ten pairs of sneakers, and a schoolyard, and an interesting game can develop with only two players and a backboard. Parents or educators have to organize and coach Little League baseball or Pop Warner football, a procedure involving the setting of schedules and much ferrying of kids around in station wagons. Nobody, except the players themselves, organizes inner-city pickup basketball games.

For a variety of reasons, some involving racism, basketball has ranked as the runt in the litter of pro sports. Revenues and TV interest in basketball were the lowest for any major league sports, and team franchises went for comparatively low sums. In 1982, almost two-thirds of basketball revenue came from gate receipts, which provided only $105 million—about half of baseball or football gate receipts. Most painful of all, TV and radio revenue brought in only 27 percent of basketball's total revenue; that's a mere $46 million as compared to $119 million for baseball and $332 million for football.

However, basketball players always had the highest average salary in pro sports: in 1984, football players averaged $163,145 (we know, we know, you wouldn't complain if that were your average salary); baseball players, $329,408, or twice as much; and basketball players, $332,000— probably because basketball teams don't have a large roster larded with a number of rookie or marginal players.

That stepchild status could be changing. In April 1987, the NBA decided to add four franchises to the twenty-three existing teams: one each in Miami and Orlando, Florida, and in Minneapolis, Minnesota, and Charlotte, North Carolina. Each new team ponied up $32.5 million, to be divided among the existing teams.

Furthermore, unlike baseball teams, basketball teams can be an exceedingly profitable possession. Jerry Buss owns the L.A. Lakers (come to think of it, Los Angeles is not noted for its lakes or other bodies of water but the team used to hang out in Minneapolis, near some sizeable, indeed, Great, lakes), and it's only part of his vertically integrated sports conglomerate. He also owns a 17,505-seat stadium, a hockey team, a tennis team, an indoor soccer club, and part of a cable channel that televises sports events, among other things. The Lakers have the highest payroll in the NBA ($9.5 million) but are expected to generate pretax profits in the $10 million range for 1987.

Pretty soon, you may be able to take stock of your favorite team's latest season and also take stock in your favorite team. Forty percent of the Boston Celtics has been sold to the public by means of $46.8 million worth of publicly traded limited partnership interests. The guys who own the other 60 percent (Don Gaston, Alan Cohen, and Paul Dupee) bought the team in 1982 for $15 million, so they didn't make out too badly on the deal. The investors didn't do so hot: in May 1987, the value of the shares was down 22 percent from their offering value. One football team (the Green Bay Packers) is publicly owned, and other teams were (cautiously) considering it; we suspect that the October 1987 stock market crash put those dreams to bed.

# Hockey

What a comeback story! You'd have to turn to Rocky III for a comparable blend of violence and heart-tugging struggle to get back to the big time. In 1987, the National Hockey League actually managed to turn a profit, an event as rare as hen's teeth, or front teeth on a goalie. Between 1975 and 1983, the NHL had gone $75 million into the tank.

Like many a business before it, the NHL got into trouble by unchecked growth. In 1966, there were six hockey franchises, all in cities cold enough for the denizens to have a personal relationship with ice. By 1975, there were eighteen franchises, many of them in places where nobody much cared to watch hockey games. And if they cared to watch them on TV, too bad: there was no network coverage, which meant a loss of $3 to $4 million in television revenue as well as an unmeasurable share of the audience.

Then a rival World Hockey Association was formed, so the fans (however many there were) had thirty teams and a farm system to keep track of. Eventually, the NHL and WHA sorted things out, so there are now twenty-one NHL teams. Then it was discovered that hockey is perfect for cable television; its audience, although not as large as that for either football or baseball, is fiercely loyal and includes enough affluent sports fans to keep advertisers interested.

By 1987, 85 percent of arena seats were sold, at prices ranging from $7 to $34 (Canadian) depending on the seat and the team. That means $172 million (Canadian). Part of this was due to heavy sales of season tickets to corporations, so there was money in NHL coffers, even if many seats remained empty until the playoffs. Furthermore, the trading rules in the league tend to keep players with the same team, not stirring up interteam bidding wars, so the average NHL salary is about $170,000. (Yeah, that wouldn't bother you too much either, but we bet you hardly ever get hit with a hockey stick during a normal workday—and you don't have to skate around the office, either.)

You can tell the men from the boys by the price of their toys—and by the sums of money that change hands in connection with the games they watch. In 1987, professional sports leagues received over $1 billion from product licenses—NBA clothes hampers, NFL furniture and fur coats (but not toilet seats; the suggestion was rejected as tasteless), and T-shirts and caps from all the leagues. (The league, not the individual team, handles the licensing.) The National Hockey League trailed, bringing in only $50 million in 1987 licensing income; the NBA earned much more, at $150 million, but was far behind the NFL and the baseball leagues, at $450 million each.

Without professional sports, commercial television would be hard-pressed for viewership and would have far less advertising revenue (and cable television would find it much more difficult to line up exclusive events). In 1987, advertisers spent more than $1.5 billion on network TV ads in search of sports fans (many of them free-spending young males). General Motors chipped in $111.4 million, Ford spent a comparatively modest $27 million, and the armed forces spent over $40 million seeking a few good couch potatoes.

Without professional sports, male bonding would be a very different thing. And who knows how many marriages would crumble if spouses had to talk to each other?

# 74

# Sports Stadiums

If you want to play football, stage a championship boxing bout, or present a Prince concert, you can't do it in someone's living room; you need a venue that will seat thousands of cheering fans (65,793 will fit into Soldier Field, where the Chicago Bears play; the Buffalo Bills can host up to 80,290 at Rich Stadium). And if you're a real estate developer or a city, you may find that building a sports stadium or fixing up an existing arena in poor repair can be the best investment you can make.

It's not an inexpensive proposition: the 75,000-seat Dolphins stadium cost $100 million (all privately financed). The stadium has 10,000 club seats, which are twenty-one inches wide and have armrests; 27,000 seats on the lower deck, and 35,000 on the upper deck; and two color scoreboards, which can provide instant replays. However, a stadium can be a real money-maker: consider all those season tickets, and single tickets ($26 each, for the Dolphins games). (It costs between $600 and $1,400 to get a club seat for the season, but for that price you also get access to the air-conditioned stadium club.)

The Dolphins are the only NFL team to own and operate their own stadium. Only one other NFL stadium is privately owned: St. Louis's Busch Memorial Stadium, which belongs to the Anheuser-Busch corporate family. The other teams play in publicly owned stadiums, although the Packers, Bills, and Cowboy franchises are involved in stadium operations.

It's been estimated that the forty-eight executive suite boxes in Seattle's Kingdome cost $5.5 million, but the boxes, which seat 10 to 12 people, rent for anywhere from $50,000 to $75,000 a season. That price includes a dozen football tickets, five baseball ducats, and an option to buy more tickets. The Kingdome was a busy place, with 156 events in 154 days in 1986; nearly 2.5 million people attended, and all the Seahawks football games were sold out.

So far, the highest-grossing single event at a stadium was the Hagler-Leonard championship fight on April 6, 1987, whose 15,336 tickets brought in $7.9 million to the Caesars Palace Outdoor Stadium of Las Vegas. That's more than the Super Bowl grossed, but then the fight tickets ranged in price from $100 to $700 apiece.

The fight fans bought all the merchandise in the arena: the average merchandise sales were between $20 and $40, although a real devotee could buy a $100 jacket to commemorate the event. The gross for the fight was $76 million, with the largest source of income being the right to broadcast the fight on closed-circuit television. The fans also ate 8,000 hot dogs and drank 15,000 beers.

Dogs 'n' suds, of course, are traditional sporting fare, usually at a cost of at least $1 per hot dog, $1 to $1.50 per soft drink, and $2.40 for a twenty-four-ounce beer. But some stadiums feature more exotic fare, from fish and chips to antipasto salad; stuffed potato skins have also been tried but were found too labor-intensive to be profitable. The twenty-six baseball stadiums had a new crusade in the spring of 1988: cutting down on beer consumption in the stands in order to limit altercations and littering. Teams such as Los Angeles and Detroit stopped sales of beer in the stands altogether—even at the cost of significant revenue from alcohol sales—in the interest of crowd control.

The Louisiana Superdome had its best season in 1986 (revenues up 39 percent, to $3.9 million) as a result of events as disparate as the Sugar Bowl, Super Bowl XX, Julio Iglesias and Monkees concerts, and the Lions International Convention. The next year was expected to be even better because, according to *Amusement Business* (the trade journal for several entertainment-related industries), "the NCAA Final Four and the Pope have signed dates at the dome." The Final Four brought in about $2.2 million by selling 63,000 tickets at $20 to $50 each, but we don't know what material results His Holiness achieved.

For about five years in a row, Madison Square Garden has brought in about $100 million in revenues to the Gulf & Western Entertainment Corporation, its parent company, and yearly profits ranging from $5 to $10 million.

## POLITICAL FOOTBALL

There are plenty of reasons (many of them flat and green) why a city wants to have professional sports franchises. A first-rate sports team enhances a city's image; politicians like to hang out with jocks; and local merchants simply love to provide hotel rooms, stadium parking, meals and souvenirs for sports fans. It's been estimated that the Tampa, Florida, area earned $250 million in four days when the Super Bowl was last held there, in 1984.

That's why cities are willing to float bond issues of tens, even hundreds, of millions of dollars to repair existing or build new stadiums. (Politicians can point proudly to team recruitment and stadium building when they're asked what they've accomplished. It's often far more interesting to voters than sewage treatment or road repair.) Maryland will issue up to $235 million in bonds (and will start a new lottery to pay off some of them) to build a football stadium (in case anyone wants to move to Baltimore) and a baseball stadium (to keep the Orioles from flying away, the way the Colts bolted to Indianapolis in 1984).

Team owners are crazy about these intercity struggles. After all, if you want to produce a Broadway show, you have to pay the owner of the theater to let you use the theater; but cities not only offer great deals to team owners, they are willing to build to suit and float another bond issue as soon as the stadium starts looking a little shabby. The late 1980s should be a time of crackling stadium construction, with some cities spending more than $100 million "on spec" in the hope that a major team will eventually move in because, unless Congress relents, bond issues to build stadiums will no longer be tax-exempt after 1990. That'll make bond buyers much less willing to buy them (unless the cities can manage to pay a hefty interest rate).

## STADIUM DESIGN

Maybe a football player with a multimillion-dollar contract doesn't mind busting his buns outdoors on a cold autumn day, but the fans usually prefer to be a little more comfortable. That usually means an enclosed stadium, which should, optimally, be a good venue for baseball, football, basketball, hockey, large conventions, religious events, and concerts. (Baseball fans, the convertible drivers of the sports world, tend to prefer fresh air, so new stadiums being built in Toronto, Cleveland, Phoenix, and San Antonio really are "rag-tops"—stadiums with retractable fabric roofs.)

But the owner of the stadium, whether municipal or private, wants the prestige of a huge stadium and the possibility of booking gigantic rock shows and play-off games. The teams also want a large seating capacity but would rather have a sold-out season, preferably with lots of season-ticket sales to bring in capital at the beginning of the season and lots of revenue from TV and radio broadcasts, than a few lonely fans sprinkled around a gigantic arena. Then there's the problem that a baseball diamond is, well, a diamond, and a football field or basketball court is rectangular. You can't very well play basketball on Astroturf, either.

Moreover, to have a hard dome on a stadium costs about $18 million, and the stadium will probably have to be round to keep the roof up. An inflated fabric roof costs only half as much and puts fewer constraints on design, but it raises the heating bill, creates a risk of collapse under heavy snowfalls, and can turn the stadium into a giant wind tunnel.

In short, designing a stadium involves the very difficult problem of reconciling the conflicting objectives of architecture and crowd control.

Sports stadiums are intimately related not only to cities' political climates, but to the balance of power between the broadcast media and the sports teams themselves. The teams want broadcast revenue, but they also want the encouragement of live fans cheering them toward victory. The fans themselves have to balance the cost of tickets and the inconvenience of going to the stadium (and missing the instant replays and color commentary) against the immediacy of live sports action. Perhaps future sports events will be purely media events, played out on a soundstage, entirely for broadcast.

# 75

# Health Clubs

| | |
|---|---|
| Number of establishments: | 3,975 "health clubs and reducing salons" (not inc. 7,549 "membership sports and recreation facilities"; 3,331 "dance schools") |
| Total receipts: | $.94 billion (not inc. $2.5 billion for sports/recreation facilities; $220 million for dance schools) |
| Average net sales: | $237,029 (not inc. $329,750 sports/recreation facilities; $66,234 dance schools) |
| | (Department of Commerce, '82) |

At first, there were gyms—seriously sweaty places in which guys with lots in the biceps department and not much in the neck department went to have a serious relationship with their barbells. And there were exercise studios, where ladies in leotards essayed a timid leg lift or two en route to a facial. And of course there were dance studios, where worshippers of the arts aspired to ballet or good old-fashioned hoofing.

Then, lo and behold, running around in your underwear became jogging, and then there was aerobics, and now here we are. "Fitness" is an everyday word, and millions have plunked down hefty membership fees to join health clubs. In 1985, according to the National Sporting Goods Association, more than 8 million people started doing workouts with low-stress equipment; 4 million people joined the ranks of regular calisthenics sufferers; and nearly 6 million people started a program of aerobic dancing. Although the National Sporting Goods Association didn't take count, health clubs also offer classes in yoga, tai chi chuan, stretching, and other movement styles.

Some of the new club members really do adopt a program of regular exercise. Others look on the club as a sort of singles bar, where you can drink all the freshly squeezed grapefruit juice you want and still drive home (probably alone, but a person has to try) without worrying about breathalyzer tests. The rest will start out with a burst of enthusiasm, then take a good look around and notice that the carpet in Studio B is a trifle frayed, or that the seven o'clock class is awfully crowded, or that it isn't as easy as they thought to take a noontime exercise class and go back to work. The jogging track to Hell (or at least obesity) is paved with good intentions.

## THE ATTRITION FACTOR

There are two kinds of clubs. One of them charges a membership fee for the year, or perhaps offers short-term deals, two memberships for the price of one, or a special price for a three-year membership. These clubs depend on attrition for much of their profit; that is, the more members they can sign up—and the fewer members actually bother to show up—the more profitable the club will be. This is the typical model for health clubs and gyms, where the membership fee covers unlimited use of the facilities, and members do not have to pay individually for the services they use.

For example, Living Well Lady, a chain of seventeen health clubs for women with 72,000 members in the New York area, expects an average attrition rate of 70 percent. According to the company's financial documents, it costs anywhere from $10,000 to $100,000 to renovate the space used for a club; improvements cost about $200,000, and exercise equipment costs $50,000 more.

The second kind of club (typically a racquet club, dance studio, or facility that gives aerobics classes) charges both a membership fee and a fee per class or hour of court time. For these clubs, the key to profitability is keeping the facilities full but not overly full. Sometimes the clubs do this through marketing; sometimes they set differential prices to encourage people to show up when the club would otherwise be empty. For these clubs, attrition means financial ill-health. Members of the International Racquet Sports Association average 15 to 34 percent attrition, a rate noticeably lower than that of many clubs charging a flat fee.

## A CHELSEA CASE HISTORY

The Chelsea Racquet and Fitness Club in New York City opened in 1986. For the purposes of this book, its claim to fame is that Dana is one of its less promising members. The 13,000-square-foot club has 850 members (about two-thirds of them male): 500 have racquet memberships only (nearly all of them are racquetball players, but there are a few unregenerate squash players); 250 use the Nautilus machines. According to owner-manager Leslie Cymrot, the perfect enrollment would be 1,100 members.

There's no arcane formula for deciding the proper balance of racquetball to squash courts, and in fact a number of racquet-club owners are converting squash courts to chambers for Nautilus equipment. It's just that a regulation racquetball court takes up more space and requires a higher ceiling than a squash court. Nautilus machines, free weights, and aerobics classes are even more accommodating: all that's required is a strong floor for the machines and weights or a springy, flexible floor for aerobics—a racquetball or squash court does nicely.

Indoor tennis courts take up as much room as five racquetball courts and so are a rare and exotic blossom. (Manhattan tennis court time can run as high as $66 an hour—and people pay it.) Any metropolitan area with enough tennis players to support a club is likely to be metropolitan enough to charge high rents; in general, one of a health club owner's biggest problems is always to find enough space for the necessary facilities and to keep paying the atrocious rent month after month.

Health clubs also have utility bills way above the owners' comfort level—what with burning lights twelve to eighteen hours a day; cooling small, enclosed spaces full of sweaty people; keeping the blow dryers burning; heating water for long, steamy showers; maintaining whirlpool spas, saunas, and steamrooms; and washing load after load of wet towels.

Another high business expense is insurance. Health club owners, like other business owners, can find it hard to buy liability insurance and nearly always find it expensive. However, the liability insurance problem is a little less severe for health clubs than for some other businesses because health club owners are legally liable only for injuries that are caused or contributed to by the club's negligence, not for injuries that are a normal risk of the sport. In other words, you have a chance to win a suit against a health club if a loose tile falls on your head in the shower but not if you get slugged by your opponent's squash ball.

Leslie Cymrot pinpointed one of the major factors in running a successful club: payroll control. An unsuccessful club has layers of administrators, instructors, instruction supervisors, physical plant managers, and the like. Chelsea has three owner-managers: Leslie and Gary Cymrot, and Schnoodle, the consumer relations manager, who moonlights as a cat ("pure-bred alley") and can usually be found sleeping either at the front door or on the reception desk. In other words, Schnoodle works as hard as some consumer relations managers . . . and never says anything to annoy a club member.

Four workers handle the desk (most of them young actresses, recruited through ads in *Backstage*), and there are one squash and racquet-ball pro, a Nautilus instructor and backup instructor, four aerobics instructors, and cleaning personnel.

The club also provides a snack bar and pro shop, but they're primarily convenience services for members, not major contributors to profits.

## JAZZERCISE: A FRANCHISING SUCCESS STORY

Starting a conventional health club—dressing rooms, Jacuzzi, and all—is a high-capital affair. However, Jazzercise, Jacki Sorenson's aerobic dance system, permits its nearly 3,000 franchisees to go into business with an investment of $10,000 or less.

The initial franchise fee is only $500 (one of the least expensive in the entire spectrum of franchising). New franchisees (nearly all of whom are women) must spend a further sum for training and for a microphone, record player, and VCR to use the Jazzercise class materials. Some franchisees lease a storefront or other space for the classes; others rent school gymnasiums by the hour, bypassing a long-term commitment to pay rent.

An energetic Jazzercise franchisee in a good territory (preferably one with a large population of exercise-oriented women but without too many competing facilities) can gross about $37,500 a year and net about $15,000. It's not a huge sum, but many of the franchisees consider it an excellent return for a part-time business that can be arranged not to conflict with family obligations. The flip side of the low franchise fee is the very high monthly fee: 30 percent, one of the highest in the entire franchising spectrum.

In comparison, there is no minimum franchise fee for the 255 franchised Arthur Murray Dance Studios; the capital requirements for starting up are about the same as for Jazzercise (approximately $10,000), and the monthly fee is 5.8 percent.

States license a bewildering, and sometimes comic, variety of professions. But they don't license or regulate personal trainers or instructors of aerobics, dance, yoga, or other physical skills. Before you trust your body to the tender mercies of an instructor, find out his or her back-

# CONSUMER TIPS

Be wary of a low, low price for membership. It could be part of a sincere—but desperate, and eventually unsuccessful—attempt to resuscitate a club gasping for funds. Or it could be an unscrupulous attempt to grab as much money as possible before closing down the operation. Eighteen states (including New York) require health club owners to post a bond to protect customers' rights to refunds if and when the club closes. Furthermore, membership fees must be put in a separate escrow account, and customers are entitled to cancel their contracts under conditions set by law. Look for a well-established club (but even then, don't discount an honest financial crisis or a flight to Bolivia with your money). Even if your state doesn't require an escrow account or a bond, it's a good sign if the club uses these protective devices voluntarily.

If there are several clubs in your area, it's likely that each club will have a slightly different pricing policy; for instance, one racquet club may charge a higher membership fee but lower hourly court rates, or higher court rates overall but lower rates at the time that's most convenient for you. Be sure to make a realistic assessment of how often and when you'll use the club in order to decide which offers the best bargain for your anticipated pattern of use.

Price is not always a guide to quality or convenience. Certainly, you won't be happy if the club's prices are too low for the club to buy and maintain adequate equipment and a full schedule of classes. If money is no object, you may be able to find a superelite club that restricts its membership to a small number of people willing to pay extra-high fees for uninterrupted access to facilities.

But a higher membership fee may go into the owner's pocket, not into the facilities; or it may be used to enhance the quality of the makeup mirrors in the women's locker room and the juicers at the snack bar, not to buy more Nautilus machines. The size of the health club facility sets strict limits on the amount of equipment and the number of classes that can be offered at one time. The bottom line is that a good club is almost certain to be crowded at peak hours, and the best teachers' classes are likely to attract a following.

ground. A college major in physical education or courses in anatomy and exercise physiology are good signs; so is training and continuing education provided by one of the organizations formed by people trying to professionalize the exercise field. It's a bad sign if the instructor is a dedicated narcissist who goes through a routine that makes his or her physique look good but that is inappropriate for the goals and fitness levels of the students in the class.

Part of the problem is that surprisingly little is known about healthy human bodies and how to keep them fit; even orthopedic surgeons have widely conflicting opinions on these matters.

# 76

# Casinos

1984 casino revenue: $5.0834 billion—$5 billion of which was the casino "win" (the amount the casino won from gamblers, not vice versa). The revenue was divided into $3.0752 billion for Nevada ($2.008 billion from Las Vegas, the rest from Reno and other gambling towns), $1.952 billion from Atlantic City. Gaming revenue in 1987 for Atlantic City is estimated at $2.5 billion.

As of mid-1988, there were only two places in the United States—Nevada and Atlantic City, New Jersey—where casino gambling was legal, although Miami Beach, Detroit, and New Orleans were considering legalizing it. As well as being very concentrated geographically, the casino industry is also concentrated in terms of ownership, since only a few players own most of the casinos. The five top casino companies—Bally's Park Place, Inc., Trump, Caesars World, Inc., Hilton Hotels Corporation, and Circus Circus Enterprises, Inc.—are likely to continue the trend toward concentration, buying out the failures such as the Dunes Hotel & Casinos, which filed for Chapter 11 bankruptcy protection in April 1987. (At least, that's who nominally owns the casinos. It's an open secret that organized crime is highly involved in legal as well as illegal gambling, but naturally enough respectable business people are signing the checks and having their pictures taken for the annual report, instead of members of the Mothers' and Fathers' Industry Association.)

In 1979, only two companies—Resorts International, Inc., and Cae-

**Where the Money Came From**
**(Fifty-nine Nevada Casino-Hotels,**
**with Revenue Over $2 Million, 1983)**

| | |
|---|---|
| (1) Casino department: | 58.7% |
| (2) Lodging services: | 13.9% |
| (3) Meals: | 12.9% |
| (4) Drinks: | 8.3% |
| (5) Other revenues: | 6.2% |

**Where the Money Went (The Same Fifty-nine Nevada Casinos)**

| | |
|---|---|
| Cost of sales: | 8.2% |
| Gross margin: | 91.8%, divided into direct expenses (45.3%) and departmental income (46.5%), the latter consisting of total general and administrative expenses (43.9%) and net operating income (2.6%) |

(Vogel '86)

sars—had a meaningful market share in casino gambling. By 1984, Resorts' market share was down to 13.2 percent; Caesars', to 11.5 percent. Other major companies included Bally, with a 12.2 percent share of the market; Golden Nugget, Inc., with 12.9 percent; Sands, with 8.2 percent; Harrah's, with 10.8 percent; Tropicana, with 11.0 percent; Atlantis, with 7.6 percent; Claridge's, with 6.3 percent; and the up-and-coming Trump Plaza, with 6.5 percent.

## LOOKING AT THE INDUSTRY

Some of the largest corporations in the United States are involved in casinos: both Hilton and Holiday Inns, Inc., are casino owners, for instance, although neither is thought of primarily as a gambling operation. Four casino companies made *Business Week*'s Top 1000 listing for the year 1987; here's what their figures look like:

| | Circus Circus Enterprises | Caesar's World | Bally Manufacturing Corporation* |
|---|---|---|---|
| Sales | $459 million | $818 million | $1.73 billion |
| Profits | 61.9 million | 58.2 million | −6.4 million |
| Market value | 603 million | 583 million | 472 million |
| Assets | 542 million | 786 million | 2.52 billion |
| Profit margin | 13.5% | 7.1% | NM |

*Also manufactures pinball machines and related amusement devices.

## FINDING A MARKET

Casino-hotel complexes have identified three segments of the casino market; usually a particular operation will be designed to attract and satisfy one or perhaps two overlapping segments, instead of trying to be all things to all gamblers.

The most palatial operations (and when a casino-hotel strives for lavishness, they get *lavish*—hotel suites that are larger than many stores and that cost $650,000 or so to equip with giant Jacuzzis, wet bars with sphinxes, and winding Lucite staircases) are aimed at the high rollers, who toss around the "black chips" (the largest denomination of chip, worth $100). Paradoxically, high rollers (who are either rich or have a short life expectancy—bad debt expenses are notoriously low in casino operations) get "comps," or complimentary services—free airfare, free hotel suites that would normally rent for $500 a night, free big-name entertainment, and free meals and drinks. It's good business for a casino to spend $10,000 to put someone in a good enough mood to lose $200,000; some high rollers frequently, and cheerfully, lose more than a $1 million at a clip. (Of course, they must win sometimes; otherwise, they'd stop gambling, free junkets or no.)

If the casino's "hold" (the amount won by the casino divided by the amount "dropped," or gambled) is 20 percent, and if the casino wants to earn $100, it must get a gambler to bet at least $2,500 for typical junket expenses of $400. The win rate is usually 10 to 22 percent of the drop, but this depends on the game; some games are notoriously bigger sucker propositions than others.

The middle of the gambling market includes a mixture of those who play with cash and those who get credit (if you can get credit from a casino, you've made it financially). Operations such as Holiday Inns' Las Vegas Riverboat and Harrah's in Reno and Atlantic City that deal mainly with this class often appeal to tourists, who see gambling as part of a vacation that includes a trip to a resort and nightclub entertainment. There must be plenty of such people. In 1987, hotel occupancy in Las Vegas was 83.3 percent, and owners of eight casino-hotels were planning to increase or even double the number of rooms available. The largest, the 2,090-room Imperial Palace, planned to add 547 rooms, and four new facilities, Golden Nugget on the Strip, Circus Circus, Carnivaal, and Southstart, were scheduled to open with at least 3,000 rooms apiece.

The "low rollers"—gamblers with a small budget, who play for cash only and often favor slot machines—are catered to by facilities like Las Vegas' Showboat and Circus Circus, which operates in several Nevada cities.

## WHAT A DIFFERENCE A GAME MAKES

The whole purpose of casino design is to create a world away from the world, where nothing matters—or even exists—except entertainment. That's why there are no clocks and no windows in casinos: time doesn't exist there.

The actual decoration and setup depend on the games being played and the type of gambler the casino wants to attract. The mood could be quiet European elegance for hushed, high-stakes baccarat games, or a rowdy, down-home cowboy ambience for slot machines or keno. One Las Vegas casino features a flying circus overhead, although one would think that it would distract the punters' attention from the important business at hand.

In the early 1980s, it cost a Nevada casino about $5,000 to buy a slot machine—and the machine generally "won" more than $20,000 a year, before expenses. Blackjack typically brought in more than $250,000 in revenues; a craps table, about $750,000. Atlantic City tables, once casino gambling was legalized in 1978, brought in even more. And a good thing, too: New Jersey state taxes on gambling operations are much higher. Nevada's tax rate is 5.75 percent of gross winnings; in New Jersey, it's 8 percent of gross winnings and a surcharge of 1.25 percent of gross revenues to be applied to urban development. (In a little more than a decade of legal operations—1976–1987—Atlantic City gained 65,000 new jobs as a result of legal gambling; $3.2 billion was invested in the area; and $2.5 billion in state and local taxes were paid. However, as opponents of legalized gambling in Detroit point out, the development was very limited in scope and area; the city as a whole hasn't benefited much.)

The two gambling areas have a somewhat different image. In 1983, about twice as many people visited Atlantic City as went to Las Vegas (26.4 million as compared to 12.3 million). On the other hand, the average visitor stayed 1.3 days in Atlantic City but more than 4 days in Las Vegas. And Las Vegas had over 50,000 first-class hotel rooms in 1983; Atlantic City had only one-tenth as many.

The differences between the two sets of figures can probably be explained by the fact that Atlantic City is close to many cities on the eastern seaboard, and trips there can be combined with vacation trips to New York City or simply with the old-fashioned pleasures of beach and boardwalk. Hardly anyone is ever in the neighborhood of Las Vegas, so getting there from most places takes long enough to justify a longer vacation stay.

## PITS AND SLOTS

Without slot machines, most casinos would be far less profitable than they are. Slots (invented in 1887 by Charles Key), on an average, bring in more than 40 percent of revenues and close to half of profits. In Nevada in 1983, for instance, slot machines brought in 41.4 percent of total gaming revenue for the largest casinos (those with over $20 million in gross gaming revenue) and 57.2 percent of gaming revenue for smaller casinos.

You can find a one-armed bandit to take anywhere from a nickel to a buck at a time; quarter slots were the most common and brought in the largest revenue. There are still poker tables here and there, and legendary poker players still fight titanic battles in Las Vegas, but American casino gambling is dominated by slot machines, blackjack, and craps. Table games—card and dice games—earned about half the large casinos' revenue and about a third of the smaller joints' revenue.

James Bond played chemin de fer; twenty-one (blackjack), which is pretty much the American equivalent, is far and away the most popular card game in U.S. casinos. In thirty-five of the larger casinos, you could find 1,639 tables, and 388 tables in twenty smaller casinos. Blackjack is pretty popular with casino owners, too: about one out of every four dollars (in large casinos) or every five dollars (in small ones) of revenue comes from blackjack.

Another kind of Seven-Eleven—crap tables—is a real convenience for casino owners. The large casinos had 228 tables altogether, which brought in about one out of every seven dollars in casino revenue. The small casinos had only forty tables altogether but still earned about one out of every eleven dollars of revenue from craps. So blackjack is more popular with gamblers, but crap tables are more profitable for the owners.

In Nevada, in 1983, the "pit" (the area for card games and craps) was by far the most profitable. The larger casinos brought in about $2,815 gaming revenue per square foot devoted to this purpose. Smaller casinos brought in only about half as much per square foot ($1,526). The largest area was devoted to slot machines, with revenue per square foot of $1,109

## CONSUMER TIP

(If you care about being an enlightened consumer while you're gambling): New Jersey law requires slot machines to pay out at least 83 percent of the drop; Nevada doesn't regulate this.

in the larger casinos, $1,325 in the smaller ones. (This is probably true because smaller casinos often attract low rollers, who often prefer slot machines.) Remember, though, that slot machines don't require dealers or dealer salaries, nor do they present the risks of possible dealer embezzlements or participation in cheating, so they give the casino an extra profit edge.

Keno and poker attracted far less floor space, probably because they brought in much less—a puny $600 to $800—per square foot. This seems pretty disappointing in the gambling context, but remember that most store owners would be in paradise if they could bring in $300 a square foot, much less $600, with no inventory.

Casino stocks are also attractive to many investors. They figure that casinos do well in both good economies (people celebrate their stock-market winnings by trying for other kinds of winnings) and bad (people look for an economical vacation that offers the chance to win next year's mortgage payments, preferably not at the cost of this year's). Besides, casino-hotels can always be operated as ordinary hotels if the casino business falters; and if everything else fails, they sprawl over some valuable real estate that can be turned into residential property, offices, or shopping malls.

Is it risky to run a casino? Not in the long run. Gambling—and, for that matter, insurance—depends on the mathematical "law of large numbers." You can't predict the next turn of the cards or the next throw of the dice, but you can forecast accurately how many of each possible combination will turn up in the course of a year. The payoffs are adjusted based on the odds, with a comfortable margin for the house. There are two zeroes on the roulette wheel, and no one is allowed to bet on them (European roulette wheels have only one zero); the house wins whenever a 0 or 00 turns up. Then there are games like poker, where the players win each others' money, not the house's, and the house gets a sort of rental fee for providing the table and the dealer.

Theoretically, it's possible that the gods will smile on the bettors, and for a while a gambler or two will have a fantastic winning streak. The casinos are well enough capitalized to cope with these temporary aberrations. They don't even mind them—after all, what could be a better advertisement to bring in plenty more gamblers who hope to share in this stroke of fortune?

# 77

# Amusement Parks

Number of amusement parks: 466
Total receipts: $1,823,728,000 (Department of Commerce, '82). In 1987, *Business Week* referred to the $4 billion in annual revenues for amusement parks in the United States.

Of the sixty-six establishments surveyed, gross profit was 60.8% of net sales; but in lieu of a net profit after tax, there was a net loss of 0.3%. Return on sales ranged from a 1.2% loss to 7.3%; return on assets, from too small to measure to 7.7%. (D & B '86)

Top earner: Michael D. Eisner, CEO of Walt Disney Company, earned $3,398,000 in 1986: $3,377,000 in salary and bonus, $21,000 in deferred compensation—which made him the second-best-paid CEO in the leisure/ recreation industry; only twenty-two other CEOs, in any sector of the economy, did any better. But then, in 1986 Disney had 31,000 employees, sales of $2.47 billion, and profits of $247.3 million, so Mr. Eisner wasn't exactly captaining a sinking ship. (*Forbes* '86)

An amusement park or theme park is designed to be a place where the whole family can spend a delightful day sampling the rides and other attractions, snacking, and buying souvenirs. To the delight of other local

**Where the Money Came From**

| | |
|---|---:|
| (1) Admissions and rides: | 50% |
| (2) Food and beverages: | 22% |
| (3) Merchandise (T-shirts, stuffed toys, etc.): | 20% |
| (4) Miscellaneous (parking, leases, etc.): | 8% |

(Vogel, '86)

**Where the Money Went**

| | |
|---|---:|
| (1) Labor costs: | 33% |
| (2) Food and beverage costs: | 17% |
| (3) Costs of merchandise for resale: | 10% |
| (4) Maintenance, insurance, telephones: | 15% |
| (5) Depreciation and amortization: | 5% |
| (6) Interest: | 5% |
| (7) Property taxes: | 5% |
| (8) Pretax net income: | 10% |

(Vogel, '86)

entrepreneurs and local taxing authorities, the family may drive long distances (buying gas and meals en route), stay a night or two at a motel, and shop at other businesses in the area.

The main attraction can be anything from a re-creation of the plantations in *Gone with the Wind* or Dolly Parton's humble girlhood home, to reconstructions of Biblical scenes or scenes from American history, to a safari park full of lions and giraffes. The park developer's challenge is to come up with attractions more exciting than the usual roller coaster—for example, a white-water rafting ride; or something like the $4 million Vortex, with its six upside-down turns, at Kings Island near Cincinnati; or a high-tech "interactive ride" that gives riders some control over their experiences.

In 1986, approximately 97.2 million admissions fees were paid to the top forty parks, including about 37 million visitors to Disneyland and Disney World alone. The visitors spent $1.5 billion in Disney hotels when they visited the parks. (There's already one Disney park outside the United States, in Tokyo, complete with a kimono-clad Minnie Mouse. Disney is spending $2 billion to open a "leisure park" near Paris, which is estimated to attract 10 million visitors once it's in operation.)

Four million people went to Sea World in Orlando, Florida, that year, while Dorney Park, in Pennsylvania, drew about 1.25 million visitors.

Admission to a major park is apt to cost $15 to $35 a day; discounts for multiple-day visits, for kids, and for senior citizens are common.

## FINANCIAL RESULTS

In 1983, the eight major corporations operating amusement parks had total revenues of $1.793 billion and pretax operating income of $324 million. That made their operating margin 18.1 percent—an impressive figure, although they had to deploy a lot of assets—nearly $3.2 billion—to get it. For each visitor, the major parks had revenue of $24.49 and operating income of $4.42; however, if you exclude the unusually successful Disney operations from the calculations, revenue drops to $18.80 per person and operating income to $3.13. (The parks contributed nearly three-quarters of Disney Company's 1986 operating income, even though Disney's revenues from movies and videos more than doubled between 1984 and 1986.)

The sixty-six amusement and theme parks in the 1986 Dun & Bradstreet survey had gross profits averaging 60.8 percent of net sales. However, the industry as a whole showed a net loss of 0.3 percent of sales, instead of a net profit after tax. The amusement park industry suffered from a small return on sales: the highest figure reported was 7.3 percent, and the least successful parks showed a 1.2 percent loss. Return on assets ranged from too small to measure to a modest 7.7 percent.

## CORPORATIONS CHIP IN

Amusement parks have a major source of income that most customers never think of: corporate sponsorship. Major corporations underwrite the building of parks or the development of new attractions. For instance, Disneyland's Club 33 is named after the thirty-three corporations that were its original investors. Tupperware Products paid for a new seal feeding pool at Sea World in Orlando (made out of plastic with a tight-closing "seal"?); Nestle's Raisinets and Crunch bars paid for the Splashwater Falls ride at the Six Flags Great Adventure Parks. The twenty Six Flags sponsors generally pay $50,000 to $150,000 for a multiyear sponsorship deal.

The corporate underwriters often provide products, such as uniforms or athletic shoes, for use in the park. In return, the park and the sponsors exchange use of their trademarked characters. Disney underwriters can use Disney characters in their ads, and General Mills has Count Chocula and Frankenberry providing crowd control at Opryland USA.

Apropos of crowd control: we trust that your manners are impeccable, wherever you go. But if you have occasion to visit the Great America amusement park in Santa Clara, California, you'd *better* behave yourself. The park belongs to the city of Santa Clara, and if you cut into a line, shove your fellow amusement seekers, or otherwise act up at the park, you face a $1,000 fine or six months in jail.

# 78

# Bowling Alleys

| | |
|---|---|
| Number of bowling alleys: | 6,483 (with a total of 131,786 lanes) |
| Number of paid lines bowled: | 1,253,614,000 |
| Total receipts: | $2,184,043,000 |
| | (Department of Commerce, '82) |

Bowling alleys have long served two purposes, providing a place both for people who like to bowl, and for teenagers to hang out, impress other teenagers with their prowess in the lanes, and generally act cool. For a while, in the late 1960s, these purposes fit into the social structure so well that Brunswick Corporation, manufacturer of bowling equipment, was one of the most successful stocks on Wall Street. Everyone wanted to bowl, hence everyone wanted to open a bowling alley, hence the price of Brunswick went up, up, up.

Social trends have created some tough times for bowling alleys. The stress on aerobic exercise has made tennis, squash, aerobic dancing, and other sports far more popular than bowling. Bowling alleys, like so many other businesses, are at the mercy of high real estate values. The land could be used for stores or for other, more popular and lucrative sports. The owner of an indoor tennis court in New York can collect $60 an hour

**Where the Money Comes From**

| | |
|---|---|
| (1) Bowling: | 63.13% |
| (2) Food and drinks (e.g., beer): | 29.98% |
| (3) Sale of other merchandise (such as team shirts): | 3.35% |
| (4) Other sources (e.g., shoe rentals): | 3.52% |

(Department of Commerce, '82)

for prime court time, while the owner of a bowling alley can get a magnificent $2.25 per game from bowling enthusiasts.

Thus, the 428 bowling alleys in Dun & Bradstreet's survey showed high gross profits—72.3 percent of net sales—but net profit after tax was only 3.6 percent. Most businesses show a lower gross profit, but 3.6 percent is a fairly average net profit figure. Bowling alleys have few expenses that count as "cost of goods sold" and thus lower gross profits, but they do have enough other expenses to keep profit levels moderate.

## REGULARS AND FADDISTS

One problem for alley owners is that the demand for bowling fluctuates. There *are* serious bowlers who are devoted to the sport whether it's fashionable or not. Bowling alleys depend heavily on business from leagues, which are organized groups of bowling teams that maintain a competition schedule and book regular hours for competition; in addition, league members often book extra time to practice. Leagues attract spectators, too, who are enthusiastically welcomed by bowling alley owners because they drink beer and sodas, scarf hot dogs, and buy team T-shirts and caps. But alleys that don't have a hard core of enthusiasts are at the mercy of fashion. If bowling drops out of vogue, teenagers start either hanging out someplace else or engaging in pastimes far from those of Andy Hardy. And today many potential adult bowlers can't spare an evening; by the time they get home from work, get dinner on the table, and say "hi" to the kids, it's time to attack the briefcase full of work brought home, watch the ten o'clock news, or just turn in for the next day's grind.

Manhattan is now down to four bowling alleys; there are a mere fifty-five in the rest of New York City and only seventy-four on Long Island.

Still, there are said to be 70 million bowlers throughout the nation; and the game is enjoying a minor renaissance in the late 1980s, with celebrities like Dustin Hoffman and Kathleen Turner indulging. After all, if miniskirts, *Honeymooners* reruns, and 1950s-style furniture are popular, why not bowling alleys? (And if complex electronic technology is everywhere else, why not in bowling alleys? A group of high-level technocrats of the personal computer industry attending a conference in early 1988 decided to relax by bowling a few lines, but they couldn't figure out the mysteries of the automatic scoring system. An employee of the bowling alley had to bail them out.)

# 79

# Vending Machines and Coin-Operated Video Games

| | |
|---|---|
| Number of establishments: | 5,646 |
| Total receipts: | $4.7 billion |
| Average net sales: | $600,000 |
| Number of employees: | 83,500 |
| Total payroll: | $934 million |

(Department of Commerce, '82)

## Vending Machines

Vending machines are usually little businesses within a business. An office, bar, factory, or store is the "host" business. A vending machine company, which installs and services the machine, either pays rent for the space the machine takes up or divides the "take" with the owner of the host business.

Vending machine companies must constantly assess the productivity of their machines' locations. Although some costs are fairly stable no matter where the machine is located (such as the merchandise in the machine), other factors fluctuate depending on location. Some locations sell much more merchandise than others; vandalism and other causes for repair vary. Some host businesses drive harder bargains than others. All these factors determine how fast the machine owner can recover his capital.

Let's take a look at some figures developed at the National Automatic Merchandising Association's February 1987 financial management workshop. Let's say that buying a machine requires an investment of $11,400. In an average month, the vending machine sells products whose wholesale cost is $2,381.84, bringing in $4,483.55. (That is, the cost of goods sold is 53.1 percent of sales.) The gross profit is 46.9 percent; direct labor in stocking the machine is 7.7 percent of sales, or $348.69. (The 1982 Department of Commerce survey found even higher payroll costs—19.8 percent of sales; but that figure includes office personnel as well as those who actually drive around replacing the packages of gum and cans of soda that have been sold.)

It costs 5.8 percent ($262.70) to maintain the machine; commissions paid to host businesses are another 5.2 percent ($236.81). Depreciation is another 2.7 percent ($124.35). All the overhead on the vending machine is 23.2 percent, leaving a pretax profit of $88.06 for the operator and a 1.9 percent return on sales. According to the seminar instructor, this was a pretty decent return on sales, although steps could be taken to increase profitability.

The vending machine business is about as labor-intensive as they come. One can't simply install a machine and forget about it: an employee has to appear at each site regularly to make sure the machine is working, to make sure that each slot is filled, to see if the balance of items is right (if everybody wants chocolate-almond bars, it makes sense to have two facings of those and to eliminate the salted peanuts that nobody wants), and, last but not least, to collect the money.

# Video Games

Not all coin-operated devices sell sodas, ice cream bars, or rental video-cassettes. Many of them don't sell anything tangible at all but provide entertainment—in the form of jukeboxes, pinball machines, and video games. Although video games have declined greatly in popularity since their peak in 1983, video arcades are still doing business. In 1984, the average weekly gross for a pinball machine was $41; for a video game, the corresponding figure was $53. Surprisingly, a nonvideo arcade game did a little better, averaging $59 a week; but laser-disc video games wiped them all off the map, at an average of $120 a week.

What some video game fanciers are after is the often somewhat sordid atmosphere of the arcade. (What could a teenage boy enjoy more than a cavern filled with other teenage boys, the opportunity to make the said other teenage boys look bad, and lots of things that eat money, flash lights, and make noise?) But for those who prefer the comforts of home, Japan's Nintendo Company makes a "fami-com," or family computer, that brings sophisticated arcade-type games to the home television set. And if that doesn't grab you, Nintendo will sell you a game cartridge that lets you design knitting patterns on your fami-com.

# Health,
# and the Alternatives

# Health Care Delivery: Doctors, Hospitals, HMOs

|                          | *Doctors' Offices*                                                                                          | *Dentists' Offices*                                                                                      |
| ------------------------ | --------------------------------------------------------------------------------------------------------- | ------------------------------------------------------------------------------------------------------- |
| Number of establishments: | 234,832 (116,133 individual practices; 8,632 partnerships; rest professional corporations)                | 114,352 (73,759 individual practices; 3,245 partnerships; rest professional corporations)               |
| Total receipts:          | $53.2 billion                                                                                              | $16.8 billion                                                                                           |
| Average net sales:       | $226,700                                                                                                   | $141,500                                                                                                |
| Number of employees:     | NG                                                                                                        | 402,900 (43,197 salaried associate dentists; 168,098 dental assistants; 64,289 dental hygienists; 9,687 dental technicians; 117,218 dental workers) |
| Total payroll:           | NG                                                                                                        | $5.8 billion                                                                                            |

(Department of Commerce, '82)

Where the Money Goes

| | Doctors' Offices | Dentists' Offices | Hospitals | Nursing Homes |
|---|---|---|---|---|
| (1) Cost of operation: | 8.5% | 15.7% | 17.4% | 22.4% |
| (2) Officers' compensation: | 40.2% | 29.1% | 0.7% | 2.8% |
| (3) Pensions and benefits: | 10.4%* | 6.8% | 3.5% | 2.0% |
| (4) Rent: | 4.0% | 4.8% | 1.9% | 5.3% |
| (5) Repairs: | 0.4% | 0.5% | 1.1% | 1.0% |
| (6) Depreciation, depletion, amortization: | 2.3% | 2.9% | 8.0% | 3.6% |
| (7) Interest: | 0.5% | 0.7% | 6.6% | 4.0% |
| (8) Bad debts: | 0.1% | — | 1.3% | 0.3% |
| (9) Advertising: | 0.1% | 0.6% | 0.2% | 0.3% |
| (10) State, local taxes: | 2.6% | 3.4% | 4.0% | 5.8% |
| (11) Other expenses: | 30.1% | 33.2% | 56.9% | 50.1% |
| (12) Net profit before tax: | 0.8%** | 2.3% | not disclosed | 2.4% |

*Doctors make heavy use of retirement plans as a tax-saving and financial planning device.
**But remember, the "owner" of the business–the doctor–has already gotten paid.

(Troy, '83–'84)

Hospitals were developed in the Middle Ages, as places where the exceptionally poor and miserable went to die. There have been doctors for almost as long as there have been people, although for millennia about all they had to offer their patients were the consolations of religion, leeches and other methods of drawing blood, and a few herbs and charms. In those days, medicine was not a high-paying profession, since people usually expected to get their religious comfort for free and compassion for low fees.

In traditional Chinese medicine, the patient pays a doctor a fee as long as he stays healthy; illness is evidence that the doctor is falling down on the job. (As we'll see, this concept has had some influence on the development of the Health Maintenance Organization, or HMO.) In the early nineteenth century, Western doctors earned a living by selling pills, powders, and nostrums to patients; no one would pay for anything as abstract as advice. (See page 363—some doctors are going back to selling prescription drugs.)

In today's America, health care is one of the very biggest businesses. In 1986, it absorbed almost 11 percent of the Gross National Product; that's $458 billion, or $1,837 per person, and in 1988 health care costs were still rising at more than twice the rate of inflation. Hospitals got $180 billion, or 39 percent, of the total, with $92 billion going to doctors, and $38 billion to nursing homes.

Part of the problem is that modern medicine has quite a lot to offer: many diseases can be cured, and many sick people can be restored to a useful and enjoyable life. So people want to take advantage of these benefits whenever possible. Then again, as the population ages and its life expectancy increases, people need more health care and more drugs.

Another part of the problem is that few people pay their own medical bills. The government picks up much of the tab: $75 billion a year for Medicare (with 31 million beneficiaries who are elderly or disabled or both). Health insurance picks up most of the rest; and, for most people, the boss pays most or all of the health insurance premium. That means that people have only a vague idea of how much health insurance costs and wince every time they have to pay a deductible or pay for a procedure their insurance doesn't cover, but they aren't exposed to the full cost themselves. (If they were, they'd probably storm the hospitals and doctors' offices with torches, like the peasants stormed the doctor's lab in *Frankenstein.*)

Employers, only too conscious of how much health insurance costs, are making desperate efforts to cut costs by carrot-and-stick methods. The "carrot" is encouragement for employees to stay healthy, by means of free or subsidized exercise classes and assistance in giving up smoking and drinking. The "stick" is a requirement that they pay more of the premiums and a higher percentage of each medical bill.

## THE DOCTOR'S DILEMMAS

In most of the world, doctors are low-paid, salaried drudges. In the United States, most doctors are entrepreneurs in a high-capital, high-prestige, but high-risk business. (However, an increasing number of recent med-school graduates are opting for salaried posts, with regular hours, to escape the crushing burden of debt and to be able to have a better family life.)

The average young doctor has borrowed up to the earlobes to pay for his or her medical education. Once his training is finished, the doctor who chooses to set up a private practice has to borrow lots more money, open an office (with monthly rent and utility bills and office staff payroll), and fill it with furniture and equipment. Then it's time to wait for the patients to trickle in. A few months with nothing to do but chat with drug company salesmen is an unnerving time for the fledgling medico.

That's one reason why so many doctors form group practices or affiliate with HMOs: they tap into an existing network of patients looking for doctors. And besides, doctors who are part of a group can share office expenses and consult with colleagues in other specialties; nor does a single doctor have to deal with all the weekend, evening, and holiday emergency needs of the patients. Between 1980 and 1985, the number of new solo medical practices went up 18 percent, and the number of new group practices went up 43 percent.

A group practice in upstate New York that was profiled by the *New York Times Magazine* ("Why Your Family Doctor Is a Group," June 7, 1987) had a patient list of 27,000, income of $4 million in 1986, and expenses of $2.5 million (including $375,000 a year in malpractice insurance premiums). The fourteen doctors in the practice earned both salaries and profit shares, with total compensation for individual doctors ranging from $60,000 to $160,000. Doctors who join the group "buy in" with $1,000 worth of shares in the professional corporation and earn a higher percentage of the corporation's equity based on the fees they bring in.

Life for the successful doctor (whether a solo or group practitioner) can be emotionally and financially rewarding: the average compensation for U.S. physicians is $100,000 a year, and many make much, much more. However, a doctor's life is far from easy and far from stress-free. The obligations of a successful doctor don't end with office hours: there can be emergency calls or visits to hospitalized patients. Many doctors also teach or do volunteer work. And, of course, there are the reams and reams of paperwork: medical files that prove the doctor was not negligent and the never-ending piles of forms for insurance, Medicare, and Medicaid reimbursements. (Doctors have to do some of the paperwork themselves and must make sure the office staff or service bureau does the rest of it properly.)

Dun & Bradstreet's 1986 survey included 1,409 doctors' offices and 301 dentists' offices. The doctors surveyed earned higher gross profits (73.6 percent of receipts as compared to 58.8 percent of receipts for dentists), but the dentists got to keep more. Dentists' net profits after tax averaged 10.3 percent, while doctors' net profits were only 8.3 percent (which is still higher than that earned by most businesses).

The ancient relationship of trust between doctor and patient has completely broken down. Patients (legitimately) expect that doctors will be careful and thorough; they also (ridiculously) expect that doctors will not only be infallible but will perform a miracle in every case, no matter how hopeless.

Malpractice suits not only penalize (some of the) negligent doctors but also subject a number of highly competent doctors to huge legal fees and endless trouble, and (sometimes) make them liable for large damage awards by juries. The threat of malpractice suits hangs heavy over all doctors. They have to spend on insurance premiums more than most people ever earn; they order an endless procession of tests and consultations with other doctors to demonstrate that they left no possibility unexplored. They then have to interpret the test results and examine other doctors' patients referred to *them* for second opinions. All of this costs money, so fees go up, insurance premiums go up, and patients get increasingly more hostile and determined to limp to the courthouse unless a miracle is forthcoming.

## HMOS

The Health Maintenance Organization (HMO) is an attempt to break the cycle of high-cost health care and high-cost insurance. The 25.8 million members of the approximately 625 U.S. HMOs don't pay fees for the particular services their doctors render: instead, they (or, more commonly, their employers) pay a yearly fee that covers comprehensive medical care and hospitalization. Some HMOs also provide eye exams, dental care, physical therapy, prescription drugs, or a combination. Others have their own offices, with doctors who are salaried employees (about 5 percent of U.S. physicians) or who contract with the HMO; other HMOs set up networks of doctors in the community who treat HMO patients at their own offices. More than two-thirds of America's 450,000 doctors have contracts of some kind with HMOs.

That doesn't mean the doctors are ecstatically happy with the arrangement. As HMOs try to earn profits in a tougher economic environment, they also crack down on their participating doctors, who then retaliate with increased negotiating demands, lawsuits, and even the possibility of forming a union.

The advantage of HMOs to the patient (and whoever is paying the health insurance bills) is the assurance of medical treatment for a single yearly fee. However, disgruntled employers often find that the costs of providing HMO coverage for employees are no lower than the costs of traditional "indemnity" medical insurance—unless there are so many competing HMOs that they have to cut prices to keep employers happy (and make sure that they renew their contracts with the HMO). The disadvantage of the HMO to the patient is that the patient may be assigned a doctor instead of having the right to choose one.

Doctors like HMO practice because of the steady supply of patients and the regular hours it offers but dislike having HMO managers tell them how many patients to see, what tests they can and can't order, and what procedures to follow.

The HMOs themselves are facing heavy competition and heavy marketing costs to attract business: it takes at least 25,000 members to run a profitable HMO. When U.S. Health Care entered the New York market in 1986, it spent about $10 million on advertisements and managed to round up over 100,000 enrollees in the New York metropolitan area. (HealthNet, the Blue Cross HMO, has 102,000 New York members.)

Fifteen HMOs are public companies, but their stocks, like other health care stocks, have not been a Wall Street favorite. So HMOs are beginning to merge and become the subjects of acquisitions.

Maxicare Health Plans, Inc., is the largest HMO operated for profit. It has over 2.3 million members, many of whom got aboard as a result of Maxicare's acquisition of two other major HMOs, HealthAmerica Corporation and Healthcare USA, Inc. It made *Business Week*'s Top 1000 list, at position #894, with 1986 receipts of $881 million and profits of $4.3 million. However, it was not a high-return enterprise, realizing only a 1.7 percent return each on invested capital and common equity. By 1987, trouble with the acquired HMOs was leading to red ink—three consecutive quarters of losses.

U.S. Health Care, Inc., another HMO rival, has 685,000 members and was #935 on the *Business Week* list. It had 1987 sales of $627 million and took home profits of $1 million, leading to return on common equity of only 0.7 percent. Its profit margins, while an incredible 35.5 percent for the fourth quarter of 1986, dropped to a mere 0.2 percent for 1987.


## HOSPITALS

The evil capitalist in Richard Condon's novel *Winter Kills* called them "hotels for pain," and he went around buying up as many as he could, figuring that his money would be well invested. Hospitals in the United States certainly take in a lot of money every year, and they sure charge the patients for every aspirin, bandage, and alcohol rub (in addition to enormous daily charges—sort of like the phone company charging you for the calls you make and assessing fees for equipment rental, monthly use, and the telephone wire), but the profit picture isn't quite so unclouded. In fact, the financial health of U.S. hospitals today is on the downslide, with a record seventy-nine hospitals closing in 1987 (up from forty-nine closing in 1985 and seventy-one in 1986). Of those that closed, half were in inner cities and half in rural areas, where hospitals are most needed. (About 12 percent of U.S. hospitals are owned by investors and operated for profit; the rest are operated by not-for-profit organizations or government entities.)

One of the biggest causes for hospitals' financial troubles is less-than-adequate payments under government Medicare and Medicaid programs. For years, hospitals' major "customers"—health insurers and the United States government—paid through the nose when every new rate rise was announced. Now they're demanding a role in setting prices. Insurers are demanding second opinions before they'll pay for surgery or hospitalization. Federal Medicare payments for patients over sixty-five are based on a DRG (Diagnosis Related Group) system: the hospital gets paid a flat fee based on the patient's diagnosis, not a per diem rate. The hospitals do get a chance to claim that a particular patient is unusually difficult to treat and therefore the hospital should be paid more; but in general DRG makes it hard for hospitals to make money treating really sick people, who hang around the hospital for a long time. Of course, people who aren't really sick are unlikely to stay in the hospital a minute longer than they have to: it's a lot cheaper to check into the Waldorf Astoria and get caviar from room service at hourly intervals.

Other cost pressures on hospitals include those damned malpractice insurance premiums. Injured people (or their estates) naturally sue the hospital as well as the doctors when something goes wrong. Juries may feel sympathetic to kindly Dr. Kildare and understand how his scalpel slipped just a little, but they don't mind sticking it to the cold, impersonal hospital. Hospitals are also finding it so hard to recruit nurses that they're doing what was previously unimaginable: raising nurses' salaries.

If all that wasn't bad enough, hospitals are now in the peculiar position of soliciting actively for patients. In a sense, building a hospital is a lot like putting up an office building. When investment funds are available and there are tax incentives, the towers go up. Frequently, once construction is over, people look around and discover that, to meet a need for 10,000 offices (or 10,000 hospital beds), seven companies have each built structures with 10,000 offices or hospitals with 10,000 beds. Furthermore, if there's a new piece of equipment for diagnosis or treatment, every hospital in town wants one; no one wants to be left behind. That means that an area can end up with more hospital beds than it needs, or more CAT scanners, nuclear magnetic resonators, or other diagnostic or treatment devices.

Hospitals used to have a really compelling motive to invest: their Medicare reimbursement rates used to be based, in part, on the amount spent for capital items such as construction and equipment. But Congressional cost cutters are likely to limit Medicare reimbursement to hospitals for capital costs.

Nature, or medical science, has struck an even crueller blow: not only are more people remaining healthy (in part because of preventive behaviors such as exercise and eating sensibly), but a number of ailments that once were treated with operations, or with lengthy hospital stays, can now be treated with medication or in the doctor's office. From the mid-1970s to the mid-1980s, hospital occupancy rates (beds filled each day) were close to 75 percent; now only about 60 percent of hospital beds are occupied each day.

Taking this in connection with the building explosion, you'll understand why many hospitals are so desperate for patients that they're mounting massive consumer advertising campaigns (91 percent of hospitals advertise, a process now accounting for about half of the billion-dollar-a-year industry of marketing hospitals) to prove that their hospital is the place to be—they're in with the ill crowd. St. Elizabeth's Medical Center in Dayton, Ohio, throws "Tupperware parties": a group of friendly doctors and nurses travel to a potential patient's home and chat with potential patients and their friends to boost the hospital's image. Thirteen other hospitals have bought a package showing them how to throw parties of their own.

New York's Mount Sinai Hospital is improving its service to private patients by offering the services of a concierge, newspaper delivery in their rooms (and the chance to have business meetings catered in the room—if they have the savoir faire to do business clad in pajamas or, worse, a hospital gown), food ordered from a restaurant-like menu, and even an optional VCR and movie rentals. A few spoilsports have suggested that the hospital could spend the marketing money more profitably by raising the salaries of the staff who actually care for the patients, but nobody much listened.

Of course, you can't just check yourself into a hospital whenever you feel the need, but you can nag or pressure your doctor into getting you admitted into Hospital A rather than Hospital B if you do need inpatient treatment.

In the late 1970s, a number of chains of private hospitals were created, and Wall Street had great hopes for their stock. However, health care stocks have been consistently disappointing in the market. There's a story going around that one doctor suddenly found six new patients on his hospital rounds, only to discover that they were "ringers": employees who were ordered to lie down and look sick on the day that potential investors toured the hospital. Hospital chains have learned that bigger isn't always better: in fact, some of the larger chains (such as Humana, Inc., Hospital Corporation of America, and National Healthcare) spent the mid-1980s spinning off groups of hospitals, selling the least profitable ones to concentrate on managing the others. Private psychiatric hospitals, especially those treating addictions and eating disorders, are a "growth industry," so they're likely to be retained, while smaller general hospitals (with less potential for profit) are spun off.

The consumer movement has affected health care as well as other areas. Patients are demanding support groups run by and for those with similar health problems; a combination of conventional "allopathic" medicine with alternative therapies such as chiropractic and nutrition therapy; and birthing rooms that are less technology-dominated than conventional labor rooms. Motivated by some mixture of compassion, belief in the new synthesis, and desire to protect revenues, hospitals are beginning to respond to consumer demands in the hopes that they can be translated into increased hospital use and higher revenues.

## FIGURES FOR GENERAL HOSPITALS

On page 358 are figures for three of the country's largest general hospital groups—National Medical Enterprises, Inc., whose hospitals include psychiatric hospitals; Hospital Corporation of America, the largest for-profit supplier of health care; and Humana, Inc., which pioneered many of the management techniques now used in hospital chains, which means that it suffered most of the financial problems besetting hospitals (note its pathetic profits for 1986). Humana owns, in addition to eighty-seven hospitals, an insurance plan (Humana Care Plus) and a network of doctors' offices (MedFirst)—both major losers in fiscal 1986, perhaps because Humana royally infuriated many of the doctors it did business with, and Care Plus ended up paying for more patients in non-Humana than in Humana hospitals. (In spite of poor profits, however, Humana still had enough clout to force the "St. Elsewhere" television show to stop using the name "Ecumena" for a fictional group of soulless, money-grubbing hospital acquirers and to run a disclaimer on each show saying that there was no connection between the nasties portrayed on the program and the nice, caring folks at Humana.)

## THE FUTURE?

It seems unlikely that the "supermeds"—vast conglomerates of hospitals, HMOs, health insurers, and doctors' offices—will ever come to pass. Humana and others have tried it and gained nothing but red-ink stains on their surgical greens. Declining patient loads and decreasing government funding mean that hospitals will have a tough time making a buck in the 1990s.

The Medicare program is being expanded to tackle senior citizens' catastrophic illnesses. That's good news, because it means that payment for these costs is more certain when it comes from Uncle Sam than when it comes from individuals. It's also bad news, because the Medicare program puts a high priority on cutting costs; a spokesperson for the American Hospital Association says that 40 percent of hospitals lose money on Medicare patients.

It also seems clear that group practices and HMOs are here to stay: if the kindly family doctor, who always had a sympathetic ear and plenty of time to chat about life's problems, ever existed outside the MGM lot, he's gone now. And hospitals are seeking "vertical integration"—relationships with medical practices that provide reciprocal referrals between doctor and hospital—or even opening "medical malls" of outpatient clin-

| | Hospital Corporation of America* | Humana | National Medical Enterprises |
|---|---|---|---|
| Number of hospitals | 400 + worldwide | 87 | 400+ |
| (and beds) | | | 50,000 |
| Number of employees | | | 75,000 |
| Net operating revenues | $4.178 billion | $3 billion | $3.304 billion |
| Contract allowances and doubtful accounts | $679 million + | $686.75 billion | — |
| Operating and administrative expenses | $2.663 billion | $1.5 billion + | $2.568 billion |
| Depreciation and amortization | $192 million | $147 million + | $111 million |
| Interest paid | $188,000 | $119 million | $114 million |
| Operating income | $455 million | $376.1 million | $241 million |
| Investment earnings | | | $2.6 million |
| Total pretax income | $505.3 million | $376.1 million | $267 million |
| Income taxes | $200 million | $160 million | $118,000 |
| Net income | $296.759 million | $216.22 million | $149 million |
| 1986 sales | $4.93 billion | $2.67 billion | $3.19 billion |
| 1986 profits | $174.6 million | $38.6 million | $109.1 million |
| 1986 return on capital investment | 6.5% | | 7.5% |
| Return on equity | 8.7% | | 11.1% |
| CEO salary (1985) | $300,000 and $353,000 deferred | $539,000 and $87,000 deferred | $972,000 |

*Largest for-profit supplier of health care.

ics that provide both immediate profits and referrals of patients who need hospital treatment.

Employers—and employees who have to pony up more each month in premiums and more each visit in deductibles and co-insurance—will continue to search for ways to cut health care costs. One positive factor in their quest is the fact that lots of fledgling doctors graduate every year, perhaps enough to create both a glut and meaningful price competition.

Meanwhile, there's always chicken soup.

# 83

# Drugstores

| | |
|---|---|
| Number of establishments: | 46,661 |
| Total receipts: | $34.9 billion |
| Average net sales: | $748,800 |
| Number of employees: | 477,900 |
| Total payroll: | $4.461 million |

(Department of Commerce, '82)

"Drugstore cowboys," who never got close to a horse, used to hang out in them. Lana Turner got discovered in one (well, maybe). Beyond providing nostalgia, drugstores combine two very profitable forms of business. They sell prescription drugs (1.5 billion prescriptions filled in 1986), a high-profit enterprise that does require professional staff (pharmacists are licensed by the state and must have postgraduate education in pharmacy) and long hours, but that is not very labor-intensive for the pharmacists. They also sell a multitude of other items—aspirin, mouthwash, shaving cream, panty hose—that require no professional expertise, just stockroom employees and clerks earning low wages.

The pharmacist's task is to decant the pills from a small bottle to

Top Chains, 1986

|  | # of stores | Sales ($M) | Net Income ($T) | Net Income as % of Sales |
|---|---|---|---|---|
| Walgreen Company | 1,183 | 3,390 | 94,169 | 2.69 |
| Rite Aid Corporation | 1,392 | 1,560 | 62,547 | 4.00 |
| Longs Drug Stores Corporation | 210 | 1,480 | 37,718 | 2.55 |
| Perry Drug Stores, Inc. | 194 | 563 | 9,575 | 1.84 |
| Fay's Drug Company, Inc. | 146 | 445 | 2,787 | 0.63 |

(Fairchild, '86)

Top Earners, 1986

|  | Salary, Bonus | Deferred Compensation |
|---|---|---|
| C.R. Walgreen III (Walgreen Company) | $604,000 | $242,000 |
| Alex Gross (Rite Aid Corporation) | $545,000 | — |
| Robert M. Long (Longs Drug Stores Corporation; also had stock gains of $122,000) | $286,000 | $9,000 |

(*Forbes, Business Week,* '86)

a large one and type the label, or, increasingly, get the label printed by a computer, which can alert the pharmacist and the patient to the possibility of dangerous interactions with other drugs already being taken. As the percentage of senior citizens in the population increases, so does the need for prescription drugs, since the average senior citizen takes fourteen prescription drugs. Almost every medical breakthrough creates a need for expensive new drugs, so the outlook for pharmacies is pretty good.

Drugstores also sell cosmetics, over-the-counter (OTC) medications such as nonprescription cold remedies (a $9.2 billion market in 1986, but only 40 percent of which was spent in pharmacies), and sundries such as light bulbs, hair ribbons, and other small items. They also sell nonprescription contraceptives: about 80 percent of sales come from condoms, rather than foams, gels, or sponges. Condom sales are highly beneficial to drugstores: manufacturers provide them with "family planning center" displays that take up only a few feet, and profit margins can be 60 percent or more. The only problem is keeping the condoms someplace where they're tough to shoplift, but that may require placing them where a

Where the Money Comes From

| | |
|---|---|
| (1) Prescriptions: | 27.2% |
| (2) Over-the-counter drugs/proprietary medications: | 14.5% |
| (3) Toiletries: | 10.8% |
| (4) Cosmetics: | 5.3% |
| (5) Stationery: | 4.8% |
| (6) Tobacco: | 7.5% |
| (7) Candy: | 3.5% |
| (8) Housewares: | 6.7% |
| (9) Toys: | 2.5% |
| (10) Photographic supplies and prints: | 4.4% |
| (11) General merchandise: | 4.2% |
| (12) Do-it-yourself supplies: | 1.5% |
| (13) Grocery items and liquor: | 4.5% (probably a hangover from Prohibition days, when whiskey was sold by prescription) |
| (14) Miscellaneous: | 2.6% |

*(Drug Store News, '85)*

customer must ask an employee for them, which would prevent sales to the easily embarrassed.

## IT'S NOT ALL ROSES

However, drugstores do have problems, especially in the heavy competition they face from the supermarkets, discount stores, and specialty stores that provide customers a large selection of cosmetics and sundries at lower prices. There are discount drugstores that merchandise on price, and about 300 U.S. drugstores are "deep discount" operations, using every possible shopping technique to get lower wholesale prices so they can offer lower prices to buyers.

For instance, the deep-discount drugstore will wait until a cosmetic company offers a special promotional deal, then buy enough merchandise to last until the next special promotion. They'll buy the merchandise *after* Christmas that everyone else overstocked before Christmas. If need be, they'll make a deal with a hotel that buys prestigious brands of merchandise for use in its amenities program (see page 279), then resell the "giveaway" merchandise, or they might even buy expensive perfumes at duty-free shops outside the United States.

## RX COMPETITION

There's a threat of competition at the other end of the business, too, if physicians are given the unrestricted right to sell prescription medications to their patients for a profit. It's estimated that a doctor can earn an extra $15,000 to $40,000 a year by selling prescription drugs. More than two hundred firms sell doctors packaged assortments of drugs for resale, and some state laws let hospitals get in on the act by opening pharmacies to the public, a move that infuriates drugstore owners, who point out that hospitals can buy drugs at lower wholesale prices.

Pharmacists are also aiming at turf traditionally occupied by doctors. The state of Washington allows "therapeutic substitution" by pharmacists; that is, pharmacists are allowed to substitute a different, usually less costly, drug for the drug prescribed by the doctor. Washington State requires the doctor's consent before this can be done; but other states are considering allowing the practice even without consent. (This is different from switching to a generic drug, which is the same drug manufactured by a different company.) Institutions such as hospitals already use therapeutic substitution to cut costs; the question is whether retail drugstores should be allowed to do it.

There's a growing trend toward mail order pharmacies, which sell drugs to customers over a wide geographic range; have a central facility instead of many retail stores; and pass along some of the cost savings to the users of the prescription drugs. This is OK with patients—as long as they can get their prescriptions on time (and more than OK if they're homebound and so find it easier to order by mail than to go to the pharmacy)—and loudly applauded by health insurers, who want to cut costs. As you can imagine, pharmacies don't like it much. They point out that a personal relationship with a local pharmacist is an excellent source of information about prescription and nonprescription drugs, their dangers, and how to use them safely and effectively.

## CHAIN STORES

In 1987, according to A. C. Nielsen Co., total drugstore sales for the United States were $53 billion. The 20,977 chain drugstores captured 61 percent of the market, with average sales per chain unit of over $1.5 million.

Here's a look at how the leading chains performed:

Top Drugstore Chains, 1987

|  | Walgreen Company | Rite Aid Corporation | Longs Drug Stores Corporation |
|---|---|---|---|
| Sales | $4.436 billion | $2.273 billion | $1.772 billion |
| Profits | $109.1 million | $86.7 million | $49.2 million |
| Assets | $1.525 billion | $1.246 billion | $475 million |
| Profit margin | 2.5% | 3.8% | 2.8% |
| Return on investment | 15% | 15.1% | 16.6% |
| Return on common equity | 17.3% | 16.1% | 16.6% |

(*Business Week,* April '88)

## SPOTLIGHT

Let's take a look at a couple of successful independent stores and the way they do business. Reses Pharmacy of Pleasantville, New Jersey, was the subject of a 1987 *New York Times* piece ("Pills—and Peas—at the Pharmacy," May 31, 1987). The store, which has been in the Reses family for generations, has fifty-seven employees (seven of them pharmacists), grosses $4 million a year, and has an above-average profit margin of 3.5 percent. The boss, Arthur Reses, earns $140,000 before taxes.

More than half of that $4 million ($2.5 million) comes from sales to twenty-five nursing homes in the area; the pharmacy fills 65,000 prescriptions a year ($1 million worth to individual customers) from its stock of 4,300 drugs and sells $500,000 worth of OTC drugs, cosmetics, and other items a year. Prescriptions are priced at cost plus a $4 prescription fee, with an additional 10 percent surcharge for prescriptions that cost more than $15 because of the necessity that the store tie up capital in expensive medications.

Kentucky drugstore owner Chet Parker wrote an article in *American Druggist* (April 1987), in which he outlined his strategy for keeping insurance premiums for his 6,000-square-foot drugstore (which grosses more than $6 million a year) below 1 percent of total sales. Just under half of Mr. Parker's business (45 percent) comes from prescriptions, and the consequences of mixing up prescriptions or providing a low-quality generic drug instead of a brand-name or better generic drug could be dire. Not only could the patient be harmed, or even killed, but the pharmacist could face one heck of a malpractice suit. As a result, Mr. Parker pays $2,322 a year for liability and malpractice insurance, which gives him $1 million coverage for each occurrence (that is, if he is found liable for any action in an amount up to $1 million, it's the insurance company's problem, not his). Any business also needs insurance against ordinary risks such as fire, flood, and breakage of plate glass. He pays $2,583 a year for a package of insurance providing $210,000 replacement cost for his business property, the loss of income sustained for up to twelve months, the state-required liability insurance on the company car used to deliver prescriptions, and unemployment insurance and workers' compensation for his employees.

Now that consumers have more options, they can shop for the best deals too: they can compare local prices to mail order prices for prescription drugs they must take on a continuing basis. Depending on local law and practice, they may be able to buy prescriptions from hospital pharmacies or directly from the doctors prescribing the drugs. And they can decide whether to buy health and beauty aids when picking up a prescription or a nonprescription cold remedy, or whether to wait until the next visit to a discount store or supermarket (see pages 182 and 89).

# 84

# Optical Goods Stores

Number of establishments: 10,586
Total receipts: $1.73 billion
Average net sales: $163,200
Number of employees: 34,200
Total payroll: $403 million

(Department of Commerce, '82)

Optical goods stores sell and repair eyeglasses, sunglasses, and contact lenses; they also provide eye exams (including exams for drivers' licenses) and glaucoma tests. The business has been helped mightily by the development of "designer" eyeglass frames, which are fashion accessories rather than hideous necessities, expensive (at least $75; sometimes over $200), and changed every year, if not more often. Improvements in contact lenses make it possible for more and more people to wear them instead of glasses or as a fashion accessory: nowadays improved tinted contacts can even be used to change the color of the wearer's eyes. Another helpful fashion trend is the use of "plano glasses" (plain glass, with no prescription) in serious-looking gold or tortoiseshell frames, to

---

## CONSUMER TIP

An ophthalmologist is a medical doctor who specializes in the care and treatment of the eye; an optometrist has postgraduate training in testing vision and prescribing corrective lenses. Either of them can write you a prescription for glasses or contact lenses. If you have to consult an ophthalmologist for an eye problem anyway, ask his or her advice on the quality of the various optical goods stores in your area.

An optician has technical training in preparing lenses. Some optical goods stores rely heavily on old-fashioned hand craftsmanship; others mechanize and computerize the process to a greater or lesser degree so they can use less-experienced personnel or those with less training. Either approach can produce good-quality eyewear—provided that the equipment is good and well maintained and provided that skilled and experienced people give careful supervision.

You can buy simple reading glasses without a prescription; places like drugstores and five-and-tens sell them. These nonprescription sales are opposed by the optical goods industry. Its argument is that an eye exam is needed to provide the proper prescription and to detect eye disease; the opposing argument is that consumers can select the appropriate magnification themselves and should be allowed to save money.

---

make a youthful yuppie look like the kind of person you'd like to take on your legal case or invest your money for you.

Optical goods shops can do business in small storefronts, with a sales counter in front and examination rooms in back, especially if the shop can have the lenses ground at a factory and then assembled into eyeglasses either at the factory or in the shop. Of course, a chain or franchise can take advantage of a central factory as well as central purchasing and volume discounts. Optical goods stores are often located in malls or on major retail streets—not that glasses are an impulse purchase, but to make sure that customers are aware of this particular store and how it stands out from its competitors. Franchises and chains have the advantage of central advertising, too, to create a corporate image.

Pearle Vision Center is one of those franchises: since 1980, it's opened 420 company-owned and 384 individually owned centers. Franchisees must pay a minimum fee of $10,000, and the minimum capital required to start up can range from $31,000 to $350,000. There's a continuing monthly franchise fee of 8.5 percent and a monthly advertising fee of 6 percent.

The aging of the population is good news for optical goods stores: many people who had perfect vision in earlier years start wearing reading glasses in middle age or later. The only cloud on the horizon is the increasing sophistication of surgery to correct misshapen eyes (and therefore make glasses unnecessary), unless, of course, more and more people take to wearing sunglasses at night or "windowpanes" to look scholarly.

# 85

# Medical and Dental Testing Labs

It's literally a matter of life and death. Testing labs process samples of blood, tissue, and various unappetizing bodily secretions to find out if patients are suffering from infectious diseases or whether a tumor is benign or malignant. On a more cheerful note, some tests diagnose whether a would-be mother is pregnant, but much of that market has been taken over by simple test kits that can be used at home or in the doctor's office.

The medical-testing market is estimated to be worth $6.2 billion (AIDS testing alone is a $50 million market and is, unfortunately, growing every day). According to the 1982 Department of Commerce survey, there are 5,869 medical laboratories in the United States with receipts totaling $2.87 billion, and 11,310 dental laboratories with receipts totaling $1.38 billion. In 1988, Dun & Bradstreet collected data from 393 medical laboratories and 242 dental labs. The medical labs had gross profits of 51.4 percent of sales and an after-tax net profit of 6.7 percent; dental laboratories had higher gross profits (54.4 percent of sales) but had lower expenses or controlled them more tightly or both, so their after-tax net profits were higher (10.0 percent of sales). Thus, both kinds of laboratories were more profitable than the average business.

There are many competitors in the medical/dental laboratory in-

**Where the Money Goes**

| | |
|---|---|
| (1) Cost of operations: | 30.7% |
| (2) Officers' compensation: | 14.3% |
| (3) Pensions and benefits: | 4.1% |
| (4) Rent: | 4.4% |
| (5) Repairs: | 0.9% |
| (6) Depreciation, depletion, amortization: | 4.6% |
| (7) Interest: | 2.4% |
| (8) Bad debts: | 0.7% |
| (9) Advertising: | 0.4% |
| (10) State, local taxes: | 3.9% |
| (11) Other expenses: | 38.2% |
| (12) Net profit before tax: | Not disclosed |

(Troy, '84–'85)

dustry, since it's pretty easy to open a lab—perhaps too easy, as we'll see below. State control over testing labs is limited and in some cases nonexistent. A testing lab certainly doesn't need a chic office suite or television ads—just a few rooms and the machinery or chemicals needed to perform one or more types of tests. Marketing is done by making connections with doctors and hospitals, not by appealing to the public.

The leading company in supplying diagnostic test materials is Abbott Laboratories, which has 14 percent of the market and brings in $850 million in sales; it has a research budget of over $150 million a year. Abbott and its competitors develop and sell testing chemicals and machinery to read test results. In 1986, Abbott brought out seventy new tests; it's neces-

## CONSUMER TIP

If you use a home pregnancy test, or a test for blood sugar, bleeding in the colon, or other medical problem, remember that these tests are not a substitute for clinical diagnosis and medical treatment. They're intended to provide early warning signals only; even the most accurate test (whether in the home or a laboratory) sometimes yields both "false negatives" and "false positives" (incorrect test results—either identifying a sick person as healthy, or vice versa).

## CONSUMER TIP

In addition to orthodox medical tests, mail-order labs often specialize in "allergy" tests or tests of hair samples to detect various "toxins" (so that the person being tested can gulp down vitamins or treatments recommended by unorthodox healers). Gullible health seekers have paid hundreds of dollars for these tests. As part of a lawsuit investigation, the New York State attorney general's office sent $350 and a blood sample to California's Bio-Health, which charges that much to test for food allergies. The donor was identified as being allergic to milk, cottage cheese, and yogurt—which is really tough for her because she's a cow. So check with a medical practitioner (there are holistic doctors, in case you don't trust orthodox medicine) to see if the tests you're contemplating have any scientific validity—and make sure that your doctor monitors the mail order laboratories he or she uses to process test samples.

Does the doctor know if the lab is the subject of proceedings by consumer protection or licensing authorities? What is the lab's record of accuracy—how many false positives and negative results come through? Who processes the test samples? Are their working conditions bad enough to make it unlikely that they can do a good job of testing and screening? Remember, medical tests determine whether patients must submit to surgery or whether an operation has been successful. People take powerful, often dangerous, drugs to treat conditions identified by testing. Before you undergo risky, painful, and expensive treatments, you have a right to know that your doctor's judgment is based on well-selected and accurately interpreted tests.

sary to continually develop tests since they tend to become obsolete in three to five years.

Speaking of machinery, an increasing trend, and one that jeopardizes the testing-lab industry, is for doctors to buy in-office testing equipment. About 40,000 doctors (out of about 125,000 doctors with private offices in general medicine, internal medicine, and pediatrics) do some testing at the office. Some of them use simple solutions to measure sugar in urine specimens; others use computerized instruments to check up to twelve characteristics of a patient's blood sample.

There are several reasons why doctors do this: it's a service for which they can charge (although many testing laboratories are owned by doctors, obviously not every doctor owns a testing laboratory); it's a kindness to the patients, who can have some of their anxiety relieved immediately, instead of waiting days or weeks for test results; and doctors are often (justifiably) skeptical about the accuracy of testing lab results.

An investigative report by the *Wall Street Journal* ("Laxatories: Harried Screening of Pap Smears Elevates Error Rate of the Test for Cervical Cancer," November 2, 1987) reveals that the Pap test (a routine test for cervical cancer) is frequently inaccurate, in part because once doctors take the samples they are sent for analysis to "Pap mills" that rely on overworked, low-paid employees who are often expected to examine one hundred samples per day. Sometimes the labs even let the examiners take the slides home and study them there!

It's common for doctors to charge up to $35 for the test; the lab, in turn, charges the doctors as little as $1.50 per test to perform the analysis and pays the screeners who judge whether the tissue is normal or abnormal as little as 45 cents per slide. It's getting harder and harder to find skilled technicians to work under those conditions.

It's common for the testing firm to bill the patient directly. There are price differences among labs, but the relationship between price and quality is uncertain. Anyway, the fact that the doctor selects the laboratory makes it impossible for the patient, who eventually pays the bill, to comparison shop.

# 86

# Funeral Parlors

Number of establishments: 18,701
Total receipts: $3.93 billion
Average net sales: $210.5 thousand
Number of employees: not available
Total payroll: $927.1 million

(Department of Commerce, '82)

In the bad old days, as exposed in Jessica Mitford's muckraking classic *The American Way of Death,* funeral shoppers were confronted with only one choice—that of a casket—and only one, nonnegotiable price since the cost of the casket was the cost of the entire funeral. Hidden in the price might be a number of services that the bereft family was unaware of or perhaps didn't even want.

In April 1984, after a decade of controversy, the Federal Trade Commission (FTC) issued a rule compelling funeral directors to disclose itemized prices for the various components of the funeral service and to give quotes over the telephone, if requested. According to Glenn Gould, a funeral industry analyst with the Florida firm of M. K. Jones and Associates, the rule has had a paradoxical result.

**Where the Money Goes (As a Percentage of Operating Expenses)**

| | |
|---|---|
| (1) Personnel (including owners' salaries): | 45.3% |
| (2) Cost of facilities (rent, utilities, interest, etc.): | 29.9% |
| (3) Automotive expenses: | 10.29% |
| (4) Promotion and marketing: | 5.8% |
| (5) Business services (accounting, legal, etc.): | 3.2% |
| (6) Supplies ("preparation room," miscellaneous): | 2.9% |
| (7) Bad debts and discounts: | 2.0% |
| (8) Other: | 0.6% |

(Federated Funeral Directors of America '86)

Customers now pay more for funerals than before; according to the Federated Funeral Directors, the average "regular adult funeral" cost $1,439.15 in 1976 and $2,766.26 in 1986. Yet they are now more satisfied and have a higher opinion of the funeral industry—in 1984, 45 percent of consumers thought funerals were "too expensive," and 28 percent thought funeral prices were "reasonable"; 1987 figures are 39 percent and 32 percent, respectively.

The availability of more information and greater negotiating options permits consumers to select the type of funeral services they want; itemized prices also make it possible for them to understand the many processes involved in a funeral service. What funeral buyers don't always understand is that about ninety percent of every funeral dollar goes to pay operating costs and that about 75 percent of those costs are fixed costs, leaving only limited scope for reduction by better management.

However, since the FTC rule came into effect, spending on funeral vehicles, visitation, and embalming has decreased. The toughest, most price-conscious shoppers tend to be in the larger cities; in small towns, where all of Aunt Edna's friends are likely to turn up at the funeral to see if her family has done her proud, funerals tend to be more elaborate.

For the economy-minded who want to make a good impression, about 25 percent of funeral directors queried in one survey make elaborate caskets available for rental, with the actual burial or cremation taking place in a more modest container, but few buyers take this option.

## FAMILY BUSINESS

The traditional image of a funeral parlor is that of a small, family-run business. The average operation handles about sixty funerals a year—not enough for roaring profitability, unless the funerals are quite elaborate. Although today's business trend is toward concentration (chains of funeral homes), it's still overwhelmingly a family business. The most efficient, best-run funeral homes tend to buy up their less profitable competitors.

Another trend in this most horizontal of businesses is vertical integration: either cemetery operators buy funeral homes, or vice versa. "Combinations" have marketing strength because the idea of buying funeral plots well in advance of need is well accepted.

However, there are two large, public corporations in the funeral industry. (So far, franchising has failed to make a mark.) The larger, Service Corporation International (SCI), owns 316 funeral homes and 80 cemeteries, cornering 5 percent of the funeral market. Its gross profit margin is 33 percent—about three times that of the industry in general. For the fiscal year ending April 30, 1986, SCI earned $40.9 million on sales of $263.9 million. About a quarter of this sum came from prepaid funerals (another increasing trend). A prepaid SCI funeral averages $2,600 (that is, close to the national average), but that price doesn't include the burial plot, which can cost anywhere from $200 to $2,000 more.

The other public company, Morlan International, Inc., earned a healthy $41 million on fiscal 1986 sales of $264 million (in other words, about the same as SCI). Morlan hit the big time by selling "opening and closing" (trade talk for the actual process of burying someone) to the owners of burial plots, on a preneed basis. Traditionally, this sale had been handled by the funeral director, when needed.

It's hard to tell who brings home the biggest paycheck in the funeral industry because the many privately owned funeral homes don't have to report earnings figures to anyone. But Marvin Demchick, Morlan's chairman, earned $196,000 in fiscal 1985, making him a strong candidate for the title of top earner. Morlan's five top executives earned an average of $141,000 in that year.

## PRENEED SALES

A growing trend is "preneed" sales; that is, people arrange their own funerals, specifying the services they want and those they prefer to be omitted, and pay for them in advance. Some funeral directors find that one-quarter of their business is preneed.

Preneed purchases can save money; but, according to industry analyst Gould, only 4 percent of preneed buyers have that in mind. Eighty percent are interested in the peace of mind of knowing the funeral is already arranged.

For the cost-conscious, another alternative is the memorial society: a group of people (often members of a religious denomination) join together to prearrange simple, economical funeral services. It's like a food

## CONSUMER TIP

Most states regulate preneed sales and require funeral directors to put the money into a trust or escrow account. If you're preneed shopping, find out your state's provisions about getting your money back if the company goes out of business, if you change your mind, or if you move to another state.

co-op, translated to another idiom. In 1984, there were about 200 memorial societies, with 900,000 members.

The cemetery industry has been selling plots in advance of need for many years. According to Dun & Bradstreet's 1986 figures, gross profit for "cemeterians" (cemetery subdividers and developers) was 58.2 percent of net sales; net profit after tax was a comfortable 7.5 percent. However, funeral homes were significantly more profitable than cemeteries: they earned 66.9 percent gross profit and 10.1 percent after-tax net profit.

But not every funeral requires a burial plot: about one "dearly departed" in eight is cremated; half of California's deceased opt for cremation, which is either a sociological phenomenon or a result of high real estate prices. Originally, the funeral director acted as an intermediary in arranging cremations, which either were performed by the funeral home, if it had the necessary facilities, or by a specialized firm that either had a business relationship with the funeral home, paid a commission to the referring funeral director, or charged the funeral director a wholesale price, which was billed to the deceased's family at retail.

Since the 1970s, a few firms have specialized in "direct cremation," without intervention of a funeral director (and with one fewer middleman to get paid). The best-known company in this industry segment is Nep-

## CONSUMER TIP

If you must arrange a funeral for a relative, look through the deceased person's papers to see if there's a cemetery plot deed—a burial plot is real estate, just as a house is.

tune, Inc. (vividly referred to by its detractors as "Bake and Shake"; its owner, Dr. Charles Denning, is sometimes referred to as "Colonel Cinders").

The funeral of the future? It's been suggested that one commercial application of the space shuttle would be the launching of small metal containers of cremation ashes into space.

# Services, Et Cetera

# 87

# Law Firms

| | |
|---|---|
| Number of establishments: | 115,407 |
| Total receipts: | $34.32 billion |
| Average net sales: | $297,400 |
| Number of employees: | 569,359 [This does not include 146,078 sole practitioners and law-firm partners, who are members of the firms, not employees. It does include 150,266 associates (who *are* employees); 58,424 paraprofessionals; and 360,699 clerical and other workers.] |
| Total payroll: | $7.15 billion |

(Department of Commerce, '82)

You won't learn how law firms really work by watching Perry Mason reruns or even by watching this season's "L.A. Law." (But then, you've probably noticed that Marcus Welby wasn't much like your doctor, and life in the Huxtable household isn't all that much like life in yours.) For one thing, litigation (pursuing cases in court) is the most visible part of a lawyer's work, but it's only the tip of the iceberg; most of the "ice" is below the surface.

Many lawyers never go into court at all, but focus on providing legal

## Where the Money Goes (Before Federal Taxes)

| | |
|---|---|
| (1) Cost of operations: | 7.7% |
| (2) Officers' compensation: | 33.4% |
| (3) Pensions and benefits: | 6.1% |
| (4) Rent: | 5.7% |
| (5) Repairs: | 0.5% |
| (6) Depreciation, Depletion, Amortization: | 6.3% |
| (7) Interest: | 0.7% |
| (8) Bad Debts: | 0.1% |
| (9) Advertising: | 0.2% |
| (10) State, Local Taxes: | 3.3% |
| (11) Other Expenses: | 39.8% |
| (12) Net Profit Before Tax: | — |

(Troy, '83–'84)

advice for businesses, negotiating contracts, setting up mergers, converting rental apartment buildings to condos, and other kinds of planning, advising, and negotiating. Even litigators (courtroom lawyers) spend much more time preparing for cases than trying them.

Anyway, the vast majority of cases that are filed never get to trial. Either one side succeeds in getting the case dismissed because it's so legally inadequate that a full trial is not available, or both sides would rather cut a deal than wait for the case to drag through the courts. As an example of the frustration involved for the lawyers (and the anxiety involved for the clients), Dana, a lawyer, spent a sunny weekend in August at the computer, drafting an appeal brief, and the next sunny weekend revising it. The following Tuesday, the case was settled, so she could have been at the beach for all it mattered.

There are four main ways that law firms earn money (honest, dishonest, sleazy, and questionable, you say? Okay, there are four ways *honest* lawyers earn money). Sometimes there's a flat fee for carrying out a particular task (for example, drawing up a will or handling the closing on someone's co-op apartment). Other ways of billing are more common when the law firm goes to court on behalf of a client. Lawyers may charge for their services by the hour with the bill payable win, lose, or draw, and whether or not the advice helps the client. Or they earn contingent fees (a portion—usually one-third, but perhaps more in difficult or risky cases—of the amount the client recovers from the opponent; of course, if the lawyer or law firm loses the case, it collects nothing except its expenses from trying the case). The fourth option is for the client to pay a retainer (a flat fee, either covering all legal services during a particular period, or covering certain specified legal services with other services to be billed by the hour).

The way a particular client will pay depends on the client (large corporations often put a firm on retainer), on the law firm's status (smaller firms and solo practitioners tend to handle a lot of flat-fee work and take a lot of cases on contingency), and especially on the kind of case. Usually, personal injury cases are contingent because few victims of personal injuries could afford to hire a lawyer otherwise. But the law firm must take a big risk (the case may be lost—or it may be won, but only after years of grinding labor), which at least theoretically entitles them to a big part of the recovery (the amount the party responsible for the injury is required to pay).

However, for obvious reasons, contingent fees are forbidden in criminal cases; otherwise, law offices would be full of clients loudly protesting their innocence and offering a percentage of the swag.


## THE SMALL FRY

In 1980, there were 542,205 lawyers in the United States. About two-thirds of them (68 percent) were in private practice, either as sole practitioners or as employees or members of law firms. Ten percent worked for businesses; 9 percent were employed by government agencies. One lawyer out of every twenty-five worked for a special interest organization (such as a legal aid society). Four percent of lawyers were elected or appointed judges. The other 5 percent did something besides practicing law to earn a living.

At one end of the legal economic spectrum are the sole practitioners (lawyers who practice by themselves, not in firms) and the small firms (a few lawyers). Two-thirds of practicing lawyers are either sole practitioners or practice with one or two partners. They rent modest offices, with enough room for themselves, for one or more paralegals or secretaries and for a conference room; they buy a few lawbooks, order new stationery when the old box runs out, and hope that they can take a reasonable "draw" each week or month and end up with some profits at the end of the year.

According to a 1984 study by the consulting firm Altman & Weil, firms of two to eight lawyers tended to spend over half their income (56.1 percent) paying lawyers' salaries; 15.2 percent on paying support staff; 3.3 percent on paralegals; 7.3 percent on rent and related expenses; 3.2 percent on equipment (such as computers and elaborate telephone systems); 1.6 percent on reference materials (lawbooks, journals), and 13.3 percent on other expenses. Their 1986 survey shows an average income of $119,944 for small-firm partners and $46,090 for small-firm associates. But very small firms in rural areas offered as little as $8,733 as a starting salary.

## THE BIG FISH

At the other end of the economic scale are the large firms, with lawyers by the hundreds. These typically survive on retainers from major corporations and institutions and on hourly fees of, say, anywhere from $85 for the lowliest associate to $350 for leading partners. One theory is that rates for associates keep inching up faster than those for partners because corporate clients look at the top of the bill first and are more likely to react with horror if the partners' hourly rate goes up.

If a law firm gets too grabby, its corporate clients can turn to another firm or expand their own legal departments. The "house counsel" typically get paid salaries, perhaps bonuses, and not hourly rates, so they can be a real money-saver. In 1984, the median salary for house counsel was $65,800 (that is, half earned more, half earned less); in 1986, the average base salary for corporations' chief legal officers was $135,000 (but one out of five earned $200,000 or more).

Pretty generous, you may say, but these salaries look like lunch money compared to what lawyers at the top firms earn. Of course, the firm's earnings are higher than the total salaries paid, but there are other expenses to worry about. A law firm is a "people" business, and a high proportion of its income (60 to 70 percent) goes for salaries. It's hard to say who the top earners are; the best-known, most successful trial lawyers certainly earn in the millions of dollars a year, but they don't have to report just how much to the public—and they don't. However, in 1986, the most profitable law firm in the United States (New York's Wachtell, Lipton, Rosen & Katz) earned $1,440,000 in profit per partner. Of course, the partners didn't get all of it (it costs lots of money to run a major law firm), but it's safe to say they got more than $1.95 apiece.

But every associate (salaried lawyer) in a law firm is a "profit center." Let's say that a lawyer earns $65,000 a year to start (that's about what big firms in New York pay young lawyers just out of law school—and some firms pay substantial bonuses as well; however, the average starting salary for law-firm associates in 1986 for the country as a whole was a little under $34,000, rising to about $43,000 after four years). And the neophyte lawyer had to make a substantial investment to compete for those salaries: law school takes three years full-time, four years part-time, and typically costs $5,000 to $10,000 a year for tuition, and more when living expenses and lost income are figured in.

For every "billable hour" of the new lawyer's time, a major firm gets, let's say, $85. The young lawyer will not survive at that firm to become an old lawyer, much less a partner, unless he or she puts in at least 1,650 billable hours a year; that would bring $140,250 into the firm's coffers. But most firms expect at least forty billable hours a week and, say, 1,900 a year (even associates get days off and vacations, sometimes), which would total $161,500.

Even counting Social Security taxes, pension benefits, and overtime, associates are an excellent economic bargain for firms. That's why they say that a law firm has three kinds of lawyers: "finders," who bring in the clients; "minders," who keep them happy (in the boardroom and on the golf course, as well as in court); and "grinders," who are banished to the back room and the darkest law library to actually do the work. Although there are exceptions, the third task usually falls to associates, the first two to partners. A common ratio is about three associates to every partner.

## MAKING PARTNER

To an associate in a big firm, making partner is like finding the Holy Grail. Senior associates in big firms are well paid (after seven years at a major New York firm, lawyers make about $133,000 a year), but a partner also shares in the firm's profits (although a new partner will probably be required to contribute a hefty amount to the partnership's capital) and has some say in decision making (how much depends on the firm's policy— some are run autocratically by a handful of managing partners; others give all the partners a meaningful voice). On the average, partners earn about two and a half times as much as associates.

However, like all good quests, the quest for partnership is difficult, and many fall by the wayside. Usually, they go to work for other firms, open their own practices, or join a corporation's legal department. Of New York's thirty largest law firms, the proportion of associates "making partner" ranges from one in twelve to about one in three.

Traditionally, law firms maintained a policy of "up or out in seven years": those who didn't make partner in that time got the heave-ho. Today, more firms allow senior associates to remain, or some firms create two or more kinds of partnerships, with different (or no) voting rights and profit shares.

## BIG-FIRM ECONOMICS

According to the *American Lawyer* (like *Forbes,* it's a special interest magazine, authoritative if a bit gossipy), in 1986 twenty-one law firms took in revenues of $100 million or more; and thirteen firms managed to have pretax income of over $50 million for their 1986 fiscal year. The top ten firms had profits of over $500,000 per partner and profit margins of over 33 percent. One firm even managed a 73 percent profit margin.

Where does this amazing prosperity come from? Much of it results from mergers and acquisitions. A really juicy takeover battle generates thousands of lawyer-hours of document searching, haggling, screaming, and hammering out of the eventual settlement. A lot of the rest comes from the new tax code: first the big firms have to explain the provisions to their clients, then spend time before the IRS and in court defending their interpretations of the new law.

## TRADE TALK

▶ Billable hour: an hour spent on work that can be attributed to (and billed to) a specific client. Billable hours do not include keeping up with general legal developments, attending continuing education classes, doing administrative work for the firm, or telephoning one's stockbroker or girlfriend. It's been estimated that about two-thirds of a lawyer's office hours are billable, with about 11 percent of the remaining time spent on office administration, 11 percent on nonbillable legal research, 9 percent on community and public service work, and 4 percent on "miscellaneous." They say that one young associate was proud of billing a twenty-four-hour day by working around the clock on a case until another associate topped that by flying from New York to California, working on a case round the clock, and billing the client for a twenty-seven-hour day.

▶ Rainmaker: a lawyer in a prestigious firm—usually a partner or retired partner who is "of counsel" to the firm—who specializes in bringing major clients (for example, his prep-school squash partner's chemical corporation) to the firm and in getting things done at the highest levels (for example, talking to his college roommate, who is now a major Department of Commerce policymaker, about a little problem the chemical corporation is having).

▶ White Shoe Firm (or "shoe" firm): a prestigious, usually large, law firm with large corporate clients, high billing rates, and high salaries. Heaven only knows where the name comes from since anyone actually wearing white shoes would not only never make partner but would probably be dropped in the moat.

▶ PC: Professional Corporation. Most law firms are set up as partnerships, a structure which has certain legal and tax consequences, but some years back, law firms rushed to become PCs to gain tax advantages (especially better pensions for the top lawyers). Those tax advantages have pretty much evaporated; in fact, some firms are now switching back to partnership form.

Many legislators and nearly all judges are lawyers. That could explain why laws and court decisions are so hard for nonlawyers to understand. The basic philosophy of the legal profession is that human beings can control every event, or at least specify who will be obligated to do what whenever any possible event occurs. This orientation has given lawyers the reputation of being "deal-killers": the endless pettifogging negotiating has driven many a businessperson to abandon many a project. It's given lawmakers a bad name, as they churn out hundred-page statutes with exceptions to exceptions to exceptions. They joke about this situation that when someone asked a country lawyer what color Farmer Jones' barn was, the lawyer said, "It's red *on this side.*"

Clients and others who must deal with lawyers are understandably frustrated when they can't get straight answers to simple questions or when it takes many (billable) hours to accomplish a seemingly simple task. But remember that precision and planning take time.

# 88

# CPA Firms

| | |
|---|---|
| Number of establishments: | 51,900 |
| Total receipts: | $14.6 billion |
| Average net sales: | $281,000 |
| Number of employees: | 330.2 thousand |
| Total payroll: | $5,933,000,000 |

(Department of Commerce, '82)

Accountants (aka "bean counters") figure out how an individual's, organization's, or business's transactions should be treated under a set of rules about income, expenses, and taxes. Businesses employ armies of accountants to handle these chores. Public accountants practice accounting for clients.

A Certified Public Accountant, or CPA, has studied accounting in college and passed a two-and-a-half-day exam administered by the American Institute of Certified Public Accountants (AICPA). In 1987, the AICPA had 240,000 members, not all of whom worked for accounting firms: many were in-house accountants for corporations or self-employed.

There are times when it makes a lot of sense for an individual to hire an accountant: to prepare a complex tax return, give tax advice for future transactions and guidance in business, real estate, investment, or

Where the Money Comes From

| (1) Accounting services: | 49.2% | |
|---|---|---|
| (2) Tax preparation: | 22.3% | |
| (3) Bookkeeping services: | 12.8% | |
| (4) Management advisory services (MAS): | 7.9% | |
| (5) Tax planning and advice: | 5.4% | |
| (6) Other: | 2.4% | (for instance, computer consulting; designing software) |

(Department of Commerce, '82)

Where the Money Goes

| (1) Cost of operations: | 15.2% |
|---|---|
| (2) Officers' compensation: | 22.3% |
| (3) Pensions and benefits: | 3.3% |
| (4) Rent: | 5.2% |
| (5) Repairs: | 0.5% |
| (6) Depreciation, depletion, amortization: | 3.8% |
| (7) Interest: | 1.9% |
| (8) Bad debts: | 0.3% |
| (9) Advertising: | 0.7% |
| (10) State, local taxes: | 3.7% |
| (11) Other expenses: | 39.5% |
| (12) Net profit before tax: | 3.6% |

(Troy, '83–'84)

divorce matters, for instance. But it isn't legally required, and people can get through an entire lifetime without ever hiring one.

But corporations whose stock is publicly traded *have* to hire CPAs to prepare the annual financial reports that are released to the public and to the SEC. Then other accountants—who are independent both of the corporation and of the accountants preparing the reports in the first place—must audit the figures. As you can see from the above, CPA firms depend heavily on audit business. That puts them in a very delicate position because although there are complex systems of rules, accounting involves a lot of personal judgment about the way particular items should be treated (is this amount deductible? how many years will this machinery last? how likely is it that this debt will be paid?).

An accountant, or an auditor, naturally wants to find ways to keep the client happy (or the client will turn around and hire another accounting firm), but CPAs not only have to worry about violating professional ethics but about getting sued by those who are harmed by a corporation's departures from standard accounting practices (for instance, stockholders who were told the corporation was prosperous when it was broke, or lenders who believed what the balance sheets said about the company's assets).

## THE BIG EIGHT

There are dozens of huge law firms and handfuls of gigantic advertising agencies, but there are only eight really major accounting firms, all of which are international, earning about half their revenue outside the United States. By far the largest is Peat Marwick Mitchell, with U.S. revenues of $1.35 billion and world revenues of $2.5 billion, which merged with the ninth-largest firm, KMG Main Hurdman, in 1987. (KMG stands for Klynveld Main Goerdeler, which was Main Hurdman's international organization when it was a separate firm.) Arthur Andersen & Company, the number two firm, had U.S. revenues of $1.35 billion out of total revenues of $1.9 billion.

The other firms—Coopers & Lybrand, Ernst & Whinney, Price Waterhouse (which handles the balloting for the Oscars), Arthur Young & Company, Deloitte Haskins & Sells (familiar to New Yorkers as the auditor of their state lottery), and Touche Ross & Company—had U.S. revenues ranging from $570 million to $860 million, and worldwide revenues in the $1.2 to $1.7 billion range.

Starting salaries at the top accounting firms are much lower than at the top law firms (see page 381): a beginning auditor or tax accountant who holds a B.A. degree is likely to earn around $30,000. However, some firms pay a bonus for overtime worked by young accountants; if law firms did that, their starting attorneys would earn about as much as basketball stars. Smaller firms tend to pay starting salaries of $18,000 to $26,000. A senior accountant, with more experience or an advanced degree or both, might earn $26,000 to $34,000 a year; a manager in an accounting firm might earn $33,000 to $51,000. These aren't startling amounts of money, which is why large accounting firms have such high turnover: it's common for young accountants to get the experience they need to take the CPA exam, then quit and open up their own accounting practices or sign on as comptrollers or chief financial officers for corporations.

## BEYOND THE AUDIT

Accounting firms cherish their audit business. However, most corporations aren't public and don't require auditing; the corporations that do require it often select a major firm as an auditor. That means that smaller accounting firms must find either a way to get audit assignments or other ways to make a living.

The 1,335 "accounting, auditing, bookkeeping" firms responding to the 1986 Dun & Bradstreet survey evidently managed to earn high gross profits (58.2 percent of sales) and exceptionally high after-tax net profits: 15.6 percent, one of the highest figures in the entire survey. (After all, if accounting firms can't take care of money, who can?)

Of course, tax work is a perpetual source of income, for private individuals as well as corporations. For accountants, tax season is an annual horror, beginning right after the New Year's Eve party and continuing without a break until April 15th; there's a mini-tax season for the following four months, for clients who have an extension on tax filing. One of the major problems for any accounting firm is having enough staff during this recurring madness yet keeping everyone busy during the summer and fall doldrums.

One solution is to use temporary personnel and wave bye-bye after tax season.

Another solution is to supplement traditional accounting practice with consulting services: for instance, computer consulting, pension advice, investment counseling, and management advisory services. However, these newer sources of income are not without problems: nobody but a CPA can handle an audit and hardly anyone but a CPA can represent clients before the IRS, but anybody who thinks he knows anything can be a consultant. It's also tough for a firm to maintain its independent stance as an auditor if it has already given the client a lot of other advice because it might be placed in the position of forcing the client to recognize the adverse accounting consequences of that advice.

Business transactions are growing more complicated. International trade raises difficult problems of how currency fluctuations should be treated. Every attempt at "fairness" or, Heaven help us, "simplification" only seems to make the tax code more convoluted. There'll be plenty of accounting work to be done in the future. The challenge for solo practitioners and small accounting firms will be to become visible and market their services effectively, so that the "big guys" don't get all the desirable engagements.

# 89

# Tax Preparers

There are four routes to getting your federal tax form taken care of. If you have a simple tax return, you can actually have the IRS prepare it for you, simply by filling out part of the return yourself, signing it, and mailing it in. The friendly federal folks will compute your tax liability, compare it to the amount already withheld from your salary, and either send you a refund (the most common case) or a bill for the difference.

If your tax situation is a little more complex, and you are intrepid or too cheap to hire someone, you can fill out your tax return yourself. The IRS provides ample free publications and recorded telephone tapes explaining taxpayers' obligations; and, at least theoretically, you can get free advice by calling the IRS or going to an IRS office. (But from January to April 15, good luck getting through—the phones ring off the wall.)

If you have a very complex tax situation or if you're interested in long-range planning strategies that will reduce your taxes, you'd be better off with an expert tax lawyer or accountant to advise you and prepare your tax returns. Or you might turn to an "enrolled agent": a nonlawyer, non-CPA who is allowed to do tax planning (and to represent taxpayers at audits) as a result of experience with the IRS or comparable training.

That leaves millions of people who don't fit into any of these categories. Maybe they can't afford an accountant, or they can afford it but don't want to spend the money. Maybe they could prepare their own tax returns (and might even be surprised at how easy it is), but they're afraid. So they go to commercial tax preparers, who are permitted to prepare other people's tax returns but who are not lawyers or accountants.

There's pretty much only one game in town: H. & R. Block, Inc., the "author" of 10 percent of 1986 returns. It's the only major nationwide company in the tax-preparation business. Small lenders like Avco Corporation, Beneficial Corporation, and Household Finance all tried to enter the business but couldn't make a go of it.

There are almost 9,000 Block units worldwide and over 7,500 in the United States (3,539 owned by the company and 4,243 owned by individual franchisees). Block has been franchising since 1958. Starting an H. & R. Block franchise can require as little as $1,000 to $2,000 in capital, and franchisees don't have to pay advertising fees. After that, it's all negotiable: the minimum franchise fee and monthly fee are variable.

In 1985, Block filed 10 million tax returns, yielding revenue of $500 million. Revenues for 1986 were $606,740,000, with pretax earnings of $113 million, over half of which—$60,104,000—was after-tax profit. The average return cost the taxpayer $50 and took up about an hour of the preparer's time.

Tax "simplification" (that's pretty theoretical, too) decreases the number of taxpayers, which is bad for business; it even drives some taxpayers to prepare their own returns. But even if the tax law keeps changing, throwing everyone into a constant state of confusion, it's tough to run a profitable business when all your customers charge in during the first three and a half months of the year. That's why Block is diversifying, entering fields such as data-base management. The strategy is paying off: in 1986, 43 percent of its revenues and 23 percent of its profits came from nontax businesses.

In 1987, Block tried a new marketing strategy, joining forces with a related product: Alka-Seltzer. They did a commercial together, showing a distressed taxpayer chowing down on indigestible snacks as he writes up his tax return. The next day, he deals with his consequent alimentary problem by relying on Alka-Seltzer, the tax problem by calling H. & R. Block. The two companies also set up a sweepstakes, with a prize of a Bahamas vacation, $5,000, and a lifetime of complimentary tax return preparation. (Of course, the value of the prize is taxable.)

# 90

# Day Care Centers

| | |
|---|---|
| Number of establishments: | 27,683 |
| Total receipts: | $1.4 billion |
| Average net sales: | $50.9 thousand |
| Number of employees: | — |
| Total payroll: | — |

(Department of Commerce, '82)

It's easy to spot the contradiction, but it's tough to deal with it. Working parents need reliable, affordable day care. They want their kids to spend their days at a place that isn't just hazard-free but attractive. The staff should really care about kids and make sure they have an enjoyable and educational day—it's not enough that the kids aren't mistreated or exploited. Yet, this convenient, warm, idyllic place must charge fees that the parent can afford. According to the Census Bureau, in 1987, 50.8 percent of women with babies under a year old were either working or looking for jobs. There were 13.4 million two-income couples with children and a need for day care: that's over 40 percent of all married couples of child-bearing age.

Something's got to give. Often, the parents leave their kids with a friend or neighbor, paying $50 to $100 a week for "family day care," an informal arrangement that frequently is not licensed or supervised by any agency. Day care centers usually charge in the range of $35 to $150 a week; the rate depends on geography, the local cost of living, and whether the center is operated by owners working for profit or by a not-for-profit agency, or whether it is subsidized by a corporation as a benefit for its employees. (This is an increasing trend: employees lose productivity if they're either late because the school bus didn't arrive, or take the day off to care for a sick child, or simply worry about how the kids are doing.)

One of the hottest political issues of the 1980s is the role that government should play in day care. In a sense, state and local governments already provide a massive day care system, in the form of public schools. But should they also help out working parents by providing pre-school day care, and centers that are open before and after normal school hours? Conservatives say no, believing that such efforts would be far too expensive and, even worse, would undermine the traditional family. Liberals say yes, citing the need of families—traditional or otherwise—for these services. A limited amount of free or almost-free public day care is already available, but it is usually restricted to families on the welfare rolls or with a very low income; it is seldom available to working-class or middle-class families. Census Bureau figures show that 1 percent of kids under five with two working parents are cared for in kindergartens or grade schools; 23 percent use the estimated 60,000 to 70,000 organized child care facilities, whether public or private. Thirty-one percent are cared for in their own homes by a housekeeper or child care worker; 15 percent, at relatives' homes; 22 percent, at other homes; and 8 percent, at centers operated by a parent's workplace.

## COSTS AND QUALITY

To keep child care affordable, costs must be cut, and one of the first areas to be trimmed is salaries for day care workers. Pay of $8,000 a year is typical. That's about what dog-kennel attendants make and less than parking-lot attendants earn. Not surprisingly, turnover is high: 40 percent a year is a typical rate. Three-quarters of the workers at Kinder-Care (discussed below) are hired at the minimum wage, and many of them work part-time. The director of a center often earns less than $20,000 a year for his or her stressful and responsible job; the pay offered to teachers with college degrees is usually under $15,000.

Local regulations vary. Frequently, a center can legally be run with a licensed administrator and a small number of licensed teachers; the rest of the care can be provided by unlicensed aides. Or licensure may be required of all personnel, but licenses will be issued to anyone who applies and who claims not to have a criminal record. The licensing agency may or may not check.

However, one way that costs can be cut without cutting corners is to achieve economies of scale through central management and central purchasing of everything from finger paints to paper towels. Several chains and franchises are now operating in the day-care field (detractors call them "Kentucky Fried Children"), and a few of them are public companies, with stock available to the public. At least one, Kinder-Care Learning Centers, has achieved outstanding financial success.

## KINDER-CARE

Kinder-Care is nearly a nationwide operation, with 1,100 day care centers in forty states (but not in New York, which has exceptionally tough licensing regulations). For 1987, it ranked #713 on *Business Week*'s Top 1000 listing, with sales of $507 million and profits of $26.3 million. It had assets of $1.941 billion, much higher than its market value of $579 million. It achieved a respectable return on common equity of 8.3 percent and a profit margin of 5.2 percent. The chain plans to add at least one hundred new centers a year and already owns part of a chain that provides tutoring for school kids with academic problems. It also owns some unrelated businesses, including a savings and loan institution and an insurance company, simply because the day care centers generate so much cash that outlets are needed to use it productively. In September 1987, it announced plans to buy a chain of shoe stores and another of discount stores.

In short, Kinder-Care has come a long way from its start-up in 1968, although its founder, Perry Mendel, started with the not inconsiderable sum of $200,000. He earned over $907,000 in 1987 and owns almost 1.5 million stock shares. The company's president, Richard J. Grassgreen, earned more than $800,000.

The competition includes La Petite Academy, a chain of 615 centers in twenty-seven states, and much smaller chains such as the thirty-seven Rocking Horse Child Care Centers of America. Franchisees can purchase an Alphabetland unit for an initial franchise fee of $20,000, with approximately $65,000 in start-up capital required; the continuing franchise fee is 7 percent monthly.

The future of day care centers should be nothing less than sensational. There's a small baby boom occurring now because the original baby boomers are having babies at last. Then there's enormous profit potential at the other end of the life cycle: day care centers for elderly people (another growing group in the population) who need companionship and some help with everyday tasks, but don't need nursing home care. But, strong as the market is overall, it's easy for an individual operator to fail. The estimates of the cost of starting up a day care center for children range from $150,000 to $300,000, and profit margins can be slim. (The 1986 Dun & Bradstreet figures show average gross profit of 49.2 percent of sales and net after-tax profit of 5.2 percent.)

The key to success is attracting just the right number of children: enough to provide a good cash flow but not so many that the facilities are strained or that the children exceed the number that can be cared for under state or local law. Hard-pressed parents must shop for the best price. It costs money for a center to provide more and better-trained care-givers and to include better equipment for recreation and education. Yet, if the centers increase their monthly charges (the Bright Horizons day care chain charges $780 a month to take care of infants, $460 a month for preschoolers), parents can either find cheaper alternatives or opt out of day care centers entirely and hire a housekeeper or nanny. To succeed, a day care center must set its prices within a narrow corridor: high enough to cover expenses, low enough to compete with other forms of child care.

# Advertising Agencies

They've been called the "hidden persuaders," the "hucksters," and the "mirror makers"; they're the people who draw on our fears and insecurities and greed to get us to buy more products, preferably those made by their clients. Few businesses have as much effect on consumers as the advertising business: the changeover from people buying what they needed for subsistence to consumers buying for status and the sheer pleasure of it would not have been possible without advertising. The whole idea of a "brand" would be meaningless without advertising. Unless you know that Ivory soap is "99 and 44/100 percent pure" or that Wisk "fights ring around the collar," what's to stop you from going into a store and buying merely "soap" or "detergent"—the first or the cheapest brand you see?

Advertising agencies are in a peculiar predicament. They traditionally earn their money by collecting a 15 percent commission based on the cost of the media advertising placed by their clients. (However, a really aggressive client can beat the commission down to 10 to 12 percent.) The media rebate the commission to the agency; the client doesn't pay the agency directly. In a way, this encourages the client to expand the number of different advertisements rather than to run a smaller number of ads more often because the agency's services seem "free" (it isn't necessary

**Where the Money Goes**

| | |
|---|---|
| (1) Cost of operations: | 60.6% |
| (2) Officers' compensation: | 5.6% |
| (3) Pensions and benefits: | 1.9% |
| (4) Rent: | 2.4% |
| (5) Repairs: | 0.3% |
| (6) Depreciation, depletion, amortization: | 1.7% |
| (7) Interest: | 0.9% |
| (8) Bad debts: | 0.3% |
| (9) Advertising: | 0.4% |
| (10) State, local taxes: | 2.0% |
| (11) Other expenses: | 22.5% |
| (12) Net profit before tax: | 1.4% |

(Troy, '83–'84)

to write a check to the agency for the hundreds of hours of creative work put into a major campaign). But it also makes it very difficult for the agency to recommend that the client cut back on its print or broadcast ads, even if marketing strategy suggests that this would be cost-effective.

Not all agencies earn their money by means of commissions. Sometimes the agency bills its clients for the employee hours and expenses spent on the campaign and adds on a 15 to 25 percent markup for overhead. Or if it's easy to measure results (such as the number of people who subscribe to a magazine after an ad campaign), the agency may get an incentive fee for each subscription or a share of the magazine's new subscription revenue over a certain amount.

## THE DEVELOPMENT PROCESS

Ad agencies, like lions and tigers, spend a lot of their time hunting—but for new clients, not dinner. The process of wooing a client varies greatly, depending on the agency's resources and the potential "billings" (the amount that the client spends on placing ads in the media) that the client may generate. At its simplest, the "pitch" consists of showing a client clips of ads the agency has already produced. At its most elaborate, an agency can spend hundreds of thousands or even millions of dollars to create a complete ad campaign for a major company, then use this extravaganza of writing, design, photography, and film to compete with other agencies for the account.

An agency needs a tremendous amount of capital to do so much work "on spec" (in hopes of securing a contract) but it's worthwhile if it lands a multimillion dollar account. Ad agency experts estimate that U.S. advertisers will devote almost $128 billion to U.S. advertising, and $119 billion to advertising in other countries. If that prediction proves true, agency commissions could total nearly $20 billion.

Once an account is landed, the agency's account executives work with the client to devise an advertising strategy. What image does the company want to project? Who already buys its products? Who are its desired customers? What's the advertising budget, and how should it be divided between print and broadcast advertising? When should the ads run?

The creative personnel handle the actual design and copy-writing. There are some free-lancers in the advertising business, but they usually work for the small agencies that can't afford to maintain a year-round staff. The larger agencies usually have a large enough creative staff to handle their (and their clients') needs. As long as an agency has the capital and cash flow to pay year-round salaries, it usually is cheaper in the long run to pay the creative staff salaries and bonuses than to pay them by the job.

## THE AGENCY WORLD

Many of the leading agencies are international, but New York (though not necessarily Madison Avenue) is still the capital of the advertising world. Nine of the top ten agencies have headquarters there. (The tenth, Leo Burnett Company, is headquartered in Chicago.) In April 1987, *Advertising Age* (which rivals *Adweek* as the trade paper for the advertising industry) reported that the 179 major agencies with New York offices racked up almost $20 billion in billings in 1986—9 percent more than the 1985 figure. (Compare this with the $9.2 billion receipts for all 41,690 advertising agencies reporting to the Department of Commerce in 1982.)

The number one agency, Young & Rubicam, grossed $536 million in 1986; the runner-up, Ogilvy Group, was way behind at $481 million. The fifth-ranked agency, Saatchi & Saatchi Compton, is a British import, with 1986 gross income of $441 million.

## MERGER MANIA

Although there are agencies of all sizes, from one or two people working at the kitchen table to paste up the ad for Suzie's Shoe Shop that will appear in the local penny-saver to the Madison Avenue office with millions of dollars in revenues and thousands of employees, the biggest agencies tend to be the most successful (and vice versa). It takes a lot of capital to script, design, and film a TV commercial and then to wait around to be paid by the network once the television time has been purchased. Print ads used to be a simple matter of drawings, photographs, and type: today, they can involve a perfume sample, a record bound into a magazine, even a three-dimensional pop-up that can cost $1 million to produce.

To a certain extent, then, merging two or more large agencies into a huge one is a natural business move. In 1984 there were eight ad agency mergers, twenty-six in 1986, and fifty-one—an average of almost one a week—in 1987. Saatchi & Saatchi bought up Ted Bates Worldwide (1986's third-largest agency), Dancer Fitzgerald Sample (#17), and Backer and Spielvogel (#23), and its pretax profits for its 1986 fiscal year were up 73 percent ($103 million). That outpaced revenue, which climbed 47.2 percent to $652 million; net income was $35.1 million. However, Saatchi lost at least $400 million in billings as a result of the acquisitions because some clients switched to other agencies.

Clients switch because ad agencies can develop conflicts of interest. If you make GluggyCola, you don't want to have your ads done by the same agency that does the ads for hated rival Drench Cola and risk them finding out your entire corporate strategy. And when you pull the GluggyCola account, you'll also take a hike with the advertising for Crispy Cheese Chips, your hotel chain, and the Slammo Tennis Racquet.

For example, in November 1987, the Goodyear Tire & Rubber Company, an account with $25 million in billings, switched ad agencies from J. Walter Thompson to Young & Rubicam (sounds like a daytime soap opera, doesn't it?), so Y & R had to give up its work for Uniroyal tires, a mere bagatelle of $16 million in billings. Panasonic stopped going to Ted Bates Worldwide because Bates merged with Backer & Spielvogel, which represented North American Philips, a rival appliance manufacturer. James J. Jordan, head of the agency Jordan, Manning, Case, Taylor & McGrath, has estimated that over $1 billion in accounts have been shifted because of merger-induced client conflicts.

## CRASH!

In 1982, about 35,000 people were working in the advertising business in New York City. In the summer of 1987, *Adweek* estimated that unemployment among advertising people was a frightening 13.3 percent. By November 1987, the number thus employed was down to about 30,000, and the top ten agencies laid off more than 1,000 people in 1987. Many of them had decades of experience, earned six-figure salaries, and had just become too expensive to keep on since clients were frightened by economic conditions and were cutting their ad budgets left and right. Also, agencies with sophisticated desk-top computers could produce rough, or even final, versions of copy and artwork with a lot less manpower than they could in the precomputer days.

Even before the October stock market crash (which happened just as clients were drawing up ad budgets for 1988), the agencies were going through hard times: fifty-five-year-old William Esty Company lost two-thirds of its business in 1987: billings shrank from $510 million (and gross income of $75 million, with a 440-person staff) to $150 million (with one-third of the staff getting the heave-ho).

J. Walter Thompson also cut its staff, which cost the agency $4.1 million in severance pay. Its commissions and fees for the fourth quarter of 1986 were up 6.3 percent, to a total of $175.8 million, but the agency still reported a loss of nearly $5 million for the quarter. (It also suffered a loss, albeit a smaller one—$1.5 million—for the first quarter of 1987.) Its pretax profit margin for 1986 was 4 percent—only half the industry average. The agency blamed clients' stingy spending for the problems; the agency also lost the $200 million Burger King account to N. W. Ayer, in the biggest "switch" in advertising history. During the summer of 1987, British financier Martin S. Sorrell bought the agency's parent corporation for $566 million, hoping to turn it around.

Only seven ad agencies are publicly held corporations, and in 1986, only two of them (Interpublic Group of Companies, Inc., and Saatchi & Saatchi) managed to earn a profit. Will the ad business ever recover from its doldrums, or will it end up like the automobile industry, with only a few surviving colossi (and with bad years even for those giant companies)? As they say in the ads, tune in next week for the conclusion.

# 92

# Public Relations Firms

Public relations firms help determine the image that consumers have of businesses; they create interest in new records and movies; they do their best to make us think that a particular political candidate is reliable, or a tough guy who can stand up to the Russians, or whatever image he chooses. They issue press releases, usually printed, but sometimes on videotape, that provide basic information (if not the entire article) for many journalists. Publicists also handle press conferences, develop publicity campaigns, and write and design materials such as brochures.

Like advertising agencies, PR firms are hidden persuaders; understandably, many are owned by advertising agencies. For example, Hill & Knowlton, the largest public relations firm in 1986, which employed 1,800 people and earned fees of more than $100 million, is owned by the JWT Group, Inc. (the initials stand for ad agency J. Walter Thompson). Burson-Marsteller, owned by advertising firm Young & Rubicam, had 1,875 employees but didn't disclose its billings. Ogilvy & Mather PR, which is part of the Ogilvy Group (advertising and so forth) was way behind with 640 employees and $31 million fee income. The largest independent firm, Daniel J. Edelman, earned $20.9 million in fees and had 336 employees.

A survey by the Public Relations Society of America shows that corporate PR budgets are rising (in part, to make sure that stockholders think highly of the current management in case a takeover battle gets underway). However, mergers and takeovers are decimating in-house public relations and corporate communications units. When a company has to start cutting costs, it often starts in the PR department. That makes it possible for PR firms to hire the "outcasts" at comparatively low salaries. In fact, the average salary in the PR field actually declined in 1986, to $42,000 (it had been $1,000 higher the preceding year) because there are enough eager newcomers to depress the going rate.

It's possible for a company, or an individual celebrity or would-be celebrity, to hire a publicist for a single transaction—perhaps the promotion of a new product or a freshly released record (in which case the publicist would probably charge an hourly rate and expenses). Nevertheless, much of the public relations business involves continuing retainer relationships with clients, which means that the publicist gets a monthly fee for handling all of the client's publicity needs (which sometimes include keeping names *out* of the paper as well as getting them in). Publicists must also develop long-term relationships with the media. Reporters and editors are deluged by information from people and organizations who want coverage. Their attention can be captured by a really creative publicity device, or by the letterhead of a publicist who is known to have a pipeline to a major corporation or celebrity or who has developed a reputation as a reliable source.

Press releases used to be sent by mail or messenger; today, they're likely to be transmitted electronically by "newswire," with the demand for electronic transmission increasing 10 to 15 percent a year. Having a story run on a newswire costs between $45 and $325. The original newswire company, New York's PR Newswire (founded in 1954), lost its monopoly when San Francisco's Business Wire, Inc., went into business in 1976. PR Newswire earned $15 million or so in 1986 (which makes it a super bargain: London's United Newspapers PLC bought it from Western Union in 1982 for $9.5 million, so they've already earned back their investment). Business Wire sells about $7 million in services a year.

Much of the business news you read or see on TV comes from press releases. So do many of your ideas about new products. In fact, you may have heard about this book through David's show or a television appearance; but you may also have read about it in a magazine or newspaper article spurred by a press release.

# The Job Business: Employment Agencies and Headhunters

## Employment Agencies

| | | |
|---|---|---|
| Number of establishments: | 9,608 | (plus 3,324 "office help supply services" and "help supply, except office workers' services) |
| Total receipts: | $9.37 billion | (plus $5.14 billion for office; $2.91 billion for other help supply services) |
| Average net sales: | $975,900 | (plus $547,200 for office; $996,300 for other help supply services) |
| Number of employees: | NG | |
| Total payroll: | NG | |

(Department of Commerce, '82)

Employment agencies and recruiters are very much like real estate brokers and especially like the services that match up would-be tenants with available apartments. In either case, the agency is paid a fee (either a certain number of dollars, or a percentage of the first year's rent or

405

salary). Often, the fee is nominally paid by the employer or the owner of the real estate, but, of course, the salary paid or the rent charged will be raised or lowered as needed to recoup the fee. Although the employees or the tenants may seem more eager (or even desperate) for the jobs or apartments than the employer or landlord is to fill them, the fact of the matter is that the employer and landlord must find suitable candidates in order to stay profitably in business. And, of course, in both cases the brokers are tempted to exaggerate a little, or downright lie, in their advertisements and in material given to applicants. Some of the jobs gloriously trumpeted forth in the newspapers' Help Wanted pages never existed; others existed but have already been filled by qualified candidates and are used to lure the job seeker to the agency.

## TEMPORARY AGENCIES

Businesses often have short-term or seasonal needs for extra workers, such as extra department store clerks to meet the onslaught of Christmas shoppers or extra accounting clerks to cope with tax season. It may be necessary to replace an employee who's out for a while, whether sick, vacationing, or otherwise indisposed, but will be back. In these situations, it doesn't make sense to hire and train a permanent employee and pay for his pension, health insurance, and other benefits only to fire the worker when the temporary crunch is over. It does make sense to hire temporary workers; and employers are usually willing to pay an agency's fee to avoid the nuisance of the hiring process. If a "temp" worker doesn't show up or turns out to lack the skills or temperament needed for the job, the employer can call the agency and get a replacement quickly. If the employer had hired an ordinary employee, he or she would have to be fired—and the time-consuming hiring process started all over again.

The temporary employment agency business grew about 20 percent in both sales and earnings between 1982 and 1987. Nearly 800,000 people worked in temporary services in 1986 (an 11.3 percent growth in jobs since 1980). Temporary assignments can last a day or a year; and companies often offer permanent jobs to especially efficient temporary workers. Some "temps" want the freedom to go to auditions or time to spend with their kids; others look at temp work as a chance to "audition" companies before accepting a permanent job. Still others want a variety of different jobs or just can't find permanent employment.

How good are temps? That depends on the agency as well as on the individual workers. The agency may require an intensive test of job skills before adding a worker to its rolls; it may also provide training in how to work with the most common types of computers and word processors. Or the agency may take a worker's word for it that he or she can type seventy words per minute and tackle every known computer program.

Here's What the Numbers Look Like for the Next Largest Temporary Firms

| | Revenues 1986 | Earnings Per Share | Estimated 1987 Earnings |
|---|---|---|---|
| Kelly Services | $1.03 billion | $2.27 | $2.85 |
| Olsten Corporation (400 offices) | $313 million | | $2.85 |
| Adia Services (600+ offices worldwide; 200 in United States) | $243 million | .76 | $1.05 |

The National Association of Temporary Service estimates the payroll for 770,000 temporary jobs in 1986 at $7 billion. The employer pays the agency directly, and the agency pays the temporary worker. Usually, the employer pays a certain number of dollars per hour; the worker receives a significantly smaller number of dollars, with the rest going to the agency.

By far the largest temporary agency (not just in the United States, but in the world; about half its revenue comes from the offices in thirty-three countries around the world) is Manpower, Inc., part of Britain's Blue Arrow international empire of employment services. It earned $31.1 million, on revenues of $1.2 billion, for its fiscal year ended 28 February 1987.

## FRANCHISES

A growing force in the industry is Uniforce Temporary Personnel Inc., a franchise which earned $1.8 million in 1986 (growing 63 percent a year since 1983) on sales of $60 million. Ten of its sixty offices are company-owned, with the others owned by franchisees who must spend a week at "Temp University" learning the business. Uniforce provides the franchisees with financing for payrolls and other bills in exchange for a hefty 45 percent of gross profits.

Franchisees can strike a similar arrangement with Personnel Pool of America, Inc., or Medical Personnel Pool (subsidiaries of H. & R. Block, which is trying to generate year-round income to supplement its seasonal earnings from tax preparation). The franchisee can choose between a traditional franchise (requiring $100,000 to $150,000 in capital and a 5 percent monthly royalty) and a "growth loan": Personnel Pool itself handles the billing and other back office functions in exchange for 35 percent of gross profits.

Franchisees can purchase either a Snelling Temporaries franchise (there are seventy of them, with 330 projected by 1990) for an overall investment of $60,000 to $110,000, or add to the 444 franchises of the

Snelling and Snelling permanent employment agency for a fee of $29,500. In 1986, when there were only forty-three Snelling Temporaries franchises, the franchisor itself had revenues of $27,102,074 and net income of $472,307. Or franchisees can combine both: Eve Austin, a Decatur, Georgia, franchisee has three permanent and one temporary services franchise. Her permanent franchises bring in monthly revenues of $50,000 to $60,000; her temporary one, $40,000 to $60,000.

Buying a Manpower Temporary Services franchise (the company itself owns 573; franchisees own 455) costs up to $75,000 in start-up capital; there's a $4,500 initial franchise fee, and franchisees also pay a 3 to 6 percent monthly franchise fee but no advertising fee.

Another franchise, J.O.B.S., is taking another approach. Its franchisees need only about $35,000 to start up (including the $22,500 franchise fee); the franchise targets semiskilled job hunters who earn less than $25,000 a year (a group ignored by most personnel agencies). Employers list their jobs for free, and job seekers pay $75 for a list of job opportunities produced by the franchise's nationwide computer linkup. J.O.B.S. doesn't screen the job seekers: it's up to the job hunters to arrange an interview, and up to the employer to decide whether or not to take them on. The J.O.B.S. franchisees average monthly sales of $6,000 to $20,000, with expenses of $4,000 to $8,000 (they are not too high because there aren't any accounts receivable or inventory involved).

# Headhunters

One difference between executive recruiters (nicknamed "headhunters") and other employment agencies is that most employment agencies wait for job seekers (who are usually unemployed) to come in and ask for help in finding a job. If the agency's clients are job applicants, its duty is to find suitable openings for the applicants. But headhunters search the business press and watch TV feverishly to find the best executive talent for a particular job opening; then they go after the best man or woman for the job—even if he or she had no intention of changing jobs before the headhunter dangled the tempting bait of increased salary, more perks, and golden parachutes.

The headhunter works for the employer and has a duty to find suitable applicants for the job, not vice versa. The employer must pay a substantial fee, but in return he or she is spared the task of sorting through thousands of resumes and deflecting calls from desperate candidates.

Headhunters fill about 15 percent of all executive jobs, at an average salary of $50,000 a year. About 20 percent of jobs that pay more than $100,000 a year in the largest corporations in the United States are filled by headhunters; the rest, by internal recruiting and promotion. A study by the Association of Executive Search Consultants, Inc. (AESC), the head-hunters' trade association, shows that a really successful thirty-year-old executive should be earning $62,000; at forty, he or she should be earning $132,000; and a forty-five-year-old who's managed to stay on the "fast track" without crashing should earn $179,000.

Headhunting is a fairly small business (revenues of $2 billion a year), but it is also fairly diverse (there are about 1,500 search firms) and very lucrative. According to John Byrne's 1986 book *The Headhunters,* the Top 10 headhunting firms' seven hundred or so "consultants" performed 8,500 executive searches a year—less than 10 percent of the total executive search market. The top firm, Korn/Ferry International, handled about 1,500 searches, and its consultants billed an average of $379,000 each; the company's 1985 billings were $58 million, with revenue of $50 million for the fiscal year. In 1985, the firm had more than one hundred partners, about two hundred associates, and seventy-five researchers. The associates earn between $35,000 and $70,000 in salary; in a good year, they can get bonuses of 40 percent of their base salaries. The partners earn at least $75,000; the top partners earn in the high six figures.

The number-two firm, Russell Reynolds Associates, did 1,600 searches, and its consultants averaged $392,000 in billings, but its revenues were only $47 million.

There are no special educational qualifications required of potential headhunters, but they do need certain personal characteristics. They must work well with people, have the patience to make constant inquiries in the face of rebuff, and have the ability to quickly learn an industry's terminology and leading members if they have not worked in the subject industry before becoming headhunters.

Executive searches can be handled on either a contingency or a retainer basis—that is, the client-employer either pays a fee only when a suitable "match" is made (the usual method for jobs paying under $60,000 a year) or pays a fee for the headhunting firm's services even if no suitable candidate turns up (the usual method for the highest-paying jobs). The typical fee is about one-third of the executive's first-year salary and bonus. Contingency fees tend to be higher than retainers because of the uncertainty involved.

Headhunters spend much of their time on the phone, calling not only executives who could be hired away but "sources" who can recommend potential search candidates. Most people used to hang up on headhunters; now 90 percent of their calls are returned.

According to the AESC, the typical executive search research director (that is, a fairly well-placed headhunter) is in his or her thirties (20 percent are over forty), has four years experience, has worked for only one firm, and has spent about seven years in another field before taking up headhunting.

What's the future of temporary agencies, employment agencies,

## TRADE TALK

A firm's "completion rate" is the percentage of searches that lead to an executive's being hired; for top firms, the completion rate is about 60 to 65 percent.

and headhunters? After the 1987 crash, temporary agencies did well as some companies shifted from permanent to temporary workers to avoid paying employee benefits (although the tax act of 1986 limits the tax advantages of "leasing" employees on a long-term basis) or to wind up the affairs of a factory being closed down or a bankrupt division. Since most businesses are getting rid of, not hiring, top management, it isn't a great time for headhunters, but we can predict that 100 percent of their calls will be answered by executives whose own positions are increasingly tenuous.

# 95

# Credit Bureaus

When a business allows a customer to open a charge account or use a credit card, or when a bank lends money or grants a mortgage, it's putting a lot of faith in the customer—and that faith is often misplaced. An ad for the credit bureau CBI/Equifax showing a gun and a charge slip points out that crooks stole $120 million in 1985 with guns and $500 million with charge slips.

In order to reduce the credit grantor's risks from suicidal to merely perilous, businesses turn to credit bureaus. A credit bureau is a central exchange of information: businesses that subscribe tell the bureau about their bad experiences with particular customers. (To protect customers' confidentiality, credit bureaus assign code numbers to subscribers and require the code number before giving out information.) In 1982, the Department of Commerce located 5,894 "credit reporting and collection agencies" in the United States. Most of them (4,383) were collection agencies, which had total receipts of $1,156,730,000. There were 298 "mercantile reporting agencies" to inform businesses about the creditworthiness of other businesses, and 1,233 were "consumer credit reporting agencies." Together, the two types of reporting agency earned $948 million.

When a business that subscribes to a credit bureau asks about a credit applicant, the bureau searches its files for adverse reports from other members, then adds other information that can be obtained by searching court and other public records. For instance, the bureau checks to see if the customer has ever been sued for nonpayment of debts, or if, most important, he has ever filed for bankruptcy. The credit bureau also verifies the information that the customer provided on the credit application, such as employment history and the customer's other outstanding charge accounts.

If it's a plain, ordinary credit report, not an "investigative" report (which is usually ordered by potential employers or insurers, not in connection with loans or charge accounts), the credit bureau confines its search to the records and verification of information supplied by the customer. Investigative reports are compiled by interviewing people—a potential source of inaccuracy, if the neighbors find it necessary to retail every rumor ever floated about the subject of the report. Federal law requires that consumers be informed whenever an investigative report is ordered and also lets them check their credit files and protest inaccuracies.

Credit bureaus also keep track of addresses (to make sure that accounts and credit cards aren't issued to post office boxes, check-cashing services, accommodation addresses, or even prison cells—all of which have been known to happen) and check to see if Social Security numbers are invalid (either invented by a crook with an inadequate knowledge of the way the Social Security system works or issued to a person who is listed as "deceased" on the credit bureau's records).

The credit bureaus themselves don't grant or deny credit to consumers; they provide businesses with information about consumers, which the businesses then fit into their "scoring" system in order to decide whether the customer meets criteria such as length of employment, home ownership or stable tenancy, and freedom from outstanding debts. Credit bureau employees, who don't have to have any special education, training, or qualifications, thus have a lot of power. If they mix up Honest Consumer Jones with Deadbeat Jones (or vice versa), if they don't bother to update files, or if they ignore accurate information provided by the consumers under investigation or by other sources, they can have the effect of unjustly depriving consumers of credit—or of giving the green light for the granting of credit to a con artist or someone with a history of late payments.

## TO THE TRADE

The credit bureaus' and collection agencies' trade association, Associated Credit Bureaus (ACB), has 1,219 credit bureau members out of an estimated 1,500 credit bureaus in the United States. (The ACB also has 919 collection agency members.) All these credit bureaus depend heavily on computerized information, which comes from six major sources: ACB Services (part of Associated Credit Bureaus, Inc.), Credit Bureau Incorporated, Chilton Corporation, Trans Union Credit Information Company, Associated Credit Services, Inc. (which has a data base with records for 110 million consumers in twenty-six states), and TRW Credit Data.

In 1985, TRW's net sales were $86,479,000 (for collection services and the sale of credit insurance as well as credit reporting). The cost of sales was a somewhat modest $32,440,000, so that gross profits were $54,039,000 (62.4 percent, or rather above the average for the businesses discussed in this book). Selling, general, and administrative expenses were $35,486,000, and operating income was $18,553,000. Other, smaller expenses were depreciation and amortization of $5,945,000 and interest of $125,000. Pretax income was $12,483,000, about one-third of which went to income taxes, leaving a net income of $7,841,000 (9.0 percent—quite high for the businesses in this book).

TRW has a new enterprise: offering consumers a program called Credentials. Consumers who subscribe and pay $35 a year (250,000 Californians already have) get free copies of all their TRW credit reports and free notification whenever a report on them is requested from TRW; they are also insured against unauthorized use of their credit cards and get a chance to supplement TRW's files with additional information. The catch is that all of these privileges are available either free or for a small fee (a few cents per page of information) under the federal laws that govern all credit bureaus.

Credentials provides TRW not only with extra income but with extra information: TRW asks Credentials subscribers for information about their medical history, personal income, and investments; that information makes up a powerful (and saleable) data base. Although federal law controls the dissemination of information about identifiable consumers, it doesn't place limits on the sale of statistics gathered from samples of consumers.

1984 has come and gone, and we're all enrolled in Big Brother's computers, but the computers are maintained by credit bureaus that service businesses, not by a tyrannical government.

# 96

# Private Investigators

Total receipts:   $3,424,266,000

(Department of Commerce, 1982)

The private eye (the name comes both from the "i" in "investigator" and the unsleeping eye in the logo of the Pinkerton Agency) is an American icon. With his trench coat and dangling cigarette, his endless circle of guilty clients, shady dames, and goons with blackjacks, he has nothing to sustain him but a pint of rye in the desk drawer and the wisdom that comes from a knowledge of human frailty.

There are about 50,000 *real* private investigators in the United States, and they don't have much in common with the fictitious private snoops. In 1982, the Department of Commerce's investigators found 7,011 "detective agencies and protective services," with $3.42 billion in total receipts.

Often, private investigators are former police officers or former military personnel (especially former MPs); but they may also be people dissatisfied with desk jobs in journalism, accounting, or law, or recent high school or college graduates looking for a job that offers at least a whiff of adventure.

The new-style eye needs to be more expert with a telephone and a computer than with a .38. Plenty of information can be gotten with those two tools: for instance, who owns a car with a particular license plate (or even a blue Chevy Nova with a plate with the letter K and the numbers 8, 2, and 3 in some order) or whether somebody named Walter Hapgood has a bank account in a particular town. It saves a lot of legwork. (If all investigators had a strict regard for privacy laws, and lacked contacts willing to bend the rules, the investigators would be back to the legwork, and frequently stymied even then.) Fred D. Knapp, a New York City investigator profiled by the *New York Times* ("Fred Knapp, Private Eye, Scourge of Illegal Tenants," May 9, 1988), specializes in using court and Department of Motor Vehicle records, among other public documents, to find out if tenants of apartments whose rent is kept down by the city's rent regulations *really* live in those apartments. If he can prove that the tenant has a primary residence somewhere else, the landlord can evict the tenant and rent the apartment to someone else for much more money.

In 1930s detective stories, private eyes charged $25 a day and expenses (and hardly ever collected that, since the usual result of their hard work was to prove that their client was a murderer). Today, the going rate is more like $75 to $100 an hour, though private investigators, like lawyers, often have retainer clients who pay by the month or year. Overall, it's estimated that the industry takes in $10 billion a year. A "debugging" job can cost $500 or more; a complete investigation of alleged employee fraud can cost the client $5,000.

Who'd need a detective all the time? A corporation needing security services, or a credit-card company or lender in constant need of "skip tracing" (finding customers who wish to make themselves scarce), or a law firm with a constant need to have witnesses interviewed or personal injury claimants followed to make sure they're not out dancing on legs allegedly paralyzed by the negligence of the law firm's clients. One estimate says that lawyers' commissions pay for 90 percent of investigations. Insurance companies also retain or employ many investigators for the same purposes. On a pleasanter note, missing heirs may have to be found to give them their inherited loot; or it may be necessary to find all the potential heirs on the off chance they may want to object to the probate of a will. Private investigators hunt for "bugs" and other surveillance devices. It's a good guess that they also plant them.

Before the liberalization of divorce laws in the late 1960s and 1970s, investigators spent a lot of their time proving that one spouse was committing adultery so the other spouse could get a divorce. Today, given no-fault divorce, only about 15 percent of private detective work concerns divorces. But it still may be necessary to find out where a spouse is concealing assets; and a really nasty custody case can require proof of a parent's moral unfitness.

Getting a "P.I." license is a lot like getting a real estate broker's license: it requires a period of apprenticeship under the supervision of an already licensed person before the investigator can set up in business for himself or herself, a written exam, and a background free of arrests or convictions.

Until recently, there were very few female private investigators: it was considered, in P. D. James's ironic phrase, "an unsuitable job for a woman." Besides, hardly any women had military or police experience. But today, about 10 percent of private investigators are female (20 percent in New York—probably because citizens of crime-conscious New York won't talk to a strange man, fearing that he's a mugger or worse).

Marilyn Greene of Schenectady, New York ("When Others Fail, Marilyn Greene Finds the Body," August 11, 1987) is successful enough to have earned a profile on page one of the *Wall Street Journal.* In twenty years, she's tracked down over two hundred missing persons, in many cases after the police or FBI have given up. (There's nothing the police can do in the case of an adult who *wants* to be missing.) Her smallest fee to date: the $6.50 proffered by a fourteen-year-old babysitter.

Her experience allows her to see patterns: for example, people bent on suicide can often be found within a quarter mile of the last place they were seen—and at a higher elevation, so they can look down and think things over; elderly wander-aways seldom get more than four miles from the last sighting. She uses records of library cards, drunk driving arrests, and traffic tickets as well as telephone directories as tools; she also has trained dogs who can track scents in the air (not just footprints).

The P.I. of the future may have a "trained" tracking robot; it's a certainty that he or she will use computers to trace a missing or runaway person or missing or misappropriated funds.

# 97

# Package Delivery

How do those millions of mail-order shipments ever get to the consumer? Well, some of them *don't* get there, either because the seller had no intention of delivering or because they got lost in transit. Some of them (but only one out of twelve) arrive by means of the post office's parcel post service. Federal law places limits on the package delivery business: legally, the post office is the only agency allowed to deliver "first-class mail," that is, letters and packages receiving certain kinds of handling.

But private businesses are allowed to handle other kinds of deliveries, and many businesses have sprung up to deliver packages and information faster than first-class mail (for instance, Federal Express overnight courier service), more carefully, and sometimes more cheaply than the post office can. The post office has responded by introducing overnight Express Mail.

The market has responded, too, with new businesses and new services provided by existing competitors. The larger delivery services maintain their own airlines: Federal Express has seventy-two jets; United Parcel Service (UPS) had ninety-five in early 1987 and had placed orders for twenty more. There are about three hundred air courier services, but not always the same three hundred, since companies quickly go into the business (it doesn't take much—just some couriers, a few ads, some

417

Market Share for Delivery
of Packages Under 70 Lbs.

| | |
|---|---|
| (1) Federal Express: | 52.8% |
| (2) United Parcel Service: | 13.2% |
| (3) U.S. Postal Service: | 8.0% |
| (4) Purolator Courier: | 7.4% |
| (5) Airborne Freight: | 6.6% |
| (6) All others: | 12% |

(Legg Mason Wood Walker Inc., '87)

wheels, and a good travel agent) and out again (there's plenty of competition for the market). The smaller carriers have to specialize (one specializes in bank documents, for instance) or offer unusual services (such as delivering overseas bulk-mail faster and cheaper than the postal service).

In financial terms, the largest player in this $6 billion-a-year game is Federal Express, with annual revenues of $3.2 billion. UPS has a dominant position in shipping items that weigh more than seventy pounds and also does well in air deliveries. Federal Express ranked as #249 on *Business Week*'s Top 1000, with 1987 sales of $3.52 billion and profits of $176 million. In 1987, its return on invested capital was 10.8 percent, and its return on equity was an even more impressive 14.4 percent. Although business in 1986 and 1987 was excellent, profit margins were way down: the operating profit margin of almost 9 percent in the now fondly remembered year of 1983 had sagged to 5 percent in 1987.

What happened? Business customers who used to flock to send overnight letters by means of Federal Express now often have their own facsimile machines and simply "fax" the documents, which is nearly instantaneous and avoids the annoyance of waiting for pickups and deliveries. Federal Express tried to set up its own "Zap-Mail" fax network: it was a notable failure, costing the company $350 million in losses and write-offs. However, that decline in profitability is not caused by a decline in service: Federal Express continues to have an excellent record of on-time delivery. There's no secret to the way it does it: it has enough personnel and equipment to do the job right, and enough supervision to make sure that no one slacks off.

Although the package delivery market continues to grow, the rate of growth is slowing down. Besides, other companies are cutting prices to attract corporate business. A package delivery company's marketing strategy depends on its size and the market segment it hopes to attract. The largest companies advertise in print and on radio and television, both to appeal to members of the public who have occasional package delivery needs and to keep their names before business decision makers who see

## CONSUMER TIP

Did you order something that never arrived? First, call the seller. Maybe your order form never arrived either, or the seller is waiting to see if your check bounces before the shipment flies. If the seller has the shipment date and a carrier, you can ask the seller to trace the package. If the package was delivered by being dropped at your doorstep or that of a neighbor, without being signed for, the shipper, and not the consumer, is responsible. The shipper must pay back the seller, who then either ships out another package or sends the customer a refund.

the ads. A smaller company couldn't afford enough ads to make an impression. It might market by direct mail (a letter to directors of medical testing labs, if the service wants to specialize in delivering samples), by cultivating business relationships that can lead to major accounts, or by taking a booth at a conference where its potential clients congregate.

The United Parcel Service is a private company, owned by its 14,000 managers. It has 65,000 drivers and a fleet of 84,000 familiar round-topped trucks painted an awful shade of brown. Its drivers, in equally hideous brown uniforms, are required to maintain an almost military, or IBM-like, dress code and code of discipline.

Federal Express and UPS each have about 12,000 "mailboxes" in which customers can drop shipments for delivery. Federal Express has far more offices: 371 storefronts and 165 drive-in centers; UPS has only fifteen air-express counters for customers who don't qualify for pickup service or who are in too much of a hurry to wait.

In 1984, Airborne Express was #2 (behind Federal Express) in overnight delivery of documents and small packages, with revenue of $417,854,000. Operating expenses were $395,011,000, leaving operating income of $22,843,000. Once the company had paid interest (over $1.5 million) and profit sharing (close to $1.5 million), its pretax earnings were $19,736,000. Taxes took an unusually high $8,907,000, leaving net earnings of $10,829,000.

# 98

# Hair Care Salons

| | |
|---|---|
| Number of establishments: | 179,439 |
| Total receipts: | $14.6 billion |
| Average net sales: | $81,400 |
| Number of employees: | 410,500 |
| Total payroll: | NG |

(Green Book, '86; 1985 figures)

Changes in society have been both bad and good for the hair care business. Traditionally, the barber shop served as a cherished spot for male bonding (and surreptitious glances at the *Police Gazette* and other periodicals not welcome in the front parlor at home) as well as the site of the twice-a-month haircut that kept a gentleman's hair above his celluloid collar.

It took longer for beauty salons to get established; but by the time permanent waves were perfected (in the 1920s), the beauty parlor served a comparable function for women. It was a place to meet, learn the secrets of the newest modes of beauty, and exchange gossip (although the magazines maintained a decidedly higher tone).

Opening a beauty parlor was a genteel sort of business, suitable for a widow in modest circumstances or a respectable maiden lady; the capital requirements were low because the owner-operator could do all the work herself, perhaps in a spare room of her own home. The potential for profit was there because many respectable ladies went to the hairdresser once a week for a shampoo and set. (Dana's mother used to report to the beauty parlor every Saturday, then sleep with her head wrapped in toilet paper to preserve the lacquered-in-place set for the rest of the week.)

The 1960s could have been the death knell for the beauty business. Fashion decreed long, straight, free-swinging hair for both sexes—no more short back and sides, and no more pin curls. But, paradoxically, swinging London was also the birthplace of the celebrity hairdresser. Hairdressers joined pop singers and photographers in the lineup of People to Know.

Today, the traditional team of barber shop and beauty parlor has been joined by the unisex salon, where the hand-held blow dryer replaces the earlier "conehead" model. The haircut, once two bits, or two dollars, depending on time and place, now can cost anywhere from $5 to several hundred. The salon may offer a wide variety of services besides haircuts, such as coloring, facials, manicures, addition of artificial nails by various means, pedicures, and waxing.

The salon is also a retail store for a bewildering variety of products described as "professional caliber." There used to be one kind of stuff, called shampoo. Then it was joined by another kind of stuff, called creme rinse. Men could polish their hair with brilliantine, VO-5, or Brylcreem. Today, you can slosh things through your hair to soften it, stiffen it, degrease it, make it shiny, or temporarily turn it green. Many of the most expensive brands of hair care products are sold primarily or exclusively at salons—adding another source of profit to the salon operation.

Salons can show strong profits. Respondents to a 1986 Dun & Bradstreet survey of beauty shops averaged 61.6 percent of net sales and an after-tax net profit of 9.9 percent. Barber shops did even better, with 76.5 percent gross profit and 12.1 percent net profit after tax—one of the strongest showings of any of the industries described in this book. Probably the difference can be explained by the fact that salons offer far more services to women than barber shops do to men; those services require more equipment and are more labor-intensive, which cuts down on turnover.

Franchising has reached the world of hair care. If you want your own Haircrafters franchise (just like 274 other individual owners; the company owns thirty shops), you'll need at least $18,000 for the franchise fee and must pay a monthly fee of six percent and an advertising charge of 2 percent a month to the franchisor. Start-up expenses are estimated to range from $71,000 to $125,000.

## SERVICES AND PROFITS

The *Green Book* (an annual trade publication) defines a full-service salon as one that provides at least ten services (for example, haircutting, shampoos, conditioning, perms, moussing, hair coloring, relaxing excessively curly hair, styling toupees or wigs, makeup, manicures, and pedicures). In 1986, salon services brought in almost $20 billion dollars; retail sales accounted for another $1.164 billion. Retail sales were the fourth greatest money-maker, with haircuts, hair styling, and tinting in the first three places.

Men's services brought in 12.47 percent of unisex salon sales in 1986 (about $2.5 billion). Nearly all the money ($1.75 billion, or 70.5 percent of the total for men) went for haircuts; surprisingly, the next largest percentage was for perming ($541,962,000—21.8 percent of men's spending). The rest was divided among hair coloring, hair removal, manicures, and hairpiece styling.

Also in 1986, salon services to women brought in $17,445,947,000. About one-fifth of that ($4,552,477,000) bought haircuts; about one-tenth ($2,709,808,000) went for coloring. Permanent waves brought in almost $4 billion; hairstyling, $3.3 billion. Other services included shampoos, conditioning, and moussing (at a total of nearly $1 billion, which is not really a representative figure because these services are often included in the price of a haircut); manicures ($500 million or so), pedicures ($292,588,000), and hair relaxing ($261,307,000). Wig and hairpiece styling, hair removal, skin care, and makeup made comparatively minor contributions to salon revenues.

## LOCAL VARIATIONS

The salon business depends a lot on the whims of local customers. New York, for instance, has the most salons (4,233 in 1986) and the largest beauty work force (13,482). Naturally, that means it has the highest salon receipts ($560 million). But it's not the profit leader: Washington, D.C., is, with the country's highest average receipts ($189,000 per salon; New York's average is $132,000; Detroit and San Francisco each average only $128,000).

There's a growing emphasis on treatments and products for healthy hair and skin. Busy executives (both male and female) also sometimes look to salons for their share of pampering (neck massages, facials, manicures). Perhaps the salon of the future will link up with the health club—a place where you can read Italian fashion magazines, receive telexes, exercise, and drink a papaya milkshake, or rub it on your hair to moisturize it.

# 99

# Laundry/ Dry Cleaning

| | |
|---|---|
| Number of establishments: | 43,912 |
| Total receipts: | $9.32 billion |
| Average net sales: | $264,000 dry cleaning plants |
| | $151,153 coin laundries |
| Number of employees: | NG |
| Total payroll: | $3.224 million |

(Department of Commerce, '82)

In rural areas and in suburbia, nearly every family has its own washing machine. Many families have dryers, though clotheslines still have their advocates: fresh air makes laundry smell great, and it doesn't increase the utility bills. However, in the closely packed cities where there's hardly enough room in tiny apartments for a washer and dryer (even if the landlord would allow them), and in two-career families where nobody has time to do the ironing, laundromats, laundry services, and dry cleaners make their mark.

Starting a laundromat from scratch is an expensive business because there are all those heavy-duty machines to buy. (*Why* don't laundromats ever have enough dryers? They insist that you use at least two

423

dryers, but they always have more washing machines than dryers.) The business provides an immediate cash flow in the form of all those dimes and quarters in the machine. There are other sources of income, too: sales of laundry detergent and bleach; snack vending machines; and laundry service for those with more cash than time on their hands.

At least one laundromat chain includes a pub and several rent videocassettes, but they're exceptional. Starting a Duds 'n' Suds laundromat (there are about forty of them already), replete with beer, nachos and other snacks, pool tables, and video games, costs about $175,000, including a $25,000 franchise fee. The Alaskan town of Homer serves the summer population of cannery and fishery workers as well as the year-round population by providing not only dry cleaning, washing machines, and dryers but showers for the tent colony.

Usually, a laundromat can be run by one person or by members of a single family: someone does have to be around to make sure nobody robs the Coke machine, vandalizes the dryers, or punches out whoever took the laundry out of someone else's machine the second it stopped running. But it usually isn't necessary to hire a paid staff. The machines have to stand up to heavy traffic and occasional abuse (sure, you're supposed to put in a sneaker when you wash down quilts or garments, to fluff up the down, but the sneaker gives the machine a beating), which means either a service contract or an endless flow of repair bills. There's the rent, of course; but laundromats must be located in residential neighborhoods (nobody's going to travel very far with bushel-baskets full of laundry), so rents are usually lower than for prime commercial space. Advertising isn't a big part of the budget: people either go to the closest laundromat, or to the cleanest neighborhood facility, or the one with the best gossip.

The Department of Commerce's 1982 figures show that the 10,943 coin-operated laundry and dry cleaning operations had total revenues of $756.8 million: $395.4 million from coin-operated self-service machines and the rest from "service" laundries that wash and iron clothing and other textiles and handle diaper service. Much of the commercial laundry business comes from linen service for hotels and restaurants, not directly from consumers. Although many people have their shirts washed and pressed by a laundry, it's just too expensive to have an entire load of wash done that way. Dun & Bradstreet's 1986 figures show average net sales of $151,153 for the 159 coin laundries and cleaners who reported. Gross profit was 70.1 percent of net sales; net after-tax profit, 10.0 percent of sales—both above average for the businesses discussed in this book.

The economics of the dry cleaning business are a little different. It's possible to open a storefront equipped with those wonderful motorized racks, a service counter, and a cash register, but without dry cleaning machinery. That makes the initial investment lower but imposes a continu-

## CONSUMER TIP

If your clothes smell of dry cleaning fluid, the plant doesn't change the chemicals often enough; really conscientious cleaners send your clothes back odor-free.

A really good dry cleaner will find out what caused the spots on your clothes and how long they've been there; cleaners have a multitude of trade secrets, tips, and tricks for dislodging dirt.

ing expense on the owners. The garments can be sent out to a cleaning plant, where they're immersed in giant washing machines filled with chemicals like "perk" (perchlorethylene) or "carbon tet" (not the national holiday of Vietnamese dry cleaners, but carbon tetrachloride) and pressed, then trucked back to the "drop store" to be reclaimed by customers. The 1982 figures show that $2.468 billion in revenue was earned by doing dry cleaning work directly for customers; approximately $286 million, by "drop shops" doing dry cleaning for resale. The 658 dry cleaning plants participating in the 1986 Dun & Bradstreet survey reported average net sales of $264,272, with gross profit equal to 58.2 percent of sales, and after-tax net profit of 8.0 percent. Although sales are greater, dry cleaning plants are less profitable than laundromats, probably because laundromats are often family-run businesses with little or no paid staff; dry cleaning plants need employees.

Many dry cleaners are individually owned, single operations because convenience and service matter a lot more than advertising budget

## CONSUMER TIP

What if your clothes come back ruined, instead of revivified? If it's a precious or cherished garment, you can have it analyzed by the International Fabricare Institute (Silver Spring, Maryland) for a smallish fee. The institute performed 40,000 analyses in 1985. About one-sixth of the problems were blamed on dry cleaners, the rest on careless manufacturers or owners.

when people choose a dry cleaner. However, there are strong franchises in this business, such as the One Hour Martinizing Dry Cleaning system (established in 1949); its 1,269 stores are all owned by individual franchisees, who pay an initial fee of $16,000 or more, and $1,500 per year for use of the name. When expensive clothes are involved, customers often feel reassured by a well-known name.

Of course, really fastidious customers can follow the example of the czars: they sent their laundry to Paris, to make sure it was done just right. (Let's hope the customers enjoy a kinder fate than that of the czars.)

# 100

# Copy Shops

Okay, let's all sing, to the tune of "Ten Cents a Dance": "Eight cents a page, that's what they pay me, gosh, how they weigh me down . . ." (Eight cents a page for copying service was the basic going rate in New York City in mid-1988, although some stores have a lower basic rate, positioning themselves as "discount stores.") A copy shop is usually a not-too-large storefront, preferably located near a college (all those student papers to copy) and near a commercial area, to service businesses that can't afford, or don't want to bother with, their own copiers.

Opening a copy shop usually involves leasing three or four sophisticated copier-duplicators (technically, a "copier" makes a small number of copies; a "duplicator" prints large runs), machines that can collate automatically, print on both sides of a page, reduce, enlarge, and practically whistle "The Yellow Rose of Texas." However, to take advantage of these miracles, the copies must be "machine feedable": on 8½-by-11-inch paper and free of pasteups, staples, or clips; otherwise they need expensive and labor-intensive hand-feeding. Some shops have machines that will copy in color; the standard machines, alas, handle only black and white.

The machines are nearly always leased, not purchased, because they're expensive babies, and few copy shop owners can afford so large

427

an initial investment. Then the shop needs hundreds of giant boxes of paper, from whatever manufacturer or distributor offers the best deal; a staff (often college students, or young actors and dancers who find it more congenial than waiting on tables), thousands of fliers to attach to local lampposts, and perhaps a few newspaper ads.

Then, it's time to open the doors and (probably) get involved in a vicious price war with the other copy shops in the neighborhood. The "weapons" in the war include lower basic prices; discounts on long runs (many copies of the same original); special "manuscript" rates (for a few copies of something over one hundred pages long); and discounts for orders left overnight (so that the workload can be evened out, instead of the shop having busy times and slack periods). Some stores offer "house accounts," so a frequent customer can be billed once a month instead of paying at each visit; some even offer free pickup and delivery service to good clients (usually businesses).

Copy shop operation is both a fairly new business and a fairly small pebble in the stream of commerce, so neither the Department of Commerce nor Dun & Bradstreet analyzes it separately. The DOC found 3,011 "blueprinting and photocopying services" in 1982, with total receipts of $856.6 million. The 223 "blueprinting, photocopying" establishments surveyed by D & B in 1986 had average net sales of $437,626 and gross profits of 50.4 percent of net sales. Net profit after tax averaged a very nice 7.6 percent.

The photocopying business is a natural for combining with other businesses: typing and secretarial service, for instance. If the shop has access to a computer, it can provide resume service and other forms of word processing (perhaps even sophisticated typesetting). A simple binding machine makes it possible to jazz up the reports that have just been copied (and, perhaps, word-processed) on the premises. A fax machine turns the shop into a center for sending and receiving documents electronically. Copy shops often provide mailboxes for rent, as an "accommodation address"—for instance, for a small home business that needs a more impressive address.

Copy shops frequently join forces with other businesses, too. For instance, the shop may take orders for stationery (business cards, wedding invitations) to be printed outside; the customer pays the copy shop and picks up the stationery at the shop or has it delivered. Sometimes word processing is handled on this basis.

The predictions that computers would provide a "paperless office" (and a paperless home and school) certainly haven't come true. At least until electronic transmission becomes the predominant means of communications, students will still need copies of their term papers; businesses will still need copies of laudatory articles about themselves; complaining consumers will need copies of the angry letters and supporting documents fired off to lagging businesses. True, the price of copying machines has dropped so that they can, conceivably, be owned by people other than multimillionaires; but the neighborhood copy shop seems secure, at least for the time being.

# Trade Associations

(Note: Because most trade associations are called either the "American Whatsis Association" or the "National Whatsis Association," these are alphabetized according to the first significant word.)

ASTM [materials testing] 1916 Race Street, Philadelphia, PA 19103 (215) 299-5400

American Amusement Machine Association [video games, etc.] 205 The Strand, Alexandria, VA 22314 (703) 548-8044

Amusement and Music Operators Association [juke boxes] 111 East Wacker Drive, Chicago, IL 60601 (312) 644-6610

National Automatic Merchandising Association [vending machines] 20 North Wacker Drive, Chicago, IL 60606 (312) 346-0370

National Independent Automobile Dealers Association [used cars] 600 East Las Colinas Boulevard, Suite 314, Irving, TX 75039 (214) 556-0044

National Automobile Dealers Association, 8400 Westpark Drive, McLean, VA 22102 (703) 821-7000

American Bankers Association, 1120 Connecticut Avenue NW, Washington, D.C. 20036 (202) 663-5000

Consumer Bankers Association, 1300 North 17th Street, Suite 1200, Arlington, VA 22209 (703) 276-1750

American Bar Association [lawyers, not pubs] 750 North Lake Shore Drive, Chicago, IL 60611 (312) 988-5000

American Beauty Association, 111 East Wacker Drive, Chicago IL 60601 (312) 644-6610

American Booksellers Association, 135 West 25th Street, New York, NY 10001 (212) 463-8450

National Association of Broadcasters, 1771 N Street NW, Washington, D.C. 20036 (202) 429-5300

Associated Builders and Contractors, 729 15th Street NW, Washington, D.C. 20005 (202) 637-8800

431

Building Owners and Managers Association International, 1250 I Street NW, Suite 200, Washington, DC 20005 (202) 289-7000

Association of Specialists in Cleaning and Restoration [fabric and furniture cleaning] 5205 Leesburg Pike, Suite 1408, Falls Church, VA 22041-3802 (703) 845-1400

National Association of Convenience Stores, 1605 King Street, Alexandria, VA 22314 (703) 684-3600

Associated Credit Bureaus, 16211 Park Ten Place, Houston, TX 77084 (713) 492-8155

Credit Union National Association, 5710 Mineral Point Road, Box 431, Madison, WI 53701 (608) 231-4000

American Culinary Federation [chefs] Box 3466, 10 San Bartola Road, St. Augustine, FL 32084 (904) 824-4468

American Dental Association, 211 East Chicago Avenue, Chicago, IL 60611 (312) 440-2500

Direct Marketing Association, 6 East 43rd Street, New York, NY 10017 (212) 689-4977

Do-it-Yourself Research Institute, 400 Knightsbridge Parkway, Lincolnshire, IL 60069 (312) 634-4368

National Association of Chain Drug Stores, 413 North Lee Street, P.O. Box 1417-D49, Alexandria, VA 22313 (703) 549-3001

International Drycleaners Congress, Box I, Cupertino, CA 95015 (408) 252-1746

Edison Electric Institute [utilities] 1111 19th Street NW, Washington, D.C. 20036-3691 (202) 778-6400

National Association of Executive Recruiters, 222 South Westmonte Drive, Suite 110, Altamonte Springs, FL 32714 (305) 774-7880

Association of Executive Search Consultants, 17 Sherwood Place, Greenwich, CT 06830 (203) 661-6606

American Financial Services Association, 1101 14th Street NW, 4th Floor, Washington, D.C. 20005 (202) 289-0400

National Association of Floor Covering Distributors, 13-126 West Merchandise Mart Plaza, Chicago, IL 60654 (312) 467-0116

Florists Transworld Delivery Association, 29200 Northwestern Highway, Southfield, MI 48037 (313) 355-9300

Society of American Florists, 1601 Duke Street, Alexandria, VA 22314 (703) 836-8700

Food Marketing Institute [supermarkets] 1750 K Street NW, Suite 700, Washington, D.C. 20006 (202) 452-8444

American Franchise Association, 2730 Wilshire Boulevard, Suite 400, Santa Monica, CA 90403 (213) 829-0841

National Funeral Directors Association, 11121 West Oklahoma Avenue, Milwaukee, WI 53227 (414) 541-2500

American Fur Industry, 101 West 30th Street, New York, NY 10001 (212) 564-5133

Garden Centers of America, 1250 I Street NW, Washington, D.C. 20008 (202) 789-2900

Gift Retailers, Manufacturers and Representatives Association, 1100-H Brandywine Boulevard, P.O. Box 2188, Zanesville, OH 43702-2188 (614) 452-4541

National Retail Hardware Association, 770 North High School Road, Indianapolis, IN 46214 (317) 248-1261

National Home Furnishings Association, 220 West Gerry Drive, Wood Dale, IL 60191 (312) 595-0200

Hobby Industry Association of America, 319 East 54th Street, Elmwood Park, NJ 07407 (201) 794-1133

American Home Sewing Association, 1375 Broadway, 4th Floor, New York, NY 10018 (212) 302-2150

American Hospital Association, 840 North Lake Shore Drive, Chicago, IL 60611 (312) 280-6000

American Hotel & Motel Association, 1201 New York Avenue NW, Washington, D.C. 20005 (202) 265-4506

American Society of Interior Designers, 1430 Broadway, New York, NY 10018 (212) 944-9220

Investment Company Institute, 1600 M Street NW, Washington, D.C. 20036 (202) 293-7700

Jewelers of America, 1271 Avenue of the Americas, New York, NY 10020 (212) 489-0023

American Council of Independent Laboratories, 1725 K Street NW, Suite 301, Washington, D.C. 20006 (202) 887-5872

Coin Laundry Association, 1315 Butterfield Road, Suite 212, Downers Grove, IL 60515 (312) 963-5547

National Limousine Association, 1275 K Street NW, Suite 800, Washington, D.C. 20005 (202) 682-1426

National Liquor Stores Association, 5101 River Road, Suite 108, Bethesda, MD 20816 (301) 656-1494

Marketing Research Association, 111 East Wacker Drive, Suite 600, Chicago, IL 60601 (312) 644-6610

American Medical Association, 535 North Dearborn Street, Chicago, IL 60610-4377 (312) 645-5000

Menswear Retailers of America, 2011 I Street NW, Suite 600, Washington, D.C. 20006 (202) 347-1932

Alliance of Motion Picture and Television Producers, 14144 Ventura Boulevard, Sherman Oaks, CA 91423 (818) 995-3600

No-Load Mutual Fund Association, 11 Penn Plaza, Suite 2204, New York, NY 10001 (212) 563-4540

Opticians Association of America, 10341 Democracy Lane, Box 10110, Fairfax, VA 22030 (703) 691-8355

Public Relations Society of America, 33 Irving Place, 3rd Floor, New York, NY 10003 (212) 995-2230

National Association of Realtors, 430 North Michigan Avenue, Chicago, IL 60611 (312) 329-8200

National Association of the Remodeling Industry, 1901 North Moore Street, Suite 808, Arlington, VA 22209 (703) 276-7600

National Mass Retailing Institute, 570 Seventh Avenue, New York, NY 10018 (212) 354-6600

American Retail Federation, 1616 H Street NW, Washington, D.C. 20006 (202) 783-7971

National Retail Merchants Association, 100 West 31st Street, New York, NY 10001 (212) 244-8780

National Association of Securities Dealers, 1375 K Street NW, Washington, D.C. 20006 (202) 728-8000

Securities Industry Association, 120 Broadway, 35th Floor, New York, NY 10271 (212) 608-1500

National Shoe Retailers Association, 9861 Broken Land Parkway, Columbia, MD 21046-1148 (301) 381-8282

International Council of Shopping Centers, 665 Fifth Avenue, 11th Floor, New York, NY 10022 (212) 421-8181

National Sporting Goods Association, 1699 Wall Street, Mount Prospect, IL 60056-9968 (312) 439-4000

American Telemarketing Association, 5000 Van Nuys Boulevard, Suite 400, Sherman Oaks, CA 91403 (818) 995-7338

National Association of Temporary Services, 119 S. St. Asaph Street, Alexandria, VA 22314 (703) 549-6287

American Land Title Association [title searches and title insurance] 1828 L Street NW, Washington, D.C. 20036 (202) 296-3671

American Society of Travel Agents, 1101 King Street, Suite 200, Alexandria, VA 22314 (703) 739-2782

Video Software Dealers Association, 3 Eves Drive, Suite 307, Marlton, NJ 08053 (609) 596-8500

# Trade Journals

(Arranged alphabetically by area of interest; Q = quarterly, M = monthly, BM = bimonthly, BW = biweekly, W = weekly.)

[Accounting] Accounting Review, American Accounting Association, 5717 Bessie Drive, Sarasota, FL 33581 (813) 921-7747 Q

[Advertising] Advertising Age, the International Newspaper of Marketing, Crain Communications, Inc., 220 E. 42nd St., New York, NY 10017 (212) 210-0100 W

[Air Freight] Air Cargo World, Communications Channels, Inc., 6255 Barfield Road, Atlanta, GA 30328 (404) 256-9800 M

[Airlines] Airfare Discount Bulletin, 1629 K Street NW, Washington, D.C. 20006 (800) 345-8112 M

Aviation Week & Space Technology, McGraw-Hill, Inc., 1221 Avenue of the Americas, New York, NY 10020 (212) 512-3288 W

Frequent Flyer Official Airline Guides, Inc., 2000 Clearwater Drive, Oakbrook, IL 60521 (800) 323-3537 M

[Amusement Industry] Amusement Business, Billboard Publications, Inc., 1515 Broadway, New York, NY 10036 (212) 764-7300 W

[Auto Dealers] Automotive Report & Auto Week, Automotive Auction Publishing, Inc., 1101 Fulton Building, Pittsburgh, PA 15222 W

[Auto Rentals] Car Dealer & Leasing Insider, ATCOM, Inc., 2315 Broadway, New York, NY 10024 (212) 873-5900 W

[Banking] ABA Banking Journal, Simmons-Boardman Publishing Corp., 345 Hudson Street, New York, NY 10014 (212) 620-7200 M

American Banker, American Banker, Inc., 1 State Street Plaza, New York, NY 10004 (212) 943-6700 Daily

Journal of Commercial Bank Lending, Robert Morris Associates, 1616 Philadelphia National Bank Building, Philadelphia, PA 19107 (215) 665-2850 M

[Beauty Salons] American Salon, Service Publications, Inc., 261 Madison Avenue, New York, NY 10016 (212) 818-9400 M

[Bookstores] ABA Newswire, American Booksellers Association, 122 East 42nd Street, New York, NY 10168 (212) 867-9060 W

Weekly Record, R. R. Bowker Co., 205 East 42nd Street, New York, NY 10017 (212) 916-1600 W

[Carpet Stores] Floor Covering Weekly, FCW Division of Hearst Business Communications, Inc., 919 Third Avenue, New York, NY 10022 (212) 759-8050 W

[Casinos] Gaming & Wagering Business, BMT Publications, Inc., 254 West 31st Street, New York, NY 10001 (212) 594-4120 M

[Catalog Showrooms] Catalog Showroom Business, Gralla Publications, 1515 Broadway, New York, NY 10036 (212) 869-1300 M

[Clothing Stores] Apparel Industry Magazine, Shore Publishing Co., 180 Allen Road NE, #300 S. Building, Atlanta, GA 30328 (404) 252-8831 M

Earnshaw's Infants, Girls & Boys Wear Review, Earnshaw Publications, Inc., 225 West 34th Street, New York, NY 10001 (212) 563-2742 M

Women's Wear Daily, Fairchild Publications, 7 East 12th Street, Book Division, New York, NY 10003 (212) 741-4000 5 times weekly

[Computer and Software Retailing] Computer & Software News, Lebhar-Friedman, Inc., 425 Park Avenue, New York, NY 10022 (212) 371-9400 W

Computer Retail News, CMP Publications, Inc., 600 Community Drive, Manhasset, NY 11030 (516) 365-4600 W

[Consumer Lending] Credit World, International Consumer Credit Association, Box 27357, St. Louis, MO 63141-1757 (314) 991-3030 BM

[Credit Unions] Credit Union Magazine, Credit Union National Association, Inc., Box 431, Madison, WI 53701 (608) 231-4000 M

[Debt Collection] Collector, American Collectors' Association, 4040 West 70th Street, Minneapolis, MN 55435 (612) 926-6547 M

[Discount Stores] Chain Store Age, Lebhar-Friedman, Inc., 425 Park Avenue, New York, NY 10022 (212) 371-9400 M

Discount Store News (same publisher), BM

[Drug Stores] American Druggist, Hearst Publications, Inc., 60 East 42nd St., New York, NY 10017 (212) 557-0410 M

Drug Store News, Lebhar-Friedman, Inc., 425 Park Ave., New York, NY 10022 (212) 371-9400 M

[Florists] Florists' Review, Florists Publishing Co., 3105 South Michigan Avenue, Chicago, IL 60605 (312) 782-5505 M

[Franchises] Franchising World, International Franchise Association, 1025 Connecticut Avenue NW, Suite 707, Washington, D.C. 20036 (202) 659-0790 Q

[Funeral Parlors] Director, National Funeral Directors Association, 11121 W. Oklahoma Ave., Milwaukee, WI 53227 (414) 541-2500 M

[Furniture Stores] HFD, Fairchild Publications, 7 East 12th Street, New York, NY 10003 (212) 741-4000 W

[Furriers] Fur Age Weekly, Fur Vogue Publishing Co., 127 West 30th Street, New York, NY 10001 (212) 239-4983 W

[Garden Supplies] Garden Supply Retailer, Miller Publishing Co., 2501 Wayzata Boulevard, P.O. Box 6, Minneapolis, MN 55405 (612) 374-5200 M

[Gas Stations] Automotive Service Reports, Automotive Service Councils, 188 Industrial Drive, Suite 112, Elmhurst, IL 60126 (312) 530-2330 M

[Gift Shops] Giftware Business, Gralla Publications, Inc., 1515 Broadway, New York, NY 10036 (212) 869-1300 M

[Headhunters] Recruiting Trends, Enterprise Publications, 20 North Wacker Drive, Chicago, IL 60606 (312) 332-3571 M

[Health Care] Health Marketing Quarterly, Haworth Press, Inc., 28 East 22nd Street, New York, NY 10010 (212) 228-2800 Q

Medical Economics, Medical Economics Co., Inc., Box 1004, Oradell, NJ 07649 (201) 262-3030 BW

[Hotels] Hotel & Motel Management, 7500 Old Oak Boulevard, Cleveland, OH 44130 (216) 243-8100 M

[Insurance] American Agent, Commerce Publishing Co., 408 Olive Street, St. Louis, MO 63102 (314) 421-5445 M

Best's Review, A. M. Best Co., Ambest Road, Oldwick, NJ 08858 (201) 439-2200 M

Journal of Risk and Insurance, American Risk & Insurance Association, Brooks Hall, U. of Georgia, Athens, GA 30602 (404) 542-4290 Q

[Investment Banking] Corporate Financing Week, 488 Madison Avenue, New York, NY 10022 (212) 832-8888 W

[Jewelers] Jewelers Circular-Keystone, Chilton Publishing Co., 1 Chilton Way, Radnor, PA 19089 (215) 964-4496 13 times per year

National Jeweler, Gralla Publications, Inc., 1515 Broadway, New York, NY 10036 (212) 869-1300 BM

[Laundry and Dry Cleaning] American Drycleaner, American Trade Magazines, Inc., 500 N. Dearborn Street, Chicago, IL 60610 (312) 337-7700 M

Coin Launderer & Cleaner, Scheldko Corp., 4512 Lindenwood Lane, Northbrook, IL 60062 (312) 272-8490 M

[Law Firms] Law Office Economics and Management, Callaghan & Co., 3201 Old Glenview Road, Wilmette, IL 60091 (800) 323-1336 Q

[Liquor Stores] Beverage World, Keller International Publishing, 150 Great Neck Road, Great Neck, NY 11021 (516) 829-9210 M

Liquor Store Magazine, Jobson Publishing Corp., 352 Park Ave., South, New York, NY 10010 (212) 685-4848 9 times a year

[Nursing Homes] Long Term Care Management, McGraw-Hill, 1221 Avenue of the Americas, New York, NY 10020 (212) 463-1672 SM

[PR Firms] Public Relations Journal, Public Relations Society of America, 33 Irving Place, New York, NY 10003 (212) 826-1757 M

[Real Estate Brokers] Real Estate Today, National Association of Realtors, 430 North Michigan Avenue, Chicago IL 60611 (312) 329-8490 9 times a year

[Real Estate Management] AOMA Newsletter, Apartment Owners and Managers' Association of America, PO Box 238, Watertown, CT 06795 (203) 274-2589 M

[Restaurants] Restaurant Business, Bill Communications, Inc., 633 Third Avenue, New York, NY 10017 (212) 986-4800 W 18 ×/yr.

Restaurants & Institutions, Cahners Publishing Co., Cahners Plaza, 1350 Touhy Place, Des Plaines, IL 60018 (312) 635-8800 BW

[Sporting Goods Stores] Sporting Goods Business, Gralla Publications, Inc., 1515 Broadway, New York, NY 10036 (212) 869-1300 M

Sporting Goods Dealer, Times-Mirror of Los Angeles, 1212 Lindbergh Ave., St. Louis, MO 63132 (314) 993-7767 M

[Supermarkets] Progressive Grocer, McLean Hunter Media, 1351 Washington Boulevard, Stamford, CT 06902 (203) 325-3500 M

Supermarket Business, 25 West 43rd Street, New York, NY 10036 (212) 354-5169 M

[Television—cable and network] Broadcasting/Cable Yearbook, Broadcasting Publications, Inc., 1705 DeSales Street NW, Washington, D.C. 20036 (202) 659-2340 annual

Cable Age, Television Editorial Corp., 1270 Avenue of the Americas, New York, NY 10020 (212) 757-8400 BW

[Title Companies] Title News, American Land Title Association, 1828 L Street NW, Washington, D.C. 20036 (202) 296-2671 M

[Toy Stores] Toy & Hobby World, 124 East 40th Street, New York, NY 10016 (212) 953-0950 M

[Travel Agents] ASTA Travel News, Communications International, 488 Madison Avenue, New York, NY 10022 (212) 826-9450 M

[Utilities] Public Utility Fortnightly, Public Utility Reports, Inc., 1700 N. Moore Street, Suite 2100, Arlington, VA 22209 (703) 243-7000 BW

[Vending Machines] Vending Times, Vending Times, Inc., 545 Eighth Avenue, New York, NY 10018 (212) 714-0101 M

[Videocassette Rentals] Video Store: The Journal of Video Retailing, H & J Publications, 7500 Old Oak Boulevard, Cleveland, OH 44130 (216) 243-8100 M

# Index